Make Me a Map of the Valley

Yours truly Jed. Hotchkiss

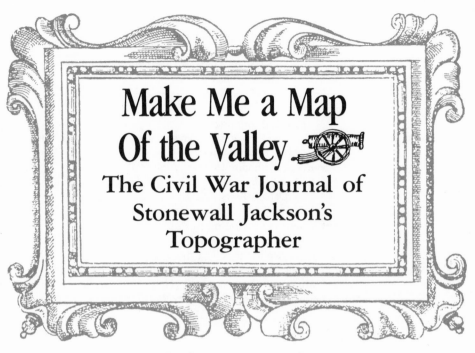

Make Me a Map Of the Valley

The Civil War Journal of Stonewall Jackson's Topographer

Jedediah Hotchkiss

Edited by ARCHIE P. MCDONALD
Foreword by T. HARRY WILLIAMS

Southern Methodist University Press

DALLAS

Fourth printing, 1989
Requests for permission to reproduce material from this work should be sent to:
Permissions
Southern Methodist University Press
Box 415
Dallas, Texas 75275

Library of Congress Cataloging in Publication Data
Hotchkiss, Jedediah, 1828-1899
Make me a map of the valley; the Civil War
journal of Stonewall Jackson's topographer. Edited
by Archie P. McDonald. Foreword by T. Harry Williams.
Dallas, Southern Methodist University Press [1973]

xxxvii, 352 p. illus. 24 cm.
Bibliography: p. 323-332

1. Hotchkiss, Jedediah, 1828-1899. 2. United States—
History—Civil War—Personal narratives—Confederate side.
3. Shenandoah Valley—History—Civil War. I. McDonald,
Archie P., ed. II. Title.

E605. H796   973.7′82   73-82036
ISBN 0-87074-137-3   MARC
ISBN 0-87074-270-1 (pbk.)

To
VENIE, JONNIE, and NEM,
and to ELLEN CHRISTIAN
For faith not spent in vain

Contents

Foreword

WALT WHITMAN called the Civil War "that strange sad war." The poet was thinking of the tragic aspect of this conflict between Americans, of the passions that had led to disunion and of the costs that had to be paid for reunion. But there were many elements of strangeness about the war, and these have fascinated military historians—the constant fraternizing between the men in blue and the men in gray, to give one example; the remarkable combination of traditional and modern methods of war that makes it seem two wars in one, to give another. But surely one of the strangest facts about it, a fact vital to an understanding of what happened in many battles, is that both sides began the struggle with no reliable maps of the area in which they would fight.

The reasons for this lack are readily apparent. There seemed to be no great need for maps, certainly not for detailed ones. Most Americans lived east of the Mississippi River and rarely traveled far from their homes. When they did go any distance, they used steamboats or railroads, and everybody knew where these conveyances went. There was simply no mass market for commercially produced maps. Certainly agencies of the national government engaged in mapping, but they made maps of restricted areas for use by a limited and largely official personnel. The army's Topographical Engineers had designed many and good maps of the Great Lakes region and the Far West. The Coast and Geodetic Survey had mapped thoroughly the Atlantic and Gulf coasts. No agency in the government had thought to map the part of the country where the war would be fought. Either nobody had thought that a civil war would come, or nobody could afford to admit that one would come.

But now war had come, and on both sides insistent demands arose from generals for good maps. These maps were a long time in arriving, and some of the apparently aimless movements made by commanders during the war's first years can be ascribed to the inaccuracy of their maps. Eventually very good maps were produced, as the *Atlas of the Official Records* attests, and were reproduced for wide usage in the armies by means of a photographic process. In the race to turn out maps the North, with greater resources in this as in other areas, had the advantage. But the South was not far behind. Some very capable map-makers appeared in the South, and one of these was possibly the foremost mapper of the war. His name was Jedediah Hotchkiss. At least half of all the Confederate maps in the *Atlas of the Official Records* were done by him. Douglas S. Freeman, in casting up Hotchkiss's contribution to the Southern cause, said that he had "a place in Confederate service almost unique."

Hotchkiss had almost a unique career. Born in New York, he came as a young man to Virginia on a walking tour. He was so attracted to the environment that he decided to settle in the state. He opened and operated several academies and taught in them. On the side he studied engineering and mapping. If he seems to have come to his profession somewhat by chance, he was following a course fairly common in the nineteenth century, a time that saw the emergence of a number of self-instructed geniuses.

At the beginning of the war Hotchkiss entered the military service of Virginia and was then mustered in the Confederate service. Again chance seemed to shape his life. Stonewall Jackson sent for him and ordered him to make a map of the Shenandoah Valley. Thus began his association with Jackson and his real career. He rendered invaluable service to Jackson and to the latter's successors in command of the Second Corps of the Army of Northern Virginia. His knowledge of the ground was in large part responsible for the surety of Jackson's moves in the Valley, as it was later for the initial success of Jubal Early at Cedar Creek. He had an unrivaled eye for terrain, and this gift made him more than a map-maker. He was an expert at reconnaissance. "With Hotchkiss away," Freeman wrote, "Jackson was not blinded, but his vision was dimmed."

Hotchkiss kept a journal during the war. For almost three-quarters of a century it remained in the possession of his family and was not available to scholars. Only Freeman was permitted to see it, and on it he based his fresh account in *Lee's Lieutenants* of the Valley campaign. Eventually the journal came into the possession of the Library of Congress, but even then it was not widely or systematically used by students of the war. Now Archie P. McDonald and the Southern Methodist University Press have made the diary available in published form, ably edited by Professor McDonald. In so doing, they have performed a service to scholarship. The journal is a mine of information about many persons and events—Jackson and Lee, the problems of command, the battles in Virginia, and last but very important, the work of a heretofore unrecognized but necessary man in the Confederate war machine. This is one of the superior Civil War diaries, possibly one of the superior American personal records.

T. HARRY WILLIAMS

Baton Rouge, Louisiana
March, 1973

Preface

THE COPY of the Hotchkiss journal used by the editor was a typescript prepared under Jedediah Hotchkiss's personal supervision. The mere bulk of the journal, massive as it was and covering most of Hotchkiss's adult life, imposed severe problems. A complete edition would not have been feasible, and therefore only the entries specifically dealing with Hotchkiss's military service during the Civil War are included in this volume. The period covered is from March 10, 1862, through April 18, 1865.

The editing has been largely a task of identification. Christian names and proper military rank had to be found for the many personalities identified only by family names. Where possible, identification has been provided for battles, events, and little-known locations. Misspellings have been corrected when necessary for ease in reading; but Hotchkiss's syntax has in all cases been preserved, and certain peculiarities and inconsistencies of spelling, punctuation, and other aspects of style have been retained in order to preserve the flavor of the original. Occasionally, items of information which Hotchkiss omitted or stated incorrectly have been inserted or corrected within brackets. The chapter divisions are the editor's, although certain obviously natural cleavages have been utilized.

I wish to express my gratitude to a number of people for their kind assistance. Mrs. R. E. Christian, now deceased, of Deerfield, Virginia, and Charles Hotchkiss Osterhout, of Jefferson City, Missouri, graciously made available much of the biographical material on Jedediah Hotchkiss. Frank E. Vandiver and T. Harry Williams were especially helpful and encouraging. My gratitude for their technical assistance also goes to the staffs of the Fondren Library, Rice University; the Louisiana State Library and Archives; the Duke University Library; and the Library of Congress; to Dr. C. K. Chamberlain, William J. Brophy, and especially Miss Jan Todd, Stephen F. Austin State University; and also to Benjamin Smylie, typist, Mrs. Helen Fay Lewis, who aided with proofreading, and Mrs. Jo Wright, who helped me with the index. For many kindnesses and timely encouragements I am especially indebted and especially grateful to my wife, Judy, and to my friend T. Barrett.

ARCHIE P. MCDONALD

Nacogdoches, Texas
March, 1973

Introduction

TO CONFEDERATE SOLDIERS in Virginia he was a familiar sight—one leg cast over the pommel of his saddle, a tall man bending laboriously over his sketchbook and drawing curious lines on a scrap of paper. Glancing occasionally at hastily taken notes, he skillfully formed a map which accurately located peculiarities of terrain, residence, and troop positions. When it was finished, this map would be used by General Thomas Jonathan Jackson; eventually it would be returned to its creator, Jedediah Hotchkiss, topographical engineer of the Second Corps, Army of Northern Virginia. He was more than an engineer—companion to Jackson, courier, often a fighting soldier—but essentially he was an engineer and the best topographical engineer in the Confederate Army. He was the man more responsible than any other for Jackson's ability always to proceed in sure knowledge of the terrain, and during the war he performed many services that would have been a credit to officers of much higher rank.[1]

Hotchkiss was not a native southerner. He was originally from New York, and he traced his ancestry through Connecticut back to Stirling, Scotland. Sailing with John Davenport on "the good ship Hector," members of the Hotchkiss family first reached New England on June 26,

1637.[2] Samuel Hotchkiss settled in New Haven, Connecticut, in 1642.[3] The Hotchkisses were an important family in Connecticut, serving in various civil and military posts, and they were active in the commerce of the area.

The call of the West drew David Hotchkiss in 1787 to the Susquehanna Valley of New York. Settling a short distance from the Pennsylvania line, he bought thirty-four hundred acres of virgin land and helped to lay out the townsite of Windsor, New York. He became the village benefactor by donating land for the town square and serving as the town's first justice of the peace.[4]

David Hotchkiss had three sons, Amraphael, Cyrus, and Gilead. Very little is known about these brothers. Amraphael was the father of Stiles Hotchkiss, who married Lydia Beecher, a distant relative of Henry Ward Beecher and Harriet Beecher Stowe.[5] Lydia Hotchkiss bore several children for her husband. A son, Nelson Hill Hotchkiss, was born on December 3, 1819, and some time later a daughter, Jenny, was born. The second son, Jedediah Hotchkiss, was born on November 30, 1828, at the family home near Windsor, Broome County, New York.[6]

Young Jedediah was instructed by his parents in the Christian religion and contemporary methods of agriculture. His mother had been, since her eighth year, a devout Methodist, but she allowed her children to be reared in Presbyterianism, the faith of their father.[7] Farming did not interest Jed. He much preferred to roam the New York countryside examining plants and rocks and observing the land. Frequently chores prevented these wanderings. But sometimes, while performing farm duties, the young boy could enjoy another diversion, books. While tending the cows or out of sight of his father, Jed would lie in the tall grass— preferably in a spot still warm from a sunning cow—and pore over the printed pages.[8]

Stiles Hotchkiss decided that his son's fondness for study should receive proper direction. After attending the local public school, Jed was enrolled in Windsor Academy. He celebrated his graduation from the academy in 1846 by joining a group of young men in a walking tour in Lyken's Valley, near Harrisburg, Pennsylvania. The valley's coal mining operations interested him, and he secured a teaching position among the German miners for one year. His leisure was profitably spent in study of the geology of coal deposits and the business of extracting the fuel.

When the term was completed, Jed began another tour in the company of a fellow teacher. They explored the Cumberland Valley of Pennsylvania and the western portions of Virginia. Stopping briefly in Page County, Virginia, Hotchkiss met Henry Forrer, one of the owners of an iron furnace near Luray, Virginia. Forrer invited him to Mossy Creek to meet his brother, Daniel Forrer, who was looking for a young scholar to tutor his children.[9] Jed accepted the position. His pay was to be $300 annually, plus board, room, washing, and a horse. He had plenty of time for reading and study, and during this period he taught himself the principles of map making and engineering.[10] A great deal of native talent and desire made this possible; formal education in these subjects was available only at military schools.

Forrer was pleased with Jed's work, and in conjunction with other Mossy Creek residents he initiated a movement to build the Mossy Creek Academy. On August 26, 1852, a building committee of seven met and pledged $100 each for the construction of the school. Hotchkiss was to head the building committee and remain as principal of the school.[11]

These activities in Virginia turned Jedediah Hotchkiss into an established young man. By 1853 he had an education, a community position, and a promising future as a teacher. Mossy Creek was good for him; it gave him honest labor in the instruction of the young, pleasant diversion in a beautiful lake, and a field laboratory for his geological and engineering interests. It was here that he took the two most important steps in his life—church membership and marriage. Trained in the theology of the Presbyterian church, he was already imbued with the religious convictions which remained throughout his life. On May 22, 1853, he went before the board of the Mossy Creek Presbyterian Church to confirm his affiliation with that congregation. The Reverend William B. Brown presided over the examining committee, and satisfied with Hotchkiss's faith in Christ the committee members received him as a member of the church.[12] He was soon characteristically in harness, teaching a men's Bible class which proudly claimed one hundred members.

In December, Hotchkiss traveled north to Lanesboro, Pennsylvania, to claim Miss Sara Ann Comfort as his wife. He had met Sara in 1846 while touring Pennsylvania. They were introduced by Sara's beau, Raply McKune. Her family had lived in Pennsylvania since Richard Comfort had settled there in the mid-eighteenth century. Born on February 10, 1833, Sara Ann was the daughter of John and Anna Hunt Comfort. Educated at Kingston Seminary, she was an intelligent woman, proficient in languages, and fully capable of aiding her husband in his school. They were married on December 21, 1853, and returned to Mossy Creek.[13] They quickly settled in a home at the foot of a hill near the academy. On May 6, 1854, Sara was received by letter into the church of her husband.[14]

Hardly a year had passed before the family was enlarged by the birth of Nellie. After two more years Anne, the second and last .child, was born. Anne's birth was difficult for Mrs. Hotchkiss, and the ordeal left her in poor health for several years. In 1858, Hotchkiss sold his interest in Mossy Creek to Thomas Moore and moved his family to Stribbling Springs, Virginia. Mrs. Hotchkiss drank the healthful waters at the springs and quickly regained her strength. Jed joined his brother-in-law, William McKune, in business. He also taught one term in a small local school,[15] but with Sara's improvement he decided to move on.

In 1859, Jed was joined by his brother, Nelson H. Hotchkiss. Together they purchased a farm near Churchville, Virginia. Here the brothers erected several buildings, and in the fall they opened the Loch Willow Academy. Jed, assisted by his wife and a small staff, had charge of the administration and instruction. Nelson attended to the farm and the boarding of the scholars.[16] Loch Willow proved very successful. For the 1860-61 term fifty-four students enrolled, bringing the school a total revenue of over $1,700.[17] The Hotchkiss family changed their church membership to Union Church in anticipation of a long residence at their new home.

The Hotchkisses concerned themselves very little with the national crisis. Absorbed in the new school, Jed spent most of his time close to his work. His brother Nelson, however, was an outspoken Unionist; but both were cemented to their new home. Jed had lived in Virginia for fourteen years and was economically tied to that state. His roots were in New York—both parents still lived in Windsor—and he undoubtedly lamented a situation which so completely separated him from them; but Virginia was his home, and it was to Virginia that he turned when forced to choose.

Despite the gathering war clouds, Jed tried to keep Loch Willow in operation as long as possible. But when Virginia seceded from the Union on April 17, 1861, an assistant teacher organized an infantry company and several pupils joined him. Shortly afterward several more students enrolled in a cavalry company. In June, Hotchkiss acknowledged the inevitable by dismissing the remaining students and offering his services to the Confederate Army.[18]

Hotchkiss reported to Lieutenant Colonel Jonathan M. Heck at Rich Mountain in western Virginia on July 2, 1861. The first Federal thrust into the area was rolling the Virginia forces back, and General Robert Selden Garnett hurried to that region to stop the invasion. There was the added problem of unrest in the army that required his attention. On July 3, Hotchkiss began his service by initiating a survey of "Camp Garnett" and the vicinity preparatory to making an accurate topographical map. In the matter of maps the Confederacy had to begin from scratch. The few maps they had were inaccurate and out of date.[19] Hotchkiss had almost completed his survey when the enemy arrived in force; the Confederates were soon under attack. Hotchkiss remained in the entrenchment during the attacks of July 10 and 11. Militarily the situation was serious for the Confederates; "Camp Garnett" was separated from the main force by Rich Mountain. In order to reestablish communication with the main force it would be necessary to cross the mountain under enemy fire. At midnight on July 11, Colonel John Pegram ordered Heck to assume command and to rejoin Garnett. Heck selected his engineer to lead the march over the mountain.

Led by Hotchkiss and the Augusta-Lee Rifles of Captain Robert Doak Lilley, the hurriedly formed column began its slow trek. "Indian," the enemy countersign, was passed back in the darkness. After the marchers had proceeded some distance in the stillness, a whistle brought them to their knees. Hotchkiss managed a low reply. It was later learned that a Federal regiment had been stationed parallel to the line of march and only the whistled reply had enabled the Confederate band to complete their escape. The summit of the mountain and the safety of the other slope were reached as the first streaks of dawn appeared. The light revealed that Hotchkiss led but fifty of Lilley's men, instead of the much larger column that had begun the march. It was later established that the others had been halted by a courier from Pegram. The messenger had traveled only as far as the rear of Lilley's company, and his caution and the need for silence had prevented the order from being passed to the head of the column. Only those men who had not received the order made it to safety.[20]

In the hasty departure Hotchkiss had been forced to leave behind his valuable engineering equipment. As soon as possible he filed a claim with the Confederate government for "1 Barometer (Aneroid), 1 set of Mathematical instruments," and two sets of compass and chain for a total value of $83.00.[21]

Back in camp, Hotchkiss was made acting adjutant, but he wrote to his wife that he expected to relinquish the post when General Robert E. Lee arrived to take command.[22] When Lee arrived, he put Hotchkiss to work on a map of Tygart's Valley. By working furiously, Hotchkiss finished the map by early August. But the effort to complete the work had sapped his strength, and he became easy prey for typhoid fever. For five days he suffered with severe headaches, pains in the limbs, and insomnia.[23] He decided to return to Loch Willow to convalesce and to finish the map in the leisure of home. In October he was notified that he would receive the monthly pay of a lieutenant of engineers, $93.33, for services rendered to date.[24]

By March, 1862, Hotchkiss considered himself again fit for service. When Governor John Letcher called out the militia of the Shenandoah Valley, Hotchkiss decided to return to the army if he could obtain engineering duty. He wrote to Colonel W. S. H. Baylor, a member of General T. J. Jackson's staff, to inquire if the colonel could secure his appointment. Baylor replied that the prospects seemed good, and he urged Hotchkiss to apply in person to the general.[25] Hotchkiss obtained letters of introduction and left with the Augusta County militia on March 17 for Jackson's camp. The militia was commanded by Colonel William S. Sproul, and its officer corps also included Colonel John H. Crawford and Major William M. Wilson. These officers were as inexperienced as their men, and Hotchkiss accepted a position as adjutant to help clear up problems of the march.[26]

Soon after he arrived at Jackson's camp, Hotchkiss was dispatched on a preliminary reconnaissance of Woodstock and vicinity. He was accompanied by Lieutenant James Keith Boswell, chief of engineers, who ultimately became Hotchkiss's closest friend. On March 21 he helped Boswell muster the militia into the regular service, and on that day he also received the happy news that Jackson would detail him for engineering duty.

The momentary joy of his appointment to staff duty was shattered by grave news from home. An epidemic of scarlet fever was sweeping the valley, and already Nellie and Anne were its victims. For many days he lived with the fear that his children were dying, if not already dead.[27] He became resigned to their loss and put his faith in God. At last word came that his daughters were spared, and Hotchkiss found time to comfort Major John A. Harman, Jackson's chief quartermaster, who had lost two children and expected the death of others.

There was hard work to fill Hotchkiss's mind after Jackson summoned him to headquarters on the morning of March 26. After a general conversation about engineering, Jackson spoke the words that made Hotchkiss his topographical engineer: "I want you to make me a map of the Valley, from Harpers Ferry to Lexington, showing all the points of offence and defence in those places. Mr. Pendleton will give you orders for what ever out fit you want. Good morning, Sir."[28] Lieutenant A. S. ("Sandie") Pendleton detailed William Humphreys as Hotchkiss's assistant and secured a wagon and supplies for the reconnaissance. Thus was formed a partnership between general and engineer. The engineer, with his quick perception of terrain could swiftly supply accurate sketches to the general, who had no real facility for grasping the lay of land.[29] Hotchkiss, aware of this lack of ability in his chief, was always prepared to explain his maps. Before movements of the army he was frequently called in to give advice on terrain. He made sure that he was able to furnish graphic representations of any point on which Jackson was not clear. He used different-colored pencils for greater clarity in the definition of surface features.[30]

In April, 1862, Hotchkiss received leave to visit his home while on a trip to confer with General Edward ("Allegheny") Johnson, who was encamped near Staunton. Hotchkiss was already tired of war, and the pleasantness of home made the front-porch rocking chair twice as hard to leave. But he hurried back to camp, for Jackson needed specific maps of the valley. During the famous Valley Campaign of 1862, Hotchkiss was engaged in reconnaissance and map making. From mid-June through July he spent nearly a month in Staunton drawing maps of the campaign. On July 15 he was ordered to join Jackson at Gordonsville with full equipment. Knowing this would mean a long absence, he wrote his wife careful instructions regarding the care of Loch Willow. He urged her to continue the children's education. "The 3 R's," he wrote, "are the foundation of education . . . and they must be well learned to begin with . . ."[31]

Hotchkiss joined the Second Corps for the engagements at Second Manassas and for the Maryland invasion. As in the past, his duties were mainly limited to reconaissance and the sketching of field maps. It was while in Maryland near Frederick City that Hotchkiss performed a curious service for Jackson; he bought his commander a new hat. Hotchkiss requested permission to go into town to purchase a new hat, and Jackson asked him to buy him a new headpiece also. The general determined the correct size trying on Hotchkiss's hat—"What fits you will fit me." When Hotchkiss returned with Jackson's new hat, "a tall black hat,"[32] he took the general's old gray cap and put it into his saddlebag for safekeeping. The cap was, on another occasion, a subject of conversation between the two men. Just before the battle of Fredericksburg in December, 1862, Jackson asked Hotchkiss the whereabouts of his old cap and remarked that it had fit him better than any other he had ever owned. When he suggested, nonetheless, that he might have it destroyed, Hotchkiss grew bold enough to ask for it as a souvenir. Jackson was pleased and after a while said, "I reckon you may have the cap." Before Hotchkiss sent the cap home, he gave a button from the headband to S. Howell Brown, a fellow engineer.[33]

In December, Hotchkiss was again ill. Plagued by colds, he suffered from fevers and was yellowed by jaundice. He stayed at the job and spent most of January, 1863, making detailed maps of the battles of Kernstown and McDowell. On February 3 he applied for leave of absence to take care of the sale of the farm in Augusta County, and "to attend to business which has been neglected since June, 1861."[34] An added incentive was Sara's birthday, only seven days away on the tenth. He left on the fifth for Loch Willow and arrived there three days later. The journey was delayed by a broken locomotive, but the talkative Hotchkiss had little trouble passing the time with the other passengers.

The sale of the farm was necessitated by a rift between the brothers Jed and Nelson Hotchkiss. Just what caused the misunderstanding is not known, but their political differences would seem a good guess. Whatever their disagreement, they were still in sufficient accord to reject the price offered at the sale on February 10. Another sale was scheduled for February 28.[35] While he was home, Jedediah settled other outstanding business. For instance, he paid his taxes, $26.61. The tax receipt lists five slaves among his assets.[36] In addition he had Christian Beer sign his note to Mrs. Jane Kiger for the annual hiring of William Gearing, a servant boy.[37]

The trip back to camp was difficult. Hotchkiss's watch was a half hour late, and he arrived at the station just as the train was leaving. Jumping aboard, he found that his luggage was too heavy to pull onto the moving car. Hotchkiss got off the train at Waynesboro and rode a freight back to get the box. The following day the engine derailed. Back on the track, the train was delayed overnight by another stalled carrier. The one pleasant event of the trip was an offer from a fellow passenger, a Mr.

Van Meter, for Hotchkiss to teach school in Hardy County. He was to have fifteen students and receive $100 per student. He declined the offer, saying that Hardy County was too far north for the safety of his family.[38]

The family position was nevertheless weakened at home. Nelson wrote to Jed on February 27, informing him that he had purchased a farm near Howardsville.[39] In March Nelson sold the farm at Loch Willow. The terms of the sale included the provision that Jed's house and laboratory were not to be sold, and he was to retain half the vineyard. Hotchkiss was pleased; he wrote his wife that "no better way exists than to take different roads when the one traveled does not suit the disposition of brethern—and we can only pray that each may, in God's fear, deal justly & righteously with the other."[40]

As winter thawed into spring, Hotchkiss thought of home and wrote to his wife of camp life. He subscribed to the *Central Presbyterian* and the *Southern Literary Messenger* and had them mailed to Loch Willow for Sara. Hotchkiss wrote his wife that he had at last been able to take a warm bath and put on clean clothes, since William did the washing, and he now felt "quite civilized."[41] Occasionally his letters revealed the grim side of army life. On March 1 he wrote of a deserter being shot. "Discipline," he noted, "is going on—a good many have been shot, some whipped, some drummed out of the camp and then put to labor with a ball and chain, some branded on the backsides with letters D. or C. for desertion or cowardice."[42] Hotchkiss was mortified to find Samuel Forrer, the son of his Mossy Creek benefactor, charged with desertion. Forrer had been apprehended while crossing the lines, but he contended that he was going for medicine. Hotchkiss visited Forrer and spoke to the military court on the youth's behalf. Whether or not Hotchkiss was responsible, Forrer did escape the death penalty, and he was thereafter grateful to his old friend. As late as 1908, on the occasion of Mrs. Hotchkiss's death, he wrote to the family, expressing his gratitude to Hotchkiss.[43]

In early April Hotchkiss found a small farm for sale that he liked. It was perfect for his needs—large enough for subsistence agriculture and a small school. He wrote to the owner, a Mr. Lindsay, to inquire his terms. They were apparently to his liking, for he considered borrowing the money to purchase the farm if he could obtain a good interest rate. Sara was unwilling to move, however, and in the end Jedediah bowed to her wishes. Later in the month he sent William home for supplies. The servant brought back the news that all at home was well, and his glowing accounts made Hotchkiss homesick.[44]

The reverie of home was snapped by the cold reality of battle. As April passed into May, a major engagement was imminent. On May 2, 1863, a Federal force under General Joseph Hooker fought the Battle of Chancellorsville against the Confederate units of General Robert E. Lee and his "right arm," General T. J. Jackson. During the day the battle went well for the Confederates. By a flanking movement, Jackson took his whole corps to Hooker's rear and, after hard fighting, won the day. As night fell, the troops began to secure their positions. Jackson rode out with members of his staff on a personal reconnaissance. Just beyond General A. P. Hill's position he learned from Federal prisoners that Hooker was throwing up obstacles to the advance. Wheeling at an alarm signal, the little band trotted back toward the safety of their own lines. It was a dark nine o'clock, and the random firing had created tension. As Jackson and his staff approached the positions of a North Carolina regiment, they were mistaken for a Yankee cavalry charge, and a nervous line of men opened fire. Jackson held up both hands and ordered the men to cease firing. He was struck in the right hand and again in the left arm. Jackson's racing horse was caught by Captain R. E. Wilbourn, and the limp general fell into his arms.

Hotchkiss and Pendleton arrived on the scene shortly after the firing ceased. Seeing the general on the ground, Hotchkiss turned his horse and raced for Dr. Hunter Holmes McGuire, Jackson's medical director and personal physician. He then hurried on to find a stimulant. When he returned, Hotchkiss was dispatched to General Lee to inform him of the development. Lee had already heard the news from Wilbourn, who had preceded Hotchkiss by thirty minutes.[45]

Hotchkiss rested awhile and then went to look for James Keith Boswell. He found the place where Jackson had been wounded, and there, too, he found his friend's body sprawled about twenty paces from where Jackson fell. Boswell lay by a side road, pierced through the heart by two rifle balls. He was also wounded in the leg. Hotchkiss started to get Boswell's personal effects for his family but found that the body had been "riffled of hat, glass, pistol, daguerreotype, & c." He secured an ambulance and took Boswell to Wilderness Tavern, where Jackson had been taken. Here he employed two men to dig the grave in the Elwood family cemetery near the spot where Jackson's amputated arm was buried. The Reverend Tucker Lacy offered "a feeling prayer."[46]

Hotchkiss was deeply affected by Boswell's death. The two had been more than superior and subordinate; they had been friends. Sharing the same tent and mess, they had the kind of association known only to soldiers. Now the friend was gone, taken away by the war that brought them together, and it was all happening too fast for Hotchkiss to understand. Jackson still lived, and that helped for a while. But he had to be taken to the rear for recovery. Lacy aroused Hotchkiss early on May 4 to select the route and lead the way to the home of Thomas Coleman Chandler near Guiney's, where Jackson was to convalesce. Hotchkiss selected a route to Todd's Tavern, through Spotsylvania Court House, and thence to Guiney's Station. He went ahead of the ambulance with a small party to clear the rocks from the road and to order the wagons out of the way. A few of the wagoners were obstinate until they were informed of the identity of the patient. Then, with hats in hand, some weeping, they gave way. The party arrived at Chandler's about eight o'clock.[47] Hotchkiss soon hurried back to headquarters to resume his topographical duties. Jackson's last words to him had promised that he, too, would soon be returning to duty. But when Hotchkiss learned that Jackson was not expected to recover, he was resigned: "I do pray Heaven to spare him unless, in the wise council of eternity, he has accomplished the end for which he was created."[48] Within a week Jackson was dead.

Shaken by the loss of Boswell and Jackson, Hotchkiss wrote to his wife that "the charmed circle in which General Jackson and his staff moved is broken & the break is a heavy one."[49] He missed Jackson very much; headquarters was dreary, to him most of all, "for," he wrote, "my tent mate is gone as well as my General."[50]

General A. P. Hill was appointed temporary commander of Jackson's corps. Hotchkiss welcomed him as a good military man, but he was worried because Hill was not a "Man of God," and did not wear the "Sword of the Lord and of Gideon."[51] Shortly afterward a general reorganization of the command structure placed General Richard S. Ewell in command of the Second Corps, and General Jubal A. Early eventually replaced him. But Hotchkiss always missed Jackson: "I was in no great battle subsequent to Jackson's death" he wrote, "in which I did not see the opportunity which, in my opinion, he would have seized, and have routed our opponents."[52]

Hotchkiss had scant time to reflect on his losses. He soon was busy preparing for Lee's second northern invasion. As the army marched toward Pennsylvania and Sara's home, Hotchkiss saw scenes which probably filled him with nostalgia and with fear. Stopping to talk with a woman who had been robbed three times by Federals and left with one dress and nothing to eat, he heard her vindictive prayer "that there might never be another Yankee child born & that not one of the race might be left on the face of the earth by the first day of next June."[53]

Hotchkiss traveled with the army as far north as Carlisle, Pennsylvania. Taking over the United States barracks there, the Confederates raised their flag and listened to the Reverend Mr. Lacy deliver an appropriate sermon. As the army neared Gettysburg, Hotchkiss was engaged in reconnaissance, serving Ewell in much the same way as he had Jackson. During the first day of the battle he acted as a courier, but he was soon ordered to Seminary Ridge to observe the troop positions so that he could draw an accurate map of the battle. On July 4 he was up at two in the morning working on a map of the country that had to be crossed on the return to Virginia. On the retreat to the Potomac River he helped move the wagons and took careful notes on the terrain. On July 14, the army recrossed the river into Virginia.

Being back in Virginia made Hotchkiss anxious for Sara and for Loch Willow. On July 14 he wrote that he longed for the "repose and quiet" of home, but could see no chance of getting there.[54] In early August Hotchkiss applied for his first leave in six months. His request took about a month for final approval, and the nearness of home made army life even more distasteful. Food, consisting mostly of corn, beans, and stewed peaches, was limited and monotonous. When not working, Hotchkiss passed the time by reading and conversing with fellow soldiers, doubtless finding solace in their mutual complaints. From the Reverend Mr. Lacy he bought Nellie and Anne each "a set of the Gospels, four pretty little volumes," and Sara a "nice . . . Testament."[55] But still the leave was delayed.

In early September the Reverend R. L. Dabney visited headquarters, collecting information for a forthcoming biography of Jackson. Hotchkiss guided him over the battlefield at Cedar Run. He was pleased that Dabney was writing the biography: "I think he will make a good life of Gen. J. and still leave room for another work,"[56] said Hotchkiss. Apparently he was already nurturing the ambition to write about Jackson himself.

As the furlough continued to be postponed, Hotchkiss grew bitter. His health was declining while able-bodied men sat out the war at home. He angrily wrote to his wife that she would make a better soldier "than 75 per cent of the -stay-at-home-and-wont-organize people."[57] By September 8 his health was such that he was granted an emergency medical leave by order of Hunter McGuire. He had to ride from Staunton to Loch Willow in an ambulance. Dr. Wilson, a local physician, called daily for five days after Hotchkiss's return and prescribed "some active medicine" to treat a condition diagnosed as dysentery. The case was assumed by Dr. Robert S. Hamilton on September 13, and Hotchkiss rapidly improved. But by late September he was not considered sufficiently recovered to return to service, and he was granted an additional ten days for convalescence. On the twenty-eighth he went to Court Day in Staunton and greeted his friends. Louis T. Wigfall and "Extra Billy" Smith made political speeches.[58]

Before he returned to the field, Hotchkiss received a curious letter from Governor Letcher's aide, S. Bassett French. French wrote on behalf of Mrs. Anne Jackson, who requested that Hotchkiss send her the general's old gray cap. It had been a present from her, and she was willing to trade him Jackson's gauntlets for its return.[59] The following day James Power Smith wrote him, for Mrs. Jackson, "I really can see no other way to do than to give it up."[60] But Hotchkiss decided to retain possession of the cap, and it was preserved by his family until October 25, 1939, when it was presented to the Virginia Military Institute.[61] No reason for this denial of a widow's request, except a soldier's affection for his commander, can be advanced.

Hotchkiss returned to camp on October 5, 1863, disgusted with war and, although only a few hours removed, already anxious for home. Matters were complicated by the theft of his horse, but fortunately a Mr. Harnsberger, a former pupil, supplied him with another mount.[62] Gradually Hotchkiss settled down to the map work that was to become his routine during the fall of 1863. In early December he and Pendleton made an extensive reconnaissance to select winter quarters. But Hotchkiss did not like the idea of winter in the field. On December 20 he requested and received a twenty-five-day leave to "attend to business and copy a map of the Valley."[63] The business he transacted demonstrates wartime inflation in Staunton. The price of hiring the servant William Gearing for another year had risen to $300, and Hotchkiss sold a horse for $600.[64]

After nearly a month at home, Hotchkiss was ordered on January 18, 1864, to report with his assistants and baggage to General Jubal A. Early in Staunton. Early wanted a map of all the approaches to Staunton and Lexington from the west. Beginning work on the map, Hotchkiss

requested Early and General John D. Imboden to detail a guide and a
courier to him. Early sent A. D. Moore, a cousin of Major William Allan,
to be his courier, and Imboden ordered that "Private James L. Williams,
Company 'G,' 18th Va. Calvary . . . report to Capt. Jed Hotchkiss . . . in
the capacity of guide."[65]

Hotchkiss was mindful of home as winter passed to spring. In late
January he had to write to Nelson of the death of their sister, Jenny, who
died in New York from childbirth; and from home a toothache com-
plaint brought forth an old soldier's remedy.[66] He became apprehensive
when letters from home were delayed, and he gently chided his wife, "Be
sure to write to me often, if only a few words at a time—that I may not
fail to know of your welfare."[67]

In midsummer Hotchkiss was with Early on his famous raid on
Washington. Penetrating to the suburbs of the Federal capital, the Confederates came to within six miles of the White House, close enough to
worry President Abraham Lincoln. Early had promised his men that he
would take Washington; but the hot July sun and the dusty roads had
taken their toll, and he was forced to retreat with only a moral victory.
As the army slowly pulled back, Hotchkiss took advantage of the low
prices and the abundant supplies in the North. He bought some bonnet
ribbon and forty yards of calico for Sara and a fresh Maryland horse for
himself. Surprisingly, he had no difficulty in using Confederate currency
for these purchases. He also wrote a letter to his parents, who still lived
in Windsor, New York.[68]

Hotchkiss remained with Early until after the battle of Cedar Creek
in October. Early and Sheridan were fighting for supremacy in the valley,
a contest eventually won by Sheridan. On the eve of the battle, Early sent
Hotchkiss and General John B. Gordon to the summit of Massanutton
Mountain on reconnaissance. Hotchkiss made a field sketch showing
heavy defenses on the Federal left; the sketch also revealed the relatively
unguarded right wing. When the attack came, the Confederates were
initially victorious; but they failed to follow up this advantage. Gordon
blamed Early for the failure, while Early laid it to Gordon's not being
ready. Hotchkiss was dispatched to General Lee with the news of the
action, but he was instructed by Early not to mention the halted advance
to the commander.[69]

When he had delivered the report to Lee, Hotchkiss was able to get
home for a visit. For some time he had maintained an office in Staunton,
and he needed to attend to affairs there. On November 30 he celebrated

his thirty-sixth birthday, sorrowed that the rapidly passing years brought only more war. "God grant that they may not have been spent in vain,"[70] he wrote.

Hotchkiss was home again for Christmas, as he had been each year of the war. It was again time to pay accounts and to hire his servants for the coming year. This time, however, he determined to purchase William Gearing from his owner. He felt an obligation to William, who, like many another who had gone away to war, had acquired a taste for spirits. Hotchkiss was able to raise $2,000 and borrow $3,000 more to purchase William from Mrs. Kiger.[71]

Returning to the field in January, Hotchkiss was used more frequently now for reconnaissance and in supervising a small staff in the making of maps. He and his assistants worked with the same devotion and patriotism as before, but the years of war were beginning to tell in economic loss and in the appearance of an understandable apprehension about the future. This was evident when in late February, 1865, Jed wrote to Sara that he had traded his *Webster's Dictionary* to Christian Beer for a barrel of flour. "I thought you would like the bargain," he commented. "It is a good one & you can hide the flour & keep it—I think."[72]

During the final spring of the war Hotchkiss was engaged in reconnaissance duties for General Thomas L. Rosser and General Lunsford L. Lomax. He was with Lomax at Lynchburg on April 9 when the first rumors of Lee's surrender reached there. Lomax rode to Danville to confer with Secretary of War John C. Breckinridge and then returned to dismiss his command.[73]

Hotchkiss arrived at Loch Willow at dusk on the eighteenth. A meeting of the Soldier's Aid Society of Churchville, held in his home, had just adjourned. His family was well but surprised to see him. They had thought that he might go to North Carolina to join General Joseph E. Johnston. He found many soldiers already home, bewildered about what course to follow. Theoretically still soldiers, they lacked leadership and initiative. Lincoln's proposition that Virginia come back into the Union without conditions "worked a revolution in sentiment" and helped them make up their minds to stay in their homes. Another factor in this decision was the marauding Federal troops who rode over the countryside stealing anything that struck their fancy.

April 20 brought the first rumor of Lincoln's assassination. Indignation and regret greeted confirmation of the news. There was fear, for

"Johnson, of Tennessee, ha[d] become President and breathe[d] out wrath against the South."[74]

A Federal provost marshal arrived in Staunton on May 1 and began paroling Confederate soldiers. Hotchkiss's parole fortunately is preserved in the collection of his papers, and it furnishes a description of him at war's end. He stood five feet ten inches, was probably a little thin, and had a fair complexion, with dark hair and brown eyes.[75] His lower lip was slightly extended. His eyes were a little sterner, a little deeper than they had been—but their view was forward. Jedediah Hotchkiss was a man of determination whose faith in Virginia was boundless. He never forgot the past, and in memory he found strength for the present. The past was a tool to be used in the building of the future; it was not a model to be reconstructed but a lesson learned so that a better future might be realized.

Virginia and the South had permanently claimed Hotchkiss, but there was too much Yankee in his spirit to allow idleness for long. On May 8 he attended a meeting in Staunton at which armed resistance was declared at an end and an attempt was made to restore civil government. The following day Hotchkiss was hard at the work of restoring Loch Willow Academy. The academy had not suffered real war damage, only neglect, and the labor consisted mainly of tidying up the classroom. On the tenth of May Hotchkiss began classes with four students, each of whom payed a tuition of $100 for a ten-month term. Things went well at school; and when Hotchkiss went into Staunton on June 10 to take the amnesty oath, he paid little attention to the Reverend R. H. Phillips and others who were trying to organize an expedition to Brazil. On June 20 he closed the school for the summer, but he expected to reopen it on September 1.[76]

While the Hotchkiss finances appeared to be very low, what Jedediah would have termed Providence was looking over his shoulder. On July 4 his old friend William Allan wrote that he had some engineering business for Hotchkiss in Staunton. Colonel M. G. Harman had some land that he wanted surveyed and probably would have other similar work. "Don't fail to attend promptly to this & I think I can work things to your satisfaction,"[77] Allan wrote.

Hotchkiss took Nellie along when he went to see Harman, and on July 6 they visited Jackson's grave in Lexington. Harman wanted Hotchkiss to come to Staunton to operate a select school for boys. His salary was to be $1,500 for teaching fifteen students. He was to receive an additional

$270 for Harman's two children.[78] Hotchkiss gladly closed the bargain and made arrangements for the move to Staunton. He literally traded houses with W. H. Waddell, who moved to Loch Willow and collected an additional $300. Hotchkiss's new home in Staunton was at the corner of Lewis and Water streets, and his school was conducted in a long building in the rear of the house.[79]

School was officially opened on September 6 with all fifteen students present—"Apparently a very pleasant set of boys."[80] Hotchkiss operated the school for two years, devoting most of the morning to classroom instruction and the afternoon to what engineering work he could pick up. In addition, he managed to find time to lecture in the sciences at the Augusta Female Seminary, also in Staunton. S. B. Robinson, who had been associated with Hotchkiss's field-engineering wagon during the war, came to live with Hotchkiss during this period and to assist him in his two professions. Beyond education and topography, Hotchkiss had one other big interest—religion. He lost no time in affiliating his family with the local Presbyterian Church. The pastor, the Reverend R. C. Walker, soon had him teaching a Bible class.[81]

The new home was brightened by the frequent visits of Hotchkiss's niece, Alansa Rounds, and her new husband, Captain F. F. Sterrett. Allie, as Alansa was affectionately named, was a favorite of her Uncle Jed's. She had visited him often before the war and had been adopted by the family. Hotchkiss's war letters reveal his deep concern for Allie and her rocky romance with Sterrett, and he happily received the newlyweds in October, 1865, as they made their way to Sterrett's home near Staunton.[82]

The arrival of a Federal detective from Richmond broke the serenity of the Hotchkiss home. A military order required Hotchkiss to surrender his collection of war maps to the detective for removal to Washington. Hotchkiss refused to relinquish the maps, but he promised to go to Richmond on the following Thursday and take them personally to the authorities. On October 28 he traveled to Richmond to protest the confiscation of his maps. Receiving no satisfaction there, Hotchkiss obtained letters of introduction to General Ulysses S. Grant and boarded the train for Washington. He found Grant most cooperative. Hotchkiss had been thinking of the historical value of the maps, while Grant was interested only in their practical value. A compromise was easily reached. Grant examined the collection and selected those maps that he considered valuable for future military use, and Hotchkiss consented to copy them. A fair price was agreed upon, and Hotchkiss returned to Staunton a victorious Rebel.[83] He hired C. W. Oltmanns, who had worked for him during the war, to prepare the maps for Grant.

Prosperity was apparently returning to Hotchkiss. In late November he selected a site on Oak Hill in Staunton for a home; however, this place, "The Oaks," was not completed until 1888. Hotchkiss was beginning to spend more time in engineering and literature than in the classroom. Already he had become a reference source for old soldiers who wished to write about their war experiences. The first postwar call came from General Early, who wished to borrow Hotchkiss's extensive diary and map collection to write a pamphlet on the Valley Campaign of 1864.[84] Later in the year William Allan enlisted Hotchkiss in an effort to write a history of the campaigns in Virginia. Allan generously allowed Hotchkiss three-fifths of any profits they might realize to get him to furnish maps and his diary.[85] The result was *The Battle-fields of Virginia; Chancellorsville*, published in New York in 1867. It actually included all operations since the battle of Fredericksburg in December, 1862. In January, 1866, Hotchkiss began the research for a book dealing with the operations of the armies in Virginia during the war. His old comrades were delighted that he had undertaken the work. General Rosser wrote his congratulations and added: "The loss of all records on our side and the one-sided statements which are now going to the world as history make it very necessary . . . that some officer like yourself . . . should undertake the work. And surely none could do it with greater prospects of success than yourself."[86]

In the summer of 1867 Hotchkiss permanently deserted the classroom for engineering duties. Except for a few lectures at Washington College and an occasional lecture to literary societies and college groups about his service under Jackson,[87] Hotchkiss devoted the remainder of his life to engineering and development work. He was probably more familiar with the topography and geology of Virginia than any other; he was therefore well qualified to launch there in 1867 a thirty-year personal crusade of restoration and development. Rich soil and relatively untapped mineral resources remained largely unused because there was a lack of local investment capital. The obvious course, therefore, was to lure capital to Virginia.

Brother Nelson Hotchkiss provided Jedediah with an early opportunity to advertise his crusade. In the spring of 1871 Nelson organized a tour of Virginia for a group of northern newspaper editors. He was then a traveling agent with the Chesapeake & Ohio and Richmond and

New York River railroads. To Nelson the tour represented a promotion effort by his employers; to Jedediah it was an opportunity to talk about Virginia to a group of influential men. Both brothers operated under the mantle of reconstruction, and an altruistic motive was prevalent in each. Nelson's health required him to leave the tour before it was completed, and Jedediah took his place as guide. Always ready with information about topography, soil, minerals, and the industrial resources of Virginia, he was described by a member of the tour as "a man of much intelligence, a most genial companion, and every inch a gentleman."[88]

Two development projects occupied Hotchkiss in 1872. First, he was engaged in a survey of the natural resources of McDowell, Mercer, and Wyoming counties for Captain Isaiah A. Welsh.[89] Later in the year he crossed the Atlantic to England as an unofficial ambassador from Virginia. His mission was to attract capital by advertising the mineral and timber resources of the Virginias. Hotchkiss liked England; he wrote home that the large turnip fields and exceptionally green grass made "the whole country look like a garden."[90] England was a challenge to his fertile mind. After purchasing a new suit, he acted like any tourist and visited Buckingham Palace, Marlborough House, and Westminster Abbey. The Abbey caused him a "strange" sensation when he realized that he was in the building with "England's long list of illustrious dead."[91]

In early January, 1873, Hotchkiss wrote to his wife that he had met the editor of the *London Times* and the mayor of Exeter. This letter also establishes Hotchkiss as a thoughtful husband; he informed Sara that he had bought her a set of china. His work seemed to be going well, he informed her, for he had been invited to address the Royal Society of Arts and Sciences. The address earned him much-needed recognition in business circles.[92]

Hotchkiss returned to Virginia later in the year, but 1874 found him back in England on a similar mission. Going first to Scotland, Hotchkiss made this trip for pleasure as well as business, and Nellie accompanied him. He found English capitalists begging for investments but reluctant to cross the Atlantic. Still, he had some hope that his trips would eventually draw some capital to Virginia.[93] Hotchkiss, and hundreds of other agents like him, did obtain some capital-investment immigration for the Virginias; but the established lines of movement, plus the concentration of steamship facilities in New York, kept these states from realizing a full return on their investments.[94]

On Hotchkiss's return, the Virginia Board of Immigration selected him to prepare a geographical and political summary of the state demonstrating the advantages of climate, soil, and production offered to foreign settlers. He was selected

because, in the pursuit of his calling as a topographical and mining engineer he had devoted much time to the acquiring of accurate knowledge of geography, the varied physical elements, the internal improvements and capabilities, the agricultural, manufacturing and general industrial condition and resources of the state, and was believed to possess greater experience and aptitude for the work than any person known to the Board.[95]

During the decade of 1880-90, Hotchkiss was extremely active in the development of western Virginia, both as promoter and as investor. He organized a company to develop iron and timber extraction. A prospectus revealed that he planned to lease 100,000 acres in Page and Rockingham counties and eventually expected to mine iron, manganese, and limestone. He told prospective investors that he could mine the ore for $44.44 per ton and sell it in Baltimore for $52.00 a ton. From his home in Staunton he published at a financial loss *The Virginias: A Mining, Industrial, and Scientific Journal*. It included articles by learned geologists describing the rich deposits of manganese, copper, iron, clay, and ocher to be found in the region. He was careful to point out the low cost of local labor, especially that of Negroes already adapted to gang labor.[96]

Hotchkiss was instrumental in securing a railroad connection for Pocahontas, West Virginia, and railroad service for the surrounding region. He learned that the line was in need of coal from its president, Frederick J. Kimball; and by promising that the Norfolk and Western Railroad could secure cheap fuel in inexhaustible quantities, he obtained the connection for the region. This increased the value of land Hotchkiss held in McDowell County. In 1884 he sold twenty-one tracts of land comprising 7,407 acres to Samuel A. Crozier of Upland, Pennsylvania, founder of the Crozier Land Company.[97]

Mining and development were not the only things that occupied Hotchkiss's time or his interests. Gradually during the 1880s he became more interested in telling the story of the Civil War, particularly from the vantage point of T. J. Jackson's staff. His appetite for publication was encouraged when in 1885 he and Joseph A. Waddell published a *Historical Atlas of Augusta County*. In addition, Hotchkiss contributed nearly half of the Confederate maps that appear in the *Atlas of the War of the Rebellion: A Compilation of the Official Records of the Union and Confederate Armies*.

Hotchkiss became acquainted with the British militarist and biographer G. F. R. Henderson, whose work on Jackson stood for half a century as the basic biography of its subject. In its preparation Hotchkiss was indispensable. He generously made his maps and his journal available, he painted word pictures of how the Confederate army lived and fought, he sought out old staff members and urged them to cooperate with Henderson, and he answered innumerable queries. Henderson wanted to know how dependent Jackson was on maps, how he looked in battle, and all the personal items for which a biographer yearns. Hotchkiss was patient and generous. He helped Henderson capture the spirit of Jackson and of the war as few have done.[98]

The historical and literary assistance was not all one way between Hotchkiss and Henderson. Since the fall of 1865, Hotchkiss had been working on a history of the military operations in Virginia. Much travel and the urgency of business left him little time for working on this project until the 1890s. When Henderson learned of Hotchkiss's project, he urged his friend not to make the work too short. Details that seemed trivial to Hotchkiss, he said, would be of exceeding interest to soldiers and to the vast army of enthusiastic volunteers. His letter included requests that Hotchkiss discuss the character, demeanor, and appearance of generals and of their troops, the nature of entrenchments, the way enemy intelligence was obtained, the methods of Confederate marksmen, and other items of military interest. "The more military your book is the better it will go down over here, as, owing to our number of volunteers and our constant little wars, the people generally understand and enjoy all details connected with the grand art of killing one's fellow man,"[99] wrote Henderson.

During the period of preparation, Hotchkiss conducted a voluminous correspondence with former associates in an effort to gather as much information as possible. Typical is the correspondence with Thomas T. Munford. A series of twelve letters were exchanged over the period from 1892 through 1898, in an interesting exercise in historiography.[100] A central theme runs throughout the correspondence. While other matters are raised and solved, each letter repeats the request sounded in the first. In reading his journal, Hotchkiss discovered a reference to a mission he had undertaken for Jackson. He was to meet Munford at the foot of Mt. Sidney and to order, "Go ahead." Time had faded his memory, and could Munford tell him what he then did, and what else passed between them that night? Repeatedly Munford denied knowledge of the encounter.

Hotchkiss's manner grew anxious, often even chiding, in his efforts to spur Munford's memory. Finally Hotchkiss acknowledged the error; he had been sent to meet Munford, but he had spent the night alone—and the encounter never happened.

Through methods like those used on Munford and through his own experiences, Hotchkiss gradually acquired the information and literary skills that made his *Virginia*, which appeared as Volume 3 of *Confederate Military History*, one of the better works of the series. It is a standard work of Civil War historiography and deserves to be considered as a primary source in certain areas because of Hotchkiss's participation in the war and familiarity with the terrain. Clement A. Evans, editor of the series, paid this tribute to Hotchkiss, who died shortly before the work was published:

As topographer and staff officer under Garnett, Lee, Jackson, Ewell and Early, he was undoubtedly more familiar with the battlefields of Virginia than any other man, and it is fortunate for the students of today and of future generations that his account of the war in that region should be here preserved. Particularly in regard to the Valley campaigns of Stonewall Jackson and Early, and the campaigns of the Second corps of the army of Northern Virginia, he was an historical authority.[101]

As Hotchkiss's beard grew whiter, he came to be a much honored man. In 1893 he was selected as a judge of mining at the Chicago Exposition. He was in demand as a lecturer, and in June, 1894, he was commissioned "Brigadier-General and Chief of the engineer corps, staff of General J. B. Gordon," who signed the mock commission as commander of the United Confederate Veterans.[102] To list the many organizations to which Hotchkiss belonged would be exhausting. A joiner of professional and fraternal groups, he carried on an extensive correspondence with many men of prominence in varied fields.

The years had brought Hotchkiss one office of which he was extremely proud. He had always been interested in religious work, and he took his position as Sunday school superintendent of the Second Presbyterian Church of Staunton seriously. He had been one of the original thirteen petitioners to the Lexington Presbytery for the establishment of a second church in Staunton. Selected as the first superintendent of the school, he held the post for twenty-four years. Business frequently took him away from home, but he always tried to be back for the Sunday service. Late one Saturday in the fall of 1898 he could find only a freight train making the run to Staunton. Hotchkiss knew that a Christian soldier could not always be comfortable, and he boarded the freight for home.

The jolting of the engine cab was too much for the seventy-year-old Hotchkiss. When the train arrived, he had to be helped to his home. His condition did not improve, and he was moved to St. Luke's Hospital in Richmond. His old friend Dr. Hunter H. McGuire came to take charge of his case. McGuire decided that an operation was necessary. Hotchkiss was soon well enough to write Munford that he was "rapidly recovering from an operation by which Dr. McGuire crushed from my bladder a stone $2\frac{1}{2}$ inches long by 1 wide and 1 thick."[103] With McGuire's kindly treatment and the pleasant company of old friends like James Power Smith, he seemed to improve. In late December he came back to Staunton for the Christmas pageant performed by his Sunday school. The new year brought bad weather, and Hotchkiss fell victim to the grippe with a mastoiditis complication.[104] He peacefully fell asleep on January 17, 1899.

Nellie and Anne were married now, and Sara came back to "The Oaks" pretty much alone. Nellie, married to George S. Holmes, lived in Charleston, South Carolina; Anne, who still lived in Staunton, was the wife of Allan M. Howison. For nine years Sara presided over "The Oaks" with graciousness. She joined her husband on Febraury 28, 1908.

At a Lee-Jackson Day meeting shortly after Hotchkiss's death, Hunter McGuire said in eulogy of his friend: "I would like of all things just now to pay my simple, loving, heart-felt tribute to the last one who has just now crossed over the river, brave, noble, and faithful Jed. Hotchkiss."

Make Me a Map of the Valley

1. MARCH 10–APRIL 14, 1862

"I want you to make me a map of the Valley"

ON THE 10TH OF MARCH, 1862, Gov. John Letcher by proclamation, called out all the militia of the Valley and adjacent counties to the west from the Potomac to and including Botetourt and Craig counties; this included the county of Augusta in which I resided.[1] The militia were ordered to report at once to Gen. T. J. Jackson, at Winchester. After the recovery of my health I had determined to enter the army again, volunteering for military engineering duty. Desiring to be as near my home as possible I opened correspondence with Lieut. Col. Wm. S. H. Baylor, of the Fifth Virginia, who I ascertained was on staff duty with Gen. Jackson,[2] and whom I knew well, to ascertain whether I could secure a place for such duty on the staff of Gen. Jackson. He replied that he thought there would be no difficulty in my securing such service and advised me to tender it in person; therefore, when the militia of the county were ordered to report to Gen. Jackson I determined to accompany them to his camp as I was well acquainted with the officers of the one hundred and sixtieth Regiment of Virginia militia, commanded by Lieut. Col. John H. Crawford, within whose bounds I resided and also with those of the Ninety-third Regiment commanded by Col. Wm. S. Sproul, and those of

3

the Thirty-second Regiment, commanded by Maj. Wm. M. Wilson, the other regiments from Augusta Co. These regiments, by orders, assembled in Staunton ready to march on Monday Morning, March 17, 1862.

I accompanied the three regiments of [Augusta] County, Virginia Militia, the One Hundred and Sixtieth and the Ninety-secondth, John H. Crawford, Col. of the One Hundred and sixtieth and Wm. S. Sproul, Col. of the Ninety-secondth, as Captain and Adjutant, at request and by appointment of Col. Crawford, the senior officer present. These regiments had been ordered to report to Gen. T. J. Jackson, down the Valley. The command numbered about 400 when it marched from Staunton, about the middle of the day, but members were falling in during the day as we marched along. The command marched to C. Landes', near Mt. Sidney, where the men slept in Mr. L's large barn and the officers in his house, having marched about 10 miles.

The day was warm and the Valley Turnpike quite dusty. We met large numbers of wagons loaded with machinery from the Harper's Ferry Armory[3] and with army stores. There were whole trains of wagons loaded with Richmond flour that had been sent to Strasburg, and even to Winchester, for the army! Also wagons of citizens loaded with furniture and carriages filled with families, many of them accompanied by servants, moving up from the Lower Valley which the Federals had not occupied.— The men of our command are in good spirits; many of those that ran away have concluded that they had best come along and not wait to be drafted. The report we met was that Gen. Jackson was holding the Narrow Passage, which is said to be very defensible against the enemy (Gen. Jackson's headquarters were at Israel Allen's, near Hawkinstown).

I recall that when I reached Staunton Monday morning I found the officers of the militia conferring as to what they should do, none of them having seen any actual military service, and very much at sea even as to how they should begin the march down the Valley. Seeing me among those at hand, Col. Crawford exclaimed, "Why, here is the man to help us out he knows all about it, having been in service in West Virginia. I will appoint him Adjutant of the command." This he at once did, and I accepted and proceeded to issue orders which soon straightened out matters and enabled us to begin the march down the Valley by about midday.

March 18th. "I wrote home at six and a half o'clock A.M. We broke camp at an early hour and marched, about 16 miles, to the large steam mill, just beyond Harrisonburg, in which our troops quartered, the three regiments together. I spent the night, by invitation, at Mr. A. B. Irick's, in company with Col. Sproul, Dr. Dunlap and others.—The day was warm and pleasant and the road dusty. The Rockingham militia are very averse to going to the army.[4] The order to them has been suspended for 10 days pending negociations, by George E. Deneals for Indian substitutes. The army is reported to be near Woodstock."

In my letter home I wrote: "We spent last night here, at C. Landes', near Mt. Sidney. Had a large barn for the men. The three regiments are here, of not more than 400 men have as yet come up, but they are constantly falling in. I slept in the house by the fire, slept soundly, but Mr. Hays said the floor was too hard. The men are in very good spirits and many of those that at first ran away have concluded that it is best to come on and not wait to be drafted for the war. I saw the Revs. Register, Martin, and Tebbs, yesterday. There is much excitement about the movements of our army up this way, and the road yesterday was full of wagon loads of servants, furniture, machinery, etc., on its way up the Valley. Gen. Meems' household went up. It is said that Gen. Jackson has come back to the Narrow Passage this side of Woodstock. The road there shuts up the whole Valley and he can easily defend the Passage. I do not suppose he will come any farther this way, though there may be a necessity for coming up to Staunton. Mr. Arnold comes back to Churchville. There were some forty preachers there and not many changes were made." The Baltimore Conference of the Methodist Episcopal Church South had been in session in Harrisonburg and the references to preachers were in consequence of that, those mentioned being known to my wife.

"*Wednesday, March 19,* started at nine A.M., and marched [?] miles to Dr. Williamson's, about two miles southwest of New Market; the men encamped in his large barn and the officers were entertained at his house." I wrote home this morning: "We reached Harrisonburg last night. The day was very pleasant though a little too warm and dusty. The three regiments encamped together in the steam mill just below town and I went out to Irick's with Col. Sproul, Dr. Dunlap and others; five of us. We were very comfortably entertained. We leave this morning at nine. The Rockingham militia has been released for 10 days. They are quite adverse to going. Our army below here is near Woodstock. *"Thursday, March 20th,* we marched to "Mount Airy" the celebrated Meem estate, about [?]. Our men found quarters in the large barns and the officers in the house of Gen. Gilbert C. Meem. We reached camp about noon. The day was quite cold with a raw wind. Maj. Poague[5] and myself rode forward to H. D., Qurs. at Israel Allen's near Hawkinstown, and reported the arrival of the Augusta militia to Gen. Jackson. He received us cordially and had many questions to ask about our men, the condition of things in the Upper Valley, etc. The First Brigade Gen. R. B. Garnett's,[6] marched back, late in the afternoon, from Camp Buchanan, to Rude's Hill; the rest of the army in near Hawkinstown."

This was my first meeting with Gen. Jackson since the beginning of the war. I had previously met him at the house of his father-in-law, Dr. Junkin, in Lexington, where I was a guest while on duty as one of the examining committee of Washington College in [185?].

March 21st. "Had a very busy day enrolling and organizing our men, part of whom were, today, mustered into service by Lieut. Col. Wm. S. H. Baylor, of the Fifth Virginia Infantry, who is the Acting Inspector General of the Valley District, with my assistance as Adjutant after he had proposed to the men that they should volunteer and join such of the old regiments of the army as they might choose. A good many did volunteer. One hundred of the militia were organized into a company with James C. Cochran[7] as Captain. Gen. Jackson came over to "Mount Airy" about noon and looked at the militia, then, accompanied by Lieutenant J. K. Boswell[8] of the Engineers he rode to Rude's Hill and examined that position, after which he returned to H. D. Qrs., but sent Boswell to examine the country further back towards New Market. He wanted a dam built in the river near Rude's to back up the water to the New Market and Forestville Road, as a protection to his flank if he should occupy Rude's Hill. In the afternoon the First Brigade marched back to camp between Mr. Jackson and Hawkinstown.—A cold day with a driving rain. It is reported that the enemy has fallen back from Winchester to quell a riot in Maryland; but there is no finding out what the truth is. I suppose that after tomorrow I will be a "private soldier" as there are not men enough to form a regiment and so Col. Crawford will not have a command but he has offered me the adjutancy of the regiment when that is made up. Col. Baylor says Gen. Jackson will have me detailed for engineer duty."

In the evening of March 31st, I wrote my wife: "We have now been a day and a half at the old Steenbergen place, the most magnificent farm in Virginia—some 1100 acres of level meadow land, the house a fine stone one on the first terrace above the level and a mile back from the turnpike. Mrs. Meem is a sister of Macon Jordan. They sent their servants to Lynchburg; nine ran away the day before they were to leave. Macon has gone home to see about his sisters. We had two days of fine weather to come [here] with [*sic*] and one of bad. We stayed the second night at Harrisonburg at the mill there. I went to Irick's with Col. Sproul; we had a nice time there. The next day came here. I have been very busy and had had to write a great deal, but expect to get through tomorrow, when I shall be a private, I suppose, as there are not men enough for a regiment and so the Colonel (Crawford) does not command, but he has offered me the adjutancy of the regiment when it is made up. Baylor says Gen. Jackson will have me detailed on engineer duty. The militia were partly mustered in today by Col. Baylor. They are putting the companies at one hundred each. Some of the men that ran away from home were caught by Ashby's[9] cavalry and brought to jail here. Gen. Jackson has been falling back but today he moved forward. A postscript on the 22nd adds: "This morning is some improvement in the weather. Yesterday was very bad, the mud is deep, but we are very well cared for, as we have houses to stay in, though crowded. There are about 12 of us that sleep in one room, with all sorts of sleeping fixing and some with no sleeping fixings. Gen. Jackson came up to see us yesterday; he looks care-worn, though he is a very pleasant man. I went down to see him the day we got here. He is very busy.—I called at Mr. Ruffner's (Rev. William) the morning we left Harrisonburg, for a few minutes. He gave me a very [nice] pocket compass and letters to some of his friends here. He wants my Johnston's Physical Atlas[10] and [if] he sends for it do it very carefully and send it. See that the Maslin boys[11] return my Marlborough and Allison if they go away. Tell them I have not yet seen their father, or the Hardy militia. I hope you are well yet I am in much suspense about you all and do not know when I shall hear from you, the mails are so deranged; half of the time the mail bags are not brought. Write to me by private hands if you hear of anyone coming here. They are falling every day.[12] The arresting of some start the others. They have taken the bank away from Harrisonburg. God bless you all. Kiss the dear children for papa.—I am very well indeed. Write, if by mail, to care of Lieut. Col. W. S. H. Baylor, Mt. Jackson."

The Macon Jordan above referred to was one of my pupils at Mossy Creek Academy. His father was one of the most prominent citizens of Luray. Macon had raised a cavalry company which was part of Ashby's command. The Maslin boys were the sons of Mr. Thomas Maslin of Moorefield that had spent the winter at my brother's, at Loch Willow, near Churchville, and I had taught them some each day while at home.

March 22nd. "Continued in camp at "Mount Airy"; some 12 of us

sleep in one room, crowded, but glad that we are in a house. The rain
ceased last night, but it is cold and the roads are very muddy. Col. Baylor
continued mustering in the militia. I aided him by writing the muster-
roll.—The First Brigade marched, some [?] miles, to Hupp's Hill, beyond
Strasburg; the other brigades, Fulkerson's, and Burk's, to Fisher's Hills.
Hd. Qrs. were in Strasburg. Ashby and his cavalry had an engagement
with the enemy, near Kernstown, and drove them to within a mile of
Winchester, then fell back across the Opoquon. Gen. Shields[13] of the
Federal army lost his arm in this action.

Writing to my wife at half-past five, on the morning of March 23rd,
(Sunday) from Camp Meem, near Mt. Jackson, I said: "We were yesterday mustered into the service of the Confederate States, for the war,
unless sooner discharged. A large number volunteered, but we made up
380, into companies, and a batallion was formed and put in command
of Maj. Poague, who is the senior major. I retain the adjutancy for the
present and may keep it after the regiment is filled up from other
counties. We formed a mess, today, with Col. Sproul and Arch. Christian.
They have a black boy along and a white boy hired, so I shall do very
well. Gen. Jackson came over to see us last Friday. He is a fine looking
fellow. Baylor mustered us in. Gen. Jackson moved his army back down
the Valley today, the enemy having falled back, it is said below Winchester, on account of the reported trouble in Maryland. We have any
amount of rumors, but know nothing. We have orders to march this
morning at eight o'clock, and I have to go to see Col. Baylor at seven,
and have writing to do before going, so excuse this. I suppose we shall
go to Strasburg but will write. It is cold."

Sunday, March 23rd: Garnett marched, at daybreak, followed by Fulkerson and Burks; closed up and formed [a] line of battle beyond the
Opoquon at Bartonsville; advanced and met the enemy just beyond
Kernstown; a flanking column moved far to the left to get on Sandy
Ridge; a portion of the army moved across to the left in front of the
enemy; Ashby, supported by infantry and artillery held our right. We
repulsed several attacks of the enemy on Sandy Ridge, but, near night,
were forced to relinquish the battle-field at Kernstown and fall back
across the Opequon the line of which Ashby held. The army bivouaced
between Bartonsville and Newtown; the General slept in a fence corner
not far from Bartonsville.—I was up early and wrote to my wife at half-
past five, then wrote an official report and took it to Col. Baylor at seven.
At eight we marched, by orders, from Camp Meem, to Mt. Jackson,

where arms were issued to our command by Ordnance Sergeant William Wholey, after which we marched just beyond the town and went into camp. The day was chilly.

I suppose I was mustered in with the rest of the [battalion] and as Adjutant with the rank of Captain but I have no remembrance concerning this matter.

Monday, March 24th: Marched at an early hour and were going up the hill beyond Tom's Brook, near the Round Hill, when we met Gen. Jackson, riding by himself and he ordered us to march back to Narrow Passage. Our battalion was thrown into a great panic by some one who shouted out that our army was routed and the Yankees were coming on rapidly. At Woodstock we began meeting ambulances with our wounded; among the first was one with Lieut. Col. John Echols of the 27th Virginia regiment. We were much exhausted by our advance and retreat. The army fell back to Cedar Creek and Hupp's Hill and halted to cook rations but the enemy came on at half-past two in the after noon and forced it to resume the retreat; it then fell back to between Narrow Passage and Woodstock. Hd. Qrs. were at Scheffer's Hotel in Woodstock.—Got letters, after dark, informing me that my children were very ill with scarlet fever.

From Camp Narrow Passage, Near Woodstock, Shenandoah County, Tuesday, March 25th, I wrote home: "My afflicted wife: I read with streaming eyes, by the camp fire, where we stopped after a long advance and a weary and rapid retreat your two letters, both mailed the 21st, and the first news I have received from home. Sad, sad indeed. May God forgive me for the sorrows of last night and may He, in mercy, spare my child. But I am now resigned. May you be supported in your extreme sorrow. I would that I could be with you, but it is forbidden me and it is now too late to reach you before the crisis is passed. I wait in painful solicitude the further news.

"We had a bloody battle Sunday resulting disastrously to our arms, though our retreat was conducted in good order, and our front only fell back a few miles. Jackson was deceived as to the numbers of the enemy when he started after them, and they came on him with overwhelming numbers. The Fifth Virginia stood the shock of battle and stopped the advance of the foe. We lost some [forty] killed and some 300 wounded. The enemy refused to let us bury our dead or bring our wounded, saying they neither asked nor gave quarter. We met ambulances all day yesterday with wounded men, wounds of all kinds, in them. Col. Echols was one. It was a sad sight for us to meet them but we went on until we met

Jackson and were ordered to retreat. We are now some 10 miles from the enemy and about 60 miles from Staunton. I will write again tonight and hope to hear more today.

"May God bless our neighbors for their kindness to you under the burden of sorrow falling upon us. None of the West Augusta Guards were wounded. . . . Write to me to Mt. Jackson, to be sent on if the Augusta Battalion of Virginia Militia is ahead of there. May God be with you. My love to all and kisses for my children if any are spared to me, and God be praised that they have been dedicated to [Him]"

25th: We stood to arms all day. In the afternoon our battalion was ordered back to near Mt. Jackson. We marched at five P.M. The rest of the army remained near Narrow Passage. Ashby skirmished with the enemy's advance. Hd. Qrs. were in a field above Woodstock.

I recall that our batallion was under arms at a little church near the top of the hill southwest of the Narrow Passage Creek. It was quite a trying ordeal for raw militia to be thus placed on duty at the very beginning of their service but it is noteworthy that all discharged their duty faithfully and were cheerful and ready for any emergency that might occur.

March 26th, 1862: In the morning our battalion was ordered back to Narrow Passage, to near the rest of the army. Hd. Qrs. were established at Miss Stover's, in the stone house, near Narrow Passage Creek. Soon after we reached camp Gen. Jackson sent me a message that he wished to see me. I promptly reported, when he said, after some general conversation about my topographical work in Northwestern Virginia last year, "I want you to make me a map of the Valley, from Harper's Ferry to Lexington, showing all the points of offence and defence in those places. Mr. Pendleton[14] will give you orders for whatever outfit you want. Good morning, Sir." I obtained orders for a wagon and driver, tent, etc., and bidding goodbye to my battalion rode back to Mt. Jackson to secure my outfit so I could get to work on the "big job" entrusted to me. Ashby is skirmishing with the enemy; the army is having much needed rest in tents.

This was the beginning of [my] career as Topographical Engineer of the Valley District of the Department of Northern Virginia while that was Jackson's separate command and then as Topographical Engineer, of the Second Corps of the Army of Northern Virginia, under the respective commands of Gens. Jackson, A. P. Hill,[15] Ewell,[16] and Early.[17] The transportation that I secured for myself, a wagon and two horses, and the driver that I had detailed, at the suggestion of Col. Crawford, William Humphreys, remained in my service during all the war up to the defeat of Gen. Early at Waynesboro, on the 2nd of March, 1865, when the wagon train of the remnent of the Second Corps was captured, although I saved my large collection of maps which I had taken the precaution of placing upon a train of cars bound for Richmond and which through various vicissitudes I managed to retain possession of and all of which I still have at the time of this writing, Nov. 26th, 1898.

I think Gen. Jackson was pleased with my conduct as Adjutant in repressing the semi-panic in the battalion of Augusta militia, which he witnessed when we met him near Tom's Brook; and that he subsequently conferred with Col. Baylor, who was familiar with my service in Northwestern Virginia, in reference to my fitness for discharging the duties of topographical engineer. That day I met for the first time Lieut. A. S. Pendleton, one of Gen. Jackson's aides, who was acting Assistant Adjutant General, with whom from that time on I had the most intimate and pleasant relations and whom I learned to respect and admire for his sterling qualities as a man and as an officer. It was not far from the place that I first met him that he received his mortal wound while attempting to rally our men retreating from the disastrous battle of Fisher's Hill.

Before marching, on the morning of the 26th, I wrote to my wife, from our camp just northeast of Mt. Jackson: "Yours of the 23rd was received last evening late and gave me some hopes of Nelly's recovery, as she lingers on so well. I gave up all hopes of hearing of her alive after your first letter that I received.

"We stood all day yesterday at the Narrow Passage waiting for the enemy to come up but Ashby drove them back and so we fell back to near Mt. Jackson. The army train, that preceded us, was very long and it was five o'clock when we started, so it was late when we got back here. I got your letter after dark. There are many that want furloughs to go home, but all refused. I have come up to Mt. Jackson, where I am writing, to ask for one by the influence of Col. Baylor, but it will have to go to Woodstock for the General's approval and I am in poor hopes of his approving it, as he wants troops so badly, and Baylor trusts the battalion to me more than to the other officers. We are poorly provided with tents and cooking utensils, but have guns enough. The battle of Sunday last was one of the hardest yet fought. The enemy had 25,000 and we 2,500 engaged. Our loss is not nearly as great as reported and many of our men are still coming in. We took 10 prisoners. Gen. Jackson said he accomplished all he expected by his move. I am in good health though I have a little cold. Do not look for me though I will come if I can. If our darling Nelly should die have her buried at Union. But God grant that she may be spared to us. I have but a moment to write and must close. Goodbye. My love to all. God bless the kind friends that aid you. Direct to Augusta Battalion, Mt. Jackson, to be forwarded."

Thursday, March 27th: Kept busy getting ready to begin examining the country for mapping it. I hear from and write home daily; am thankful that my children are better. We have news from Winchester about the heroic action of our ladies after Kernstown.

My letter of that date, from Camp Narrow Passage reads: "We spent yesterday marching back from Mt. Jackson, where we had been marched the day before at five P.M., a distance of nine miles. We are now at the same place we were before where the turnpike passes along a narrow spur or ridge, between Narrow Passage Creek and the North Fork of the Shenandoah just beyond where those two streams unite. It is thought Jackson will make a stand here. Ashby is fighting the enemy every day. One of their cavalry has just been taken a prisoner. He is a Marylander; says he is tired of the war, thought it would be only against South Carolina and for a short time. Our men get very weary, but I suppose these marches are to make them get used to marching. The Fifth Virginia Regiment (Augusta) is in a sore condition, having been marching every day and fighting also. Gen. Jackson received a letter today from Mrs. Lee, from Wincester, saying that the Mayor and ladies of Wincester had buried our dead. The loss on our side, in the fight of Sunday, was about 470 in killed, wounded and prisoners. Our prisoners marched through Wincester waving their hats and shouting: "Hurray for Jeff. Davis!"; the [ladies] cheering them at the same time. It was reported that Ashby had killed 500 of the enemy before Saturday night.

"I see a good many of the Augusta people here. They have come down to look after their friends in the Fifth, as the first accounts that reached Staunton were very much exaggerated. Henry Robertson (the Doctor's brother) is among the missing. Lieut. Dale, of Doyle's[18] company was killed. One fellow was saved by a ball hitting his pocket-knife and shivering it into some 10 pieces. James Galt had to throw away his gun and everything else he could and take through the fields. The enemy's cavalry cannot jump fences or stone walls, as ours do, therefore many of our men escaped even when cut off. The West Augusta Guards lost one of their pieces because a horse was shot and they could not extricate it. I am in great doubt about our dear little Nelly and spend much of the sleepless nights in thinking of her and your sorrowing condition. I have just been detailed by Gen. Jackson to make a map of this country and must go to work at once. I am unable to get a furlough now but I hope I may soon and that God in mercy has spared my beloved child and has consoled you in your affliction."

Friday, March 28th: Examined the country along Narrow Passage Creek, back to little North Mountain, and reported it unfavorable for defense. In the afternoon the army moved back to Pence's Hill.

It was the general opinion in the country as stated in one of my previous letters that at the Narrow Passage was a point where the enemy could easily be held in check and from the fact that Gen. Jackson had already halted there several times and that he kept his army in that vicinity, would lead to the conclusion that he entertained the same opinion. My reconnoissance westward showed that that [position] could be easily turned by several roads and that it would be difficult for an army to speedily fall back from that point from the fact that Jackson fell back that afternoon to Pence's Hill showed that he accepted my report as conclusive in reference to the feasibility of the Narrow Passage as a point of defence.

Saturday, March 29th: Got [?] Hoshour, of Woodstock, as a guide and rode over the country in front of the army from the Massanuttons to the North Mountain, having Ashby's cavalry in front of my reconnoissance. Orders came from Gov. Letcher[19] to draft all the militia as privates into the volunteer companies so as to make each Virginia regiment 1,000 strong. The day was raw and cold with rain and sleet at night.

I recall [that] this reconnoissance which was expedited by having with me a local guide who was familiar with the country and knew the names of all the people and the points to which all the roads led showed that there was no defensive position in front of Woodstock that could not be easily turned.

Sunday, March 30th, spent the day at Mount Jackson in the room of Sergeant S. Howell Brown of the [?] Virginia regiment, a surveyor of Jefferson Co. who is detailed to make a map of the Lower Valley for Gen. Jackson. Sleeting and raining continued during the day and the trees are encrusted with ice. The enemy is reported to have fallen back. My letter of this date reads: "I have just received, my dear wife, your brief note saying that Nelly is out of danger. I am truly [thankful] that a merciful God has spared us the sad affliction of depriving us of our first born. Praised be His name that He has granted this favor. I have written to you that I am now on engineer duty again, and have a good place though no rank as yet, simply Acting Topographical Engineer, of Gen. Jackson's staff. I have a wagon assigned me for my transportation and a good driver, and can get along without much exposure, though I shall have to ride about considerable in reconnoitring the country. I have a very nice Chief of Engineers, Lieut. J. K. Boswell, belonging to the regular corps. He is a fine fellow and I suppose we will form a mess together. Yesterday I was down in front of the army, though Ashby's cavalry was far in advance. Ashby is a gallant soldier and always keeps the enemy at bay. I saw Macon Jordan a few days ago: he is looking fine, says he considers himself a poor man now, so many of their slaves have run away and their fine farm in Fauquier Co. has fallen in the hands of the enemy. He has raised 240 cavalry and, I suppose, will be made a major. Yesterday the order came from the Governor to draft all the militia into the volunteer [companies] now in the field, so as to make 1,000 men in each regiment with 10 companies; and now there is much uproar among the militia. This will throw all the officers into the ranks as privates. I am sorry for some of them for they are good men, but it will be a fine thing for others for they will thus learn what the duties of a soldier are. I am glad that I have made my escape from the militia before this proclamation, for I had labored very hard to get them fixed up and had them so well supplied by strenuous efforts, that they were very well satisfied, and [expressed] great regret at parting with me. I should have been very sorry to have had to take part in disbanding them, [especially] as they wish to remain organized as they are. Gen. Jackson regrets that this order has been issued, as he was more than pleased with the way in which the militia has conducted itself.

"Yesterday was very raw and cold and last night it rained and sleeted. The militia were the only troops that had any tents. Those of all the other commands having been sent back to Harrisonburg, and the poor fellows have suffered much. Today it is raining and the trees are completely crusted over with ice. I am keeping a sort of Sunday, abstaining from work. The work of last Sunday (the battle of Kernstown) turned out so disastrously for us that I suppose we should try and keep more Sundays hereafter, though it is almost impossible to keep the day as it should be, there are so many contingencies to provide for. Of the four great battles of this war that have been fought on Sunday the attacking party has lost the day.

"I hear with regret that Gen. Edward Johnson[20] has been ordered back from Alleghany and is to come here, leaving the Alleghany line entirely undefended, and I fear the enemy will soon come to Augusta Co. We hear that the enemy has fallen back to Alexandria from Manassas; it is supposed to aid in an attack on Fredericksburg. I wish you would write as often as you can. I hope you will all get along well. I may come home after some maps; the only way I can possibly get off. Have you got your sugar yet? Write me to Mt. Jackson, as Acting Topographical Engineer on Gen. Jackson's staff."

Monday, March 31st, examined the line of Stony Creek, on the southwestern side, from the Massanutton Mountain across to the Little North Mountain and found it a good one for defence.

April 1st: Gave Gen. Jackson a map of Stony Creek and vicinity, from my personal observations of yesterday, and advised him to make a stand there. He sent me to inform Col. Ashby about this line and direct him to hold it. The enemy had advanced rapidly and in force, and [had] driven Ashby through Edenburg and across Stony Creek and I found him on the Valley Turnpike in my selected line. He rode with me along that, for some distance, was pleased with it, and put his men and guns in position to hold it. The infantry were not far in his rear. Hd. Qrs. were established at Israel Allen's near [Hawkinsville] where part of the staff [slept] on the ground. This is a fine spring day.

As Ashby and myself were riding along in front of the woods and in our line, west of the Valley Turnpike, a Federal sharpshooter, in Edenburg, fired at him but hit, in the rear, and killed the horse that a little boy, they called Dixie, who followed Ashby, was riding. As the horse fell Dixie tumbled off, then jumped to his feet to run. Ashby called him back to get his saddle and coolly waited for him under a continuing fire from sharpshooters.

As Ashby fell back he burned the bridge over Stony Creek, at Edenburg, and aided by infantry that had been sent back to him, and his horse artillery was able to hold the line of Stony Creek. Our wagons went so far to the rear they did not get back. The army fell back from Narrow Passage and marched through Woodstock. The General accepted my opinion of the much-thought-of Narrow Passage line and did not attempt to hold it.

Wednesday, April 2, I went to the front at daybreak, the General and rest of the staff came later and we spent half the day on the Stony Creek line which was held by a brigade of our infantry, with the First

Virginia Battalion deployed as skirmishers, on each side of the Valley Turnpike with Ashby's cavalry on the left. Later in the day the whole army, with artillery was brought up. [We] skirmished with the enemy all day and repulsed several advances. At night a brigade was left in front with the cavalry and the rest of the army went into camp between Hawkinstown and Mt. Jackson, and at Rude's Hill. Hd. Qrs. were removed to Rev. Rude's, "Locust Grove" at the foot of Rude's Hill, where we were cordially welcomed. As we were riding back from the front the General remarked, "We have been favored by Providence today." Four companies of infantry and three pieces of artillery were sent today to near Swift Run Gap to quell the Rockingham rebellion in the Blue Ridge.

After reaching Mr. Rude's, in the afternoon of April 2nd, I wrote my wife: "We have changed quarters today and are nearer to you than before. Yesterday the Yankees advanced this way and Ashby and his cavalry contended with them all day. They advanced some 12 miles through Woodstock and on to Edenburg where they were stopped by the burning of the bridges over Stony Creek and by meeting forces which the General sent back. I rode up along Stony Creek the day before and made a sketch of it and recommended to the General to make a stand there. Today he sent a brigade and some guns to that line and there was considerable skirmishing during the day, in which we had the advantage and when they attempted to cross the creek we drove them back howling with several killed. The General has ordered a large force back to the line of Stony Creek and I suppose a fight may take place there. 'We have been favored by Providence today,' the General said. The shells of the enemy howled dreadfully. I never heard such unearthly noises. The shells are very long, from 12 to 15 inches. Quite a number of them burst near the General and his staff yesterday but not one of our men was injured. A little boy, just behind Ashby had his horse shot by the enemy firing at Ashby. I hope he may be preserved. He is a noble man. The General sent me down last night to tell him about the roads, the Stony Creek line, etc., which he had examined. We sent our baggage to the rear yesterday and it did not get back until very late, so we slept on the ground. I slept finely, was tired enough to enjoy it. This morning we started at daybreak for the front, five miles [from] where the fight is to be and the enemy held in check. We spent half of the day there, that is the General and his staff, then I went out to see a back road and the General moved his Hd. Qrs. back of Mt. Jackson to Rev. Mr. Rude's above which there is a fine position to hold, the next one above Stony Creek.

"I am now attached to the Engineer Corps[21] and posted at or near Hd. Qrs., and have a much pleasanter position than in the adjutancy of a regiment, or in any other post in the army. The chief of the corps, Lieut. James Keith Boswell, is a fine fellow and I meet many of my old friends of Valley Mountain. There were 614 of our men killed, wounded and prisoners. The news of the battle is [more] fully related in the papers than I can give you for we only hear odds and ends of news and no very connected statements. I have not read more than one or two newspapers since I came here; in fact [I] have not seen more than one or two. I have read some Northern newspapers.

"I hope that Nelly has fully recovered and that you are all getting along well. I am enjoying good health and getting better of my cold. Sleeping on the ground seems to agree with me. If you have an opportunity you may do up and send me the Life of Marlborough. Send it by some one that is coming down here if you happen to know of anyone. I got Mr. W. H. Ruffner's barometer today and he loaned me a compass. He is very kind indeed. I have secured a mess chest, a box for my papers and maps and have a table and chairs, and also some dishes. I bought some butter today, not very good, at 30 cts a pound. I have just eaten the last of my home biscuits. I wish I had a half bushel of them and some butter from home. The militia will be drafted in tomorrow. The General has just ordered four companies of riflemen and several pieces of cannon up to Rockingham Co., to storm the camp of the militia, in the Blue Ridge, that refused to come to duty. So don't be alarmed if you hear the noise of a battle near at hand for no harm will come but to the recreants. They are said to be near McGaheysville. There will be an example made of some of those that failed to come."

Thursday, April 3rd, rode to the front and then examined the roads and the country in the rear of our Stony Creek line and towards the western side of the Valley. We are very pleasantly quartered at Mr. Rude's and I like all the members of the staff now that I am having a chance to get acquainted with them. A number of us sleep in one large room, some in beds but most of us on our blankets on the floor.

April 4th: Worked all day on a map of our Stony Creek position and its vicinity. The General spends most of the time in his room. It is said he is writing his report of the battle of Kernstown.[22] He is very quiet, says but little and eats but little. We continue to hold the line of Stony Creek with infantry, cavalry and artillery.

I wrote to my wife on the 4th: "I today received yours of the 2nd of April also the first letter you wrote me about Nelly's sickness. Strange it has been so long on the road. We are still at Mr. Rude's and the enemy is still at Edenburg, fighting with Ashby, or rather keeping out of his way. There is not much prospect of a fight though it is hard to tell what a day may bring forth. We have reports of all sorts of things happening around us but put little credit in anything. Today I saw a Philadelphia paper of March 28th. It contained an exaggerated and inflated account of the fight of March 23rd, claiming a capture of 200 wagons when we did not lose one.

The draft for filling up the volunteer companies was made today. A list of the men was first made and a number was fixed to each name, then a lot of pieces of paper with numbers on them, was thrown into a hat and the pieces picked out one by one and whoever's name was placed opposite the number drawn he was drafted in.

"Nelly's sweet little voilet [*sic*] dropped out of my letter as I opened it and I was very happy to think that my little daughter was reviving and getting new life again just as the sweet flowers [are] opening under the influence of the vernal sun. She must be very thankful to her [God] that her life is spared and we will join her in [thanking] Him and hope she may live long to be a blessing to her parents and to her friends. The birds are singing very sweetly here and I suppose they are also singing at Loch Willow and papa would like to sit out on the porch with the little girls and mama and hear them sing rather than be here where he has to see and hear so much of men killing and being killed, doing all the damage they can to one another, burning up bridges, etc. Oh, how I wish war would cease and that we might all have peace in the enjoyment of our rights and liberties; but those rights we [must] have, cost what it may. I am very well indeed; stay in the house here and eat with the General and staff. Rude is a very nice man. He is a retired Lutheran preacher, a Dane by birth. He married the widow Steenbergen, who was a Miss Capterton, a second cousin of Mrs. John Pinderton's. She is a fine lady and he is very obliging and kind. We have often very pleasant times. The Adjutant General A. S. Pendleton, is a grandson of the revolutionary Col. Pendleton[23] and is a very fine young man, a gentleman every way. The Medical Director, Dr. Hunter McGuire[24] is a very smart fellow and gives us entertaining medical prelections at our evening sittings. Gen. Jackson does not say much. He is quite deaf; spends most of his time in his room, by himself, except when in the saddle; but he is very pleasant and I like him much. I have been drawing maps all day so you will excuse me for not writing more. I [would] drop a line or two to Powell about the sugar. I send you enclosed some postage stamps. I am glad the friends are so kind to you and that Annie is still well. I do hope she may be spared from sickness. Mr. Rude says that greasing them is a speedy and safe cure.

Saturday, April 5th, spent part of the day at work on the topography of the country near Rude's Hill. *Sunday, April 6th,* a day of rest. It is getting quite spring-like; the grass and the grain are greening and the early flowers are open. *Monday, April 7th,* Worked on map and rode over a portion of the vicinity of Hd. Qrs. at Rude's. The troops at the front are changed every three days. *Tuesday, April 8th,* a rainy day. Worked on my Valley map in a room with a good wood fire. *Wednesday, April 9th,* another rainy day occupied in drawing map as usual. Very bad weather; hard on the army. *Thursday, April 10,* the rain continues and the streams are full and still rising. I wrote home in the morning and again in the evening quieting my wife's apprehensions about an advance of the enemy up the Valley directing that 30 sheets of drawing papers be sent me from my stock at home.

My letters of the 10th of April, from Mr. Rude's read: "We have had three days of uninterrupted storm, terrible to soldiers, and our men have suffered much, [though] they have been in their tents and have [kept] fires as best they could. I am still, fortunately, under a hospitable roof and by a good fire, for which I am certainly thankful. We are still in the same situation. No news. I hope Anne is doing well. I am anxious to hear from you but suppose the mail is interrupted; that is now going, so goodbye and God bless you. I am perfectly well."

"I wrote you a line this morning by mail but I have a chance to send another, by private hands, as far as Harrisonburg, so I will write again as I did not answer your questions. I do not think it worth while for you to draw the money on the check I gave you. I prefer you should not yet, for you would only get Confederate notes and they would be of but little use to you if the enemy came to Augusta. So say nothing about it until I write to you. I am in hopes I shall be able to come home before long and look after things. It is not worth while for you to borrow trouble about putting things away or to apprehend any danger. I do not think the enemy will get to our county. I feel assured they will be kept back and that our county will be held. I have great confidence in our generals, and think the Valley will not be given up. Try and keep in good spirits. Tell Allen[25] he must be a good boy and do what is required of him, or

I shall have to put him with some hard master that will make him work. I hope, though, there will be no need of that. Have Nelson[26] straighten him if he needs it. Try and keep up a friendly spirit. It will do me so much good while I am [obliged] to be away. Take care of your funds and when I draw my first month's pay I will send you more. Do not think about being cut off from me; for I do not apprehend any such thing. I am doing office work altogether now. Say nothing to anyone about your monetary affairs. Send me 30 sheets of flat-cap paper same as in my Herbarium. It is in the table up stairs. Direct as usual and to New Market. Send to General Jackson's Hd. Qrs. I hope Anne is better. The three days' storm has cut off communication. I see the daily papers. Send mine up to the house for them to see and they will send them back. I will have the paper kept on. No news on this line; we are waiting for more from the Peninsula and from the West. Send the paper to Capt. H. M. Bell, A. Q. M. at Staunton, and ask him to send it on at once to Hd. Qrs."

Friday, April 11. The rainy weather continues so I spent most of my time working on my map; Brown is also working on a map of the Lower Valley. *Saturday, April 12th.* Weather showery. Worked at map. *Sunday, April 13.* Rested, read, walked out along the turnpike, talked with fellow officers, etc. The General went to the brigade camp near Hd. Qrs. and distributed religious tracts. Gen Wm. B. Taliaferro[27] reported to command one of Jackson's brigades. The General [didn't] say so, but I am sure he does not like to have him because of the part he took with Loring after the Romney campaign. I recall that in a conversation about this time Jackson mentioned that Gen. Taliaferro had been ordered to report to him as a brigade commander and he took occasion to introduce the subject of the Northwest Virginia campaign of the previous year and asked a good many questions about the part Taliaferro had borne in that campaign but made no comments himself and said nothing about his own previous experiences with Taliaferro. I never knew a man more guarded in his speech in reference to others. I do not remember to have ever heard him say ought in derogation of anyone, at any time.

Monday, April 14th. The rainy weather continues, the mud and the high water forcing inaction. Worked at Map and reconnoitering, as usual. Wrote a long letter to my wife, describing members of our staff, etc. Maj. John A. Harman, our chief quartermaster, told me of the death of two of his children and that he expected two more would die. Poor fellow, he is completely unmanned, and I do not wonder! The letter referred to is as follows: "I received yours telling me that the children [are safe] for which I am truly thankful. I am sorry that I cannot be at home to relieve you of the severe burden of care that rests upon you and that I am fearful will make you sick also. Be careful and get some one to relieve you as much as possible. I feel sorry for poor John A. Harman. He has lost two children and told me this morning that he expected two more to die today. When will this pestilence of scarlet fever cease from our county?

"I have just been reading the Spectator; it has a good deal of interesting news in it. We caged and ironed today the leader of the militia rebellion in Rockingham. He is a tigrour [*sic*] looking fellow. We captured a Dutchman from a New York regiment. He had on him quite a number of letters one from his wife, all in German in which she berated him soundly for not writing to her, but got over her wrath before she ended and wrote to him like a loving Vrow. She had come on to Alexandria to see him. He had several letters from others in which they all spoke of being infinitely tired of the war and desirous of getting out of it.

"By the way Sam. Harnsberger, the tall young man from McGaheysville that went to school at Mossy Creek, is here in a cavalry company. He was in Western Virginia last summer with Wise.[28] He told me that J. T. Brodt was in the army, a member of the Kanawha company, and furthermore, that he was at Roanoke Island and was probably taken a prisoner there. Good for old Brodt that he proved true at last. It rains here all the time. I hope you have a better spell of weather. We are kept in doors most of the time, of late, by it.

"I am very much pleased with Gen. Jackson and his staff. He is at times very chatty, but usually has but little to say. Sunday he went through one of the brigades with a bundle of tracts and distributed them. He stays to himself most of the time; eats very sparingly; does not drink tea or coffee and eats scarcely any meat. The Assistant Adjutant General, Lieut. A. S. Pendleton, (Sandy we call him) son of the revolutionary Col. Pendleton[29] of Rockbridge, (the famous Manassas artillery Capt.) is a young man of about twenty-two and light-haired. He graduated at Washington College and has taught in Lexington. He was at the University of Virginia when the war broke out. He is talented an admirable talker, and a man of fine sense and acquirements. He is the one spoken of in the Spectator as carrying off wounded men. He says he did many things at Kernstown that he does not remember, but knows he did not carry anybody off the field. Berkeley the surgeon of the regiment, Dr. McGuire says was not there. So it is hard to tell who the surgeon was. Dr. Hunter McGuire, the Medical Director, is also a young man of fine talents. He is not more than twenty-six, but has been a professor in a Medical College at [Philadelphia] and also in New Orleans. He is a son of Dr. [Hugh McGuire] of Winchester, of whom you have often heard. The Doctor is one of my brother George sort of men, blunt, good humored, and full of honest life. Lieut. Col. Wm. S. H. Baylor, our Acting Inspector General, is a first rate good fellow, good natured and accomodating. He will, no doubt, be elected Col. of the Fifth Virginia Regt. We shall miss him much. Lieut. James K. Boswell, the Chief of the Engineer Corps, is an excellent, good natured, honest Presbyterian of Alabama, formerly of Fauquier Co. He is well off, has a sweetheart in Fauquier Co., where the Yankees are, and he talks much about her. He is my bed-fellow. One of your good bodies that everybody likes and, of course, I like him. Lieut. Henry Kyd Douglas[30] is from Maryland and has lately been put on the staff as an assistant to Col. Baylor. He is a lieutenant in one of the companies of the [Second] Virginia Regiment. He is quite young but has been practicing law in St. Louis. He is one of your wide awake, smart young men. I like him too. Lieut. R. K. Meade[31] is from Clarke Co. He was a private at Manassas where he lost his right arm and has a lieutenancy given him because of that. He is a good negative sort of man, kindly disposed and willing to do all he can. There are two clerks at Hd. Qrs. Logan, and Laird, detailed from the Washington College Co. They are good fellows too. Sergeant S. Howell Brown is engaged with the engineer corps. He is county surveyor of Jefferson Co. and is an excellent surveyor; a big stout fellow, accommodating and pleasant, but a mass of facts; painfully matter-of-fact man, at times fearfully exact. But I really like him nevertheless. Then add a half-dozen darkies of all shades and natures and put in your husband, "Mr. Lipkiss, as one of the Dutch girls here calls me (Mrs. Rude says she [can't] say Hotchkiss) and you have the General's staff, described after a fashion. I will describe mine host if we stay here much longer.

"I have nothing of interest to write. The enemy is still at the same place, beyond Stony Creek, being reinforced, we hear.

"What a set of cowards they must be to want any more troops to oppose our small army. The militia, officers, and all, have all been drafted into volunteer regiments. I have the same place I had last year with Gen. Loring.[32] I am Topographical Engineer on General Jackson's staff.

I may get a commission as the engineer corps is to be increased. I suppose I will get the same pay I did before. We get the papers here every day and the news often comes here, from over the Ridge, by pony express. I wish I could come in and see you all. Kiss the little darlings for papa. Tell Allen to have a good garden, well worked, and everything done like a good boy that I hope he is. My love to all our relations and friends. Read them my letter or send it up, for I have not much time to write. Write often—I send you enclosed the Dutchman's wife's letter to him.

"Heaven only can tell what the future has in store for us"

TUESDAY, APRIL 15TH. The indications are that the rainy spell is about over. I am occupied as usual but cannot expect such good times to last.

Wednesday, April 16th, Worked at map of Valley and rode about examing the country.

Thursday, April 17th. The enemy advanced, in force, at three A.M., this morning, and compelled us to retire from the line of Stony Creek, which we have held since April 1st. Ashby soon notified Hd. Qrs. and we got an early breakfast, packed up our wagons and sent them to the rear and awaited on Rude's Hill, where we had a force of infantry and artillery, our men retiring from the front, the coming of the enemy. I rode around to Mt. Airy on the flank of the Massanuttons and watched the deploying of the enemy on the northeast side of North River, near Mt. Jackson, then rode back and reported what I had seen, to Gen. Jackson, and the apparent intentions of the enemy. I estimated his force at about 10,000. After our men were all over the river, Ashby, in person, attempted to burn the North River bridge, but his combustibles ignited slowly, and the enemy's cavalry coming on rapidly, forced him to retire. They followed him a short distance and gave his splendid white horse a mortal wound.[1] Our artillery, from Rude's Hill, soon drove them back across the river. We remained at Rude's Hill until advised that a flanking column of the enemy was moving up the western side of North River to intercept us at New Market when we slowly fell back up the Valley, Ashby holding the rear. We formed a line of battle at New Market where we remained for a time, then fell back and halted for a while and dined at Mr. Cowan's, near [?] then fell back to Lacey's or Big Spring, where we supped and spent the night at Abe Lincoln's, a distant relative of President Abe Lincoln, having marched miles. At supper, Mrs. Lincoln, an old lady, at the head of the table, after many hesitating glances at Gen. Jackson, on her right, as she poured the coffee, said: "Gineral, are you an relation [to] old Gineril Jackson, who used to stop here?" A question that evidently pleased the General, as he was a [D]emocrat [and] an admirer of 'Old Hickory,' although he was compelled to say he did not know that he was related to him. Col. J. T. L. Preston, of the V. M. I. is with us tonight. I wrote home, although very weary from having been in the saddle so long today. The people here are very much disturbed by our falling back. The enemy came to New Market. Ashby halted and held the rear at Sparta.

My letter from Big Spring 12 miles from Harrisonburg, written last Thursday evening, April 17th, reads: "The enemy advanced, at three A.M. today and we had falled back thus far and are stopping for a day or so. I should rather say for an hour or so, for I expect we will have to move on in a few hours. The enemy is pressing upon our rear and Ashby is keeping them back. There was a little skirmishing and one or two of the enemy were killed and we lost one man. A number of shots were fired from both sides, but at a distance of two miles, and, of course, no body was hurt by that, though the noise and the explosion of the shells was anything but agreeable. I rode to where I had a good view of the Yankee troops, drawn up in line of battle from the hill-top near Mt. Airy where I was sent to see them. They have about 10,000 men I should think, and then Blenker[2] is at the end of the Valley with about the same number, so I suppose Banks feels quite safe.

I know not where we will stop, I suppose, though, when we get to Staunton for it seems to be the opinion that the inner line of the State is to be defended. We are now at the house of Mr. Cowan. One of his sons married a Miss Allabaugh, of Bridgewater. It is a very nice place. All the ladies leave tonight for Bridgewater, except a young Miss [?]. We were very sorry to leave Mr. Rude's. We had such a nice time there.

Col. Preston, of the V. M. Institute, is here now and starts back tomorrow. He intends to ask Gen. Jackson to let me go along and so come
by way of Union Church, but I do not know what the result of his application may be, so I will write. We are coming up so near home that I
am sure I shall get there before long, on some excuse or other. I send a
paper for Nelson and he will send it for you to see. I am so weary that
you must excuse my short letter, for I have been in the saddle nearly all
day and want to sleep and rest some before another start, for we may
have to travel during the night. Jackson is very cautious and I do not
think he will be caught napping. I board with the staff now and so do
not, as yet, need any provisions, though I intend to board myself soon.
Send this up so they may see it at the upper house."

April 18: The General and staff started at an early hour and rode
rapidly 12 miles to Harrisonburg, where we spent part of the day, the
General in person, giving orders to quartermasters and brigades as they
arrived. The army marched, at daylight, to Harrisonburg. The troops
cheered the General lustily, as we rode by them while on the march. The
General and part of the Staff dined at "Hill Top" the home of Rev. Wm.
Henry Ruffner, then remained for a time on the high commanding hill
south of Harrisonburg, and then, late in the day, rode to Keezletown
and took quarters at Mr. Peale's. The advance of the army came to the
vicinity of the same place. At Harrisonburg the wagon train was divided
and part of it, with superfluous army baggage was sent on to Staunton
and part of it, the regular army train, preceded the army to [Peale's]
Cross Roads. After the trains had crossed North River the bridge near
Mt. Crawford and the one near Maj. Robert Grattan's were burned as
was also the one over North River at Bridgewater. Ashby held the line
of hills northeast of Harrisonburg, on the Valley Turnpike and Maj.
Funsten, with part of the cavalry, fell back from Sparta along the Keezletown road out which I rode from Peale's, by Gen. Jackson's order to
attend to the posting of a picket. It rained very hard in the forenoon
and the mud is very deep after leaving the Valley Turnpike. Many wagons were stalled. Col. J. T. L. Preston continues with us. The enemy
followed us slowly. Hd. Qrs. for the night are at Peale's, six miles from
Harrisonburg.

Saturday, April 19. Our army marched at two A.M., via McGaheysville and Miller's Bridge, 11 miles, to the vicinity of McGaheysville. It
rained most of the day; the roads are badly cut up by the army train
and became very [muddy]. The General gave me orders, early in the

morning, to go and burn the "Red" and the "Columbia" bridges, across the South Fork of the Shenandoah, on the roads leading from New Market eastward, if they were not already held by the enemy, taking to aid me all the cavalry I could find on my way down to those bridges. I also took along S. Howell Brown for company and assistance. We found the cavalry at the Shenandoah Iron Works, many of them under the influence of apple-jack. After a short halt for refreshments at Mr. Henry Forrer's, at the Iron Works, we went on down the river. I left Brown with Lieut. Mantaur's company to get the "Red" bridge ready for burning, but directing him not to fire it until I should have time to reach the other bridge, to which I rode on with the companies of Capt. Macon Jordan and Capt. Sheets,[3] to Honeyville, near "Columbia" bridge whence I sent Capt. Sheets to reconnoitre. He reported no enemy at the bridge, so I gave permission to feed the horses and let the men get out of the deluge of rain that was then falling, where Capt. Sheets and some 50 men went to burn the "Columbia" bridge, about a mile away down the river, at the same time sending a squadron, under Lieut. Lionberger,[4] to burn the White House bridge, still further down the river, on the road from New Market to Luray. The horses were hardly fed when Capt. Sheets and a few men came dashing back, at full gallop, pursued by the enemy. I succeeded in getting Capt. Jordan's men into the road and ready to meet the attack, but at the first fire they ran away and scattered and could not be stopped. Many of the men were drunk, as was also Capt. Jordan himself. The enemy pursued us some three miles but captured only a few of our cavalry as they had at once taken to the woods. I escaped and hurried back to the "Red" bridge and got Lieut. Mantaur's company deployed to meet the enemy, but they did not come on. Brown had burned the "Red" bridge, but we did not succeed in burning the other two. The cavalry that had not stampeded came back to Shenandoah Iron Works, and late in the day, having ridden [many] miles through rain and mud, I reported to the General at Hd. Qrs., at Capt. Asher Argenbright's near Conrad's Store. It rained very hard nearly all day. Many of the cavalry that had run away even went across the Blue Ridge; the most of them got back to the army in about 10 days.

Easter Sunday, April 20th. The army rested in camp. It rained hard nearly all day. Ashby's cavalry came across the South Fork of the Shenandoah, by Miller's bridge, and encamped near Conrad's Store, his pickets remaining in front near McGaheysville. Our infantry is encamped in the woods near Elk Run Church and up along Elk Run on the road leading to Swift Run Gap. I was at work all day, by the General's order, on maps. He has none of this locality and must have one at once. Gen. Edward Johnson came here last night and had a long conference with the General. I wrote a long letter to my wife telling about my escapade with Jordan.

My letter of the 20th from Conrad's Store, Rockingham Co., reads: "I wrote you a few lines several days ago, that is two days saying that we were on our way to the Blue Ridge, having turned off from McAdamized road,⁵ Friday P.M., and that the army spent the night six miles from Harrisonburg, and the next day at two [the] army came to this point. I was sent on by the General, with 150 cavalry to burn the bridges on the Shenandoah River below here. I rode on 10 miles to the first bridge and there left a strong picket, and had the plank taken up at once, at one end, and preparations made for burning the bridge. I then went on with the rest of the men six miles, to the next bridge, concealed my men at Honeyville though I had much trouble with Jordan's men, some of which, as well as himself were drunk. I had the bridge carefully reconnoitred and it was reported that no enemy was to be seen. I then sent three men, with a capt. to burn the bridge, and ordered the rest of the men to feed their horses three-fourths of a mile distant. The men sent forward to burn the bridge put hay in the mouth of it and set it on fire, when a column of the enemy appeared and fired a volley and their dragoons charged. A messenger at once reported that they were coming and I ordered the men to their horses and told Jordan to front his men and I rode forward to reconnoitre. Jordan followed me instead of attending to his men. The enemy came charging up the road and firing when our men except some three or four, broke at once and a perfect stampede of them took place, the enemy pursuing for three miles. Every attempt to rally was unavailing. Some actually threw away their guns, many of them their coats, blankets, etc. I never saw a more disgraceful affair; all owing, no doubt, to the state of intoxication of some of the men and to the want of discipline among them. One of our men was killed, one wounded, and we have not yet found out how many were taken prisoner. When I found the men could not be [rallied I] rode on rapidly and looked after the party I had left behind and with them brought up the rear, most of the others having taken to the woods. The enemy now holds the lower bridges but we have burned the upper one. Our escape was providential considering the panic of the men and the rapid retreat over a rough road.

I suppose you all thought you were abandoned when you heard that we had left the Valley, but now you see that we saved the Valley by that very movement for the enemy at once fell back. I suppose we will be reinforced in a day or two and a battle will no doubt be fought before many days, and on that may hang the fate of our county. I do pray that it may be favorable to us. Gen. Edward Johnson of Alleghany fame was here last night and went back this morning, so concert of action will be secured by the meeting of our generals in council. The weather is still bad, very bad, and the mud deep, making it very disagreeable for our troops. There was some skirmishing at Yorktown a few days ago favorable to us, and I suppose the great fight must soon come off. The varied successes of war have been our fate and I suppose will continue to be, but of our ultimate success there cannot be a shadow of a doubt if our rulers and people do their duty, as I think they will, though we must be tried in the school of adversity before we will use our strength as we ought to and will be willing to be disciplined. Of course it is not my business to tell what I may happen to know what is to be done, for such things should not be made known. I am somewhat stiff and sore today from my long ride and exposure yesterday but am perfectly well. We are quartered in a house and therefore are secure from inclement weather at night.

I am sorry, truly sorry, that Macon Jordan was in such a condition yesterday. I do not know what may come of [it] to him, but I am sure the General will see to it that he is properly looked after. When Ashby's men are with him they behave gallantly, but when they are away from him they lack the inspiration of presence and being undisciplined they often fail to do any good.[6] Only a few days ago a company of 50 of them were taken prisoners through lack of care in guarding themselves.

The excitement among the people along the line of our march this side of Harrisonburg was intense and many left their homes. I suppose they will return now, but I do not look for quiet for some time to come. The war is only just begun and Heaven only can tell what the future has in store for us. But the Lord God Omnipotent reignth and He will do right, and if we are in the right we shall surely prosper and no matter how dark the heavens may now appear they must become brighter, and through the thick gloom I think we may see the glimmerings of a brighter dawn. God grant it may soon come.

Give my kind love to relations and friends and kiss my spared children for me. I wish I could see you but the General says I cannot be spared now. Send this letter up and let brother and family read it as I have not time to write to him now though I desire to do so. I have been busy all day, although it is Sunday, by order, making a map of this region. May I be forgiven for it. Send your next letter to Staunton, care of Capt. H. M. Bell, A. Q. M., to [be] forwarded by Gen. Jackson's courier, if we are not back into the Valley before you get this. I hope the children have gotten well and that all things are working together for good. May God grant that they do and bless you all."

Monday, April 21st. The General ordered me, at an early hour, although it was cold and raining very hard to ride to Swift Run Gap and find a concealed road by which we could make a flank attack on a portion of the enemy that he said was encamped there. I rode, by detours, very cautiously to the top of the mountain, but, to my surprise, found no enemy there. Soon after I reached Swift Run Gap the 10 Virginia infantry[7] marched up from the east of the Blue Ridge on its way to join our Valley army. I returned and reported to the General and then learned that he had named the wrong Gap. He intended to send me to Milham's, or Fisher's Gap, on the road from New Market to Madison C. H., and not to Swift Run Gap. After feeding my horse I again faced the storm and rode to furnace No. 2 where I got Mr. Henry H. Propes, a former pupil of mine at Mossy Creek,[8] as a guide, and we rode up the North Fork of Naked Creek, behind a low range of mountains between us and the South Fork of the Shenandoah to the head of that fork of Naked Creek and then across Honey Run Valley to Graves' on the head of Hawk's Bill Creek, 19 miles, on the road from Columbia Bridge to Fisher's Gap where I got information about the enemy encamped at Columbia bridge. We then rode back to Mr. Lucas', on Honey Run and there spent the night, only some three miles from the enemy's encampment at the west end of Columbia bridge. It rained and sleeted all day and the streams are much swollen. Had a hard day's duty, having ridden not less than thirty-five miles, in rain and sleet, over rough mountain roads and along bridle paths much of the way through the woods.

Tuesday, April 22nd, in the morning I reconnoitred the enemy's position at Columbia bridge from a high knob in the western Blue Ridge, the weather having cleared, then rode back, some 15 miles, to camp, and made a map of my route, the enemy's positions, etc., and reported with same to Gen. Jackson by 11 A.M. *Wednesday, April 23.* A fine sunny day. Some of us went over the river to Harnsberger's.[9] *Thursday, April 24th.* It snowed nearly all day then rained some. It was very inclement and the troops suffered much in their bivouacs in the woods, all the tents having been sent away, as we left Harrisonburg, to Waynesboro on the Virginia Central R. R. for storage. Maj. Robert L. Dabney[10] (Rev. Dr.) reported for duty as Assistant Adjutant General of the Valley District. Col. Turner Ashby sent in his resignation as commander of the cavalry because Gen. Jackson had ordered that all the cavalry companies in his command should be divided into two regiments each of these to be assigned to brigades of infantry for the purpose of disciplining them. At night Ashby and Jackson had a long conference.[11]

On the 24th I wrote to my wife: "I avail myself of a lull in business caused by the dreadful weather of today, snowing great big flakes, like all the world all day, to write to you while I can, for I do not know how long I shall have that privilege or how long before communication will be wholly cut off.

"We have just received a messenger from Winchester. He says they have an iron rule there. Soldiers visiting houses, searching through everything marauding over the country and insulting people. Most of the troops there are Dutch (Germans) and they are more brutal than any others but our women there are not afraid of them and tell them freely what they think of their conduct. We learn that they have about 21,000 men under command of Rosecrans,[12] Banks and Shields having gone away. We take a number of prisoners every day. Today we had one from Maine, one from Connecticut, one from Vermont, one from Pennsylvania, and one German. The Conn. man says the people in his state think they will conquer us by July but he does not think so now. Said he would take the oath of Allegance to the Southern Confederacy if we would let him go.

"I saw Capt. Geo. Crisman yesterday. Rallston was elected captain in his place and he has gone to Richmond. All the old officers that were not re-elected are allowed by Gen. Jackson to go home, so we have had quite a stampede of officials. W. S. H. Baylor was elected Colonel of the Fifth and Colonel Wm. H. Harman went home. There were all sorts of promotions and depressions. In one regiment the adjutant was made its colonel. Rev. Dr. R. L. Dabney came here today having been made adjutant general of this division, or rather of the Valley District. He is a fine man. Says the war has taken away all the students of the Union

Theological Seminary and he now comes to the war also. We are getting our army re-organized, and will, I suppose, soon have order brought out of chaos.

"A few of the enemy have been down this side of McGaheysville but our cavalry put them to flight. They came into Harrisonburg and have made prisoners of some of the men from the [county]. They will need more and more men to keep the country the farther they advance and will [find the] task of subjugation no easy one. Last Monday one of our cavalry companies went to within six miles of Winchester and there took some prisoners and returned. One of the enemy's sentinels at Harper's Ferry was shot. They will find as they advance foes in their rear that will annoy them as much as those in front and so the work of subjugation will have to be daily done over.

"It is reported in the Richmond papers that we are again in possession of Nashville. How true it is I know not. McClellan[13] is still idle on the Peninsula, bound down hand and foot by the mud of that region, said by those that know to be bottomless. His large army is being increased daily but still he fears to offer battle, knowing as he does, that his whole reputation hangs on the result. Gen. Jackson remarked today that he was in the same class with McClellan at West Point and that he thinks he lacks nerve.[14] The army of Gen. Ewell is in supporting distance of us across the Blue Ridge and which one of these armies will join the other to strike a blow is uncertain. This is one of our present problems of chances for discussion, for no one knows what Jackson intends to do.

"I shall come home to see you all as soon as some important moves have been made, and I hope they are not far off; I also hope that they will relieve the Valley of the presence of the enemy. We hear that Edward Johnson is at West View. Too near our home to be agreeable. We now feel what it is to have an army in our houses and an enemy thundering at our doors. But then that is the best way to have our forces where they cannot be cut off in detail but can assist each other. The day of hope may be followed by a night of despair, but that night is sure to be followed by a morning of sunshine. So trust in God's all abounding goodness and may my loved ones, in faith, pray for the day of deliverance to speedily come. If the foe should come to your door, outwardly submit, but coldly and abhor to the last those who bring to our firesides slaughter and devastation. Train our children, as you have done, in the ways of knowledge, virtue and holiness, and so fill up the weary hours of our separation; and may the Lord in mercy shorten these days of tribulation.

I hope you have no need of anything and that you are all being restored to a measure of health. I am extremely anxious to hear from you. I wrote to you to send a letter to me to the care of Maj. Harman,[15] Staunton, asking him to send it to me by Gen. Jackson's courier. The rain is now beating against our windows and it is dark without. I pity our poor shelterless men. I am enjoying excellent health; am not exposed any at night and do not intend to go into a tent until the weather is better, although it costs something more to live as we do, paying for our board, but one's constitution is saved and that is of more value than a few dollars. I hope the foe may not visit you but if they do try and keep them from destroying our property by claiming protection, as a lady, from the officers and they may give some heed to your claim. I do not think it worth while to move anything, although you might secrete your provisions if you can. My love to all. Live in the bonds of love and peace and may God's choicest blessings be upon you. Yesterday I sent Nelly an illustrated paper. Hope she may get it."

I recall that I paid Col. Ashby a visit on the 24th, in his quarters near ours. Found him sitting before the fire in a very moody humor. He complained that Jackson was treating him very badly in desiring to divide his command into two regiments and requiring him to drill them. He seemed to think that although he had so many companies he could easily manage them all himself and that it was [unnecessary] to have them drilled.

Friday, April 25th. A showery day. The cavalry were restored to Col. Ashby's command, he having agreed to discipline them. He is left at liberty to dispose of his force as he deems best.

A VISIT HOME

Saturday, April 26th. I obtained leave of absence and at 11 A.M. started for home to look after my papers and home affairs as the enemy's cavalry had been to Jenning's Gap within four miles of my Loch Willow home near Churchville. I went by way of Port Republic and New Hope. Found the roads very muddy and badly cut up by our commissary and other army wagons. It rained most of the day. I reached Staunton at 11 P.M., after a ride of 36 miles, and spent the night there. The work of reorganizing the army is now going on. Some of the enemy's cavalry came to the Shenandoah River below Port Republic. *Sunday, April 27th,* rode on home in the morning and spent the forenoon there; in the afternoon rode up to Valley Mills, near West View, to see Gen. Edward

Johnson, who has his Hd. Qrs., there at Capt. P. O. Palmer's, and to learn about the Federals in his front, as Gen. Jackson had directed me to do. One of Johnson's brigades is in camp to the west of West View and the other to the east, both along the Staunton and Parkersburg Turnpike. This is a fine spring day. *Monday, April 28th.* In the morning I rode back to Valley Mills and saw Gen. Johnson and discussed with him the enemy's position in Ramsey's Draft of the Shenandoah Mountain and the feasibility of capturing it, then rode via Staunton to Byer's on Christian's Creek, for the night on my way back to camp. A fine spring day. Heard of the fall of New Orleans which excites but little attention that having been expected.[16] *Tuesday, April 29th.* Rode on to Hd. Qrs. by four P.M., having dined and fed my horse at Gen. Samuel Lewis'.[17] Reported to the General what I had learned from Gen. Johnson, the condition of the roads, etc. At the close of our interview he gave me orders to go to the Peak, or southwest end of the peaked, or Massanutton Mountain, tomorrow, and reconnoitre the enemy's position, movements, etc., in the vicinity of Harrisonburg, and signal to Col. Ashby, who would march his cavalry up the road towards Harrisonburg, any movements of the enemy during his advance. I saw Col. Ashby and obtained a cavalry escort, then sent for Capt. Wm. B. Yancey's company of the 10th Virginia, as an infantry escort, ordering these to be at Hd. Qrs. at one A.M. tomorrow morning ready to march. Capt. Yancey I knew well as he had been one of my pupils at Mossy Creek Academy. The day was somewhat misty and rainy.

Wednesday, April 30th. I started, promptly at one A.M., with my escort for The Peak. Rode [toward] McGaheysville to the Notch at the end of the Kettle where we left our horses with a guard, and proceeded cautiously, with videttes[18] in advance and climbed a rough spur of the mountain to The Peak which we reached about daybreak, at 5 A.M., and where we remained most of the day watching the effect of Ashby's advance, with infantry, cavalry, and artillery, and his challenge to Banks[19] to battle. We saw plainly the enemy's encampments around and below Harrisonburg but no movement was made to meet our advance. Ashby went as far as Montevideo just under the end of the mountain. I got back to camp at 6 P.M. and found the General and staff in the saddle ready to start up the river towards Port Republic following the army which was already marching in that direction. Gen. Jackson, at our old quarters at Argenbrights, was having some last words with Maj. Gen. R. S. Ewell, who, with his division had just come across the Blue Ridge at Swift Run

Gap and taken the camps we had vacated. By direction of Gen. Jackson I reported to Gen. Ewell what I had seen of the enemy, from The Peak, and then followed after Jackson. The rain was falling in torrents and the mud was very deep. The troops cheered the General as we rode along their line of march, especially when the General and staff took to riding across a sandy field to flank them and get to the head of the column. The General on the Little Sorrel[20] rode at full gallop and we had a rather ludicrous staff race across this field. We rode, at a rapid pace, through the rain, mud and darkness, some 13 miles, to Lewiston the home of Gen. Lewis, where we were quite hospitably received. The day was quite pleasant until 3:30 P.M. when it began to rain and became quite cool. The troops marched some 5 miles and encamped in the woods. Many of the army wagons, following them, mired in the mud and quicksands.

Thursday, May 1st. The General and all the staff spent the day, with large details of soldiers making and repairing roads and helping the wagons and artillery along through the mud and quicksands. It rained hard and the mud and quicksands became deep and treacherous. The army marched to within two miles of Lewiston and encamped in the Piney woods. *Friday, May 2nd.* The General and staff were again engaged making and repairing roads and helping along the trains, most of the army assisted, and so by desperate efforts we got the trains and troops, by way of opposite Port Republic into the entrance to Brown's Gap. The cavalry came up and encamped near Port Republic. The General and staff went to Mr. John F. Lewis' at Mt. Vernon Furnace,[21] at the western entrance to Brown's Gap. Boswell and myself supped at Dr. Kamper's in Port Republic,[22] then rode on to Hd. Qrs. I had the 42 Virginia Regiment[23] for a working party we cut out new roads through the woods, made corduroy road, lifted wagons out of the mud by main strength, etc. The men, under Col. Ronald[24] were a fine set of workers. The day was sunny and pleasant. Hd. Qrs. in the morning at Gen. Lewis' and at night at Mr. John F. Lewis' at Mt. Vernon Furnace.

Saturday, May 3rd. The army marched at an early hour across the Blue Ridge at Brown's Gap, over a good, dry, turnpike road, the advance reaching Meechum's River Depot[25] of the Virginia Central R.R. and the rear the eastern foot of the mountain [near] Brown's Cove.[26] After dinner at John F. Lewis' the General and staff followed and over took the army at Brown's, at the eastern foot of the Blue Ridge. I saw many of the men of the Stonewall Brigade bathing in the clear, cold stream at the foot of the mountain, washing off the mud of the three days of wading from

Conrad's Store near Port Republic. Vegetation east of the Blue Ridge is starting rapidly. A fine spring day and we greatly enjoyed our ride across the Blue Ridge over a good road. We spent the night at White Hall.

Before leaving Lewis' at Mt. Vernon Furnace, three miles east from Port Republic, I wrote to my wife: "I have not had time to write to you since I got back to camp, for the General started me, at one o'clock of the night I got back, for the top of the Peaked Mountain, to observe the movements of the enemy about Harrisonburg; then just as I got back to camp the General and staff started up towards Port Republic and since then I have been busy all the time, with a whole regiment of men, mending the worst road I ever saw in the Valley of Virginia. We made miles of corduroy road. The whole army is up here now and on the way to Meechum's River, over the Blue Ridge, on the Virginia Central R.R. and I think we will go from there to Staunton, but do not know. We left Ewell's whole army at Conrad's Store. He came up as we left. I must close for the courier is going. I am perfectly well and hope all of you are. I just got two letters and Dr. Hamilton's."

Sunday, May 4th, the General started me, at an early hour, for Staunton by the Virginia Central cars from Meechum's River Depot. I followed the road along the eastern foot of the Blue Ridge to the one leading across by Jarman's Gap, then took that and crossed the mountain and reached Staunton about dark. Finding that Col. Williamson had gone on to Gen. Johnson's camp near West View I followed on after him, but soon met Gen. Johnson coming to Staunton [to] meet Gen. Jackson. After a conference with him, finding I could consistently do so, I rode on home for the night.

A fine, warm spring day. I stopped en route and bathed in the clear cold water of a stream on the western side of the Blue Ridge. The General and part of the staff, riding by way of Rockfish Gap, reached Staunton about 5 P.M. and took quarters at the Virginia Hotel. The advance of the army took cars for Staunton at Meechum's River Depot and reached that town about 11 A.M., just as the people were going to church, greatly surprising them by its coming in on the cars as they supposed that Jackson had left the Valley for good. The Stonewall Brigade marched to Afton and took the cars which had been sent back for them from Staunton.

Monday, May 5th. The General remained in Staunton where he had his hair cut and laid aside the blue (U.S.) Major's uniform which he had worn at the V.M.I. and continued to wear up to this time, and put on a full new suit of Confederate grey. I reported to Gen. Edward Johnson's Hd. Qrs. some six miles from my home, at an early hour and Col. Williamson and myself, with an escort of cavalry, and Capt. R. D. Lilly's[27] company, from the 25th Virginia infantry, went to Dry Branch Gap, in Big North Mountain on the Staunton and Parkersburg Turnpike, and then northeast along the crest of Crawford Mountain until we got a full view of the enemy's camp at Cross', which we reconnoitred with reference to an attack, then returned to Gen. Johnson and discussed a plan for our proposed attack, after which Col. Williamson rode home with me for the night. A fine forenoon but rain in the afternoon. Hd. Qrs. continued at the Virginia Hotel in Staunton.

Tuesday, May 6th. Col. Williamson and myself rode early in the morning to Jenning's Gap and thence by a bridle path to the top of Crawford Mountain. We found that the enemy had left their camp at Cross'. We then rode on to Staunton, by way of the Parkersburg road and reported to Gen. Jackson. We heard that Banks had left Harrison and retreated down the Valley after plundering the people. A fine spring day and the farmers are planting corn. Hd. Qrs. remained in Staunton.

"Our men would rather fight and march than dig"

WEDNESDAY, MAY 7TH. The General and part of the staff started very early in the morning. He first rode out on the Middlebrook road, as if he were going to Lexington, then by a cross byroad he got back into and followed the Staunton and Parkersburg Turnpike. The rest of the staff were so totally ignorant in reference to the movements of the army, that upon the [report] of some one that the General had taken the Lexington road, they also started that way, but learning that he had turned off they followed after him, but only overtook him, after a ride of 25 miles from Staunton to Rodgers' Toll-gate in Ramsey's Draft, where the advance General Johnson's Men, had fallen on the Federal outpost at that point, killed and wounded several of the enemy, captured stores, etc. The main body of the enemy's advance, had retreated up the Shenandoah Mountain, but is supposed was still holding our "Fort Johnson" at the pass on the top. The General ordered me to go up the spur of the mountain on our right, preceded by a line of skirmishers, and ascertain whether the enemy had left the top of the mountain, Col. Williamson doing the same thing on the left. We had a hard scramble up the steep slope of the spur but finally reached the top only to find the enemy all gone but seeing their

rear guard on the top of Shaw's Ridge, the next one beyond us. We returned to Wm. Rodgers', at the Toll-gate, where Hd. Qrs. were established for the night; I found there Col. Jonathan N. Heck,[1] my Rich
Mountain commander, for the night. The advance of the army, Johnson's
brigade, crossed Shenandoah Mountain and encamped at head waters on
Shaw's Fork. The rear encamped near Dry Branch Gap of the Big North
Mountain. The day was very warm and the roads dusty.

Thursday, May 8th. At an early hour the troops marched across
Shaw's Ridge, [unopposed], to the Cow Pasture River at Wilson's,[2] then
began to ascend the Bull-Pasture Mountain. The General sent me in
advance, with skirmishers, up the winding turnpike road along an eastward spur of Bull-Pasture Mountain, and when, at each turn of the road,
I found the way clear I waved my handerchief, then he came on with the
main column. So doing we soon reached the gap at the summit, two miles
from Wilson's and three miles back from McDowell, as our progress was
not opposed. Having reached the summit I took Gen. Jackson out to the
right of the gap to the end of a rocky spur overlooking the Bull-Pasture
Valley, and showed him the enemy in position near McDowell. At the
same time, he looking on, I made him a map of McDowell and vicinity,
showing the enemy's position, as in full view before us. We then rode
back to the gap and with great difficulty rode up a steep, rough way,
along a gorge, to the cleared fields on the top of the mountain to our left,
called Sitlington's Hill, where Gen. Jackson had already taken his command and placed it in concealment and was studying the enemy's position.
I rode with Gens. Jackson and Johnson across the field on the crest of
the mountain, to reconnoitre. Discovering us the enemy's skirmishers
advanced from the Bull-Pasture Valley, fired on us and forced us to retire through the Woods in our rear.

After this reconnoissance, by order of the General I found a route
for bringing up artillery from the turnpike to the summit of the mountain
in the [fields]. Skirmishing was kept up for some time by the opposing
forces, but as there seemed to be no chance for a fight that day the General let most of the staff go down to John Wilson's on the Cow Pasture
late in the afternoon, to get some dinner, himself remaining on the
mountain at the front. While we were eating we heard the sound of
artillery. I at once called for my horse and rode rapidly to the top of the
Bull-Pasture Mountain, where I found Gen. Jackson, all alone, in the
road at the gap. It was already dark. He at once sent me down the road
towards McDowell to see what was going on; he had already sent back

to Shaw's Fork for the Stonewall Brigade and seemed very anxious for
it to arrive. Starting down the road I soon met Col. Wm. H. Harman and
others bringing Gen. Edward Johnson wounded, from the engagement
that was going on on our left. I rode back and informed Gen. Jackson.
When the ambulance came up he stopped it and had a brief conversation
with Gen. Johnson then said to me: 'Go up to Gen. Taliaferro and give
him my compliments and tell him I am coming in person with the Stonewall Brigade and he must hold his position until I come.' The wounding
of Johnson had left Taliaferro the ranking officer present, in command
of the field. I rode down the turnpike to the steep gorge, or log way, down
which they were bringing the wounded to the turnpike and finding I
could not ride up it in the darkness, I left my horse in charge of Wm. F.
Snapp a private of the 25th Virginia, whom I knew, who had broken
down and had not been able to ascend the mountain with his command,
and climbed up on foot, to the field on the top of Sitlington's Hill, and
found the [rear] A scene of great confusion. It was between 8 and 9
P.M.; we had repulsed the enemy's attack on our left and our troops were
all mingled together, in the greatest disorder imaginable, like a swarm
of bees, calling out for comrades, commands, etc., no one being able to
distinguish another in the darkness. I soon found Gen. Taliaferro and
delivered my message. Soon after that Gen. Jackson himself came up
with the Stonewall Brigade; he then had a long conference with Gen.
Winder,[3] after which he and the staff that were with him rode back to
Wilson's, some three miles, getting there about two A.M. of the morning
of the 9th. The General and some of the staff walked most of the way
down the mountain, leading their horses, being too sleepy to ride. We
found the house and yard at John Wilson's full of wounded men that had
been brought down from the battle-field. The day was very pleasant but
the night very chilly. Vegetation in this mountain region is but just
starting.[4]

Before retiring the General told me I must return to the top of the
mountain at three A.M. and see about opening a road up to Sitlington's
Hill, where we had been engaged in fighting, for taking up artillery,
and must also ascertain whether the enemy had left McDowell. Our
Hd. Qrs. at Wilson's on the Cow-Pasture, were 31 miles from Staunton,
on the east and two from the gap on Bull-Pasture Mountain and 5 from
the village of McDowell on the west.

These are some of the incidents of the battle. Col. Michael G. Harman moved his regiment, the 52nd Virginia, early in the action, gallantly

up to the fight. Col. Wm. H. Harman was much excited after Gen. Edward Johnson was wounded. Gen. Johnson had about 30 skirmishers and some officers with him when he rode, early in the day, to Sitlington's Hill. When we joined him he said the enemy were visible at several points and had one or two regiments on Phoenix Hull's Hill north of the turnpike opposite Sitlington's Hill. He drove in several of the skirmishing parties which the enemy sent out to flank his left, then sent for reinforcements. The [52nd] Virginia, under Col. M. G. Harman, came up and was posted on the left as skirmishers; it drove back the enemy's advance. The 12th Georgia, Maj. Willie A. Hawkins in command was then put in front, on the crest of the hill on the right of the 52nd Virginia. The 57th Virginia Lieut. Col. Elisha H. Keen[5] was put on the right of the 12th Georgia, and the 44th Virginia, Col. Wm. C. Scott,[6] on the right of the 57th and extending in a ravine down the slope of the hill.

The enemy opened a heavy fire on our right at 4:30 P.M. At that time Gen. Johnson was on the right of the 44th Virginia reconnoitring. He moved to the right where a short engagement took place during which the 25th Virginia, Col. Geo. H. Smith,[7] and the 31st Virginia, Lieut. Col. Alfred H. Jackson, (Col. John S. Hoffman, of the 25th, although sick, came up also) came up and were posted on the right of the 44th Virginia. Just then a terrific fire of small arms and artillery opened and the enemy attempted to advance but was repulsed. Then Gen. Wm. B. Taliaferro and his brigade came up and the 23rd Virginia, Col. Alex. G. Taliaferro,[8] and the 37th Virginia, Col. Sam. V. Fulkerson,[9] were advanced to support the center where the 12th Georgia was gallantly engaged. The 10th Virginia, Col. Simeon G. Gibbons, the last regiment of Taliaferro's Brigade, then came up the hill and was ordered to support the 52nd Virginia which had repulsed the enemy from our left and was advancing to flank them. Just then the enemy advanced a heavy force and attempted to flank our right. This movement was repulsed by the 12th Georgia on the part of Taliaferro's Brigade. Companies of the 25th and of the 31st Virginia were then ordered to our extreme right, to a hill in the woods to guard our flank. Col. Arthur C. Cummings' brigade then coming up that and the 10th Virginia were sent still further to the right, down the slope towards the turnpike to further guard our right flank.

From 4:30 to 8:30 P.M. the firing was terrific. At 8:30 P.M. Gen. Johnson was wounded and left the field and Gen. Wm. B. Taliaferro succeeded to the command. He says he sent the 23rd Virginia to support the 25th and the 37th Virginia to the right to drive the enemy away.

[They] drove them down the hill and then returned. He sent 4 cos. of the 10th Virginia to support the 12th Georgia and six cos. to the right of the 23rd Virginia, and afterwards under the hill as a reserve. He says the battle lasted until 9:30 P.M. Gen. Jackson estimates the loss of the enemy under Milroy[10] at from 500 to 1,000.[11] Col. Abner Smead, Gen. Johnson's A.A.G., says there were 500 men in the 12th Georgia and 3,000 in all in Johnson's brigade at McDowell. Hd. Qrs. are at [John] Wilson's, on the Cow Pasture River and the Staunton and Parkersburg 31 miles from Staunton and two from the gap in the Bull Pasture Mountain and 5 from McDowell on the west.

Friday, May 9th. I found the air very keen and bracing and a heavy white frost and myself chilly and stiff when, after a short sleep, I started at three A.M. for the top of the mountain in obedience to Gen. Jackson's orders. On reaching the summit I soon learned from the pickets that the enemy had retreated from McDowell, so sent word to Gen. Jackson and then rode to examine and sketch the battle-field on Sitlington's Hill. I found the bushes, that were very thick in the field where our men were mainly posted during the engagement, cut into splinters by the bullets of the enemy, a good many of whose dead were still lying about, all of ours having been carried down to the turnpike at the mouth of the ravine by which we had gone up and been laid in a row along a grassy space beside the road. Col. Stapleton Crutchfield,[12] our chief of artillery and myself then rode down and examined the Yankee camps at McDowell. We found them full of all manner of things that had been gathered there. They had left precipitately after the fight, although Gen. Schenck had joined Gen. Milroy with 6,000 men after the battle. Milroy afterwards reported that we had flanked him, coming up the Valley of the Cow Pasture River, during the night.

Our troops are too tired, and besides we have no cooked rations, to pursue the enemy, so Hd. Qrs. were brought over to Mrs. [Phoenix] Hull's at McDowell and the army closed up to that vicinity and ordered to cook rations. Later in the day I rode around and sketched the topography of the Federal camps and of the country in the vicinity of McDowell. In the evening Maj. John Marshall McCue, from Mount Solon, in Augusta County, joined us at Mrs. Hull's; he and others from that region having come over to look after the killed and wounded in companies from that locality. The 12th Georgia had 40 men killed and 140 wounded in yesterday's battle. Col. Simeon B. Gibbons, of the 10th Virginia, from Luray, was killed, also a good many others of our Valley men.

Our loss was quite heavy. Today our dead were buried in the bend of the road near the mouth of our path ravine by which we went to the battle-field. The day was warm and pleasant after a heavy frost and a dense fog in the morning. Old Mr. Robert Sitlington met us, in the turnpike, in the morning as we rode forward towards McDowell, very much excited. He said: 'I thank God that you have so punished the insolent foe that has been tyrranizing over us.' The [enemy] burned several houses as they left said to have contained stores and some of them dead men. I secured a fine wall tent from those that had been left standing in and around the Federal camps.

Saturday, May 10th. We marched on, at an early hour in pursuit of the enemy, following the Parkersburg road some 6 miles towards Mon-terey then turning northeast by the road leading to Franklin, which the enemy had taken. After we had gone some 10 miles the General called me aside, riding back and into a wood road and into the woods, out of eye and ear shot, and directed me to ride back, with all possible dispatch, and blockade the roads leading through North River and Dry River gaps, from the Franklin road into the Valley, riding by way of Churchville and taking as many of the cavalry encamped near there, under Maj. Jackson,[13] as I wanted. I told him I wished to have nothing to do with that officer, as he was a drunkard. He replied: "Then take whom you please and send me a report each day." I asked that Mr. S. Howell Brown be permitted to go with me, to which he consented. We rode back, by way of Mc-Dowell and Jenning's Gap, and reached my home at Churchville by 11 P.M. I found Capt. Frank F. Sterrett's[14] company of cavalry encamped near that place and ordered them to be at my house by three A.M. the next morning and ready to march. We then took some sleep and fed our horses. I changed mine for another. On the road from McDowell today we met many citizens going to look after friends and relatives who had been in the battle. We met the stage coach from Staunton, at Capt. C. R. Manson's shanties,[15] at the mouth of Ramsey's Draft, about two miles beyond Rodgers'. A fine spring day; the peach trees are in bloom.

As I recall the circumstances connected with Jackson's sending me back to blockade the mountain passes, we were halting in the road, for the army to rest or for some other purpose, when he turned his horse towards the rear and beckoned to me to ride with him. We rode back some little distance until we came to a wood road leading up into the forest on the left. He took that and I followed him until we were out of sight and hearing of others in the woods, then he turned about and facing me, with his usual emphatic gesture with his long arm and extended index finger and said: "Banks is at Harrisonburg, Fremont is at Franklin. There is a good road between them and Fremont ought to join Banks but I dont think he will. I want North River Gaps, and Dry River Gaps, by which he could do it, blockaded by daylight tomorrow morning. I want you to go and do this. Take couriers along and send one back every hour telling me where you are. You will find cavalry near Churchville that you can take to do this work with. Now don't take any counsel of your fears."

Sunday, May 11th. I started from Loch Willow, near Churchville, with my cavalry escort at three A.M. by way of Stribling Springs across to James Todd's and blockaded the North River Gap road by falling trees into it and obstructing it in other ways, near his house, we then rode on by the way of the mouth of North River Gap and halted for a while and fed our horses at Hufford's on North River; after which we rode, by Emanuel Church and Ottobine Church to Dry River Gap and blockaded the Harrisonburg and Franklin road in the gap beyond Rawley Springs. We spent part of the night at Krousehorn's where we got supper. We heard that the enemy's cavalry had been back to Harrisonburg and had come out to Muddy Creek on the road to Rawley Springs. We procured axes and crowbars from citizens near the entrances to the gaps from the Valley and by sending details far up into the gorges followed by the road and cutting down trees and rolling large rocks into the road as we withdrew we made a very effectual blockade especially of the road leading from Franklin to Harrisonburg through Dry River Gap.

I remember that after the war when I was doing some engineering work for a Federal force at Staunton which was engaged in the preparation of a Federal cemetery near there, Gen. Thomas,[16] as assistant general of the Federal Army during the war came to Staunton on a tour of inspection and visited me at my office. During our conversation I mentioned my ride to blockade these roads. He said he remembered that President Lincoln had telegraphed to Fremont to join Banks at Harrisonburg by the road between those places and Fremont had replied that the road was blockaded and he could not do it.

Monday, May 12th. Very early in the morning I rode back with my escort to Mt. Solon and thence sent the cavalry back to Churchville and sent for my horse which I had left at home to rest. I then went to Maj. J. Marshall McCue's accompanied by Brown, and we there rested during that day and the following night. This was a fine, warm, spring day. As

we rode by Mossy Creek Church they were burying the remains of Frank
Eruitt and of Harman who were killed at McDowell. An extravagant
story was in circulation that Jackson had captured Milroy. After I left
the army Jackson advanced to near Franklin and Hd. Qrs. were located
in a meadow about 1½ [miles] southwest from that town on the road
to Monterey. By order of Gen. Jackson divine services were today held
throughout the army.

Tuesday, May 13th. In the morning started for Franklin via Briery
Branch Gap, accompanied by Maj. J. M. McCue, Joseph I. Hottle, Bell[17]
and others. Heard while crossing Shenandoah Mountain, [by] a bridle
path, that Jackson had fallen back from Franklin, so we turned up the
North Fork of the South Branch of the Potomac, taking roads leading
toward McDowell, and spent the night at Keyser's, after a ride of 40
miles over rough road and bridle paths. Brown got sick on the way and
turned back to Maj. McCue's. A fine day. Hd. Qrs. were at Solomon
Flesher's, a brick house on the south side of the river ½ mile S. W. from
Franklin.

Wednesday, May 12th.[18] Got an early start, via Doe Hill, and reached
McDowell about 9 A.M., where I found Gen. Francis H. Smith[19] and Col.
John T. L. Preston with the V.M.I. cadets, who had been left at Mc-
Dowell to guard Prisoners, etc., and who were pretty much used up by
the hard marches, guard duty, etc., mere boys that most of them were. It
rained very hard last night and most of today and the streams are rising
rapidly.

The army returned to the vicinity of McDowell and Hd. Qrs. were
again at Mrs. Felix Hull's.

Thursday, May 15th. The General started me, at an early hour, to
overtake the advance of the army, Taliaferro's Brigade, now marching
back towards Staunton and turn it towards Jenning's Gap and Stribling
Springs. I overtook the advance Col. Alexander Taliaferro's 23rd Virginia Regiment, on Shenandoah Mountain, and gave him instructions,
then rode to Lebanon White Sulphur Springs and secured quarters for
our party at King's. The General and the rest of the staff arrived about
3 P.M.; an order was issued for the observance of the next day, May 16,
as fast day.

We heard of the evacuation of Norfolk, the blowing up of the Ram
Virginia, or Merrimac,[20] and that the enemy was within 12 miles of Richmond. Gloom all around us, but we trust in God. Col. T. H. Williamson,
who has been with us on volunteer engineer duty, left us to return to

the V.M.I. It rained some and was quite cool. Maj. J. M. McCue rode with me today on his way home.

Friday, May 16th. I started home in the morning and met a wagon load of my people in Jenning's Gap coming to the army to see me; we all turned back home. Drew my pay for April. It rained quite hard last night and most of today. The army remained in camps near Lebanon White Sulphur Springs and observed the "Fast Day." Hd. Qrs. at King's.

Saturday, May 17th. The advance of the army marched at an early hour and encamped on North River opposite Bridgewater, the rear in the vicinity of Mt. Solon. Hd. Qrs. were established, in tents, on Castle Hill, just west of Mt. Solon where I joined the General in the morning. By invitation the General and staff dined at Maj. J. M. McCue's as also did Brig. Gen. Geo. H. Steuart[21] of the Maryland Line, who had come to confer with the General. Very fine day.

Sunday, May 18th. Hd. Qrs. remained at Mt. Solon. Gen. Jackson Maj. R. L. Dabney and myself rode via Mossy Creek down to opposite Bridgewater where Maj. (Rev. Dr.) Dabney preached a good sermon to Col. Z. T. Conner's Brigade, encamped in George Gibbon's meadow on the left of the road and along North River. After [the] sermon we went, accompanied by Col. Z. T. Conner, and Capt. R. D. Lilley to Mr. George Gibbons to dinner. Were told many things about the visit of the Yankees to Bridgewater. Gen. R. S. Ewell reached our camp about daylight this morning and had a long consultation with the General; after breakfast he rode with us to preaching and after that back to his command at Conrad's Store. Fine day; hard shower in P.M. which we rode back in to Hd. Qrs. Saw many of my old Mossy Creek friends on the road. Dr. H. Black[22] was acting Medical Director of the army as Dr. Hunter McGuire was sick.

Monday, May 19th. Gen. Jackson had us all up to breakfast at 3 A.M. and the troops in motion; the advance crossed North River at Bridgewater on a bridge made by pushing into the river one behind the other, closed up, wagons furnished by the people and planked over lengthways. When we rode down to the ford yesterday, after preaching, and saw how deep the water was the General asked me how he could get the men and ammunition chests across the river with safety and dry. I suggested the plan of a wagon bridge, as above stated, telling him how numerous the big four-and-six-horse wagons were in that region, where I had lived for a number of years. He adopted my suggestion and ordered Capt. C. R. Mason with his negro pioneers and the quarter-master to carry it out. The advance of the army reached Dayton and the rear encamped near Bridgewater. A fine but very warm day. Hd. Qrs. were in a tent near the old stream mill just below Harrisonburg.

By order of Gen. Jackson Lt. J. K. Boswell and myself rode on in advance of the army down the Valley, via Harrisonburg, to reconnoitre the enemy's position. We reached Co. Ashby's camp, on the bridge over Smith's creek near New Market, by 4 P.M. after a ride of 36 miles and after a conference with him in reference to the location of his pickets and the enemy's position we rode on intending to spend the night at Rev. Rude's: but found his daughter lying dead in the house, so we went on across the river [to] Negg's, a [Dundard], and found them very willing to entertain us. The enemy had treated them so badly they were glad to see our soldiers back again. We dined and fed at Cowan's, near Sparta, where Col. Daum,[23] Shields' Chief of Artillery, had been quartered and made his boasts.

Some of Ashby's men were very anxious to go to Front Royal and capture some Yankee stores, etc. The main body of the enemy is at Strasburg with cavalry pickets on the line of Pugh's Run beyond Woodstock. When Banks fell back from Harrisonburg Shields' command crossed the Massanutton mountains from New Market to Luray and then on down to Front Royal.

Tuesday, May 20th, 1862. We went on to Woodstock; the enemy is four miles below, at Maurertown: reported to be entrenching, especially at Strasburg. Boswell with Capt. Brown of the [?] Miss. to the end of the Massanutton, or Three-Topped Mt., near Strasburg, to reconnoitre, and I went back, by the "Middle road," to Myer's Forge and spent the night there with Capt. Myers[24] and his cavalry Co. The enemy makes frequent dashes into Woodstock. A fine day. (Gen. Jackson was at Tenth Legion.—Smith.[25])

Wednesday, May 21st. I went up to Columbia Furnace and took dinner; then went down the road to Woodstock and back by the "Faidly" Road; spent the night at the Furnace, which the owner has deserted and gone North; because his sons have proved traitors to the South. It is rumored that the enemy is advancing. A fine warm day. Sketched the roads. A young man went down around the enemy's lines to Middletown, last night, and will report tomorrow. Was arrested, on account of my blue dress. (Hd. Qrs. at the church beyond White House Bridge.—Smith).

Thursday, May 22nd. Got a cavalry escort and went down to the enemy's lines at Pugh's Run, near Fair view; went in sight of the Federal pickets. Came back to Columbia Furnace and found orders to report to Hd. Qrs., so started, at 3 P.M., and went to Rude's, via Mt. Jackson, 18 miles, and spent the night there. Had a pleasant visit with the old gentleman, Rev. Rude who had much to say about the recent Yankee Invasion and the immense amount of damage they had done. Heard our army had crossed over to Luray. A fine warm day. The advance of our army went to within 10 miles of Front Royal today. (Hd. Qrs. at Cedar Point. —Smith).

Friday, May 23rd. Started at 3 A.M. and went on to Luray, 19 miles, then on to Front Royal, 25 miles farther, and got there, just after we had charged on the enemy, and witnessed the fight on the hill and saw them charged on across the bridge; or, rather, came up a few moments after our men got to the bridge, the sight being obstructed by the hill. The Gen. went on beyond Cedarville, to where Col. Mumford[26] charged on the Ist Yankee Maryland Regt. with his cavalry, received their fire and routed them completely. We captured many stores, two trains of cars, etc. Ashby went to Buckton and cut off their retreat to Strasburg, but he lost many brave men there; Captains Sheets, Fletcher and [Baxter],[27] all killed. Brown and I slept in a barn at Cedarville; the Gen. went back to Front Royal. (To Richard's?—Pendleton).[28] Our cavalry went within 8 miles of Winchester. Our infantry advance, the troops of Gen. Ewell, encamped on the hill beyond Crooked Run. I ascertained, the next day, that the enemy had a picket within a mile of Cedarville where we slept and had our wounded. We took some 500 of the enemy and pursued them until a late hour. A very fine day, but cool at night.

Saturday, May 24th. It rained and hailed some in the morning and was quite cool. The army was all marched up until the rear rested at Cedarville, while Gen. Ewell and his troops, the advance, went on beyond Nineveh, where we stopped, at Mr. Mason's, and got some breakfast; then Gen. Jackson had a consultation with Gen. Ewell after which we went back to Cedarville, going by the troops which were halted. Gen. Ewell went on, by the turnpike, to within some four miles of Winchester. When we got back to Cedarville, the Gen. went a short distance with me on the road to Middletown; then directed me to take 16 cavalry [men] and go and find where Banks was, and report to him every half hour. I started and at about a mile and a half was fired on by the enemy's cavalry picket, some 60 in number, in the woods, the rain falling.[29]

By the official returns, by Gen. Jackson's Chief of Ordnance, in Dec., 1862, we captured at Winchester 9,354 small arms and 500,000 rounds of ammunition: The Chief Commissary, Maj. W. J. Hawks, received, from Winchester and Martinsburg, at that time, 103 head of cattle, gross 92,700 lbs; 14,637 lbs of bacon; 6,000 lbs of Hard Bread; 2,400 lbs of sugar; and 350 Bush. of salt (official Report).[30]

Gen. Geo. H. Steuart commanded the 2nd and 6th Va. Cavalry and was a part of Ewell's command. Gen. Jackson waited for him to come up to pursue the enemy after which they were routed, on the 25th, but as he did not come the General sent Capt. Pendleton after him. He refused to come until ordered by Gen. Ewell, so much precious time was lost before Ewell could be found, and the enemy therefore had time to form again and oppose them. Our infantry had pursued some 6 miles.[31]

Friday, May 30th. McDowell, with 30,000 men, reached Markham Friday, May 30th, and was 3 days passing, having Shields', King's and Ord's[32] Divisions, in that order.

In the morning messengers came informing the General of Shields' approach towards Front Royal, and of McDowell's approach towards Berryville and of Banks' reorganizing his force at Williamsport. The ladies of Charlestown called to pay their respects to the General. We went down to the front and the 5th Va. Regt. was advanced and skirmished with the enemy and we had considerable artillery fighting. I was down to the river where the company on picket, the "Liberty Hall Volunteers," were enjoying themselves bathing. Got chased by a Yankee cavalryman, and as I had no arms I made good use of my horse. We came back to Maj. W. J. Hawks' to dinner. After we left the front Gen. C. S. Winder's troops drove the enemy away from and occupied Bolivar's Heights, but were compelled to leave them by the enemy's artillery on the Maryland shore Heights. As we were riding back into Charlestown a Lt. of Cavalry rode up to Gen. Thos. J. Jackson and said: "General, are the troops going back?" The General replied: "Don't you see them going?" He asked, "Are they all going?" The General turned to Col. Abner Smead and said: "Colonel, arrest that man as a spy." The fellow was much alarmed, but Col. Turner Ashby, soon coming up, got him off by saying that he had not much sense. It commenced raining before noon, and rained very hard. I rode back to Winchester on my horse, the General and some others of the staff came in the cars. I got there first and met a messenger from Col. Z. T. Conner announcing that the enemy under Shields had driven Col. Z. T. Conner and the 12th Ga. Regt. out of Front Royal, capturing some of them and the stores, etc. Col. Z. T. Conner showed great want of judgment and was surprised, completely. I sent

the messenger across the field and stopped the cars and informed the General of what had happened. As I came into town I met the 12th Georgia coming in from their retreat; those that escaped. Shortly after we got to the hotel it was said the General got a dispatch in these words: "Winchester (such an hour) General: Just arrived, enemy in full pursuit, unless immediately succored all is lost. Yours Conner."; and it was reported that in the evening the General sent for Col. Z. T. Conner and said: "Colonel, how many men did you have killed, Sir?" "None," he replied. "How many wounded?" "None, Sir," said he. "Do you call that much of a fight?"; and then the General ordered him in arrest.[33] The enemy crossed some forces over the river at Berry's Ferry and are reported to be in Berryville tonight. Dangers environ our army. It was cool today. It rained very hard, with thunder and lightning.

Saturday, May 31st. The General came into our room, at 3 P.M., and said to me, first, "I want you to go to Charlestown and bring up the First Brigade. I will stay in Winchester until you get here if I can, but if I cannot, and the enemy gets here first, you must bring it around through the mountains." He feared that the converging columns of Fremont,[34] Shields, McDowell and Banks might compel him to go out and fight one of them but he was in fine spirits. I rode rapidly to Charlestown and there met Gen. C. S. Winder, just starting out to the front, and informed him of the state of affairs. He got his men and we went on by the Smithfield Road. I got Maj. Briscoe to burn the R. R. bridges and destroy the Telegraph. At Smithfield we had some alarm, a Q. M.[35] rushing back and stateing that the enemy had advanced to Bunker's Hill and would cut off our train which was in advance of us and had gone that way. It was only an alarm, which Gen. W. soon quieted and went on. The army reached Winchester about dark, by way of Brucetown. I came on to Chrisman's, near Newtown, and slept on the floor there. The First Brigade came on to near Newtown. The General left Winchester about 2½ P.M. The road was full of stragglers. A fine warm day; streams swollen some. Hd. Qrs. for the night were at Hupp's, one mile from Strasburg. Ewell's Division and Taliaferro's Brigade reached Strasburg.

Sunday, June 1st. I came on to Strasburg and found the General at Hupp's. About noon cannonading began on the Capon road.[36] Ashby had one of Chew's guns there and a few cavalry, and drove back and kept the enemy at bay. Steuart and the Maryland Line kept them back at Cedar Creek. Boswell and 5 cavalrymen were charged on by a company of Shields' cavalry on the Front Royal Road, a mile from Town, and the enemy (that is the cavalry) came to within a half mile of Strasburg. When the firing opened towards Wardenville the General Mounted and went that way with a portion of the troops until our whole army came up, then he formed them to the N. W. of Strasburg to offer Fremont battle and maneuvered the army over the hills, for some hours, while our train, in double lines, 8 miles long when well closed up, moved on towards Woodstock. We came to Woodstock and spent the night in a lawyer's office,[37] in rear of the C. H. Col. J. T. L. Preston, of the V.M.I., was with us. The General did not come up until late. He told me when I reported at Strasburg, to go and rest myself, so I went to the Yankee Signal Station, on the top of Round Hill, and from there watched the movements of the army, the train, etc. Our prisoners, some 2,300, were guarded by Col. Cunningham's[38] 21st Va., at Tom's Brook, below Round Hill towards Woodstock. Our advance came to near Woodstock. A very pleasant but warm day. There was a very heavy thunder storm in the P.M.

June 2nd. The enemy is advancing rapidly; the General went to our rear and skirmished with them all day. The train got in great confusion and the General sent me to go along with it and get it in order, and direct that no wagon shall stop to water, etc., and keep all to the right and in motion. Then he directed me to keep in front; so I went on to New Market. The advance of our train reached near there. Ashby had his camp at Fry's Point, S.W. of Edinburg,[39] and at Red Banks. The General came to Israel Allen's, near Hawkinstown. I spent the night with Kagey. A party of our men burnt the White House and the Columbia bridges, on the Shenandoah, just in advance of the enemy. Col. S. Crutchfield went to see if it had been done. There was a very hard rain in the P.M. Ashby had a fight, aided by stragglers.

Tuesday, June 3rd. I went down to Mt. Jackson in the morning, but learning that the enemy was advancing still I turned back and aided in forwarding the train, then came back to Rude's Hill and witnessed the burning of the bridge, across the river near Mt. Jackson, by Ashby; then we came on and encamped in a field of Dr. Rice's, below New Market. There was a hard rain in P.M. and at night. The Gen. was almost afloat at night from the heavy rainfall.

Wednesday, June 4th. We spent a very unpleasant night; it rained very hard and flooded our tents, so we left our camp in the morning and went up to Mr. Strayer's,[40] where we spent the day until 6 P.M. The General had me in his room twice asking about the country in the vicinity of Port Republic, the topography, etc. We thought at one time that the enemy was advancing, having put a pontoon bridge across the river near Mt. Jackson; so our men were ordered out and held in readiness below New Market, but the enemy did not come on. As they were attempting a flank movement on the other side of the North River we moved up to Williamson's, in the evening, about 6 P.M., and our forces occupied the hills near his house. It rained very hard in the morning; was quite cool in P.M. At 10 P.M. the General started me to go to the top of the Peaked Mt., towards McGaheysville, wishing me to go there and watch and report the movements of Shields in the Luray Valley, taking a signal operator with me.

Thursday, June 5th. Reached Harrisonburg at 3 A.M., rested two hours and fed my horse. Dr. McGuire came up in an ambulance and our sick were taken to Mt. Crawford and across North River in boats. The river was very high, said to have been higher that it had been in 25 years. Our sick were taken on to Staunton, ambulances coming to the river after them. Everything in Harrisonburg was in confusion. I went on at 5 A.M.; got Mr. Eiler, at Peale's, as a guide, and reached the top of the mt., "The Peak," by 8½ o'clock A.M., and spent the day there. Saw the head of Shields' column encamp 2 miles below Conrad's Store, near the Big Spring, at about 4 P.M. The day was fine; had some rain. Came down from "The Peak" about 5 P.M.; took supper at Mr. Eiler's and then went in pursuit of Hd. Qrs. Went to Harrisonburg and found that only Ashby and his cavalry were below there; everything profoundly quiet. Then went up the turnpike and took the Port Republic Road, which the army had taken and found Hd. Qrs. at one mile on the road to the left. Gen. R. S. Ewell was encamped near by, while the advance of our army was not far from Cross Keys. Out train and prisoners went to near Port Republic. It was quite late when I reported to the General.

Friday, June 6th. Went to Peale's in the morning and sent a signal man to "The Peak." Communicated some from Peale's; then, as the enemy was reported advancing, up the Keezletown Road, went to near Cross Keys and established communication to that point from "The Peak." In the P.M. I went on to Port Republic. We had a fight with the Yankee cavalry, about 3 P.M., on the ridge east of the Turnpike, on the Port Republic road. Our force was Ashby's cavalry regt. and the 6th Va. cavalry. We took the Yankee colonel, Sir Percy Wyndham,[41] an Englishman, and 30 privates, and routed them; then they came on with infantry, which was repulsed by Gen. George H. Steuart with the 52nd and 58th Va. regts. and the Maryland Line. This was about dark and two miles further from Harrisonburg. After we had repulsed the Federal infantry Ashby took some of our infantry and went forward to try and cut off the enemy's cavalry by going around through the woods. Our men had been firing whenever they saw any of the enemy. Ashby directed them to cease firing and went forward to reconnoitre; just at that time he was shot, it is supposed by one of our men mistaking him for a Yankee. So fell the gallant General Turner Ashby; a loss irreparable.[42] We were at Dr. Kemper's, on the hill, at Port Republic, and it was late at night when the news of Ashby's death came. After hearing this Gen. Jackson walked the floor of his room, for some time, in deep sorrow, greatly moved by the sad news. Col. Percy Wyndham gave his parole and slept on the floor at our Hd. Qrs. A fine day, but the roads very, very muddy.

Saturday, June 7th. I spent the day in getting up a map of the country around Port Republic and in signaling to the man I had left on "The Peak," from Fisher's Hill. The General offered the enemy battle near Cross Keys but they did not come on. We pitched our tents near Dr. Kemper's, on the bluff of South River, in the afternoon. Carrington's[43] battery was encamped near our camp, the rest of our troops were on the other side of North River. A fine day.

Sunday, June 8th. About 10 A.M. of today, while some of us were quietly in our tents and the General and a portion of the staff were on the point of going over to the army across North River, the Yankee cavalry and flying artillery, from down the river, made a dash upon Port Republic, our picket running away but some few coming through the town. The enemy appeared opposite Port Republic, across South River, and began firing at such of our men as they could see, and especially at the bridge guard, while a portion of them crossed near the factory. As soon as the firing began the General started down toward it, on foot, as his horse was not ready, and went into the town, and when the others came on. Capt. A. S. Pendleton, Col. Wm. L. Jackson, Lt. J. K. Boswell, Lt. Edward Willis[44] and Col. S. Crutchfield, and some one brought him his horse, he mounted and they all rode rapidly towards and through the bridge; but the enemy caught Willis and Crutchfield who were in the rear of the party.[45] Our bridge guard was then firing at the enemy across the main Shenandoah River below the bridge and the Yankee artillery, below Mrs. Yost's on Charles Lewis' land, opened on our troops and on the bridge. Soon as General Jackson had reached the other side of the bridge he sent Col. Jackson and Lt. Boswell to see where the enemy was; he remaining on the bluff above New Haven. Col. Jackson went to the end of the bridge and the enemy fired on him from its southern end and through the bridge; Boswell went up the river and saw them across North River and reported to the General, he then went and motioned to them, shouting, "Go away from that bridge. Go away from that bridge," and they went away. Shortly afterwards they brought up a piece of artillery and planted it at the Port Republic end of the bridge. The General thought it was ours, one of Courtney's[46] guns, though Lt. Boswell assured him that it was the enemy's. To convince himself the General went to the top of the bank and beckoned, and called out; "Bring that gun over this side." They at once opened on him with canister, one shot, that killed one of our men; then the 7th Va., Col. Fulkerson's[47] came up and opened on the Yankees and drove them from their gun, killing one of them. They then fled across the river. Just then 4 regiments of Yankee infantry came up to near Mrs. Yost's house, and we opened on them with 10 pieces of artillery, from the hill on the opposite bank of the Shenandoah River, when they retreated, both infantry and cavalry. I was lying down in my tent, sick with a violent headache, have been exhausted from duty that day by the General, when the tumult began; but I helped to strike the tents and load up our Hd. Qrs. wagons and then got on my horse and rode, quite rapidly, up the river, out of range, as the enemy were firing across the river and teams, artillery, etc., were flying up the road in great alarm. As soon as the panic ceased I went on to Weyer's Cafe and looked awhile at the battle, which had opened at Cross Keys, between our forces under Gen. R. S. Ewell, and the Federal army under Gen. J. C. Fremont. We could see the battle field quite plainly, with the aid of my field glasses, from Cafe Hill. The battle raged furiously and lasted until nearly dark. We drove the enemy's left wing from the field and repulsed all their attacks on us with great loss to them but comparatively small loss to us. Gen. Ewell managed his troops admirable. The 16th Mississippi Regt., Col. Posey's[48] commanded by Lt. Col. [?][49] of Trimble's[50] Brigade drove the enemy more than a mile and won many laurels. After watching the battle for a short time I went to Mr. Abram. Mohler's house and went to bed and slept off my severe headache. Towards night, feeling better, I guided Chew's battery to where it could guard Patterson's Ford, then spent the night at Jas. A. Patterson's. Our cavalry was on the south side of South River; the trains came over through Port Republic and went up towards Mt. Meridian and were parked there. The battle raged over a wide space; we had 30 killed and

270 wounded; the loss of the enemy was much greater. Hd. Qrs. at Dr. Kemper's. A fine cool day.

Monday, June 9th. Our troops were all brought over North River before day, only a few cavalry were left ready to check any advance of the enemy. As soon as all our troops had passed over we burned the bridge over North River and having made a foot bridge of wagons across South River, our troops crossed that and marched down towards Lewiston, to fight Shields' advance. The First Brigade, Gen. C. S. Winder's, began the fight, in line of battle towards the Shenandoah River and at right angles to that; it was soon driven back. Just about that time I came up and the General asked where I had been. I informed him; then he said: "Take Gen. Taylor[51] around and take those batteries." Pointing to the enemy's batteries near Gen. Lewis' house, which were making sad havoc among our men. The brigade of Gen. R. S. Taylor was just then coming up; so I met it and led it, in line of battle, with skirmishers in front, to the right, through the woods, until nearly opposite Gen. Lewis' house, when the brigade advanced and charged upon the battery and took it, after being repulsed several times. Gen. Wm. B. Taliaferro's Brigade came up, along the western edge of the woods, in time to give the enemy a volley or two by a flank fire. We routed them completely; took at one point a battery of 5 guns; we drove, or rather pursued the enemy, with our cavalry, some 12 miles, capturing some 300 prisoners. The day was fine until late in the afternoon when we had a tremendous rain. Fremont drew up his army in line of battle on the north side of the Shenandoah, after we had whipped Shields, and opened his artillery on the ambulances that were gathering the wounded of both armies and on the burial parties. After the battle, by order of Gen. Jackson, I led the army, by a by-road, through the woods, across to Mt. Vernon or Miller's Furnace, then up towards Brown's Gap, the train having been sent up that way earlier in the day. The army occupied the cove leading to Brown's Gap and extended across the mountain to Brown's Cove on the other side. Hd. Qrs. at Mr. John F. Lewis', at Mt. Vernon Furnace.

Tuesday, June 10th. I spent the day at Lewis' making maps of the surrounding country. We are gathering up the wounded and the arms from the battle field and burying the dead. Our loss is very heavy but that of the enemy is still more. It rained most of the day. The army is encamped on the sides of the Blue Ridge; Hd. Qrs. remain at Lewis'.

Wednesday, June 11th. By order of the General I went down in the morning and examined the fords of South River in reference to crossing; found the water too deep to enable us to cross our caissons and keep their boxes dry. Went back, collecting information about roads, etc., and reported to the General. He ordered me to take some infantry to the fords and make crossings by filling them up with stones, as I had suggested. I spent the night at Lewis', but was up most of it waiting for the army to guide it to the ford; slept in the yard; a fine day.

Thursday, June 12th. We left Lewis' at an early hour, the General going to Port Republic to see the troops across South River there and I to Weyer's Cafe to see the train across South River there. Found the river rather high for crossing at that ford so went up and made the ford at Patterson's Mill passable, by filling it with rocks and stones, having a detail of a Mississippi Co. for this purpose. Late in the day I found Hd. Qrs. in the corner of the woods where the Weyer's Cafe road leaves the Port Republic road, then went back to James A. Patterson's and spent the night; a very fine day.

Friday, June 13th. Spent the day at J. Davis Craig's, near Mt. Meridian, getting up a map of the South River country. The troops are all encamped between Middle and South rivers, near Weyer's Cafe, resting after our severe fighting and marching. The General has ordered washing and cleaning up to be done. Fremont has gone back to Strasburg and Shields to Luray. I spent the night at Mr. J. Davis Craig's. A fine warm day.

Saturday, June 14th. The General has ordered the observance of this day as one of thanksgiving and prayer on account of our victories. Lt. J. K. Boswell, Mr. J. Davis Craig and myself rode over to see the battle field of Cross Keys. We had a very interesting time; saw the miserable Dutch of Fremont's army that he had left, wounded, behind him. The enemy did a great amount of damage; plundered the houses of the people near the battle field and burned up one house in which it is supposed he had put his dead. One citizen dug up and reburied 100 or more Yankees which had been buried too near his house. Our men behaved very gallantly according to the accounts of the people near the action. I sketched the battle field for a map and we then went back to camp. A very warm day.

Sunday, June 15th. Attended preaching at the First Brigade, Gen. C. S. Winder's, camp. Maj. (Rev. Dr.) R. L. Dabney preached a good sermon. We went over to Dr. Walker's to dinner. In the afternoon we had sacrement at the Qrs. of the Third Brigade, Gen[52] on the left of the road going down to Port Republic. Dr. Dabney made some excellent remarks. It was a very impressive celebration of the Lord's Supper, in the woods, amid the din of camps hushed for a brief period to celebrate the Supper of the Prince of Peace. The General attended the meeting, humbly devout. Our camp is still at the corner of the woods. There was a storm at noon, wind very high.

Monday, June 16th. Drawing maps at camp in my tent. Some splendid re-inforcements are coming to us; some here to Mt. Meridian, and some to Staunton.[53] Quite cool for the season.

Tuesday, June 17th. Drew maps at camp all day; went over to Mr. J. Davis Craig's for supper. At 9 P.M. the General sent me with a message to Col. Thomas T. Mumford, at Mt. Sidney, 8 miles. Told me I must go there in about an hour, that I would find him on the Valley Turnpike in front of the Tavern,[54] and tell him he had arranged what he wanted to see him about. I went in time and waited for Col. Mumford the specified time, but he did not come; I then went to Mr. Jacob Roler's and spent the night; enjoyed a good quiet night's rest. The day has been cool. Gen. Jackson, accompanied by Col. Wm. L. Jackson, left camp at 10 P.M. and rode up to Staunton in the night. He told me to come back from Mt. Sidney to our old camp, though I could see that some movement was on hand. After midnight the army broke up camp and marched towards Waynesboro. The day has been cool.

Wednesday, June 18th. In the morning I rode back to Mt. Meridian but found the General and the army gone, as I had expected, so started on after them to Waynesboro, where I awaited the coming of the General from Staunton; dined at Mr. Hugh Gallagher's, where Maj. W. J. Hawks was stopping, sick. The General arrived at 5 P.M., sent off some telegraphic messages and we then went on up the Blue Ridge, as Maj. Dabney had said to Rev. Richardson, "Following our noses." The whole western slope of the mountain on both sides of the road, for over three miles, was covered with troops with camp fires burning. It was a very fine sight. We saw Gen. Whiting at the foot of the mountain and then rode on, in the darkness, looking for our Hd. Qrs. camp by inquiring at every camp fire, but could not find it. I saw Gen. C. S. Winder at the Mountain Top House, Rockfish Gap, where I went to look for our Hd. Qrs. On my return I said, "General, I fear we will not find our wagons tonight." He replied, earnestly, "Never take counsel of your fears." Go and see if you can find some place where we can stay; at least find some place where we can sleep. Get something to eat if you can." As my horse had been rested I pushed on, over the rough and rocky road, and found a place for us at Mr. James McCue's, at the foot of the Blue Ridge on the Eastern side, where we got a good supper and nice lodgings, our party being Gen. Jackson, Col. Jackson, a courier and myself. The day has been quite warm and the roads are very dusty. Our whole army is moving; some of it reached Mechum's River today. No one knows where the army is going; but some hard blow is to be struck. The General was long at his devotions after we retired to our chamber, he, Col. Jackson and myself, having each a bed in the same large room. After we had retired I amused him by telling of the various opinions I had heard during the day, from the citizens, in reference to our destination. When I was through he asked, in his own quick, sharp way, "Do any of them say I am going to Washington?"

Thursday, June 19th. In the morning we rode on towards Mechum's River; the General in fine spirits and disposed to converse. We talked about fortifications among other things. He said he "had found that our men would rather fight and march than dig." We passed some artillery commanded by an officer who had served under Capt. Duncan,[55] in Mexico. The General then went on to speak of Capt. Duncan, said: "He was very quick. He would turn up his eye like a duck in a thunder storm and give you his opinion upon any subject at once."

"O Lord, give us the biggest kind of a victory"

TUESDAY, JUNE 24TH.[1] Made maps. Dined at Maj. A. F. Kinney's and supped at Rev. R. H. Phillips; had a nice time at each place; strawberried at Mr. P's. Warm showers. (Hd. Qrs. at Beaver Dam—P.).

Wednesday, June 25th. Worked as usual. Nelson was here, also Esq. Daniel Wilson. A very warm day. We hear that Jackson is at Ashland and moving towards the enemy. (Hd. Qrs., Ashland—P.).

Thursday, June 26th. Worked all day and went home at night; got there late and had a pleasant visit. We heard, in the P.M. and until 9 o'clock, the sound of heavy artillery; the [people] are out listening to it; it sounds very distinctly. The fight has no doubt begun at Richmond. A very warm day. Moved my camp down the hill. (Hd. Qrs. at Shady Grove Church, Henley's—P.).

Friday, June 27th. Came back at an early hour; worked all day and at night slept soundly. We heard today of the fight yesterday until 9 P.M. and of our driving the enemy back 5 miles, capturing artillery, etc. A very warm day. Today was fought the battle of Cold Harbor.[2]

Saturday, June 28th. Worked all day very hard. It rained last night and until 11 A.M. today. We heard of our fighting, until 10 P.M. yesterday, driving the enemy back 5 miles further, capturing 10 batteries, 30 odd guns, 3 generals, etc., etc., and that we are still fighting and by God's blessing shall win. Much interest excited to know the result. Quite warm in P.M. (Hd. Qrs. at McGhee's, Turkey Hill P.).

Sunday, June 29th. Went home in the morning and spent the day there; my wife not well. The people much rejoiced at the news. It rained in P.M.; heavy thunder. Went back to Staunton, in P.M. we heard of the continuation of the fight and our success. (Hd. Qrs., Grape-Vine Bridge P.).

Monday, June 30th. Worked as usual. News from Richmond still good; many called to see the maps of the vicinity of Richmond, (Stuart,³ etc.). A fine day. Hd. Qrs. at White Oak Swamp. P.

Tuesday, July 1st. Worked as usual; the fight is still going on and the success of our army is quite certain. A fine day. Read the papers until quite late. Rain at night. Today was fought the Battle of Malvern Hill.⁴

Wednesday, July 2nd. It rained quite hard all day. Worked very hard and am quite tired. Took tea at Rev. Mr. Tinsley's. The fighting still going on and the news cheering. (Hd. Qrs. at Poindexter's P.).

Thursday, July 3rd. I have been at work, though feeling badly. Capt Winfield⁵ called on me today also Gen. R. A. Garnett⁶ and Col. M. G. Harman. I called to see Gen. Ed. Johnson, (who was wounded at Mc-Dowell) in the evening; he is getting along well, but regrets it very much that he cannot be in the fighting at Richmond. "Too bad," he said "to be wounded in the first little fight; I would not have cared after some of the big battles." A fine day. Gov. John Letcher telegraphed today that the victory is complete; God grant it may be a prelude to peace! (Hd. Qrs. on the road to Westover P.).

Friday, July 4th. I worked as usual. There was a suspension of business and some observance of the day in Staunton. No news of any moment. They are bringing up the remains of some of our gallant dead from Richmond; Capt. W. H. Randolph, an old pupil of mine, among the rest. We have driven the enemy to the shelter of his gunboats. A very fine day. (Hd. Qrs. at Westover, in the field P.).

Saturday, July 5th. Worked until 5 P.M. and then went home in company with my Brother Nelson, who came to town today. Had a delightful ride home. The harvest is progressing rapidly and the ladies, some of them, have gone to the fields.

Sunday, July 6th. Went to Union in the morning; took my wife and children. Mr. R. C. Walker preached about "the Bible and what it has done," and took up a collection of $63. for the Confederate States Bible Society, which is preparing to go into operation in Georgia; all seem disposed to help freely. We had a nice dinner and Brother Walker came with us; in the P.M. he preached in Churchville, on "Repentance." After preaching I came back to Staunton to my camp. A lovely day, but warm.

Monday, July 7th. Worked at maps; got materials for map from clerk's office. I dined with Maj. A. F. Kinney today. No news of importance. A rumor is afloat that we have been recognized by France and Belgium. Warm day. (Monday, [7th], Hd. Qrs. at White Oak Swamp P.).

Wednesday, July 9th. Routine of duty as usual. A very warm day. Nothing doing, but plenty of rumors. (Tuesday, Hd. Qrs. At Mrs. Price's P.).

Thursday, July 10th. At map preparing. Maj. J. M. McCue came and spent the night with us; had quite a nice visit; he brought up a wagon load of eatables for the sick at Richmond, and he goes down with them tomorrow. Very warm. (10th Hd. Qrs. at Richmond P.).

Friday, July 11th. The Major missed the cars, so remained with us. Worked as usual. Saw Capt. Curry[7] and Rev. Mr. Junkin yesterday. The Captain's presence reminded me of Rich Mt. fight one year ago today. It rained very hard in the night.

Saturday, July 12th. Worked until 5 P.M. and then went home by the way of Morris' Mill; Nelson came in and I went home with him. A fine day; the cherries and berries of all kinds are now ripe in the Valley and are very nice. Found all well at home.

Sunday, July 13th. Went to church, in Churchville, with my family. Nelson and Harriet took dinner with me at home, all very nice. I came back to Staunton in time to go to preaching there and heard an excellent sermon by Wm. Baker. A very warm day.

Monday, July 14th. Worked all day. Rev. R. C. Walker took dinner with me. In the evening I went to Mr. D. A. Kayser's to tea and had a very pleasant visit. Saw Mr. John W. Alby, and his new wife, also Gen. Imboden (John D.)[8] and wife, he coming home just then, and Miss E. Bell and some Captain.[9] The day was very warm. The rumor is credited in the A.M. that the enemy was in Gordonsville, but it is not so; there is some movement on hand for the cars are detained at Richmond.

Tuesday, July 15th. Worked at map all day. At 10 P.M. got orders from Gen. T. J. Jackson to come to Gordonsville at once; so wrote home and packed up some and retired quite late. A fine day. A storm of wind and some rain in P.M.

Wednesday, July 16th. We were up at an early hour and packed up and by 8 A.M. were on our way. The day was intensely hot. We stopped at Mountain Top, on the Blue Ridge, for dinner and rested there for some time. There was a thunder storm at 3 P.M., but we went on to near Mechum's River and slept, in an empty house, on the floor, supperless, as our wagon did not come up; but we were weary enough to enjoy it and slept soundly.

Thursday, July 17th. Went on through Charlottesville, where I saw Gen. B. H. Robertson[10] and his cavalry, from the Valley, on his way to Gordonsville. We went on to near Cobham, beyond Walker's Church and spent the night at the Rev. Mr. Boyden's, the Rector of Walker's Church, a fine stone edifice that we passed by. The day was very pleasant; some rain and mud. We feasted on cherries. All sorts of wild rumors afloat of the advance of Pope and his army and some alarm among the people. (Hd. Qrs. at Beaver Dam P.).

Friday, July 18th. Came on to Gordonsville, found the road very muddy. It rained hard all day too. We pitched our tent and built a fire in it to dry the ground some. The enemy is not far from here; is near Orange C. H. and Gen. Jackson has not come yet. Some of the troops have come here. (Hd. Qrs. at Harris', Frederick Hall[11] P.).

Saturday, July 19th. Gen. Thos. J. Jackson came up today and we reported. He said nothing about work; he looks the worse for his Chickahominy trip, and so do the troops. I went in the P.M. out to Mechanicsville, 5 miles. A very fine day, roads very muddy. The General spent the night at Rev. Ewing's[12] but the staff encamped in the woods back of Gordonsville. Capt. R. E. Wilbourn[13] came up with the General as signal officer.

Sunday, July 20th. Went to church and had a good sermon by Mr. Ewing "on the Goodness and severity of God"; the General was out to church, though looking weary. In the P.M. there came a report that the enemy had captured the up train on the Va. C.R.R.,[14] so the General ordered some forces to go to Beaver Dam Station, but we soon heard that the enemy had come to the Station, burnt it and soon left; so the troops were recalled. A very fine day; rain in P.M.

Monday, July 21st. We went out towards Liberty Mills, on the road to Madison C. H., 7 miles, N.E. of Gordonsville, to select an encampment. We pitched our tents on the hillside, 4 miles from Gordonsville; the enemy moved back towards Culpeper. Worked on map in P.M.; a very fine day. Hd. Qrs near 4 mile-post from Gordonsville. We ate our fill of blackberries; the whole army turned out and picked them, the hill sides were full of them; the General seemed to enjoy them [very] much.

Tuesday, July 22nd. Worked at map all day, some rain. The troops are getting up from Richmond.

Wednesday, July 23rd. Worked on map in A.M.; in P.M. went to Orange C. H. and came back by the Cavalry camp and Toddsburg,[15] through plantations, to Hd. Qrs. at 9 P.M. A very fine day.

Thursday, July 24th. Worked all day in tent. In the evening we had a long chat at Hd. Qrs., Col. Alex. R. Boteler[16] having come up. A fine day, but very warm. The army is drilling and resting. Lawton's[17] Georgia Brigade came up.

Friday, July 25th. Making map of country in front. The enemy showed some signs of advancing, in the A.M.; everything looks as though we might soon have a fight with Pope.

Saturday, July 26th. We were all roused at an early hour, baggage packed and started to the rear, and a portion of the army went that way too. We went across to Toddsburg, with a part of our army to intercept the enemy if he should attempt to come to Gordonsville that way, as they had advanced to Orange C. H. and threatened to fall on the Cavalry Brigade of Gen. B. H. Robertson, who was encamped near there, and who sent for an infantry support. But the enemy did not come on and late in the P.M. we came back to our former camp. There was a heavy thunder storm in the P.M.

Sunday, July 27th. Went to the 5th Va. Regiment to preaching; heard a good sermon and remained with Col. W. S. H. Baylor to dinner; he has a fine camp and has it clean. A very fine day.

Monday, July 28th. Made maps of Madison and Greene. Mr. Almond, of Stannardsville, gave me information about the country towards the Blue Ridge. The enemy is up in Madison. Warm.

Tuesday, July 29th. We moved our camp to Mechanicsville—farther away from the front and to new and clean grounds, 6 miles S. of Gordonsville. We have our camp at the old church, a little west of the Village. The enemy is making some demonstrations. We found the Division of Maj. Gen. A. P. Hill at Gordonsville, it having been sent up to reinforce Gen. T. J. Jackson; it has not all arrived as yet. We dined near the Mechanicsville (Louisa Co.) church. Rain in P.M. Bought potatoes at $5 a bush[el].

Wednesday, July 30th. Worked at map. We have a very nice place for our camp and in a region where we can get some fresh supplies. Heard from home; a good letter. Went to Gordonsville in the P.M.

Thursday, July 31st. The General put us all to making maps of the country out to the Potomac. I had a private chat with the General about a conversation [about going to his house for dinner] I had with Maj. J. M. McCue, etc. It was a very fine day, worked very closely and was quite tired.

Friday, Aug. 1st. Worked at the ordered maps. Gen. Banks, of Madison Co. called to give us information about the country and I took down a map from his description of the roads, etc. Fine day.

Saturday, Aug. 2nd. Finished up a map of the Piedmont region and then began one on a larger scale. There was a cavalry skirmish at Orange C. H. today; we had some men killed and some captured, and we killed and took some of the enemy. They came out after our cavalry and our cavalry charged on them when they fled and led our men into town where a column of the enemy, from a cross street, charged after our men when they had passed and took them in the rear. No result of importance; the enemy went back across the Rapidan. A fine day. Finished up map of the Piedmont region and then commenced one of the same region on a larger scale.

Sunday, Aug. 3rd. Wrote my wife early in the morning, then went to church with the General to hear Rev. Dr. Stiles[18] preach, in the camp of Lawton's Brigade of Georgians, in the woods a mile from our camp. The text was, "Show thyself a man," a subject which he handled ably, explaining: 1st what [a] man is; his value in comparison with earthly things, perishable things, and each man of more value than the aggregate of earthly humanity in that he will, eventually, surpass in existence the sum of all human existence, of more value than all material things, because without him they possess no value, therefore he gives them value and he must be of more value, than they themselves, etc.; then he applied this value of man to spiritual and national matters, showing how a man ought to conduct himself in reference to each, in view of his importance, etc. He prayed that there might be no straggling when we again went forth to battle, and said: "O Lord, when we go out again to fight give us the biggest kind of a victory." The old man was eloquent and his voice thrilled like a trumpet and perspiration rolled down his face. When we got back to our camp we found the Hon. Wm. C. Rives there, and in the course of conversation he spoke of the reminiscences of the spot where we were, of LaFayette's retreat across the Raccoon Ford, on the Rapidan, and on to Mechum's river, (Creek) not far from here, cutting out or widening the road, which passes through here and to this day is called the "Marquis Road." Cornwallis[19] pursued him, leisurely, until Greene[20] joined LaFayette, when Cornwallis, in turn, retreated. A fine warm day.

Monday, Aug. 4th. Drew maps as usual. A fine day; nothing of interest transpiring.

Tuesday, Aug. 5th. A very warm day. In the P.M. we moved our Hd. Qrs. back to Col. Magruder's,[21] 4 miles beyond Gordonsville. It was intensely hot and we did not reach our old camping ground until late. All slept on the ground, under the trees, except the General. Was very weary from packing up, etc. The 12th Va. Cavalry, Col A. W. Harman,[22] came over from the Valley.

Wednesday, Aug. 6th. Made a map of the region along the foot of the Blue Ridge for Col. A. W. Harman, worked very steadily and am tired. The trial of Brig. Gen. R. B. Garnett, for his conduct at Kernstown, is now going on at Gen. R. S. Ewell's Hd. Qrs., at Liberty Mills. Got letters from home and heard that a barrel of provisions had come too; a very agreeable message, for we are not on very full rations just now. All quiet; not even a rumor of news. Very warm; shower in P.M.

Thursday, Aug. 7th. Worked at maps all day and until quite late in the P.M., then we packed up and went over to Orange C. H., going through the plantations by a way I selected, by order of the General, that was concealed from observation of the enemy. The whole army is in motion, Jackson's old Division coming, secretly led by me, to Orange C. H. Gen. Ewell crossed the Rapidan at Liberty Mills as if intending to attack Pope's army at Madison C. H. The General slept part of the night on a stile in the street of Orange C. H.; after that he and some of the staff went to Mr. Willis'. Brown, Sneed[23] and I slept in the edge of the woods near the R.R. and not far from Willis'; a portion of the troops slept in the field in front of us. A very fine day.

Friday, Aug. 8th. We marched on and crossed the Rapidan at Barnett's Ford, driving the enemy's pickets from there and beyond, and then driving in quite a large body of Federal cavalry, beyond Crooked Run Church, and to near the head of Cedar Run. We captured a camp near Crooked Run Church and took some prisoners, then routed quite a body of them at Locust Dale. I went back from near Locus Dale to the Rapidan, with orders, and Maj. E. F. Paxton[24] did the same. Saw a large pile of wheat in the river which the enemy had emptied out of the mill. Gen.

R. S. Ewell, after crossing at Liberty Mills bore to his right and formed a guard to the left flank of the main body; a part of his command came in at Barnett's Ford, marching down the east side of the river. Our cavalry sleeps at the Yankee cavalry camps. [Most] of the [staff] slept in the yard at Mr. Garnett's, near Crooked Run Church. The grass in the yard was very long and nice and nearly everyone of us, except the General, slept on it. Our scouts captured Yankees in every direction; caught one with a horse load of chickens which he had stolen. A very warm day; dusty. Mr. Garnett told us much about the atrocity of Pope's army and the suffering of the people from the enforcement of his order to "subsist his army on the country." Many fine places have been nearly destroyed by the enemy. The corn fields look finely.

Saturday, Aug. 9th. We went forward in the morning and stopped awhile at the widow [?] while the cavalry reconnoitred, Gen. Jackson urging Gen. B. H. Robertson, of the cavalry, to find out where the enemy was, and Gen. Robertson complaining of the number of his stragglers. While we were there Gen. I. R. Trimble came up to see the General about a case of horrid conduct of the enemy at Culpeper C. H. Gen. C. S. Winder overtook us here, although he was not well from his sickness and looked very pale and badly, but he had heard of our advance and had come on to join his brigade. We ascertained, about noon, that the enemy was strongly posted some two miles beyond the head of Cedar Run; we then rode up on the hill near Garnett's and reconnoitred. A large body of the enemy's cavalry was drawn up in the plain and clouds of dust beyond showed that large bodies of troops were coming to the field. Gen. Jackson soon sent out flanking parties, Gen. R. S. Ewell to the right and Gen. J. A. Early to the left, and we opened artillery on them from the centre. We drove off the cavalry and engaged the infantry and artillery and drove them from the field, although they came near flanking our left and driving it back, but Gen. A. P. Hill coming up routed them in turn. We took some 300 prisoners, one cannon, 12 wagon loads of ammunition and some 3,000 stand of small arms. The General and his whole staff were exposed to the hottest of the fire and all were busy trying to rally the left wing after it fell back, the General appealing to the men to follow him, and he led a body of them to the fight. The brave Gen. C. S. Winder was killed while posting a piece of artillery and before he had [an] opportunity to lead his men into action. The cannonade continued until long after dark and was a splendid sight. The enemy left their dead and wounded on the field. The Yankee prisoners cheered Gen. Jackson as he rode past them coming back after the fight. I went back to Crooked Run Church, where our wagons were, and found Gen. A. R. Lawton there, who is in the rear today guarding it, as the enemy attempted to fall on our left flank and rear, at two points last night, but were met and promptly repulsed with loss at each place. Soon after I got back orders came for the wagons to move forward, so we came up and encamped on the hill near the battle field. We lost a good many in killed and wounded. The enemy admitted a loss of 500 killed; but they had more. The engagement lasted from 4 P.M. until late at night. The day was very warm; we slept under the trees. Col. Jas. W. Jackson[25] of the 47th Alabama, was borne to the front by two men, after he had been wounded, and went on with his command. Lt. Joseph G. Morrison, A.D.C. on the General's staff, distinguished himself by gallantly going into the thickest of the fight and urging on the men; Capt. Robert D. Lilley, of the 25th Virginia, seized the flag of his regiment and rallied its faltering men. There was a hard shower in the midst of the fight.[26]

Sunday, Aug. 10th. We have occupied the same ground all day, holding the battle field, and have been busy bringing away our wounded, burying the dead, collecting arms, etc. The enemy was drawn up in line of battle, some 3 or 4 miles in front of us, for a long time, but made no forward movement. I rode over the battle field and heard the most agonizing shrieks and groans from the many wounded Yankees that were lying exposed to the full blaze of the sun; our men moved them into the shade and ministered to them, but we had our own men to attend to first. Gen. J. E. B. Stuart[27] came up today and took the [cavalry] and went out on our right and nearly around the enemy's left. There was a very heavy rain in the afternoon. We spent the day on the hill in rear of the battlefield. By request of Gen. Jackson I made a sketch of the battle field and suggested a name for the battle, Cedar Run, which the General adopted. Col. A. R. Boteler took this sketch to Richmond, to President Davis; he started for Richmond today. It was reported at one time that the enemy was advancing, and our wagons, having gone well forward, took a panic and for awhile there was a wild stampede, the wagoners thinking the enemy had flanked us. The General mounted his horse and soon restored quiet and fixed [prepared?] to prevent any such move again. We sleep on the same hill top. Warm day.

Monday, Aug. 11th. The enemy sent a flag of truce, or rather they said the doctors had sent it, asking for a truce until 2 P.M. to carry off their wounded and bury their dead. This we granted; they afterwards asked to have it extended until 5 P.M., as they had not been able to finish, and that was granted. Once during the truce they advanced some troops, and Gen. J. E. B. Stuart, who was on the field, threatened to take all their ambulances. He told them to come on if they wanted to, for we were ready for a truce or a fight. The officers of both armies had a free conference and Gen. J. E. B. Stuart and some of his former companions in the U. S. Army sat down and had a long chat. While the enemy were carrying off their dead and wounded we were collecting arms and removing our dead and wounded. One Yankee officer rebuked another, who was a member of Gen. F. Sigel's[28] staff, for picking up arms to carry off. Soon after the enemy asked for the extension of the truce our wagons and the part of our army in the rear started back and we marched to Orange C. H. I came by a near way, to where our wagons halted a mile west of the C. H. Gen. Jackson came back to Garnett's and got supper and spent the rest of the night there. A very pleasant day.

Tuesday, Aug. 12th. I went by "Montpelier" and took a look at President Madison's former residence, then went to our old camp, near Col. Magruder's; had been there but a short time when we got orders to move towards Toddsburg to encamp; we went and encamped near Dr. Pannill's, finding the General out towards Orange C. H.; he came on to Hd. Qrs. The General told me, while we were riding along, to at once make as many maps as I could of the region from where we are on to the Potomac. We had a tremendous shower in the afternoon.

Wednesday, Aug. 13th. Worked at the ordered maps. The General said "Do not be afraid of making too many." A fine warm day. Gen. James Longstreet[29] came to Gordonsville today.

Thursday, Aug. 14th. We are still very busy making the maps reaching to the Potomac; troops in large numbers are constantly arriving at Gordonsville. Gen. Robert E. Lee came up today and encamped some $2\frac{1}{2}$ miles from Gordonsville on the Madison Turnpike; Gen. Jackson went up to see him. Gen. Lee now assumes command of the army here. Gen. Jackson has been to Richmond and aided in driving McClellan off and now the whole army comes to help Gen. Jackson in his long cherished move towards Maryland. A very fine day.

Friday, Aug. 15th. We are all busy on the maps and all think the move is soon to take place; troops are constantly arriving at Gordonsville and coming this way.

Saturday, Aug. 16th. We moved from Dr. Pannill's and Jackson's whole Corps went to Mountain Run, along the Southern slope of Clark's

Mountain 6 miles from Orange C. H. We had our Hd. Qrs. [at] Mr. Grymes', 4 miles from Orange C. H. I conducted Gen. Taliaferro's Brigade across to the Plank Road; the army was marched so as to avoid being seen. The enemy had moved towards the Rapidan in force. Col. S. Bassett French, of Gov. Letcher's staff, came to us today. Very warm.

Sunday, Aug. 17th. Went with the General to preaching at the Hd. Qrs. of the 3rd Brigade, Gen. Taliaferro's, on the southern slope of Clark's Mountain. Rev. Tebbs preached. The General, on our way to preaching, spoke of what he considered "the right sort of a man," "one always striving to do his duty and never satisfied if anything can be done better." In the afternoon I went with Gen. J. E. B. Stuart to the top of Clark's Mountain and saw the enemy marching away from Crooked Run Church; did not get back until quite late; Capt. R. E. Wilbourn, our Chief Signal officer, came back to camp with me. Gen. Stuart went down the Plank Road towards Verdiersville. I had a talk with Gen. Stuart on religion and he expressed himself very strongly, saying that he felt the need of a higher power than any he could command to aid him; we were talking of Gen. McClellan's having joined the church. A fine warm day. As we rode back from church we met Gen. R. A. Pryor's[30] Brigade and it cheered Gen. Jackson.

Monday, Aug. 18th. The General left the Engineer Corps behind to make maps and he went on to Mountain Run; we worked until nearly night and then moved over to Hd. Qrs.; found Gen. R. E. Lee encamped near by. We were opposite the churches and on the south side of the Run, on Crenshaw's farm. A fine day, but quite windy.

Tuesday, Aug. 19th. We worked at maps of Culpeper Co. Mr. Wren aided me today. Orders were issued to cook three days rations and be ready to move at moon-rising. Our forces have been concentrating in this vicinity for several days. In the afternoon some men, who had been tried and found guilty of desertion were shot. Most of the 2nd Corps was drawn up to witness the shooting. A fine day; quite pleasant.

Wednesday, Aug. 20th. We left Crenshaw's farm, on Mountain Run, 6 miles from Orange C. H., at 3 A.M., leaving our wagons, tents, etc., behind, but breakfasting before we started. We rode over to where the troops were encamped and found they had not yet marched. The General was much put out and ordered out the Ist Brigade of Gen. A. P. Hill's Division that he found ready to march, being impatient of any delay, and put a staff officer with each division to see that the marching orders were obeyed. We went across a depression in Clark's Mountain, crossed the

Rapidan at Somerville's Ford and marched on to Stevensburg, 9 miles
beyond the river. The enemy's cavalry had been in force all along the
road the day before Gen. Longstreet crossed the river on our right at [?]
Ford; Gen. Stuart and his cavalry crossed at [?] Ford, fell on the enemy's
cavalry near Brandy Station and routed them, taking prisoners, etc. Gen.
A. P. Hill's Light Division was in front today. The enemy is retreating.
[We] went to Jones' Run, 2 miles beyond Stevensburg and, supperless,
took up our lodging in the corner of a wood. The day has been very warm
and the roads very dusty. Our Cavalry, in the charge at Brandy Station
today, took 50, wounded 50 and killed 15 of the enemy. We had a number of our men wounded. We captured some prisoners and stores at Culpeper C. H., which the enemy left yesterday in great haste.

Thursday, Aug. 21st. We started from our ground bed at an early
hour and went to Gen. J. E. B. Stuart's Hd. Qrs. at Maj. Barbour's,[31] and
breakfasted with him. The army moved on to the Rappahannock via
Brandy Station and Pottsville. Found the enemy posted on the river bank
with artillery in earth-works; they opened a severe cannonading showing
that they intended to defend the R.R. bridge crossing, but we moved up
cavalry, infantry and artillery and opposed them while the main body of
Jackson's Corps moved on to Beverly's (Cunningham's) Ford where we
had a cannonade as well as at the R.R. bridge, simultaneously, Longstreet coming up to the R.R. bridge in time to occupy it, or the front near
it, tonight after we had marched on. A portion of our troops crossed the
river at Beverly's Ford and drove the enemy from it, taking some prisoners, guns, etc. Our troops are rapidly concentrating and we are en-
gageing the enemy's attention, at every ford on the river, as we progress,
so they cannot divine where we intend to attempt to cross. The cannonading from both sides was quite heavy; the Yankees shelled the wood we
were in. I was engaged getting the topography of the country and at a
late hour hunted up the General coming in from the front. We spent
the night at Mr. Thompson's, near St. James Church. The General was
very weary and much enjoyed a glass of milk I procured for him. There
was a heavy shower of rain in the night. Lt. Wm. G. Williamson,[32] of
the Engineers, joined us today.

Friday, Aug. 22nd. Gen. Jackson's Corps moved up to Wellford Ford
and crossed Hazel River there and had a fight with the enemy in "The
little-forks" of the Rivers; more of an artillery duel than anything else;
we then moved up the fork to Freeman's Ford and through Jeffersonton and down to Lee's Spring, where a part of our force crossed over. The

General spent the night near Lee's Springs (The Warrenton White Sulphur) at the "yellow house." The enemy is moving up the river also. I saw Oswald F. Grinnan, my former assistant at Loch Willow, and went over to a friend of his to dinner and shall stay at Mr. Wyman's, 3 miles from Brandy Station. Gen. Lee moved up to Wellford's, Gen. Jackson fixed up the bridge at Lee's Springs. The enemy crossed at Beverly's Ford to fall on our train, but caught a Tartar in Gen. I. R. Trimble who fell on them and gave them a sound thrashing, in the woods between St. James Church and Beverly's Ford. The firing at one time during the day was very heavy. It rained very hard in the P.M. and also in the night.

Saturday, Aug. 23rd. In the morning Gen. Longstreet drove the enemy across the Rappahannock bridge, with loss to them, but they succeeded in burning the bridge. Gen. Jackson remained at Lee's Springs all day and took infantry and artillery over to the hills across the river. The enemy came up late in the P.M. and we opened on them; they replied and a fierce artillery duel took place. When the enemy's infantry advanced a Georgia regiment charged on them with a yell and drove them away. I came up in the afternoon and found all engaged in fixing to cross the river. Gen. Stuart got back from an expedition to the enemy's rear at Catlett's;[33] he captured wagons; some 300 prisoners, money, Pope's Hd. Qrs. papers, etc. There was a heavy rain in the P.M. and the streams are getting up. We stay on the hill near the "yellow house."

Sunday, Aug. 24th. Our troops, at an early hour, were all brought back across the river towards Jeffersonton, the state of the water and no permanent bridges making it necessary, for security, so to do. The General was much out of humor with the quarter-masters and the commissaries because the army was not fed well and the provisions were not brought up in time. He told a Georgia Colonel that "field officers were intended to be useful as well as ornamental." We moved our camp back to near Jeffersonton, out of range of the enemy's guns on the other side of the river, wither they had come up in force. There was much cannonading in the afternoon; we kept artillery and a supporting force on the hill on the Jeffersonton side of the river. Gen. Longstreet came up to our Hd. Qrs. and examined the surrounding country, saying he intended to drive the enemy off and cross there; I made a sketch of the position for him. I was down to the front with orders, under a severe cannonade. A fine warm day.

Monday, Aug. 25th. We spent last [night] near the village of Jeffersonton, but there was so much disturbance, as marching orders had been issued, that we did not rest much. The enemy made some demonstrations yesterday towards Waterloo Bridge, but Stuart drove them off, aided, I think, by some infantry. The 2nd Corps, our army, was off, very soon in the morning, to beyond Amissville and there struck off eastward to a private ford, Hinson's, and crossed before the enemy had any intimation of our move. Jackson's Corps is in advance while Longstreet guards the fords at Lee's Springs and below and keeps the enemy here; he moved in before day as our Corps moved out; Longstreet moved on in the P.M. and Anderson's[34] Division took his place. I remained behind, by the General's order, and made maps. A very warm day. The enemy burnt the buildings at Lee's Springs. There was much artillery firing during the day. The enemy is in strong force between Warrenton and Waterloo Bridge. (Gen. Jackson's advance went to Salem, Fauquier [County], today and Hd. Qrs. are there for the night. P.).

Tuesday, Aug. 26th. I worked very hard at maps. The enemy shelled our position nearly all day and did some damage. We moved our wagons back, about a mile, to get out of range [of] any attack the enemy might easily make. In the night Anderson's Division moved on, leaving Lee's Springs and marching towards Amissville, and we followed with our train, as it was reported that the enemy was making preparations to cross and fall upon our rear. We marched nearly all night; Tom Snead and I took a nap by the roadside. A warm day. Jackson went from Salem, by Thoroughfare Gap and Haymarket, to Gainesville, by 4 P.M.; there Stuart overtook him and they went on and that night attacked Bristoe Station, Stuart keeping on his right flank and between him and Warrenton Junction. (Hd. Qrs. were at Bristoe. P.). The same night Stuart left Bristoe with part of his cavalry and Trimble's brigade of infantry, of Ewell's Division, and went to Manassas Junction. The army went by Salem and the Plains to Bristoe.

Wednesday, Aug. 27th. Our wagons were moved up to Gaines' X roads,[35] or rather 1 mile south of there, and we had Snead go on for orders. I worked at maps under a tree. A very fine day. We heard that Jackson had destroyed the enemy's stores at Bristoe. Stuart and Trimble attacked Manassas Junction, at daylight, and captured 8 pieces of artillery, horses and equipments complete, and many stores. Jackson and part of his command came up to the Junction, at noon, today, and fought Taylor's Brigade of the enemy, coming, from the direction [of] Union Mills, in which action, in the P.M., Gen. Taylor[36] was mortally wounded. Gen. R. S. Ewell, in the meantime, was attacked at Bristoe and he retired towards night, to Manassas Junction. Col. Thomas L. Rosser,[37] of the 5th Virginia Cavalry protecting his right flank and bringing up his rear. The cavalry was picketing and scouting, in every direction, today and tonight. Brig. Gen. H. F. Lee,[38] with a portion of his cavalry brigade and a portion of Gen. B. H. Robertson's, was sent on an expedition towards Alexandria and went to Burke's Station, capturing prisoners, etc. At night, after destroying everything at Manassas Junction, the army marched for the Stone Bridge, a portion of it going by way of Centreville. The cavalry was so disposed as to cover this movement, Rosser forming a rear guard to Gen. A. P. Hill's Division. (Hd. Qrs. were at Manassas Junction. P.).

Thursday, Aug. 28th. I went up to Bell's in the P.M., towards Washington, Rappahannock Co. In the A.M. went to Elysville,[39] where part of the army had crossed and where our train was floundering through the mud; found Brown there and we went foraging, bought honey, etc., etc., then came back by way of Flint Hill. I spent the night at Bell's, a fine man, and heard much of the atrocity of Pope's men, especially Sigel and his crew. Mr. Bell said that Dr. David Strother, (Porte Crayon) was in the Yankee army there. Spent a delightful evening; hope to meet many more such men. A fine day. (Hd. Qrs. near Groveton, P.).

In the morning the army, facing towards Groveton, Col. Rosser and his cavalry being on the left flank and in front and with some cavalry thrown out on the right as videttes, Gen. Stuart observed the enemy's movements and reported them to Gen. Jackson; then, with portions of Gen. W. H. F. Lee's and of Robertson's brigades, under Robertson, Stuart went towards Hay Market, keeping on the south side of Bull Run, by a by-pass, crossing the Run at times, and near Hay Market found a force of the enemy, which he skirmished with for some time, beginning at 3 P.M.; then returned to take part in the battle which had been going on, about dark, after the infantry and artillery firing had ceased. Stuart's attack at Hay Market was intended as a diversion in favor of Longstreet who was advancing to Thoroughfare Gap and engaging the enemy there at the time, and who later forced his way through. Jackson fought and kept the enemy back. Gens. Stuart and Jackson spent the night at a house near Sudley Mills; the wagons were at Sudley Church all day.

Friday, Aug. 29th. I came back to our camp; rumors had been rife of an attack to be made on our train by the enemy, so Maj. A. S. Pendleton, our Adj. Gen., organized the stragglers into a regiment for a guard. After dinner I went on to Amissville and saw Gen. Ripley,[40] who had just come up with his Georgia Brigade, then went on to near Waterloo Bridge and

spent the night, our picket being still there on this side of the river. A
fine day; shower in the evening. Jackson fought the enemy all day near
Sudley Mills, or between there and Groveton; a sanguinary fight. Gen.
Stuart, in riding forward towards Groveton, at 10 A.M. found that the
enemy's sharpshooters had penetrated the woods towards Jackson's ambulances and baggage wagons, which were on the road leading to Groveton, finding the Stuart [Horse] Artillery, Capt. John Pelham,[41] near by,
he directed him to shell the woods through which the enemy was advancing and also to collect the stragglers, teamsters, etc., and drive the
enemy back; he also notified Gen. Jackson and sent Maj. Wm. Patrick[42]
word to keep his cavalry between the enemy and the baggage, an order
which he faithfully obeyed, but was killed just as he had successfully repulsed an attempt of a large body of the enemy to cross the run near
Sudley. Gen. Stuart also informed Col. Wm. S. H. Baylor, whose command (Winder's Brigade) was posted along the unfinished R.R., of the
enemy's advance, and requested him to move forward and drive them off,
with the "Stonewall Brigade," which he commanded. He replied, "I was
posted here with positive orders to stay; and here I must remain." Gen.
Stuart went on towards Hay Market to establish communication with
Gens. Lee and Longstreet, ordering Pelham to report to Gen. Jackson.
Gen. Stuart was accompanied by cavalry. He found Lee and Longstreet
on the road, between Hay Market and Gainesville, marching and inquiring the way to Sudley. Gen. Stuart told them where Gen. Jackson was and
advised Gen. Lee to go by the Warrenton Turnpike towards Groveton;
after [a] discussion he acquiesced and went that way. Gen. Stuart then
went to Longstreet's right flank, with portions of Robertson's and W. H.
F. Lee's brigades, and spent the night there, some 2 miles east of the
turnpike. The detachment under W. H. F. Lee, which had been to Burke's
Station, returned in the P.M. to Gen. Jackson near Sudley Mills. Gen.
Fitz. John Porter,[43] of the Federal army, was at Manassas Junction on the
29th and when Pope was fighting he failed to come to his aid, though
he was likely to be defeated, and after advancing fell back to Manassas
Junction. This is the charge against Porter on which he was expelled
from the army. When Pelham was ordered to report to Gen. Jackson the
General directed him to ride over the field with him and after pointing
out to him the different roads gave him discretionary orders to engage
his battery when a fit opportunity should occur. About [3:30 P.M.] Gen.
A. P. Hill sent for some artillery to be thrown rapidly forward, as the
enemy was giving away. Pelham placed his battery in position, near the

R.R., and opened on some batteries and a column of infantry posted on the hills near Groveton. The wagons moved back to within 2 miles of Aldie.

Saturday, Aug. 30th. I went on, quite early, to Waterloo Bridge and then on to Warrenton, passing where the enemy had been encamped two days before. The people of Warrenton received us with acclamation, opened their houses and brought forth food, the ladies themselves did it and gave to all such as could not go to the houses to eat. They were beside themselves with joy at their release from Yankee domination. Lawton's Brigade passed through about 3 P.M. I went on to near Buckland and was kindly entertained by an Irishman, who described to me the state of alarm the Yankee army was in when there on the night of the 28th. A fine warm day, but rain in the P.M. The report of a glorious victory was in Warrenton, when I reached there. McDowell, in command of 60,000 of the enemy, when he passed through Warrenton bade a gentleman there good bye, and told him he was about to have a change of masters, which he supposed would be agreeable. Gen. Jackson fought the enemy, to the left of Groveton and between there and Sudley, along the unfinished R.R., and drove them completely away, pursuing and capturing a good many. He had his Hd. Qrs. near Sudley Church. Longstreet was on the right, along the Warrenton Turnpike. Gen. Stuart remained on Longstreet's right and when the enemy was routed [he] moved down on them "with crushing effect," he says, and drove them into and through Bull Run, at Lewis' Ford, the artillery enfilading the enemy's lines and firing into their rear, but ceased firing at dark for fear of firing into our own cavalry.

Sunday, Aug. 31st. Started at an early hour and went on to Gainesville; there saw the prisoners we took yesterday, and then on to Groveton and spent most of the day riding over the battle field and vicinity, where they are burying the dead and collecting the wounded; sometimes in heaps, wherever they came up to near our lines. Many of our gallant dead were also there; but there are many more Yankees. When I came to Gainesville there was cannonading going on toward Manassas Junction. Large parties were engaged burying the dead and removing the wounded, while hundreds, yea thousands, of the enemy could receive but little attention. Our advance was near the Stone Bridge, Longstreet's force; while Jackson's army was towards Sudley. I rode over a portion of the old Manassas, or Bull Run at Sudley Ford and went, by a by-road, to the Little River Turnpike, coming into it not far from Gum Spring. I saw

Gen. R. E. Lee, near Sudley, and Col. S. Crutchfield at the ford where
Patrick had captured some artillery. We marched on until quite a late
hour, having started about dark. The army went on to Pleasant Valley
and Chantilly, Stuart in advance. Col. S. Crutchfield and I spent the night,
under the trees, where we struck the Little River Turnpike, making our
suppers out of roasting ears. There was some rain in the P.M. Our wagons came back to the rear of the battle field.

5. SEPTEMBER 1–DECEMBER 31, 1862

"Maryland, My Maryland"

MONDAY, SEPT. 1ST. We went on and found Hd. Qrs. at a small house near Pleasant Valley. The General had just enquired for me, so I sat down and made him some copies of maps, and then, after dinner, went on. The soldiers were very bad, stealing everything eatable they could lay their hands on, after trying to buy it. They were nearly famished, our wagons being still behind. They were also very thirsty, water being very scarce. I had a hard time to keep them out of the house where I was at work. The army marched on to Chantilly and late in the P.M. had a severe fight with the retreating enemy, going towards Fairfax C. H. The fight was on Ox Hill. The Federals Kearney and Stevens,[1] and many privates were killed, and the enemy was repulsed. The fight took place during a terrific storm of rain, thunder and lightning, and the enemy, at one time, drove us back. Night put an end to the contest and we kept the field; the enemy went on to Fairfax C. H. The General had Hd. Qrs. a little beyond Chantilly, at an old house. Snead and I slept in the field near the Stuart house, making a fire and getting some hay to sleep on; supperless. It was very cold and we suffered a good deal; we also got very wet. (Hd. Qrs. near Chantilly. P.).

Tuesday, Sept. 2nd. I went back towards Aldie and procured a map of Loudoun Co., of Mr. Lee, and dined at his house. We have a host of stragglers; I find them wherever I go. When I came back [I] saw the crowd of Yankee citizen prisoners. We had our Hd. Qrs. a mile beyond Chantilly. Gen. Stuart went to Fairfax C. H. And there got back his A. A. Gen., Norman B. Fitz Hugh, who was captured at Verdiersville; he also had a warm reception from the ladies; said they all kissed him. Our men halted today and cooked rations; our wagons came up. Stuart took a large train of Yankee ambulances that were going to Bull Run: but Gen. Lee let them go on. Gen. Lee came up to Chantilly. A fine day; there was a frost at night.

Wednesday, Sept. 3rd. We went, by the "Ox Road," the "Lawyer's Road," and Thornton's Station to Dranesville, Stuart going on to Vienna. We crossed the battle field at Dranesville. I stopped at Dranesville and made a map. We slept, on the right of the road, a mile beyond Dranesville. A fine day; our route was a concealed one and we are now on the Fall's Bridge Turnpike.

Thursday, Sept. 4th. We started at an early hour and marched on through Leesburg and out to Ball's, to the Big Spring, for the night. I stopped and worked awhile at map. Saw the enemy's pickets on the other side of the Potomac. We found Goose Creek quite high and had to make a detour to cross it. We passed near the battle field of Ball's Bluff. All are in fine spirits, being sure that we are on the way to Maryland. Gen. D. H. Hill's[2] Division came to Leesburg, by a nearer route, yesterday, and went on to the Potomac to [White's Ford];[3] it is reported that it crossed the river. A very fine day; cool at night.

Friday, Sept. 5th. We started about sunrise and went, by a private road, to White's Ford and there crossed the Potomac into Maryland, Gen. Jackson on a cream-colored, or "clayback" horse, and riding on the left of the front. The 10th Va. Regt. of infantry, preceded by a band and bearing a Virginia flag, was in the advance; as the band reached the Maryland shore it struck up the air, "Maryland, my Maryland," amid shouts of the soldiers. It was a noble spectacle, the broad river, fringed by the lofty trees in full foliage; the exuberant wealth of the autumnal wild flowers down to the very margin of the stream and a bright green island stretched away to the right. The General and his staff were treated to a noble melon on Maryland shore. We went on by a lock in the canal and there intercepted a boat load of melons on the way to the Washington market, which our men bought. As we reached the top of the bluff the enemy's picket scampered away and we could see the dust of their flight at a long distance. We went by the "Furnace Road" to near Buckeystown, in Frederick Co., crossing the Monocacy. Many citizens came out to meet us, most of them professing friendship and gratification at our coming. Some were alarmed, but only a few. Our crossing was unexpected by the enemy and therefore was unopposed. Gen. J. had a fine horse presented him and we were cordially invited to many houses. The General ordered a field of corn to be purchased and the roasting ears given to the men and the husks and stalks to the horses; he also bought rails and ordered the men to have one day's rations of roasting ears cooked and in the haversacks by dawn tomorrow. We were very handsomely entertained, near Three Springs, some 6 miles from Frederick City. I spent the night in a house; the General took the ground. I worked on a map of Frederick County until midnight. A very fine bright day, but quite warm.

Saturday, Sept. 6th. We marched on towards Frederick City, by the way of Monocacy Bridge to cut off the enemy's retreat; but they had fled the night before. The General was thrown from his new horse, in the morning, and considerably hurt; so much so that he gave up the command, for awhile, to Gen. D. H. Hill, who marched into Frederick City, on the left.[4] We found many army stores on fire and took many. The General got on his horse after a time and we went to a point above the Monocacy Bridge. I heard one of the soldiers say, as we passed by, "I wonder if the General has roasting ears in his haversack too?" We soon stopped for dinner when the General took a large roasting ear out of his haversack and deliberately gnawed off the corn, and the whole army, stretched for miles along the road, followed suit. We find a good many friends. Many of the "Union" men went away, but we have made no arrests. I went into the city; some of the merchants sold freely and took Confederate money; others would not take it, but no one was constrained. Our Hd. Qrs. are some 4 miles from Frederick City, towards Frederick Junction of the B. & O. R.R. I worked at map of Frederick County in P.M. We are fixing to blow up the Baltimore & Ohio Bridge over the Monocacy. Stuart is far down in Howard Co. The army is rapidly closing up. Gen. Lee has his Hd. Qrs. near ours. There is some further move on hand. A fine warm day, but very dusty and unpleasant in the roads.

Sunday, Sept. 7th. We spent the day in camp. I worked at map by order of the General. Very warm.

Monday, Sept. 8th. Drew maps most of the day; went to Frederick City in P.M. There was quite a stir there about recruiting for our army.

The enrollment for the Federal draft had just been completed when we came. We blew up the R.R. bridge today, Williamson and Snead directing the work.

Tuesday, Sept. 9th. Drew maps, one of Washington Co., Md. Marching orders are out. Citizens from all directions crowd in to see Gen. Jackson. It is very warm. My horse is quite used up.

Wednesday, Sept. 10th. We started before day 3 A.M., and crossed the South Mountain (Blue Ridge) at Braddock's Gap and encamped, on the western slope, near Boonsboro.[5] A squad of Yankee cavalry made a dash at the head of our column, or rather on the officers carelessly riding in front, and nearly caught some of them. Col. S. Basset French hid in a cellar, or was put there by a "Union" man, until the enemy had gone; a few of Gen. Jackson's escort having put them to flight. A very warm day. Young Geo. G. Junkin, who was Gen. Jackson's A. D. C. at Kernstown and captured there, came to us today, escaped from Federal prison. Very warm. I find the "Union" sentiment stronger as we go northwest, though all are astonished at the number, discipline, and good conduct of our troops.

Thursday, {Sept.} 11th. We went on to Williamsport, turning to the left, a mile or so beyond Boonsboro, and then across the Potomac at Williamsport, by the battle field of Falling Waters, and on to Hammond's Mill, 1½ miles from the North Mt. Depot of the Baltimore & Ohio R.R. We heard the enemy's evening gun at Martinsburg. Took some prisoners at N. Mt. Depot. A warm day; showers in P.M. Part of our army went towards Hagerstown. Hd. Qrs. at Hammond's. We took the enemy's pickets at Williamsport.

Friday, Sept. 12th. Went on to Martinsburg, by the way of Hedgesville, moving cautiously, but soon learned that the enemy had fled; so we moved promptly in and were greeted by the inhabitants with a hearty welcome. Captured some stores there. The enemy strewed their salt in the streets. The ladies thronged the General and went so far as to cut a number of the buttons off his coat, and also attacked the tail of his horse, for momentos. A. P. Hill marched some 6 miles towards Harper's Ferry and Jackson's old Division encamped on that side of Martinsburg. We took supper at Mr. [?] and then went and slept in a field some five miles from Martinsburg. It rained last night and laid the dust, and this is quite a pleasant day. I bought some things in Martinsburg; new hats for the General and myself.

Saturday, Sept. 13th. The enemy from Martinsburg fled to Harper's

Ferry; we went on today and came into Charlestown and Harper's Ferry Road above Hall Town, below Brown's, and went on and occupied the position, above Hall Town, that we held last May. The General sent me to get a line of signals established to Hd. Qrs. from Gen. J. G. Walker,[6] who was to be on Loudoun Heights with his Brigade. [Snead] also received orders to go to Loudoun Heights and see about placing the artillery, and also Williamson; so we all went over the Shenandoah by Keyes' Ford; got some fine peaches by the way and went on to the top of the Mt. Found Gen. J. G. Walker just going up. During the P.M. he got his artillery in position and we heard from Gen. L. McLaws[7] who had just established himself on the Maryland Heights and driven the enemy from there into Harper's Ferry; he had a severe fight and lost many men. A warm day. We slept on the top of the Mt. We have the enemy surrounded and hope to take them tomorrow.

Sunday, Sept. 14th. We had a cold night on the Mt. Got everything ready for the enemy today; have them completely beleagured. They fired at us in all directions, many of the shots went over the Loudoun Heights. Gen. Jackson intended to advance and storm the place today, after demanding a surrender, but he did not advance; why I know not.[8] We opened on them in the P.M. from the Loudoun Heights, with 3 pieces of artillery, and made their cavalry scatter, also compelled the infantry to frequently break. The enemy stood to their arms all day, presenting a very fine appearance in their solid lines. I suppose we will attack them tomorrow, as we are fully prepared. Late at night, today, we moved more artillery across the river. Snead and I slept at McCreary's near Keyes Ford. A warm day.

Monday, Sept. 15th. The batteries that we had taken to the south bank of the Shenandoah opened on the enemy at an early hour and were followed by those on the Loudoun Heights, as well as by those on the left. The enemy replied for awhile, but just as our assaulting column, under Gen. A. P. Hill, came within attacking distance, the enemy hung out a white flag and surrendered. Our batteries kept up the fire for some little time, as the smoke and fog prevented their seeing the flag, and besides, they were some ways off. Our troops soon marched in and the Yankees stacked arms and were paroled. About dark they were marched over the Potomac and sent on to their own lines. The officers were allowed to keep their arms and horses, and private baggage was allowed the men. We took 11,090 prisoners, among them 450 officers, 13,000 stand of small arms and 72 pieces of artillery, besides a large amount of am-

munition, and commissary and quartermaster's stores. We destroyed the
B. & O. R.R. bridge and the pontoon bridge which the enemy had laid
across the Potomac. [Snead] and I came across the Shenandoah, just
after the surrender, and aided in destroying the bridges. I went among
the prisoners and conversed with them; most of them were only two
months from home and were glad they were taken. I found a N.Y. Regt,
the 111th, and wrote to my Father by the Col. Segoin.[9] A Major Smith
gave me his revolver. Quite late in the day I went up to Mr. Brown's
(S. Howell's father's) near Charlestown, and there spent the night. A
very warm day, and quite dusty; our soldiers are as dirty as the ground
itself and are nearly of the same color. The enemy looked at them in
amazement, especially when they cheered Gen. Jackson as he rode by
them. The General and part of the army went on to Sheperdstown
tonight, or to near there; Jackson's Division and Ewell's. A. P. Hill and
his Division remained near Harper's Ferry, he being in command there.
McLaws' Division came over, from the Md. Heights, at midnight and he
remained near Hall Town[10] the rest of the night.

   Tuesday, Sept. 16th. Went to Charlestown in the morning and got
fuse, etc., then back to Harper's Ferry and gave it to the Corps engaged
in blowing up the bridge, then assisted Wm. Allen[11] in collecting arms.
Came up to Maj. J. A. Harman's tent, at Hall Town, late at night, and
slept there. There was some fighting going on today over in Md., near
Boonsboro, I think. The rest of Jackson's Corps went to Shepherdstown
tonight. A very warm and dusty day. We have removed most of the
stores that we captured, and the owners have claimed most of the slaves
that we found in Harper's Ferry.

   Wednesday, Sept. 17th. Went to Charlestown in the morning and
transacted some business there, then on to Sheperdstown and found the
battle raging around Sharpsburg, A. P. Hill having just gone in on our
right. My horse was so jaded that I did not cross the river, but watched
the battle for a time and then went to Maj. Thos. E. Ballard's tent, on
the hill above the ford, and there spent the night. The General ordered
cooking utensils and provisions to be sent over, in the night, to Sharpsburg. The General slept near the battle field, on the ground; the troops
slept on the battle field. Our line extended along the course of Antietam
Creek for a long ways, on the west side. The enemy's line was some 6
miles long, on the east side of Antietam Creek. Gen. Jackson was on our
left. Gen. A. P. Hill on the right. We drove the enemy back on the
right and on the left, they beginning the attacks. They nearly broke our

center. The slaughter was very great on all the line, and we lost many valuable men. The day was very warm and the dust excessive. The battle raged from 4 A.M. to near 9 P.M., with intervals but with unabated fury. The position of the combatants was much the same at night that it had been in the morning, though we held most of the battle field. Capt. A. S. Pendleton and Dr. Hunter H. McGuire slept where I did. The General slept on the field, on the ground.

Thursday, Sept. 18. I went across the Potomac and found that the General wanted a reconnoissance made up the river, above Shepherdstown. I could not find him so obtained a guide and went up and ascertained the position of the enemy's pickets, the crossings of the river, etc. As I could not go far enough up on the Md. side I came back to the Va. side and went up to Terrapin Neck. Learned all I could there, got my supper, and started back, just after dark, meeting and directing a strong picket, of all arms, that was sent up to guard Shepherd's Fork. I did not reach Shepherdstown until quite late, when I found the train and troops coming over to the Va. Side; all the wagons having been taken to the Md. side in the morning. I made my way, with difficulty and danger, across to the Md. shore, going along the river down to the ford at Boteler's Mill, as the road was full of horses, wagons, ambulances, etc., and very narrow, with a bluff above and below and the river beneath. I found the ford full of wagons and the bank on the other side densely packed with them. I saw some pushed into the canal by the press. Getting back some distance, seeking Gen. Jackson, I found Gen. J. E. B. Stuart coming out. He wanted me to go back with him and show him the way, telling me that Gen. J. had read my report. So I threaded my way back, the General's horse falling down under a wagon once, and took him to Gen. W. N. Pendleton, Chief of Artillery, and through the ravines on to Shepherdstown and into the road to Scrabble. I then laid down in the street of Shepherdstown, by a fire some soldiers had kindled, and slept for two hours, being very weary. Our entire army, train and all, passed safely over the Potomac during the night, Maj. J. A. Harman, Q.M., "cussing" it over. The day was quite warm until the P.M. when there was a heavy thunder storm.

Friday, Sept. 19th. Our troops, trains, artillery, etc., were all safely over the Potomac by 8 A.M., having been covered by the fog, and the enemy did not find that we were all over until everything had gained the Va. bluff, when [they] came on rapidly and commenced shelling the bluff. Our wagons and men that were scattered about, speedily scampered off and no damage was done. Our artillery on the bluff soon opened on the enemy and compelled them to move back some; we went some 3 miles off, towards Martinsburg, and there encamped. I visited Col. A. R. Boteler's house; he being at home. He had his house full of men. Our recrossing the river without any loss, must be considered one of the most successful of military movements. A fine warm day.

Saturday, Sept. 20th. Last night the enemy came over in force and dispersed our picket, etc., at Boteler's Mill, captured 4 pieces of artillery and took some prisoners, causing a stampede from the Va. bank of the river of which they took possession. Today Gen. Jackson went down with A. P. Hill's Division and drove them into the river, with great slaughter, many of them being killed and wounded while fording the river. He took some 60 prisoners. I went with the wagons and made a map of Berkeley Co., which the General wanted. About dark an order came to us, at Lee Town,[12] to go to Tabler's Mill; so we went on by Martinsburg and on to where the road to Tabler's Mill leaves the turnpike, and there slept from mid-night on. The day was very pleasant.

Sunday, Sept.. 21st. We moved the wagons over to Tabler's Mill and found the General there, on the high S. bank of the Opeqon Creek,[13] which the soldiers are using freely today, washing off the dirt of our long marches and battles and washing their clothes; the vermin have become very numerous in camp. The Division of Maj. Gen. A. P. Hill was assigned to Gen. Jackson's command yesterday. Cooking and washing are the worship of today, very necessary acts, next to Godliness at least. I wrote home and lounged about the rest of the day, an unprofitable Sunday but of much the same character as the rest of these days of tribulation and war. God grant they may be shortened and that peace may come to us again.

Monday, Sept. 22nd. Drew map of Maryland. The troops are enjoying the proximity of the Opequon. The days are getting quite cool. We still occupy the hill above the creek.

Tuesday, Sept. 23rd. Our troops are all this side of the Potomac now, and we have burned all the bridges, etc., there and removed our captured property to a place of safety. A fine Sept. day. We had quite a Quarter-Master's row today about forage, etc. "Cousin Tom," alias Mr. Neal, left us and went to Imboden, the General giving him his Maryland horse.

Wednesday, Sept. 24th. We moved away from our old camp in the P.M. and came to near Martinsburg to escape the filth and vermin that were collecting around from the proximity of the army. We had quite a shower in the P.M. Boswell and I went out to Mr. Hedges and supped there. The Yankee cavalry has been making some demonstrations in Loudoun and Fauquier and captured some of our wounded men at Aldie.

Thursday, Sept. 25th. I overhauled my boxes and put things in good shape; cleaned up generally, worked hard and am quite tired. It has been a delightful day and we have enjoyed it much in our nice camp, but news comes that the enemy is advancing and I suppose we will soon move.

Friday, Sept. 26th. Went out to Mr. Hedges', some 2 miles off, and spent part of the day with him, learning about the roads, etc. I am not well; cleaned up to much after being so long dirty, I suppose. Found Thos. C. Kinney at our camp, as Eng., when I got back. Orders to march are out. Day cool and sad. I feel quite badly.

Saturday, Sept. 27th. We moved at 5 A.M., passing through Martinsburg at an early hour, and went on to Bunker's Hill and encamped back of Mr. Boyd's. The roads are very dusty. Our army is rapidly filling up from stragglers and men released from hospitals; they come in thousands. Quite warm. There is much jaundice in camp.

Sunday, Sept. 28th. Spent the day in camp, part of the time in bed, feeling badly. Rev. Dr. Stiles preached near by. Boswell, Brown, and Kinney went to Winchester. The day has been very quiet and I have enjoyed it much. Heard from home, a good letter. A fine day.

Monday, Sept. 29th. I got a letter of recommendation from Lt. J. K. Boswell, and also one from Gen. Jackson, to the Secretary of War and applied for a commission in the Topographical Engineer Corps. I had a plain talk with the General; he said he thought my great fault was talking too much, but he gave me a good testimonial and hoped that I might succeed in [obtaining] the appointment, and at the same time asked that I might be assigned to him for duty. I can but admire the General's candor in telling me what he did, and I intend, with God's help, to get rid of the fault complained of. After getting my letters of recommendation I had my wagon packed up and took it to Winchester to get it repaired, and then I intended to take a reconnoitring trip. [Snead] started with me, but Brown came up, with orders from the General, to take all the wagons and go and look for a camp; I was too sick to go along and so spent the night with Maj. W. J. Hawks. Very warm, dry and dusty; clouds are everywhere, obscuring the air and almost blinding one on the roads. The enemy made some demonstrations towards Charlestown, having reoccupied Harper's Ferry. There was some artillery fighting there. I met large numbers of soldiers returning to the army. Camp still at Bunker's Hill.

Tuesday, Sept. 30th. I transacted some business in Winchester, then mounted my horse and started up the Valley Turnpike, but turned off at the Cedar Creek road and mapped the country as far as Mr. Brumback's, 9 miles from Winchester. A fine country and a fine day. Wrote to Col. A. R. Boteler in the morning; spent the night at Mr. Funkhouser's in company with two young preachers.

Wednesday, Oct. 1st. Went on to Frieden's Church, dining at Mr. Funkhouser's near Lebanon Church where Fremont and his crew came into the Valley, last June, via the Strasburg and Capon road. The people relate many outrages committed by Fremont's men.

Thursday, Oct. 2nd. Went on by the Back Road to Fair View and took dinner at Mr. Craig's, near that place, then rode on to Woodstock by way of the road from Van Buren Furnace. Only remained a short time in Woodstock then went out, by the Middle Road, to Joseph Hottle's and there spent the night. Very warm and dusty. The soldiers are coming back rapidly from the hospitals; the roads leading towards Winchester are lined with them.

Friday, Oct. 3rd. Went out to Frieden's Church and then back by Smutz's Mill and on to Strasburg, by a very rough and hilly road. Dined at Mr. [?] near Smutz's Mill; spent the night in Strasburg. Very dry and dusty.

Saturday, Oct. 4th. Sketched the defences thrown up by the enemy at Strasburg. Paid $2.50 for self and horse over night. Went out by the Capon Grade to Mt. Lebanon Church on the Back Road; dined again at Mr. Funkhouser's; then went over to Cottontown and down back of the Little North Mountain to Mt. Hope Mills, then into the Back Road, then on to Mr. Rudolf's, near Mt. Zion Church, where I spent the night. Found my host a nice man and his home a pleasant place. The day was very warm; a heavy shower just at dark.

Sunday, Oct. 5th. Came on to Winchester by way of the Round Hill on the N. W. Turnpike. Went to the Presbyterian Church and heard a long and dry sermon from Rev. Graham.[14] In the afternoon went down to camp; a hot and dusty ride. Found Hd. Qrs. at the same place, at Bunker's Hill, 12 miles from Winchester. Everything has been quiet since I left, save a cavalry fight near Martinsburg from which we drove the enemy with loss to them and not much to us. I am quite weary from my long and dusty ride.

Monday, Oct. 6th. Spent the day in camp drawing a map of part of Washington, Co., Md. Everything is quiet. The enemy still keeps near Sharpsburg, in Maryland. Warm and dry as usual.

Tuesday, Oct. 7th. Was preparing to go off again when the General ordered some more maps, so I must again drudge in camp. I do not feel well; my head aches. A deserter came in and reported that McClellan was still in the same place. Gen. R. E. Lee came up to our Hd. Qrs this morning and he and Gen. Jackson are having a long conversation aided [by] my maps of Maryland and Pennsylvania. No doubt another expedition is on foot. It was understood, yesterday, that Maj. Gen. Ambrose P. Hill had preferred charges against Gen. Jackson, and that he in turn had preferred charges against him; so some trouble is anticipated. I hope all may blow by. Gen. Hill is a brave officer but perhaps too quick to resent seeming over-steping of authority. [Now] Gen. Jackson intends to do his whole duty. May good and not evil come out of this trouble.

Wednesday, Oct. 8th. Worked all day copying a map of part of the Valley for Gen. R. E. Lee, [Snead] helping me. We had a spicy time in the evening discussing Col. A. Snead's captured horse. Lt. Rogers,[15] of Gen. A. P. Hill's staff spent the night with me. A very warm day; dusty and fleay as ever.

Thursday, Oct. 9th. Worked at map until noon, then started for Winchester with Boswell; dined at his mother's and then we rode on and went over the Kernstown battle field, riding about until dark when he returned to Winchester and I went to Mr. Pritchard's for the night; very weary and almost sick. Hot and dry as usual.

Friday, Oct. 10th. Spent the day riding over and mapping the Kernstown battle field in the intervals of the showers that were falling all day. Had quite a pleasant time all to myself; went back to [the] same place for the night.

Saturday, Oct. 11th. Went over the S.W. part of the battle field and on to the Opequon. Dined at Mr. Glass'. He says 100 Yankees and one Confederate were killed by our last volley when the enemy pursued us from the field, about dark, near the [r]ailing fence, March 23rd, 1862, and that then the Federals fell back and if we had not retreated they themselves would have fled; and that it was only when our cavalry fell back that the Federals took straggling men prisoners. I went over to Mr. Templar's, near Bartonsville, to spend the night. Heard that Stuart and his cavalry had gone to Pennsylvania. Day showery and cold.

Sunday, Oct. 12. I spent the day by the fireside at Mr. Templar's, reading Milburn's Sketches and the Bible and conversing. Saw McMicken and Sherrard,[16] of Hardy Co., who came over with some things for our sick soldiers. Wrote home at night. It rained and was quite cold.

Monday, Oct. 13th. It rained in the morning so I could do nothing, but after dinner went to Kernstown, mapping the road from Bartonsville there, then went to Col. Wm. Glass'[17] to spend the night. Day quite cool. Some of our army came back to near Kernstown on account of the small pox, some regiments having a good many cases of it. Camp still at Bunker's Hill.

Tuesday, Oct. 14th. Went to Winchester in the morning, following the ridge that extends [west] of the town. Heard of Stuart's return and of his successful raid into Pennsylvania. Read the papers for a time then rode out to Newtown, mapping the Valley Turnpike to that point and spending the night there. A fine day. Hd. Qrs. Still at Bunker's Hill.

Wednesday, Oct. 15th. Mapped the Valley Turnpike from Newtown to Middletown; saw Tom Kinney there; met Maj. Strother Jones and went home with him to Vaucluse; had a delightful ride and he showed me much of the surrounding country. Found Mr. Allen, of Clarke Co., at Vaucluse and spent a pleasant afternoon. A fine autumn day. Hd. Qrs. still at Bunker's Hill.

Thursday, Oct. 16. Mapped the road from Vaucluse (Maj. Strother Jones') to Middletown; dine there; $1.50 for horse and self; then examined and mapped the road to Buckton on the North Fork river, on my way to Powell's Fort Valley. A cool, changeable day. There was a heavy rain at night, with thunder and lightning. Spent the night at Mrs. Cooley's. Camp at Bunker's Hill.

Friday, Oct. 17th. Started early and mapped the road towards Strasburg, to the river ford, then rode back to Buckton and went up Passage Creek to Mr. Brown's, in Powell's Fort Valley, some 7 miles, mapping as I went. I enjoyed the scenery very much. A pleasant day. Camp still at Bunker's Hill.

Saturday, Oct. 18th. Hd. Qrs. were moved to Martinsburg, to camp near town; moved there for the purpose of destroying the B. & O. R.R. and its appurtenances. I got my horse shod in the morning, 25 cts for having two old shoes put on (speculation has not reached here yet), then went on to Burner's Springs for dinner; had a nice ride and found a pleasant gentleman there. Went, late in the P.M., across the N. Massanutton Mt. to Woodstock and on to Mt. Jackson. A long ride and I am very weary. A fine day. The people are making molasses from sorghum; saw much flax spread out rotting and many evidences of domestic manufacture.

Sunday, Oct. 19th. Went on up the Valley, stopping awhile at Mr. Rude's, then on to Harrisonburg, to Mr. Robert Kyle's; reached there about dark. Had Mr. Bumgardner for company and heard from him that the army moved, on Thursday last, towards the Potomac; also heard from him the particulars of Stuart's raid through Pa. It is very dry and hardly any seeding has been done; the Great Valley is almost desolate from the drought. Hd. Qrs. at Martinsburg. We burnt the depot and the hotel of the B. & O. R.R. Co. at that place.

Monday, Oct. 20th. Camp still at Martinsburg (at night at Cooper Shop. P.) Army engaged in tearing up the track of the B. & O. R.R. I went on home by the way of Bridgewater and Mossy Creek; saw many of my old neighbors and friends on their way to the Rockingham Court. Spent a pleasant hour and dined at Mr. Daniel Forrer's.[18] Reached home at dark; all delighted to see me and I was glad to get there, if but for a day. Pleasant, but cool.

Tuesday, Oct. 21st. The General started back towards Bunker's Hill, but spent the night on the way, on the Shepherdstown and Smithfield Turnpike. I went to my brother's to dinner and we had a pleasant hour or so, then he and I went to Staunton, reaching there late; saw about some clothes and then came home.

Wednesday, Oct. 22nd. Hd. Qrs. moved back to Bunker's Hill. I spent the day at home, drawing, finishing up my notes and fixing to go to camp tomorrow. The day quite cool, but gusty and threatening rain.

Thursday, Oct. 23rd. Hd. Qrs. at Bunker's Hill. I started quite early; went to Staunton and transacted some business, then down the Valley Turnpike to Mt. Sidney, sketching the road. Spent the night at Mr. Jacob Roler's. A fine day. Many people are sending to the Kanawha Salines for salt, as the road is now open. Paid $45. for a pair of boots.

Friday, Oct. 24th. Went on down the Keezletown Road to Peale's stopping at Kemper's for dinner, passing by the battle field of Cross Keys. Things are much changed there. The people are seeding, with much difficulty, the ground is so dry. The [corn] crop on the road is very good. A fine day; windy. Hd. Qrs. at Bunker's Hill.

Saturday, Oct. 25th. Hd. Qrs. were moved to near Charlestown, part of the army going there to tear up the Winchester and Potomac R.R. Went on down the Keezletown Road and sketched it to the Valley Turnpike, near Sparta. A very rough road. Then went on to New Market.

The wind was very high and the clouds of dust, sweeping along the McAdamized Road, were almost unendurable. Gusty; many signs of rain. Found no orders at New Market.

Sunday, Oct. 26th. Hd. Qrs. near Charlestown, troops tearing up the R.R. I found that a North-Easter had burst upon us during the night with a driving wind and cold rain. I had a good fire made and spent the day in my room, reading and writing home; also went to church, Old School Lutheran. Was quite comfortable; a very bad day.

Monday, Oct. 27th. Hd. Qrs. still at Charlestown. It rained some in the morning but soon blew off cold. I went on to Rev. Rude's, but not finding him at home went to Meem's[19] at Mt. Airy, remained there awhile and then on into Powell's Valley, through the wild gorge of Riddle's Run; then on to Moston's Furnace and to Woods', 2 miles below where I spent the night, meeting with a hearty welcome; a very agreeable thing after a disagreeably cool day. Sketched the road, but found it quite cold work. Paid at hotel, for self and horse, $1\frac{1}{2}$ days, $6.40. at New Market.

Tuesday, Oct. 28th. Hd. Qrs. were moved to Mr. Pendleton's (near Blackburn's, Clarke Co.), on the Summit Point and Berryville road, some $4\frac{1}{2}$ miles from Berryville. I continued down the Fort Valley, sketching the road to Burner's Springs where Mr. Samuel A. Dannar rec'd me very kindly and I spent a very pleasant evening. The day has been fine; a genuine October one and I enjoyed it much. The bracing air, the fine wild grapes, and the Mt. scenery. My hosts of last night were very kind. Hd. Qrs. near Blackburn's house.

Wednesday, Oct. 29th. I went on across the South Massanutton Mt. to the Page Valley, that of the S. Fork of the Shenandoah. Found the slope of the Mt. towards the river, a very long one and quite steep. I went on to Milford to dinner and to Mr. Fayette Buck's, at the mouth of Gooney Run, where I renewed an acquaintance of 15 years ago and spent the night. A fine day, but cool in the P.M. Some two Brigades of our army came across from Strasburg and encamped near McKay's Ford, on their way to cross the Blue Ridge to Eastern Va. Hd. Qrs. still at Pendleton's.

Thursday, Oct. 30th. I went to Front Royal and up to "Mt. Howze," the residence of Mr. Marcus B. Buck, an old friend of 15 years ago, and whom I have not seen since that time. He is much changed, but still has much of the same genial, gentlemanly nature about him that he had then. I spent a delightful P.M. there, working up my sketches. A fine, mild day. Longstreet's Corps is passing through Front Royal to Eastern

Va. Had a pleasant evening with Mr. Buck. Hd. Qrs. at Pendleton's.

Friday, Oct. 31st. I went on, through Cedarville, [Nineveh], White Post, Berryville, and 4 miles beyond, to our Hd. Qrs. D. H. Hill has crossed the Blue Ridge at Snicker's Gap and A. P. Hill is below him, so our forces are now along the Blue Ridge, for some distance, making demonstrations on McClellan's army as it moves along through Piedmont, and disconcerting his plans. I found the General had sent for me; had a pleasant reunion at Hd. Qrs. A fine day, but quite dusty again. The enemy has crossed the Potomac and is moving towards Fredericksburg. Hd. Qrs. at Blackburn's, or Pendleton's, on the Summit Point road.

Saturday, Nov. 1st. I saw the General in the morning; found that he wanted me to look after my commission and go and see Gen. R. E. Lee and get authority for him to continue me on my present duty. As he was not now Commanding General he was not authorized to make such disbursements; so I settled up to Nov. 1st, got a statement from Gen. Jackson to Gen. Lee that I had rendered valuable service, and he would retain me if he had the authority so to do; then, in company with Capt. Edward Willis, started for Front Royal. We stopped at Berryville for dinner; saw Col. A. R. Boteler there, then went to my friend, Mr. B. Buck's near Front Royal, getting there late. We had a fine ride, the day being very pleasant, but some dust. I drew my pay for 3 months, $300. Brown, Kinney, Williamson, and the clerks made a new mess today. Hd. Qrs. at Blackburn's.

Sunday, Nov. 2nd. We went down to Front Royal to church and heard a very good sermon, the preacher giving special attention to "extortioners." We spent a very pleasant day at Mr. [M. B.] Buck's, strolled upon the Mt., read good books, etc. I wrote home in the P.M. A fine, cool, autumn day.

Monday, Nov. 3rd. It was quite cold, so I did not start out until late, then went up the Gooney Manor Road to Brownton, 9 miles and back; Mr. Buck went up with me. The day was quite raw. We enjoyed the profusion of delicate, wild grapes that grew by the road; had a nice visit at night; slept soundly. We talked until quite late. Quite raw and cold. Hd. Qrs. were moved from Pendleton's (Blackburn's on the Summit Point Road) to "Carter Hall,"[20] Millwood.

Tuesday, Nov. 4th. Started for Culpeper at 8 A.M., Willis going with me a ways and then turned back to Front Royal and Winchester, as he heard that the enemy was advancing on Jackson. It is evident that McClellan is out witted by the staying of Jackson in the Valley and is trying to find his whereabouts by force. I went, by Chester Gap, on to Little Washington, in Rappahannock Co., about 20 miles. D. H. Hill's Division came down to Front Royal, from Manassas Gap, today, and I heard that the enemy had advanced to Linden on the M. G. R.R.[21] Found the people much alarmed, driving their cattle away, etc. Saw firing back on the Mt. towards Manassas Gap, and suppose there was a fight there. The day was quite cold and I found a fire very pleasant.

Wednesday, Nov. 5th. Started at daylight and went on to Sperry-ville, intending to breakfast there, but found the town "eaten out" by the army, Longstreet's Corps, that had passed that way; so I went on and got some corn for my horse, where some soldiers were shucking some the Q.M. had impressed, fed him, and then went on until noon when I made out to get my dinner at Griffinsburg, a one-house town. Sketched the road all the way; came to Gen. James Longstreet's Hd. Qrs., at Pendleton's, a mile from Culpeper C. H., and learned from him where Gen. Lee's Hd. Qrs. were, near and south of the C. H. among some pines. Went there and spent the night with Capt. Sam Johnson.[22] Gen. Lee got back today from Richmond. Our cavalry is bringing up the rear of Longstreet's troops, which are encamped along the road, not far from the C. H.

Thursday, Nov. 6th. Saw Gen. Lee and got his approval of my em-ployment by Gen. J., then went on to the Cedar Run Battle field, mapping the road and then on to the Robertson river,[23] on my way to Madison C. H., finding myself, at night, at Smoot's, a very comfortable old widower's. Hood's Division was encamped on the old Battle field. Things looked much changed there. I took dinner at Col. Slaughter's, where our cavalry was during the Cedar Run fight. The Yankees came there after the fight and searched the house and carried off some things. The day was quite chilly and I found it difficult to map the roads, etc. Hd. Qrs. moved to "Saratoga,"[24] a point on the Front Royal and Winchester Road [two]½ miles from Winchester and at McCoy's a mile from [Nineveh].

Friday, Nov. 7th. It sleeted and rained all day, so I kept to my quarters; fixed up my notes and made the time pass quite pleasantly, with a good fire, apples, and a chatty old fellow at hand. Soldiers were passing all day, from the camp at Cedar Run, some 10 miles off, coming after apple brandy at $15 a gallon; some of them were even barefooted. Hd. Qrs. at McCoy's, Nineveh, and remained there until the 14th.

Saturday, Nov. 8th. Started on at an early hour and went to Madison C. H. to dinner, then on to Criglersville and put up at Mr. Stickler's. The roads were full of people moving from the threatened invasion of the enemy who are pressing that way, having reached Gaines' XRd's[25] today. It had been quite cool; some flurries of snow.

Sunday, Nov. 9th. Spent the day at Criglersville, read, talked, and looked at passing wagons of the cavalry, stragglers, etc. The enemy is said to be 20 miles off and we falling back. Saw much selling of liquor today and also of other things; the day has almost ceased to be "hallowed." Quite cool.

Monday, Nov. 10th. Went on across the Blue Ridge, by Fisher's Gap; had a long and hard ride; sketched the road and came to Kite's at the foot of the Mt. Met Hampton's Legion[26] on the way over the Mt., many of them were drunk, and "apple-jack" seemed to be plentiful. A fine warm day.

Tuesday, Nov. 11th. Went on to New Market, crossing the Massanutton Mt., sketching the road to N.M., then went on intending to stay at Mr. Rude's, but went there and did not find him at home, so went to Mt. Jackson for the night. Took dinner on the top of the Mt. (Massanutton). Heard that Gen. J. had gone to Bunker's Hill. A fine day, cool in the morning.

Wednesday, Nov. 12th. Went on down the Valley and mapped the road to Woodstock, dining there; then on to Strasburg, in the rain which began at noon. Found the place full, as D. H. Hill's Division is encamped near there tearing up the M. G. R.R., burning the cross ties, etc. Quite cool.

Thursday, Nov. 13th. Went on to Middletown, from Strasburg, passing through Hill's encampment, mapping the road. Went over to Vaucluse and spent the P.M., having a pleasant time. The day was a fine one. Bill for self and horse, over night, at Strasburg, $2.50. Hd. Qrs. same place as on the 6th.[27]

Friday, Nov. 14th. Maj. Strother Jones and I went on to Winchester, by the Grove Road,[28] passing over the Kernstown Battle field, which he had never visited. We had a pleasant ride. I heard, in Winchester, of the capture of Maj. J. Marshall McCue and his escape, and of the advance of the Yankees to Highland Co., Va. Took dinner with Capt. R. D. Lilley. The day was very fine. Went out on the Front Royal Road to go to our Hd. Qrs. and found they were establishing them, some $2\frac{1}{2}$ miles from Winchester, on Hogg Run. I [spent] the night with Maj. J. A. Harman, who has a stove in his tent. Had quite a chat with the General at night.

Saturday, Nov. 15th. Spent the day in my tent, fixing up my note book, etc. The General appointed the evening to see me about my visit to Gen. Lee, etc. He expressed himself as gratified at my success in obtaining Gen. Lee's approval of my employment as Top. Eng. Quite cool; had a long talk with Maj. J. A. Harman about the charges against his brother, Col. M. G. Harman, and read letters about it.

Sunday, Nov. 16th. I spent the day in camp, reading, etc. The rest went to church in Winchester. It began to rain, late in the P.M., and is quite cool; Capt. Edward Willis went to join Gen. E. F. Paxton, who has just taken charge of the "Stonewall Brigade," having been made a Brigadier General. He has been acting as our A.A.A. Gen. for some time.

Monday, Nov. 17th. Fixed up in the morning, for a new trip and started towards Front Royal, but the rain caused me to stop at Bridgeport, at noon, and I only got to Mr. Mason's at night, 10 miles from Winchester. It rained quite hard last night and much of today and the tents are quite uncomfortable without fires.

Tuesday, Nov. 18th. Went on to Front Royal; mapped the road to Cedarville, then went to my Friend M. B. Buck's, on the Mt. It rained and misted most of the day. The enemy is beyond the Rappahannock and below the Thoroughfare Mt. Had an agreeable visit with Mr. Buck. Hd. Qrs. still at Hogg Run.

Wednesday, Nov. 19th. Rode on towards Luray, mapping the Gooney Manor Road to Mrs. King's; then went across the Luray turnpike and up to Oak Hill. Met Capt. L. Randolph on the way, just from Richmond. He said Lord Lyons[29] was daily expected there with good news. A pleasant day, but a little cool. The General moved to Winchester today, to a house.

Thursday, Nov. 20th. I went on to Luray, sketching the road. Came near being arrested; quite amusing. A boy saw me sketching, by the road side, and reported me to the Provost Marshal, at Luray, as having on blue pants, etc., so he got Capt. Macon Jordan and some others to come and take me prisoner. When the Captain rode up he broke into a big laugh, recognizing me, having been one of my Mossy Creek pupils, and insisting that I should go to his house. So I spent the rest of the day there and the evening at Mr. Lionberger's. The evening quite cool. Heard many incidents connected with the occupation of the place by the enemy, before and after the battle of Port Republic. Hd. Qrs. in Winchester.

Friday, Nov. 21st. I remained at Luray. It rained last night and in the A.M. today. Fixed up my notes; was busy all day. The ladies at Mrs. G. Jordan's were quite chatty. Heard today that Gen. Lee had left Culpeper and gone towards Fredericksburg. Quite cool. Head Quarters still in Winchester.

Saturday, Nov. 22nd. Started across the Blue Ridge, via Thornton's Gap, and sketched the road on to Sperryville, though I found it very cold work, especially towards evening. Had some trouble in procuring lodgings at Sperryville; at last got quite comfortably housed. Heard that Gen. Jackson had broken camp at Winchester. Pleasant but cool and bracing. A good many cavalry passed me, coming over to Stuart. Bill for supper and lodging at Sperryville, $2.50. The General and staff left Winchester and rode over the battlefield of Kernstown, then on to Tumbling Run, beyond Strasburg, for the night. (At Old Stone House. P.). The army moving also.

Sunday, Nov. 23rd. As I could not get feed for my horse at Sperryville went on today and mapped the road to near Criglersville, spending the night at Mr. Thomas'. Did not much like the idea of working on Sunday, but have often had to do it since the war began; a military necessity. The day was quite chilly, roads bad and muddy. The General went on to near Mt. Jackson, to the house just beyond [Mill] Creek.

Monday, Nov. 24th. Went on through Criglersville, to Madison C. H., then through Wolftown and across the Rapidan to Mrs. Booton's; a delightful place. The day was quite pleasant, but the evening chilly. The people at Madison C. H. expected our army there, as a store of corn had been collected, within a few days, by some Quarter Master. Paid $7.00 for a pair of drawers. The General went across the Massanutton Mt., from New Market, then, via Columbia Bridge, across the Shenandoah, and on to within a mile of the village of Hawksbill, on Hawksbill Creek, on the road to Madison C. H. (Williamson made a sketch of Gen. J., on a log, in the rain, which he gave me. He had on the soft hat I bought for him.)

Tuesday, Nov. 25th. Went on to Stanardsville and up to the foot of the Blue Ridge, to Long's for the night. Met a mountaineer's welcome. Quite a fine day. Some of the La. Brigade of Ewell's Division were at the same place over night, having left the Brigade at Columbia Bridge and "flanked" to Swift Run Gap. I bought 10 yds of linen at $3.50 a yard. The General crossed the Blue Ridge by Risher's, or Graves' Gap, through Criglersville to Madison C. H. and to a half mile beyond, on the road to Gordonsville. Ewell's Division encamped a mile beyond Hd. Qrs.

Wednesday, Nov. 26th. I rode on across the Blue Ridge by Swift Run Gap, to Conrad's Store; got completely chilled, and was quite [cold] when I reached the fire at Argenbright's, where I took dinner and spent the night. In the evening went to a party at Miller's (where Col. Car-

roll,[30] of Shields' army, had his Hd. Qrs. before the battle of Port Repub-
lic) but had such a headache I had to go back to the hotel and go to bed.
Day quite chilly; it rained hard last night. Hd. Qrs. remained [near]
Madison C. H., at the same place in the woods.

Thursday, Nov. 27th. Rode on to Weyer's Cave, to Abram. Mohler's,
where I spent the night, having mapped the road all the way and especially noted the field of the battle of Port Republic. Had the scenes of
that bloody day vividly recalled to my mind. Evidences of the battle are
plentiful as yet. A fine day, but chilly. Hd. Qrs. still near Madison C. H.

Friday, Nov. 28th. I was up at an early hour and off for home, though
feeling quite sick as I have been since my chill. Found my wife in Staunton; we went on home, stopping for dinner at W. M. Dudley's. Found
orders in Staunton for me to report to Orange C. H. at once, but was too
unwell to obey. The day was quite chilly. Hd. Qrs. were near Orange
C. H. to the south, 1 mile away, at Haxall's;[31] the army was encamped
near by.

Saturday, Nov. 29th. Spent the day at home; was quite sick and took
medicine, but was better at night. Am getting ready to go back next
Monday. War is a hard thing, every man a slave to power and can have
no will of his own. It rained during the night. Gen. Jackson went on to
Gen. Lee's Hd. Qrs., on the Mine Road near Muscoe Garnett's, Smith and
others with him, and spent the night there, not far from Fredericksburg.[32]
He went by the Orange Plank Road, some 40 miles. The wagons and
part of the staff went by way of Orange Springs and encamped at Richard's Shop. The army marched on by several different roads; D. H. Hill's
Division by Orange Springs and A. P. Hill's by the Plank Road. It
snowed in Augusta Co. last night.

Sunday, Nov. 30th. I felt much better in the morning and so concluded to start back to camp in the afternoon. The ground was white
with snow in the morning but it turned warm and by noon the snow was
[melted]. I left home with a sad heart, for our army has gone from the
Valley and its fate is uncertain; when I may get home again I know not,
but hope all may turn out well. Left home at noon and rode to New
Hope, to Mr. James M. Stout's, where I spent a very pleasant evening
and night. The day pleasant but cool. I am 34 years old today; God be
praised for his mercies to me. Paid $35.00 for a pair of boots. Hd. Qrs.
near Mrs. French's, some 5 miles west of Fredericksburg and near Gen.
Lee's Hd. Qrs.

Monday, Dec. 1st. Went on across the Blue Ridge, at Brown's Gap, to Horace Brown's at the eastern foot of the mountain. The day was very pleasant; the temperature 55° Fahrenheit after sundown. I was quite weary but slept well. Mapped the road across the Blue Ridge. The General moved, via the Telegraph Road to Massaponax Church and then to Mr. Chandler's,[33] about a mile from Guiney's Depot, where he encamped.

Tuesday, Dec. 2nd. Got an early start and went on, by way of Nortonsville, to Orange C. H., where I arrived late in the evening. The day very pleasant and quite warm in the P.M. The army was "clean gone," hardly a "straggler" left behind. The crops for part of the way along the road are very good. Found the hotel at Orange C. H. a dirty place. Bill for lodging and breakfast $2.50. Hd. Qrs. at Mr. Chandler's, near Guiney's.

Wednesday, Dec. 3rd. Travelled, by the Plank Road, towards Fredericksburg, turned off just below Verdiersville and taking the Catharpen[34] Road through an almost unbroken forest. Went to within 6 miles of Spotsylvania C. H. A Mr. Davis, of Rockbridge Co., was with me; we got a good dinner at Mr. Wright's; found Charles Harris of the Q.M. Dept. where we spent the night. The roads are badly cut up. The day was very fine; sunshiny and pleasant. Hd. Qrs. at Guiney's, at Mr. Chandler's.

Thursday, Dec. 4th. Rode on to Spotsylvania C. H. and then, by a round about way, to Hd. Qrs. at Guiney's, some 20 miles; the hardest place to find I have sought for in some time. A man told me they used to call it 6 miles to the Court House, but they had "supervised the road lately and made it 8." Saw the General and got orders to make a map of Caroline Co., so no chance of getting back to the Valley. Dined with the General; wrote home at night. The day was very pleasant. Found Gen. R. E. Lee at our Hd. Qrs. when I got there.

Friday, Dec. 5th. It rained, snowed, and hailed all day, beginning at 9 A.M.; day very unpleasant. Made a tracing of the map of Caroline Co. At night wrote to Col. A. R. Boteler, M. C., at Richmond, and read Abe Lincoln's message to his Congress; his claptrap argument for emancipation, etc. A very hard [day] for the soldiers.

Saturday, Dec. 6th. Went on a [reconnaissance] towards Port Royal. The mud was very deep and partially frozen; it was quite chilly. The soldiers are making themselves quite comfortable. The army horses are suffering much with "greasy Heel," a sort of scratches. The General went today to Gen. Lee's Hd. Qrs. and to Fredericksburg.

Sunday, Dec. 7th. Spent the day in my tent as there was no preaching

near. At night Williamson, Kinney and myself had a long talk on religious subjects. The ground frozen, air chilly.

Monday, Dec. 8th. Rode towards Fredericksburg on a [reconnais-
sance]. Stopped to see Gen. E. F. Paxton, at the Stonewall Brigade camp,
some 4 miles from Guiney's towards Hamilton's Crossing. Got back at
dark and at night read the papers. Ground frozen quite hard and it did
not thaw much, though the day was quite comfortable. Today we paid
40 cts. a LB for bacon. Hd. Qrs. at the same place.

Tuesday, Dec. 9th. Rode over to Gen. R. E. Lee's camp, some $2\frac{1}{2}$
miles from Hamilton's Crossing and near Mr. Garnett's, mapping the
road to that point, then went on to Gen. J. E. B. Stuart's camp and got
from Capt. Wm. W. Blackford,[35] his Engineer, a surveyed map of Caroline Co. made by Capt. Grant.[36] Spent the day ruling lines for this reduction by squares. The General made me a present of the famous "Old
gray cap," worn by him from some time in December, 1861, until two
days before the capture of Harper's Ferry in 1862, having been worn
through all the marches, battles, and camps of that eventful intervening
period. I bought him a new soft hat, in [Martinsburg], Va., as we passed
through there, by his request, at the same time that I bought one of the
same size for myself. When I overtook him and handed him the hat and
he put it on, I asked him if I should take care of his cap in my saddle-
bags, as he was away from his baggage. He replied, "If you please" so
I put it among my baggage and there it remained until today, when I
heard that he had asked for it; so I took it to him and he put it on, re-
marking that it fitted him better than any other cap he had ever had, but
it was no longer fit to wear and he thought of having another one made
like it. I told him if he was going to have it cut up I wanted a button
from it as a souvenir of what it had seen. We then conversed awhile on
other topics. When I rose to depart he said: "I reckon you may have the
cap." I thanked him for it and took it to my tent where S. Howell Brown,
of Jefferson Co., Va., of our Engineering Corps, begged earnestly for one
of the buttons that fastened on the strap, and I gave him one. So much
for the "old cap," of "Old Jack,"[37] Brown accepted a proposal, about some
maps, that I had made to him in the summer. The day has been very
pleasant and the sun shone beautifully. At night I wrote in my journal.
The enemy's gunboats came up to Port Royal but were driven back by
our guns.

Thursday, Dec. 11th. The Yankees opened on Fredericksburg today,
just before dawn, and attempted to throw pontoons across the Rappa-

hannock river there, but were driven back; they made a second attempt and were foiled in that, but they finally succeeded in throwing one across at the mouth of Deep Run, $1\frac{1}{2}$ miles below the town, and effected a crossing of troops. The artillery firing in the morning woke us up; the cannonading was very heavy. The town was set on fire in three places by the cannonading and a woman was killed by one shot. The artillery firing was kept up all day and there was some infantry fighting in and near the town by Barksdale's Brigade. Gen. Barksdale[38] and his Brigade were in the town when it was set on fire by the artillery. He sent to Longstreet and asked if he should put the fire out. The reply was: "You have enough to do to watch the Yankees." At night the enemy crossed over in force. I worked at a map of Caroline Co.: the day was fine.

Friday, Dec. 12th. The General had ordered that all should be up to breakfast at 4 in the morning, and as those that slept in the eating tent were not up in time he ordered the breakfast to be set out of doors. After breakfast he started for Fredericksburg, sending for Brown and myself to come along. We followed, by the Telegraph Road, on to the brow of the hill towards Fredericksburg, where our heavy guns were placed and where we found Gen. R. E. Lee. Gen. Jackson had been there but had gone to the right. We followed and at last found him near Deep Run. Hood's[39] Division was moving into position to the left of Deep Run and A. P. Hill's Division was moving into the woods in which Hood had been and where Hill afterwards fought. Hill's Division had marched that morning from its camp some 2 or 3 miles back, along or near the R. F. & P. R.R.[40] on the road from Hamilton's Crossing; Gen. Hill had his Hd. Qrs. on a high Wooded hill, near John Yerby's. Our line of battle was formed parallel to the Mine road east of and about $\frac{1}{4}$ mile from it, the right resting on the R.R. near Hamilton's Crossing. The day was spent getting the troops into position. The enemy deployed a large force along the valley of the Rappahannock. There was some skirmishing on our left. Gen. Jackson rode all along the line, as also did Gens. Lee and Stuart. Late in the afternoon the General rode down to the river, from Hamilton's Crossing, taking me with him, and examined the country to and near the river bank; we then rode back to our camp, the General whistling as we went along. We found our wagons near A. P. Hill's Hd. Qrs. and encamped just in his rear. Gen. Early started his Division, from where it was encamped near Rappahannock Academy,[41] from below Moss Neck, at about sundown, and marched up to near the R.R., to the ridge beyond Brooke's, via Grace Church. D. H. Hill's Division moved at about the same time, it having been encamped not far from Rappahannock Academy, picketing the river front down to Port Royal. He [bivouacked] near Early. Our Hd. Qrs. are about 2 miles from Hamilton's Crossing near John Ewing's. The morning was cold but as the day advanced it moderated. The smoke and fog were very dense and concealed the army movements on both sides. Jackson's old Division (Gen. Wm. B. Taliaferro commanding) was, in the morning, encamped some 3 miles from Guiney's and a mile from Massaponax Church.

Saturday, Dec. 13th. We were up at an early hour and off to the battle field by daylight; the tents were struck and the wagons loaded up and sent to the rear. All our troops were early in position; A. P. Hill in front, Early on the right, and Taliaferro on the left as supports, and D. H. Hill along the Mine Road in reserve. At about 1 A.M. the enemy advanced and the battle opened with artillery. The Federal infantry advanced at [1:30] P.M. and an incessant firing was kept up until about 2:15, when it slackened some; it was renewed at intervals during the rest of the day. The most of the fighting was on the right of Jackson's line and on the left of Longstreet's. The enemy was repulsed with great loss; our losses were also great. The cannonading was very heavy. About sundown we opened a very heavy artillery fire on the enemy. Gen. Jackson had ordered an advance if the enemy wavered much; but, although the enemy was driven back, a delay occurred, as the orders had not been received in time by all the division commanders, consequently some confusion ensued and the advance was not made. Gen. Jackson had intended to push the enemy to the river. We took a good many prisoners and the enemy took about the same number, but their loss in killed and wounded was greater than ours. We drove the enemy back ¾ of a mile, their repulse being complete. The morning was cool but the sun rose red and firey and soon drove away the fog and the day became quite pleasant; the sky was almost cloudless. After dark we rode back to our wagons at Darnabus' Pond near Curtis' Shop, and there encamped. Found Col. A. R. Boteler there.

Sunday, Dec. 14th. Went to the battle field early this morning expecting a renewal of the fight but everything was quiet save some occasional artillery firing from both sides. The enemy opened on a battery that was being placed in Hood's line at the corner of the woods. In the morning A. P. Hill's Division was relieved from the front line of battle and Taliaferro and Early took his place; D. H. Hill was put in the second line and A. P. Hill in the third in reserve. The enemy held his position on the bottoms of the Rappahannock. Capt. Boswell, of the Engineers, dug pits on our right for sunken batteries. The General went to the front at 5 A.M. Hd. Qrs. last night at Curtis' Shop near Darnabus' Pond; during the day they were at Marye's (Hamilton's) house near Hamilton's Crossing of the R. F. & P. R.R. Last night there was a grand auroral display, one of the finest I have ever seen; the day has been very pleasant.

Monday, Dec. 15th. Hd. Qrs. removed to a place near John Yerby's on the Massaponax. The General was off to the front by 5 A.M. All again expected a battle. Gen. Stuart spent most of the day at the batteries on our right. The enemy remained all day in the same position as before. At 3 P.M. they sent in a flag and asked for a truce to enable them to remove their wounded and bury their dead. The General refused the truce until a communication, in writing, was sent, asking for it; then Gen. W. B. Franklin[42] commanding the Federal left, repeated the request in writing. Gen. Jackson commenced writing a reply, on my letter-pad, but after writing a few lines he changed his mind and granted it verbally, through Lt. J. P. Smith, one of his aides.

Tuesday, Dec. 16th. The enemy recrossed the river last night, took up their pontoons and made good their escape. Towards noon it was reported that the enemy were crossing at Port Royal far down the river to our right. As the 2nd Corps was in position nearest in that direction it was ordered to march to meet the reported movement. We started from Hamilton's Crossing at about 1 P.M., Early's Division in advance followed by Taliaferro's, A. P. Hill's, and D. H. Hill's in the rear, going by Grace Church, the advance getting to near Moss Neck where a messenger from Gen. Stuart, who had preceded up, gave information that there was no enemy at Port Royal, so a halt was called just where the head of our column was in a narrow road hedged in by dense and well-nigh impenetrable pine thickets. The troops had been ordered to go into [bivouac]. The General, who was in front, tried to get back to the rear unobserved by his men. He gave his horse to a courier and attempted to get through the woods and "flank" his line, but could not succeed, and had to come back and remount his horse and ride back along the line of march. The soldiers at once "caught on" to the situation and cheered him, vociferously, as we galloped, in single file through the opening they made for us along the middle of the road. The men were in fine spirits and kept up the cheering for the entire staff and escort that [followed] the General, adding: "Close up"; "You will get lost"; "You will never find him"; etc. After getting through the thicket-enclosed road we turned to the right and rode down, through the more open woods, to a sheltered hollow and went into bivouac where the fallen leaves were abundant. Some one started a fire at the base of a large, hollow, tulip-poplar tree, the ascending sparks of which afforded a subject for conversation to the General and staff. We tried to induce the General to go to a house, as the air was sharp and raw and we had nothing to eat; but he refused and we soon laid down, in a circle around the roaring fire in the tree, with our feet towards the fire. About 10 P.M. our chimney-tree burnt off and fell, with a crash, but fortunately did not hit anyone. By that time we were all well chilled and when we renewed our request to go to a house he yielded and Pendleton and myself rode forward in search of Corbin's place and having found it easily secured an invitation to come to "Moss Neck," the palatial home of Corbin,[43] and Hd. Qrs. were established there late in the night. A fine bracing day but the wind was chilly. The troops went into bivouac near where they were halted.

Wednesday, Dec. 17th. We all slept this morning until quite late, having been well nigh exhausted by the anxieties and demands of the preceding days. About noon our wagons came up and we encamped at the foot of the Moss Neck terrace. A fine warm day following a chilly night.

Thursday, Dec. 18th. We remained at Moss Neck; D. H. Hill's Division went into camp at Grace Church; A. P. Hill's between him and Moss Neck; Taliaferro back of Moss Neck; and Early between Rappahannock Academy and Port Royal, all not far from where they had been encamped before the last battle. I worked on a map of Caroline Co. A fine warm day.

Friday, Dec. 19th. The General rode down the river to opposite Hop Yard; Kinney and Williamson were sent to look for short routes towards Richmond. I worked at Caroline Co. map. A fine warm day.

Saturday, Dec. 20th. Worked all day at map of Caroline; Boswell applied for furlough and Gen. Jackson approved it, he then went to Gen. Lee for his approval but he refused it. Quite cold and windy.

Sunday, Dec. 21st. Rested in camp; got books from the excellent Corbin library and read. Kinney and Williamson returned today. At night had a [long] talk with the General, at his quarters, especially about the war. He lamented the calamities it had brought upon Fredericksburg; said: "War is the greatest of evils." He asked if I thought the troops could endure the cold weather, encamped as they now are and most of them without tents. Said he was much disappointed in the weather here;

it was not as warm as he expected it would be. He spoke of railroad accidents, one having happened today; said they presented the most horrid sights he had ever seen. We talked of the [state] of religion in the North and in the South, and how Providence had blessed us, and how our strength had increased during the continuance of the war and up to this time. A pleasant but cool day.

Monday, Dec. 22nd. Our troops commenced throwing up entrenchments from the mouth of Massaponax Creek down to Port Royal. I worked on Caroline Co. map. A fine pleasant day.

Tuesday, Dec. 23rd. I got permission from the General to go home on business from the Engineer Corps, and Boswell granted me 8 days leave of absence, so I packed up and went down to Guinea's Depot; reached there at noon; Maj. J. A. Harman came down also. Saw Maj. W. J. Hawks. Heard that Gen. Jones[44] had fallen back to Mt. Jackson. Learned that Capt. A. S. Pendleton has been promoted to Major and A. A. G.[45] We went on cars to Hanover Junction; read the papers, President Davis' proclamation about Ben. Butler,[46] etc. We got oysters at $5.00 a gallon. At Hanover Junction took Accommodation train of Va. Central and went to Gordonsville. A very pleasant and warm day. Gen. Lee was at Hd. Qrs., at Moss Neck, today. A train of army supplies came up from Richmond and went to Culpeper; strange! We stay at Gordonsville with Quarter Master Norris.

Wednesday, Dec. 24th. Slept until late. It looks like rain or snow. I made some purchases in Gordonsville; took first train for Staunton, reaching there at 5:30 P.M. Got a horse from Q.M. H. M. Bell and went on home; found all well and much pleased to see me. Heard that Milroy was at Strasburg. The day has been very warm; find it much cooler in the Valley than at Moss Neck . . .

Thursday, Dec. 25th. A warm and pleasant Christmas day. Brother Nelson H. Hotchkiss and myself went to Staunton, also Mr. Booth. Made some arrangements about servants for next year. The Confederate States have called for five per cent. of the slaves to work on the fortifications at Richmond; this has caused quite a stir among owners. Dined at Nat. P. Catlett's. There is much talk about the late Fredericksburg battle. Paid hire for servant boy Allen, for 1862 $35.00. Gave note for servant hire for 1863 $50.00

Friday, Dec. 26th. Went to Staunton in carriage with Mr. Booth; was very busy trying to get my matters fixed up so I can return to Hd. Qrs. No news; Mr Bear[47] called to see me. Pleasant day but threatening a storm. At night wrote to Mrs. Doctor Butcher. Paid for articles as follows: 20 lbs of candles, at $1 a lb, $20.00; 1½ doz. military coat buttons, large 12.00; . . . Pair of boots for Boswell $40.00 . . . Gold Lace .38 . . . my note to D. A. Kayser 32.57 . . Books for my children 1.35 . . . "Spectator" subscription to Sept. 1863 5.00 . . .

Saturday, Dec. 27th. Went to Staunton with Capt. F. F. Sterrett;[48] saw about a stove, servants, etc. Heard the Yankees had left the Valley and that Gen. Jones had gone back to Winchester. Dr. R. S. Hamilton and Mr. Booth dined with me at home. At night went up for awhile and heard one of the plays of the Soldiers' Aid Society.[49] Very pleasant day; storm threatening . . .

Sunday, Dec. 28. Took my family to Union Church, Where we had communion. The sermon, by Rev. Robt. C. Walker, was on "The substitution of Christ for man." A large attendance. The day was a fine one. Gave Collection $2.00

Monday, Dec. 29th. Packed up and came to Staunton. Rev. R. C. Walker came over to see me in the morning. Dined at Dr. Young's and [spent] the night at his house. A fine warm day. . . .

Tuesday, Dec. 30th. Got up at an early hour and went to depot and got my baggage on train. Saw Maj. J. A. Harman. We started at 7½ A.M. The morning was cool. Heard at Gordonsville of Stuart's move on the enemy, capture of prisoners, etc. It rained in P.M. Left train at Hanover Junction and spent the night there with Major Geo. W. T. Kearsley, the local commissary, with whom I had a long talk at night. The cars were completely filled with passengers. Paid fare to Hanover Junction $5.50; newsboy for newspaper 25 cts.

Wednesday, Dec 31st. In morning went on to Guiney's, by early train, and breakfasted with Maj. W. J. Hawks, our Chief Commissary. Boswell came over from camp and got his new suit. I did not get all my baggage on at Hanover Junction, so went back for it and spent the night with Major Kearsley. The day had been chilly; it threatens a snow storm.

"Surely the Lord is on our side"

THURSDAY, JAN. 1ST, 1863. I spent the night at Hanover Junction at Maj. Kearsley's, having come back yesterday from Guinea's to get my baggage. Maj. Johnson[1] of the Q.M. Dept. was there and we had a pleasant evening. Came up to Guinea's at 8 A.M., the cars crowded full of soldiers returning to the army and of servants coming and going to hiring and homes. The train reached Guinea's at $9\frac{1}{2}$ A.M., where I waited a while until the wagon came, then loaded up my boxes and came up to camp, 8 [miles], at Moss Neck, at Corbins; Found Gen. in the house, (one of the offices on the lawn) all the rest in tents near where I left them. Boswell had fixed up the tent. Col. Lee came up with me, to begin his duties as Judge of the Corps. The day has been warm and fine—delightful.

Friday, Jan 2nd. Spent the day in my tent, working on map of Caroline Co. In the evening we got the news of Bragg's victory at Murfreesboro,[2] as Gen. Jackson said, "Very gratifying intelligence." Allen and I took a walk late in the evening, we talked about maps of battles, etc., and discussed what added to the charm of reading history. We had a "read" of the Life of Lorenso de Medici at night and I wrote a while; wrote to

105

my wife. Called on the Gen.; found C. J. Faulkner there. A fine day,—
cool. Troops drilling.

Saturday, Jan. 3rd. There was a heavy [rain] this morning but the
day mellowed and has been very fine. Boswell and Williamson were out
superintending the erection of fortifications along the crest of the hills
above here on the river; the Gen. was up to see them yesterday and decided in favor of Boswell's line rather than Gen. D. H. Hill's, which is too
near the river. Allen spent part of the day at my tent and read for me
the life of L. de Medici. In the evening took the Gen. some apples and
chestnuts and then read him the news,—the confirmation of the victory
at Murfreesboro. All are much rejoiced at it. A donation of over $700 was
sent in, by a Ga. Regt., for the Fredericksburg sufferers, and all parts of
the army are giving liberally to the despoiled people; the Gen. gave 100.
I worked at the map of Caroline Co. Made a map of the Battle Field for
my friend Buck of Front Royal, at night.

Sunday, Jan. 4th. This has been a very pleasant, warm day, with a
sprinkle late in the P.M. I went up to Grace Church, in company with
Allen, etc.; the Gen. Had preceded us. We found the church full, too
full to enter, so, after a little chat with Mr. C. Estill, I came back and
read essays, etc. Boswell and Williamson went down to Guinea's. In the
evening Col. Lee was in my tent awhile and Allen and I took a long read
of Roscoe's Life of L. de Medici. Everything is quiet; there is a rumor
that the enemy is moving away.

Monday, Jan. 5th. A fine pleasant day; quiet, the troops fortifying
along the crest of hills. No picket firing; everything more like peace
than war; only the drilling of the men looks warlike. Heard that Gen.
Lee had ordered Imboden, Jones and Davidson³ to unite in an attack on
Winchester. Read with Allen and finished the Life of Lorenso de Medici.

Tuesday, Jan. 6th. Worked at map of Caroline Co. At 11 A.M. went
out with Boswell to witness a grand Review of Gen. A. P. Hill's Division
of the 2nd (Jackson's) Corps of the Army of Northern Va. There were
over 10,000, I suppose, on the field, a meadow, or bottom, of the Hayfield
estate. The pageant was a splendid one, though marred by the cold rain
that fell slowly most of the time. The Brigades of Lane, Archer, Pender,
Field, Gregg and Thomas⁴ were on the field and passed in review. I
called on the Gen. in the evening and got my pay acct. fixed; chatted
some about the condition of the troops, etc.

Wednesday, Jan. 7th. Worked at map of Battle of Kernstown most
of the day. It has been quite cold but clear; some flurries of snow fell

last night. Maj. Harman came back and I got two letters from home, one written on the anniversary of my marriage, Dec. 21st, the other since I was home. There is nothing going on but drilling and fortifying. The enemy at Winchester is carrying a high hand, making people take the oath, etc. . . . Lincoln's Proclamation,[5] proclaiming freedom to the slaves, excites no attention, hardly affords a subject for conversation in the army. All are disappointed, but hopeful, about the West. I drew my pay for Nov. and Dec., 1862, today and gave $15. to the Fredericksburg fund, for the relief of the sufferers by the enemy, etc. Our Hd. Qrs. have raised some $800., and A. P. Hill's Div. some $10,000.00.

Thursday, Jan 8th. Worked at map of Battle of Kernstown all day. It was quite cold. Allen came over and we read at night.

Friday, Jan. 9th. Re'cd. an order, in the morning, for a map of the Battle field of Fredericksburg to write the report of the battle by, and as I had not the requisite information I rode up to Gen. Stuart's Hd. Qrs. to see Capt. Blackford, his Eng. who had surveyed the field, and get a copy of his map. Went up the "River Road" for the first time and saw our preparations for defence along it. Passed by the battle field; many of our troops are still encamped near there and have cut much timber away from it. Found Blackford gone, concluded to come back, but met Gen. Stuart who would have me go back, almost carrying me by clasping his arm round my waist and whistling to my horse. So I went back and waited. Read the papers, chatted with Gen. S. and staff, and when Blackford came had quite a pleasant visit and we turned into his bunk for the night, in our overcoats for night gowns for lack of blankets. Maj. Fitzhugh[6] related to me the circumstances of his capture, in August, on the plank road, and his presence near the Yankees during the fight at Rappahannock Bridge,—the charge of Maj. Von Borcke[7] as seen by the enemy, etc. A fine day, cool.

Saturday, Jan. 10th. I waited until 3 P.M., to get a copy of the map, before starting back, amusing myself talking and reading. Gen. R. E. Lee reviewed F. H. Lee's Brigade of Cavalry, at 11 A.M., in a heavy rain, which began by a mist at 10½. The cavalry came up from towards Guinea's, and were anxious, for the review, so Gen. Lee went on with it. When the papers came we heard [about] Gen. Magruder's[8] capture of the "Harriet Lane" war steamer and others, at Galveston, and the news gave lively satisfaction. Stuart said Magruder was evidently guilty of a rape of (the) Harriet Lane. I started back at 3 P.M. but had not gone far before Gen. Stuart sent after me to come back and help fix some memo-

randa of the battle of Groveton for Gen. Jackson, as Maj. Pelham and
Col. Rosser were there then,—so I waited and took down the mem. as
he dictated it, and then started back at four, but at a short distance met
Jam. Fitzhugh, thrown from his horse by a slip, so I stopped and helped
him and then went back a ways with him to see him safely on, when I
turned towards camp once more, which I reached at 8 P.M., quite wet,
as it rained hard all day. It slacked down some at sundown. I wrote
some, copying the memoranda I had taken for Gen. Jackson, before
going to bed. Quite cold.

Sunday, Jan. 11th. Spent the day in camp, reading Bible, Tillotson's
Sermons, etc. Col. Wm. Harman and Davis Ball came in P.M. I took
dinner at Maj. Harman's with them. In the evening went up to Gen. J.'s
room and sat awhile and then to Col. Faulkner's, after which I came back
and wrote home. A pleasant day; one or two sprinkles, but the sun shone
some.

Monday, Jan. 12th. Made a map of the Fredericksburg Battle Field
for Col. Faulkner to write his report by; worked some at map of Kernstown. We moved our tent towards night and fixed up. I wrote to Dr.
Young about servant. We heard of the successful defence of Vicksburg
again. Kinney and Willamson moved too.

Tuesday, Jan. 13th. Worked at map of Kernstown Battle Field; a fine
day. Called on Col. Faulkner at night and saw Gen. Taliaferro there and
talked about the battle of McDowell.

Wednesday, Jan. 14th. Boswell beset me last night to go and see
Gen. J. E. B. Stuart and get him to send him up to Fauquier Co., for
some purpose, as he was dying to see his sweetheart; so I went up and
got Gen. S. to ask Gen. Jackson for him for a few days. Had a nice visit
with Gen. S. Sent off Booth and Worster's letters to the North; came
back and stopped at Gen. Lee's and saw Maj. Talcott[9] and got some maps
of Stafford and King George [counties]. Saw Gen. Longstreet and got
his position at Groveton and rode down to Hamilton's Crossing with him,
where he has his wife, and we had a nice talk. Got back to camp late,
but wrote until 12 mid't. Heard from my wife and N. H. Boswell went
up and saw the Gen. and got off. Air damp but not cold; wind high.

Thursday, Jan 15th. Worked at map of Kernstown. Boswell went off
early. The Gen. rode up to see the fortifications. I wrote up my journal
at night. Maj. Bier,[10] our Chief of [Ordnance], got orders to report to the
Sec. of the Navy and goes tomorrow. Read the President's able message.
A spring day, warm and high S.W. wind; threatened rain, but now clear.

Friday, Jan. 16th. Recd. orders from the Gen. to get a map of the whole front line of our works and to show the disposition of our pickets, etc.; so I went up to A. P. Hill: found he had gone to Richmond, by order of the Sec. of War, and Gen. Rodes[11] commanded, so saw him and then found Williamson and went along the whole of Hill's line and sketched it and got home at dark. The day was quite cool and windy. The army has rec'd. orders to cook three days rations. The enemy has made some demonstration on our front and has been making a road down to the river. It is rumored that a part of Longstreet's force is moving. The Gen. went to the front today.

Saturday, Jan. 17th. Worked at map of our front line, made a tracing, for Capt. Blackford, of Gen. Stuart's staff, Engineer, who came down to attend to some of Boswell's work while he is gone. Capt. B. took supper with me. I worked until quite late at a map of the battle field of Mc-Dowell and became very weary before retiring. The day has been quite cold and windy. Called on the Gen., Col. Faulkner and Maj. Harman in the evening. I have a bad cold.

Sunday, Jan. 18th. I spent most of the day in the house, at Mr. Corbin's, as I felt very badly from the effects of my cold—Read some and listened to some reading by Allen. A chilly day.

Monday, Jan. 19th. Col. Faulkner, our Chief of Staff, came by at an early hour for me to go up to the battle field with him; so we rode up and went over the position occupied by Gen. Jackson's Corps and that occupied by the enemy in his front. We also went to Fredericksburg and saw the great destruction made by the enemy and some of our troops during the fighting thro. its streets, and especially by the sacking of the town by the enemy;—hardly a house escaped getting a shot of some kind through it, and the sacking was general. We saw safes, everywhere, broken into and windows smashed, etc. We rode down to the river and looked at the enemy's works on the opposite hills and also at his pickets all along the shore. We saw two unburied Yankees lying near the R.R. crossing of Deep Run,—two mere boys in appearance. We had a very interesting day and Col. Faulkner expressed himself much gratified at the information he had gained, etc. The day was very fine;—clear and bright sunshine and agreeably cool until late in the P.M. when a cold wind sprung up. I came home and soon Capt. Blackford came and we called on the Gen. and then on Mr. Corbin's family. Capt. B. Spends the night with me;—our men are busy fortifying the hills across Moss Neck.

Tuesday, Jan. 20th. Worked at maps until 11 A.M. and then went to see a Cavalry Brigade, Brig. Gen. W. H. F. Lee's, reviewed by Gen. R. E. Lee. It was very fine and a large number of officers, ladies, etc., witnessed it; it was near our Hd. Qrs. After the review I made a sketch of the river for Gen. Early's Engineer, Lt. Richardson,[12] whom I had not seen for a long time, as he has been absent from his wound received at the battle of Sharpsburg. I heard from Nelson today and he sent me one of the advertisements of the sale of our farm,—which we propose to sell on the 10th of Feb. The enemy seems to have more force in front of us. Some of our troops have gone away to N.C. The day has been very chilly, a biting wind blowing from the N.E., the sky overcast; at 7 P.M. it began to rain, quite hard, and has kept it up to this time, midnight, quite steadily. I have been working at the map of the battle field of "Mannassas No. 2," or "Groveton Heights," tonight.

Wednesday, Jan. 21st. It has rained, with slight intervals, all day, and is still at it, very hard now, midnight; the streams are coming up rapidly; and the water is standing over the country. I have been engaged on map of position. Wrote to wife and brother,—wrote at night;—a cold rain.

Thursday, Jan. 22nd. Worked at map of front during the day and map of Battle of McDowell at night. Gen. Lee sent word that the enemy was moving pontoons, etc., down to Seddon's in front of us. It rained all day, but not very hard; the mud is now quite deep. My servant came in the evening.

Friday, Jan. 23rd. Worked at map of position, took it to the Gen. and we discussed the points of defence. In the evening I rode over and saw Gen. Taliaferro and he told me he intended to ask for a transfer, as Maj. Gen. Trimble is to be put in command of the Division over him, having been made Maj. Gen. and he passed by. The news from the W. is cheering, one of our war vessels has sunk a Federal gunboat. The enemy still makes demonstrations in front. It has been foggy and misty today but the sun set clear. It is muddy. Snow fell in the Valley 18 inches deep this storm.

Saturday, Jan. 24th. We packed up and moved our tents to the top of the hill; to a drier place and one more easy to pull out from if we have to move. At 10 A.M. Gen. Taliaferro came by and he and Williamson and myself spent the day on horseback examining his line of defence and the points between him and Gen. A. P. Hill that need defending. We had a long ride going to and fro,—but were quite interested in the defences, etc. Saw the enemy's pickets and one of them asked me how I liked the looks of the bank where he was and told me they were going to make a road with a pile of poles near him. I got a copy of the N.Y. Herald— which says N.Y. must speak for peace and a peaceable separation—it had in Wendell Phillips' answer to Lincoln's proclamation, in which he says that Jackson is an honest fanatic on the side of slavery.[13] We called on the Gen. in the evening and reported. I read to him the paper. A fine warm day.

Sunday, Jan. 25th. Spent the day in camp reading, etc. There was preaching in many of the camps; the day was warm and the sun shone brightly, but there was some little rain at night. I wrote home to my wife and to Nelly.

Monday, Jan. 26th. Williamson and I went down to Port Royal and examined Gen. Early's lines. Gen. E. accompanied us. His defences extend below Port Royal and we have some torpedoes in the river there also. His defences, he says, are to be held to the last if the enemy attempts to come over. We had a long talk about the Battles of Cedar Run and Fredericksburg. Gen. Early marched his four brigades from Moss Neck to Brooke's Hill the day before the battle of Fredericksburg. We did not get home until late; a fine day but changeable; got a letter from home; they are all unwell,—influenza. The papers bring us Burnside's address to his army and the news of his movement to cross, last week, which the rain frustrated. He intended to cross 6 miles above Falmouth, at Banks' Ford, and try to turn our left flank. Surely the Lord is on our side. I called on Col. F. and read the reports of the Battle of McDowell and wrote down the positions, etc.

Tuesday, Jan. 27th. Worked at maps all day. It was quite cold, very chilly, changeable, occasional rain, or misty showers, and just before dark it began to rain hard and rained all night. Dr. Cozzens came and I heard from home by him; he is at my tent tonight.

Wednesday, Jan. 28th. It has snowed steadily all day, and been very unpleasant—and the ground is covered. It rained or the snow melted through my tent and compelled me to stop work. I read the papers at night at Col. Faulkner's. We hear sounds tonight somewhat like artillery. Dr. C. started to go to Stuart, but came back, saying the roads were too bad. Took map of the fortifications to the Gen. and he examined it and said: "Good, very good." The Gen. finished the report of the Battle of Fredericksburg, today. I wrote at night and shall write to my brother by Dr. Cozzens.

Thursday, Jan. 29th. Worked at map of the vicinity of Richmond for Col. Faulkner to write the battle reports from. It has been a pleasant sunshiny day,—but cool,—the snow being about a foot deep. It broke down many trees last night and some horses were killed. It is freezing up tonight. I sent Dr. Cozzens down to the depot to go back home; he is too much of a child for me. The papers say the enemy "stuck in the mud" when they attempted to come over the 20th inst. The mud is deep.[14] I read last night until 3 A.M. of today, finishing Bulwer's "Strange Story," a really strange book, but one conveying such knowledge and showing a deep insight into many things.

Friday, Jan. 30th. Worked at map of Richmond and vicinity, all day, then at map of Groveton at night. The day was very pleasant. Boswell came home from Fauquier and reports no enemy there and deserters constantly coming from the Fed. army. He witnessed a tragic scene at the house where he went to see his sweetheart.

Saturday, Jan. 31st. Worked at map of Richmond, etc. Made a tracing of our part of the Fredericksburg fight for Boswell to make his report by. Called on Col. F. at night, then wrote awhile. Recd. a letter from Harrison asking for maps, etc., of our battles,—which I must refuse, as I intend to write myself.[15] The day has been very pleasant, thawed some but the snow is still deep. It appears that Burnside, the Fed. Commander here, was relieved from command the 26th and Jo. Hooker[16] put in his place. Sumner and Franklin have also been recalled. Success to the derangement such changes must produce.

Sunday, Feb. 1st. Spent the day in camp, reading, etc. It was quite pleasant until late in the P.M. when it rained some; more mist than rain. The roads are very deep and bad. Robt. Fisher called on me in the P.M. The snow melted rapidly.

Monday, Feb. 2nd. Worked at map of the vicinity of Richmond very closely. Boswell went to Guinea's. I read the papers at Col. Faulkner's. We have broken the blockade of Charleston for the time and captured a gunboat. The enemy seems to be moving in all directions, but we, as yet, steadily repulse them. Fine day.

Tuesday, Feb. 3rd. Worked at map of the vicinity of Richmond. It was quite clear and cold and the ground froze up solid. I called on the Gen. in the evening for leave of absence, etc. He granted it. Boswell was away all day and tonight. Worked at night on the battle of Kernstown.

Wednesday, Feb. 4th. Completed my map of the vicinity of Richmond and took it to Col. Faulkner; got my leave of absence back from

Gen. Lee and am ready to start. Boswell came back at night. I finished my sketch of the battle of Kernstown. Conversed awhile with the Gen. and was an hour or so at McGuire's. A cold day.

Thursday, Feb. 5th. I went down to Guinea's Station to go home, but my box did not get there in time, so I spent the night with Maj. Hawks. It commenced snowing at an early hour and snowed hard until noon, then it turned in and rained, and also rained hard during the night. Large numbers of soldiers go home now, daily, on the cars, on furlough. The roads are very bad and there is no prospect of a movement.

Friday, Feb. 6th. I got off at 1 P.M. for the Junction and then started from there to Gordonsville, but our engine broke down and we had to stay at Beaver Dam and await the coming of another. I got a copy of Tucker's Partizan Leader and read it through. Quite a wonder when considered in the light of passing events. But the truth, as always, is stranger than the fiction, and Virginia instead of being the last is the foremost, and the fabulous prices affect everything that is bought as well as everything that is sold. I saw a gentleman, in the morning, Mr. Bell, just from the North. He says the people there are divided, disgusted, disheartened, and utterly sick of the war.—Mad at England because she will not interfere. He thinks the war must end in the spring. Says the North has no faith in Jo. Hooker and the question is "Where have we been whipped today?" I was quite amused to hear the opinions of soldiers about the generals, the battles, etc. Of course the chief topic of conversation is the war and everything connected with it, as that is everybody's business now. One of Longstreet's men said he would rather serve under Jackson than anyone else because he was so careful of his men and was to skillful to avail himself of advantages, while Longstreet only threw his men where the hottest fire and the hardest fighting was. Jackson's men liked him because he would stop and tell any soldier where his Regiment was, and spoke of Jackson's helping to fix the road from Swift Run Gap to Port Republic and how much it encouraged the men, when worn down. An officer of Pickett's Division,[17] of Longstreet's Corps, said they were very sorry that Burnside did not cross at Banks' Ford the 20th ult., or when B. proposed to cross the river last, for we were well prepared for them there and would have opened on them with infantry and artillery where they did not look for it,—and we would have trapped them, surely. It rained some in the morning, then cleared off quite cold and froze during the night. As we came on towards Gordonsville, found the ground covered with snow.

Saturday, Feb. 7th. Got a few hours sleep at Gordonsville and a good breakfast, then started at 12 for home. There was a rumor that the enemy was coming up to the Rappahannock via Orange Road, —but I hardly think they will come far. Had quite a visit with Mr. Phillips, who was on the cars. Got to Staunton in good time and got a horse and reached home by 8 P.M. Found all well. Quite a fine day.

Sunday, Feb. 8th. Spent the day at home, talked with my brother, read, etc. The day was very pleasant.

Monday, Feb. 9th. I rode 'round and made some settlements, and made quite a visit at Mr. C, and Mr. H. Bear's. A fine day.

Tuesday, Feb. 10th. We put up our farm for sale and got a very good bid but were not satisfied at the offer, so we put off the sale to the 28th of Feb. C. Kinner and S. M. Yost dined with me. The day has been very pleasant,—quite warm.

Wednesday, Feb. 11th. Went to Staunton with brother,—settled some accounts, made purchases. The mud was deep and it misted and rained most of the day. Quite cool in P.M.

Thursday, Feb. 12th. Rode about settling, then called and dined with the Farmer's Club[18] at E. Geeding's. A warm or pleasant day;—showers in the P.M., very muddy. Quite busy at my accounts.

Friday, Feb. 13th. Spent the day at home, fixing fence, etc., to make my wife comfortable. H. Bear and wife spent the evening at my house. A fine warm day;—snow nearly gone and the farmers are plowing.

Saturday, Feb. 14th. Spent the day settling with various persons; attended a meeting in the P.M. for the purpose of sending an agent South to buy cotton. We had quite a lively discussion, but finally we sent two agents, Palmer and Hanger. The day was quite pleasant, but has a chilliness in it. I wrote accts. to a late hour, and paid a visit to my niece Allie.

Sunday, Feb. 15. Spent the day at home, as I felt badly;—went up awhile to Nelson's and we dined there. Parted with my children at bedtime, as I go early and they felt very badly. Chilly day.

Monday, Feb. 16th. Started for Staunton at 3½ A.M. but only got there just as the train was going, got on myself, but my baggage missed; so I went on to Waynesboro and then came back to Staunton and spent the day there, doing business, etc. Dined with Maj. Ball and shall spend the night with Capt. Lilley. Heard that Gen. Jones goes down the Valley, to attack Milroy, in a few days. A fine day.

Tuesday, Feb. 17th. We started on the cars at 7½ A.M. and went on very well until we were detained there several hours, then we came to near Anderson's and found the freight train off the track and spent the night there, unable to get by. It commenced snowing before day and continued, with some rain, all day;—very muddy and quite cool. Hood's and Pickett's Divisions of Longstreet's Corps are moving towards Richmond. We were much amused by a witty fellow, Jacob Abel, who related many amusing anecdotes, etc.

Wednesday, Feb. 18th. We exchanged cars and got on the train that came up from Richmond, at 10 A.M., and were backed to the Junction; there Capt. Lilley and I spent the rest of the day and the night until midnight, and then went up, in a freight train, to Guiney's. The mud is very deep and it rained nearly all day, some of the time very hard, The water is standing over much of the surface;—saw a portion of Hood's Division at the Junction, on the way to Richmond, and a train of Artillery went down on the R.R. Not very cold.

Thursday, Feb. 19th. Slept from 3 A.M. until morning at Maj. Hawk's; my horse came down and I rode up to camp, through the deep mud. Found our Corps in the same place. Had quite a visit with Col. Faulkner and the Gen. at night. Conversed on various topics, war and peace, battles and marches. It is mild today. Misted some. The enemy has been leaving opposite to us.

Friday, Feb. 20th. A fine day, wind and sun dried up the ground rapidly. I worked at map of the country near Winchester, making report of battles there; the Gen. asked for a map to write his report by and to accompany it. Col. Faulkner read me the report of the battle of McDowell, and I made some suggestions in reference to it. Three of the "Stonewall Brigade" were, today, "whipped for desertion."

Saturday, Feb. 21st. Worked at map of country around Winchester. At night I made off some memoranda for my brother and was up to a late hour. Boswell is not well. Capt. Wilbourn, of the Signal Corps, came back today; he was wounded at [Manassas.] The Divisions of Hood and Pickett have gone below Richmond and it is said that Longstreet has gone too. Col. Faulkner related to me an incident showing the strong good sense of Gen. Jackson. When the Military Court was organized here and had decided several cases, the papers relating to the cases were signed by Gen. Jackson and sent to Gen. Cooper,[19] the A. Gen. at Richmond. He wrote, very politely, to Gen. Jackson, that the papers did not show that the Court had taken the oath prescribed for Courts Martial in the Articles of War, and so he sent them back and hoped Gen. J. would have the Court conform to the law, and also sent instructions to the

Court. Gen. J. replied that it was not an omission but was in conformity with the law establishing the Courts;—and in that they differed from ordinary Courts Martial, and asking to have the matter decided by the Attorney Gen. The Court acted under the instructions of Gen. Cooper, until a few days ago it was notified that the Atty. Gen. had decided as Gen. J. had,—showing the care with which he examined everything relating to his duty as a Commander. I wrote to my brother at night. Sent to the depot for my box. Signs of a storm at night.

Sunday, Feb. 22nd. The enemy fired a salute in honor of Washington this morning, while polluting the soil of his native country by their presence. It commenced snowing in the night and has blown and snowed all day, drifting, and the snow is some 15 inches deep. I spent the day in my tent, reading, etc. It is not very cold. Called on the Gen. a few moments in the evening. He spoke of Dr. Hoge's mission to Europe to procure Bibles, and was sure he could succeed well.[20] Boswell was quite sick all day.

Monday, Feb. 23rd. It cleared off last night; the snow is quite deep in places, averaging one foot. The cars did not get up to Guinea's today. I got secret orders from the General to prepare a map of the Valley of Va. extended to Harrisburg, Pa., and then on to Philadelphia;—wishing the preparation to be kept a profound secret. So I went to reducing a map of Cumberland Co., Pa. The day was quite pleasant. Boswell was sick and in bed most of the day.

Tuesday, Feb. 24th. Worked busily at my map. Boswell went to Port Royal. A fine day, but cool. We are packing our supplies and the men are put on 1/5 of a lb of bacon a day. I recd. a letter from home. At night worked at map of the vicinity of Port Republic.

Wednesday, Feb. 25th. A winter frost last night;—cool in the morning. Worked at map of Cumberland Co., Pa. A very fine day;—snow melting.

Thursday, Feb. 26th. It began to rain last night and rained nearly all of today quite hard, melting the snow and settling the ground. The news of the passage of a conscription bill and a bill to make the banks of the U.S. take Fed. Bonds and thus men and money will be put into Lincoln's hands,[21] causes a feeling of sadness that the war is to be indefinitely prolonged, and we must go through its horrors another year, though no one desponds. Worked at map of Cumb. Co., Pa.

Friday, Feb. 27th. The snow was completely eaten up on the warm wind of last night and today, and is nowhere to be seen but in very sheltered nooks;—quite warm and pleasant and it has dried up amazingly. The enemy had a balloon up, opposite to us, today.[22] Gen. W. H. F. Lee brought in 200 Yankee cavalry he captured in Stafford Co. I heard from Nelson today;—he has bought near Howardsville. Worked at map of Cumb. Co., Pa. Wrote at night. Col. Faulkner read me a portion of the Report of the battle of Winchester which he is now preparing. Brig. Gen. Jones has had charges preferred against him for cowardice. Gen. sent for dates of marches today.

Saturday, Feb. 28th. Worked at map of Cumberland, Pa., during the day, and on map of Cedar Run Battle Field at night. A fine day, though cool. It rained at night. A deserter from the Ist. Brigade was shot today and one escaped yesterday. The Gen. rec'd. a box of presents from London, Eng.;—shirts, gloves, etc. Boswell came back in the P.M. The cavalry in the Valley has captured some 200 Yankee cavalry. It is said that Hood's and Pickett's Divisions suffered much in their late march to Richmond.

Sunday, March, 1st. Read part of the day, sauntered around part of it to enjoy the glorious sunshine and still breeze that continued all day— dined at the General's tent and after dinner took a ride with Col. Faulkner and Dr. McGuire down to the river;—the horses felt finely and we had a splendid gallop,—enjoying its exhilarating effect much. It rained nearly all night, but cleared off about 8 A.M. today and was clear and pleasant, the wind was up and the roads were much dried by it. Rev. Mr. Lacy[23] came to our Hd. Qrs. today to remain awhile;—wrote to my wife at night. The bridge of the R.R. over the Mattapony River was washed away yesterday, so we had no cars today. Heard that a Gunboat had come up into the river again.

Monday, March 2nd. Worked at map of Cumberland Co. The day was quite pleasant, but it rained at night.

Tuesday, March 3rd. A fine day and drying up. Am still at the same duty.

Wednesday, March 4th. As I had nearly finished the map of Cumberland Co. I wanted some more to add to it, I therefore went up to Gen. Lee's to obtain others, or rather to Gen. Stuart's, Capt. Blackford having them. I got the maps I wanted and then had a pleasant visit with Gen. S. We talked of the battles of Groveton Heights, etc. He said Gen. Jackson was entitled to all the credit for the movement round the enemy and Gen. Lee had, very reluctantly, consented to it. He spoke of the great results it had. He also said Gen. Jackson was ordered to follow Longstreet over the Mt. in Nov. and after Gen. Lee had gone Gen. J. requested to be allowed to stay and move along up the Valley and then cross, thus deceiving McClellan and thwarting his plans. Gen. S. hoped Gen. Lee would do justice to Gen. J.'s movements, etc. Had quite a nice visit and came back before night. Quite cool in A.M.; wind high, froze some.

Thursday, March 5th. Maj. Pendleton came down in the morning and informed Brown and myself that he had been ordered to conscript us, by a late order of Gen. Lee's, and desired us to select our company. I protested against being enrolled and went to see Gen. Jackson and drew up a paper and submitted to him which I am to take to Gen. Lee to-morrow for his remarks. Gen. J. said it was an unpleasant duty imposed on him by the laws, or orders issued, and he was sorry I had not been appointed engineer to obviate any such necessity. Gen. Lee's order was that all men in the army, not on any roll, sh'd. be enrolled at once, and Gen. Early, so Gen. Jackson told me, had enrolled nearly all his staff, as they had not been commissioned, and had made them join companies. So I am again at sea in reference to my position until I see Gen. Lee again. Gen. J. said the country was nearly ruined by political demagogues, —when speaking of my failure to be appointed. I did no work to be mentioned,—being too much disturbed.[24] Got a letter from my wife, one from my brother;—both despondent. Alas, alas, what am I coming to. But there is a just God and He always sustained me and brought good out of evil, and glory be to Him. I trust in his Holy Name. The day has been chilly, but pleasant. Boswell went down to Richmond, today,—for 3 days. The Yanks had their balloon up today, again. Maj. Harman was very kind today.

Friday, March 6th. I wrote out my statement and asked my questions, and Gen. J. made his remarks, and then I took the papers up to Gen. Lee. He was busy, so I chatted awhile with his staff and then went on to Gen. Stuart's and spent the rest of the day with him. Had a nice time and we chatted on all sorts of subjects. He says Gen. Lee came to us at Gordonsville with rather a low estimate of Jackson's ability;—but now he often wishes that he had many Jacksons. Says Gen. Lee asked him if he did not think it was very hazardous for Gen. Jackson to attempt to go around the enemy when we crossed the Rappahannock in August. I questioned one of his scouts and made a map of a portion of Fauquier Co. He told a good story on Maj. Von Borcke's first interview with Gen. Jackson. Von B. said when J. spoke to him "It did make his heart to burn." Slept in Capt. White's tent. It rained in the night;—was quite cool and damp.

Saturday, March 7th. I made a map, for Gen. S., then came down and saw Gen. Lee; got his decision that I was not liable to duty, as I was already on duty. Conversed some about maps, etc.; then I came by Gen. Early's and he told me about his position at Cedar Run Right. Says he had 1,200 men there. Came back and saw the Gen. who said he was gratified at my success;—then asked me to make a map of the battle of McDowell to go with his report. I worked at that until midnight; got his Report to make it by. The day has been chilly—it rained very hard, with thunder and lightning at night.

Sunday, March 8th. Went over to church at the chapel of the Stonewall Brigade;—the Rev. Dr. Hoge preached us an eloquent sermon on the death of Stephen;—he was listened to with great attention;—his language was very fine. The Old Brigade is a noble set of men; they lost 1,890 men in 1862, in battle alone. Dr. McGuire buried his servant today and he is very sad, mourns for him as for a brother. We had a long talk at night on various topics. I wrote home and read until late, then went to bed but was restless;—so I got up, at 1 o'clk. of the morning, and went to work on the map of the battle field. It rained;—a thunder storm at night.

Monday, March 9th. Finished my map and took it to the Gen.;—he expressed himself satisfied with it and sent it on to Gen. Lee. I took a ride to Hamilton's Crossing and back. It was quite pleasant; frogs and birds singing,—turtles crawling out in the sun. Boswell came home. Wrote in my journal at night.

Tuesday, March 10th. Worked very hard all day and until quite late at night. Finished the map of Cumberland Co., Pa., and copied the Counties of Spotsylvania and Caroline for Gen. R. E. Lee;—also worked awhile at a map of the battle field of Manassas No. 2. It snowed in the morning, cleared off,—snowed again, then rained and now it is raining again. Col. Lee came and looked at the map of the battle of Kernstown and we had quite a talk about it.

Wednesday, March 11th. Worked at map of "The Route of the Army of the Valley from Franklin, Pendleton Co., Va., to the Battle of Winchester, May 25th, 1862" to accompany the Report of the battle. There was a heavy cannonading, in the A.M., somewhere towards the Potomac. The day was quite cool.

Thursday, March 12th. Finished the "Route Map" and took it to the Gen. who was much pleased with it and pronounced it "a beautifully gotten up map," and Col. Faulkner said it was "remarkably accurate." In the evening Col. F. read Bos. and myself the Report of the battle of Winchester and we made remarks on it. I copied a map of Spotsylvania Co., for Gen. Lee, at night. Heard from home, all well. The Gen. went up to Gen. Lee's in the A.M. Quite chilly,—freezing in P.M. Crutchfield came up in the P.M.

Friday, March 13th. Reduced a map of [Stafford] Co., Va.;—worked very hard all day. Gen. Jackson went up to Gen. Lee's Hd. Qrs. yesterday and Gen. Lee went to Richmond in the P.M. The day has been quite chilly and it froze hard at night.

Saturday, March 14th. Worked at a map of Fauquier Co. After dinner packed up to move, as we are to go at dawn Monday morning if the weather is not too bad. Air chilly.—Williamson came back from Richmond, today, and Kinney was, on Thursday, ordered to report to Richmond, as Gen. J. has no use for him here. Boswell was away finishing his map of Fauquier Co. The air is quite chilly. I wrote in my journal at night.

On Thursday I made an application to the Secretary of War for a commission,—on which Boswell endorsed as follows:

"Hd. Qrs. 2nd Army Corps, March 13, 1863

Mr. Jed. Hotchkiss has been serving as Top. Eng. with this Army Corps since the 27th of March, 1862, and has rendered a large amount of valuable service. In the collection of Topographical information I have never known his superior, I therefore, respectfully recommend that he be commissioned in the Prov. Eng. Corps and assigned to this command.

(Signed) J. K. Boswell
Capt. & Chf. Eng. 2nd Corps.

Gen. Jackson approved the letter and sent it to Gen. Lee.

Sunday, March 15th. I went to church, to the Chapel of the "Stonewall Brigade," in the morning and heard a sermon from: "Occupy till I come," which was a very good one. The Gen. came there alone; he wore a plain cap having dispensed with the gold lace. Lt. Henrich was at my tent the rest of the day and dined with me. Boswell went to Gay Mont. It has sleeted, rained, and hailed all the P.M., with some thunder and lightning;—air Chilly.

Monday, March 16th. The Engineer Corps and Q.M. Corps of Gen.

J. moved at an early hour today up to near Wm. Yerby's.—2½ miles up the Massaponax from Hamilton's Crossing. The Gen. remained another day at Moss Neck. I came in company with Brown and he went to see about the camp and I went to Gen. Lee's Hd. Qrs. and chatted awhile with the staff there, (The Gen. is still in Richmond);[25] then went up to Gen. Stuart's and chatted awhile with Blackford, (Gen. S. was not there, being in Culpeper), then came to camp and found our wagons there so pitched our tent, unloaded boxes, etc. Servant Wm. was quite sick;— made him some tea. It was quite cold in the morning, the ground frozen and iced over from the storm of yesterday;—the weather moderated in the P.M. and some of the ice and snow melted.

Tuesday, March 17th. The Gen. and staff came up today and en-camped at the same place where we are. Our Hd. Qrs. have been at Moss Neck, Mr. Richard Corbin's, since the 16th of Dec. We went there the day after the Yankees crossed back after the Battle of Fredericksburg; —or rather the morning after they crossed, in the night. So we have been there 3 months, in winter quarters, and have had quite a pleasant winter, all things considered, and our men have enjoyed fine health. There are only some 1,500 sick in all the Richmond Hospitals at this time. Pendle-ton and McGuire dined with us and then Capt. Blackford and Lt. Robert-son came and dined with us to try our prepared soup. There was a heavy cannonade, most of the P.M., said to have been at Banks' Ford. The day has been quite pleasant most of it, but threatening a storm in P.M. I work-ed at map of Fauquier Co., Va. Boswell made a stable, fixed bed, etc., etc. Gen. J. and Smith called at Hayfield, Wm. P. Taylor's. Little Janie Cor-bin, of Moss Neck, called, which diverted Gen. J. very much.[26] Fight at Kelley's Ford.

Wednesday, March 18th. Worked at map of Fauquier Co., Va., during the day and on one of the vicinity of Manassas, during the eve-ning; the day was quite chilly. The cavalry fight yesterday, of which we heard the cannonading, was a very hardly contested one.—It occurred in Culpeper, not far from Kelley's Ford. We lost some 150 or 200 in killed, wounded and missing;—among them the brave Maj. Pelham, of Stuart's Horse Artillery. The enemy was driven back across the river, with much loss, leaving their hospital behind them.

Thursday, March 19th. Worked as before. Went over to Harman's and read the papers after dinner;—he told me of his troubles, about forage, with Pendleton and McGuire and the conference with the Gen. about it. We are now allowed 8 lbs of corn and 6 lbs of hay as a horse ration. It snowed in P.M. Quite cool. Boswell sent down the river today.

Friday, March 20th. Worked as above. It stormed all day,—or until in the P.M., and was quite cool.—Boswell and Williamson went up the river to look after the Yanks.—heard from home today.—Chatted awhile with Col. Faulkner about the battle of Cross Keyes,—which he considered only a part of the Port Republic fight. Says it was only a skirmish; a reconnoissance in force, and that Gen. J. by his strategy, cheated Fremont out of his battle.

Saturday, March 21st. It snowed and sleeted nearly all night and is quite cool,—so we are good for a stay of some time at this camp. Kinney left for home yesterday—to await orders there, as he is not wanted here. I pity him, but he is really of no use. It rained during the day and snowed some too.

Sunday, March 22nd. Mr. Lacy preached, in his tent, at our Hd. Qrs., an excellent sermon of the "blood of Abel and the blood of Christ"; in the A.M. the Gen. was all attention;—in the P.M. there was a prayer meeting at the same place. The morning, cool and lowering, was followed by a clearing off and sunshine and the snow melted rapidly, leaving few traces of it by night. Mr. Lacy came over to my tent in the evening and we had a long and pleasant talk, and Brown and I talked until quite late. I dined with Maj. Harman today. Everything is quiet.

March 23rd. I worked at map of Fauquier Co. in day time, and at one of the Battle of Winchester at night. Lt. Long,[27] of the 31st Va., one of my Valley Mt. friends, came to see me today. He is a fine looking fellow; said Gen. Jackson's sister, in Beverly, was a Union woman.[28] She said she could take care of the wounded Feds. as fast as brother Thomas could wound them. Heard from home;—the snow in Staunton was 2 feet deep. Gen. Jones and his command had fallen back to the Big Spring on acct. of forage. A cool day, lowering,—snow clouds. Brown went up to Gen. Stuart's.

Tuesday, March 24th. I worked at map of Fauquier Co. until dinner time then went up and spent several hours with Gen. Stuart, conversing about the late battle of Kelleysville. His loss was 10 killed, 83 wounded and 35 missing.—He says his cavalry never behaved better; fighting against great odds, they charged the enemy, posted behind a stone wall, and drove them from it, but were unable to get their horses over and so had to fall back when the enemy rallied and reinforced. He laments the loss of Pelham, who was hit in the head by a musket ball while cheering on the cavalry, through a gap in the fence, to a charge, he waiting for them to pass that he might get through to go to Gen. Stuart, having been to order in all his artillery.

Speaking of the V.M.I. he said: Gen. Jackson had been informed, in 1861, that he must go back to the Institute or resign his place as Prof.,—and that Gen. Jo Johnston had him made a Maj., in the Reg. Army of the C.S., at once.

The day was very mild and pleasant until late in the P.M. when it began a cool rain. I called at Gen. Lee's;—he was just going to see Gen. Jackson. Gen. Stuart got back today from Culpeper and Boswell and Wm'son. also came back.

Wednesday, March 25th. Worked at map of Fauquier in day and Battle of Winchester at night. Got a letter from my brother and heard he had sold our farm, and he will soon move. I am very well satisfied about matters now and hope all may prove for the best. In the evening Col. Faulkner read me his Report of the Battle of Port Republic—including the skirmish at Cross Keys;—it is very good and correct. Had a pleasant talk with Mr. Lacy. The day has been quite pleasant,—warm and sunshiny.

Thursday, March 26th. Worked at map of Fauquier.—In the evening went over [and] spent a few hours conversing with Mr. Lacy,—in which he told us some very rich anecdotes and amused us much. I then went in and spent an hour or so with Col. Faulkner, conversing about the Battle of Cedar Run of which he had just commenced writing the report. He told me the Gen. said, "Now Col. Faulkner, when a battle happens, and I hope we may not have another, I want you to get where you can see all that is going on, and, with paper and pencil in hand, write it down, so we may not have so much labor and so many conflicting statements, and then write up the Report at once after the battle." I came back and worked at map of Cedar Run until quite late. There was a little rain in the morning, but it cleared off and became quite cool at night.

Friday, March 27th. There was a heavy white frost and the sun came up clear and bright and we had a glorious day; warm and pleasant. This was the day appointed for fasting and prayer and it has been well obeyed in the army;—a Sabbath, a peace Sabbath, quietness has prevailed and worship was had in almost every camp, over 50 sermons were preached in our Corps. Dr. Lacy preached at Hd. Qrs., to a good audience,—from Matthew 21st, 44th. An excellent sermon on national responsibility to God;—he read, in connection, the 20th and 23rd Psalms. We had prayer by Gen. J. in the morning, at 8, and in the P.M. at 5 we had prayer meeting. May much good come to us, O Lord, from our united prayers this day. I wrote to my wife and daughter in evening.

Saturday, March 28th. I worked at a map of the Valley to accompany the Gen.'s Report of the battle of Winchester. Boswell wrote his Report of Eng. Operations at Port Republic, etc., and Williamson copied my map of Cumberland Co., Pa., and Brown that of Fauquier Co., Va. It rained, nearly all day, quite hard, and the ground is very soft. I went over and conversed with Dr. Lacy, for some time, in the evening and then worked at map of the Battle of Winchester.

Sunday, March 29th. We attended preaching, at our Hd. Qrs., in the morning;—had a good sermon on trusting to God but exerting ourselves also by crying unto him;—some of the audience were much affected. I read a portion of the day. At 6 P.M. we had a prayer meeting at Mr. Lacy's tent in which the Gen. prayed fervently for peace and for blessings on our enemies in everything but the war. I conversed, in the evening, for some time with Dr. Lacy and Col. Faulkner. Dr. L. said the Gen. told him "that he had almost lost confidence in man for when he thought he had found just such a man as he needed and was about to rest satisfied in him he found something lacking in him," but he added, "I suppose it is to teach me to put my trust only in God." Col. Faulkner spoke of the severe Roman simplicity of the Gen. in his Reports, admitting nothing but what he could verify as true. Col. F. said that he did not intend to make his reports laudations of anyone. The day has been clear, but cool and windy. Gen. Lee is sick and Gen. J. went over to see him in the P.M. Capt. Randolph dined with us. Bos. read to me until quite late.

Monday, March 30th. Worked all day at the map of the battle of Winchester and completed it. Boswell and I went in the evening up to see Gen. Stuart, he taking him a map of the country of Fauquier, a copy of my map. We had a pleasant hour there and after we came back I spent an hour in Mr. Lacy's tent listening to his inimitable humor. His account of Bishop Early and his collection was very good. Pendleton told about Maj. Dabney and riding according to rank as we came from Conrad's Store to Port Republic. I read over the report of the Battle of Winchester and took notes for my map. The day has been quite pleasant but cool.

Tuesday, March 31st. It commenced raining, sleeting and snowing about 1 A.M. and kept it up all night and the morning found the snow some 5 inches deep. I heard from home yesterday—a good letter. The storm continued nearly all day. I worked at map of Winchester Battle

Field to accompany the Gen.'s Report, finished it late at night. Quite a discussion arose in reference to the body of soldiers that fell on the enemy at Middletown. Col. Faulkner had put it in as Wheat's Batl'n.,[29] but I was sure it was 2 cos. of the 7th and 1st of the 9th La.,—under Maj. Penn.[30] The Gen. fixed it by stating that "some of Taylor's Brig. did it," as he would allow nothing that could be a matter of controversy to enter the report.

April 1st. It was quite pleasant today and most of the snow melted. I worked on a map to accompany the Battle of Port Republic during the day and at a map of Culpeper at night. Boswell went down to Buckner's Neck. We had a prayer meeting, at Mr. Lacy's tent, at 6 P.M.; quite a full attendance. I had a long talk with Col. F. in relation to many things;—the Gen.'s knowledge of character;—the two Joneses, appointed by his recommendation, have not turned out well, and he is troubled about it.

Thursday, April 2nd. Made a map of the route of the army to the battle of Cedar Run and position of Fed. Forces, etc., to accompany the Report of the battle. Boswell and I went up to Gen. Stuart's in the P.M. Quite a fine day. I wrote several letters at night.

Friday, April 3rd. Worked at map of Battle of Cedar Run;—worked until quite late at night. The Gen. was out of humor in the morning about the position of the forces on the field on the map. Boswell took him the map against my wishes, and he gave vent to considerable displeasure. The day was cool. Bos. was away at night.

Saturday, April 4th. Finished the maps to accompany the Report of the Battle of Cedar Run and took them to the Gen., who was satisfied with them after I had made the lines, representing the advance of our forces, a very little shorter and had put Cedar Creek down on the map of "Route." Strange man!—Everything must conform to standard of simplicity and accuracy, severe in all its outlines. Mr. Russell,[31] M. C., came to see the Gen. I had a long talk with Col. F. on various topics, especially Gen. J.'s peculiarities;—he spoke of the matter Gen. J. crossed out of the Reports, after he had used much care in putting it in,—saying that it would not do to publish to the enemy the reason that induced one to do certain things and thus enable them to learn your mode of doing.

Col. F. in his Report of the Battle of Cedar Run, had spoken very highly of Gen. Winder, and said his loss was still felt, though many brave, etc., men had occupied his place. The Gen. said it looked like a reflection on Gen. Paxton, and so crossed it out. The Col. asked him what

induced him to fight Shields instead of Fremont, at Port Republic.—He
said he had several reasons: "First I was nearer to him, second he had
the [smallest] army, then I was nearer my base of supplies, had a good
way of retreat if beaten,—and Fremont had a good way to retreat if I
had beaten him, while I know Shields had a bad road to go over." We
also talked about the Bath Expedition of Jan. 1862; of Gen. Jackson's
reticence in regard to it; not even informing Gen. Loring, the second in
Command, of the object of the expedition, when he was going, or anything of the kind;—and his Adjutant Gen., Col. Preston,[32] who slept
with him and was his brother-in-law, was not informed of it either, and
if Gen. J. had been killed no one would have known what was to be done.
In the evening Bos., Mr. Turner, Dr. McElhency and I rode up to Gen.
Stuart's. The Gen. was away,—so I called on Blackford,—took a chat
with J. Esten Cook,[33]—a romp with Maj. Von Borcke, and then back
home. Fixed up my maps of the Battle Fields of Winchester and Cedar
Run and then retired; 3 in our narrow camp bed, Dr. McE. spending the
night with us. It began to snow at 6 P.M. and snowed all night.

   Sunday, April 5th. The snow is some 6 inches deep this morning and
it is quite cold. We had preaching, in Mr. Lacy's tent, from the text:
"All things work together for good, etc.";—a good sermon. Mr. L. is a
very sensible man and one well qualified for a general missionary to the
army. I had a severe headache most of the day so did not go to Prayer
meeting in the evening. I had my hair cut and head washed and then
felt better. Heard today that Gen. Stuart's Pontoons had arrived and
that he was bringing another Brigade of his cavalry up to the base of the
Blue Ridge.

   Monday, April 6th. Finished up the map of the Battle of Cedar Run.
The Gen. was not satisfied in reference to some of the positions of the
forces at night, in the advance, and wanted me to hunt up the officers
that commanded them and find out from them, so I found Col. Peck,[34]
of the 9th La., who was the advance of Stafford's Brigade,[35] and learned
that they had advanced up to the enemy's pickets,—some 300 yds, in advance of the woods, before they halted, and there they captured prisoners.
The shot from the enemy's arty. went over them; they afterwards fell
back to the woods. I saw Capt's. Adams and Taylor,[36] of Gen. A. P. Hill's
staff, and found where Field's Brigade[37] was,—and fixed it on my map.
These two Brigades spent the night in the woods. After that I worked on
map for Report of Port Republic. A cool and bracing day. Boswell and

Williamson went up the river and were away all night. Col. M. G. Harman came down to his Reg't. today.

Tuesday, April 7th. Worked at map of part of the Valley for Report. Boswell and Williamson came back and the Gen. ordered Williamson to the Valley for temporary duty with Gen. Wm. E. Jones. Gen. J. E. B. Stuart spent most of the day with Gen. Jackson. A cool day.

Wednesday, April 8th. Nearly completed the map for Port Republic Report. Williamson went away this A.M. In the evening went over to the 31st Va. and chatted awhile with the boys from Randolph Co.; those I knew on Valley Mt. They are a noble set of fellows and fight finely. P'd Lt. Long $100, due him by Dr. O. Butcher, and took a receipt for the same. We had prayer meeting in the evening;—a very good one. Went in the Gen.'s tent and heard Hitchcock's testimony in the McDowell Court of Inquiry read. Had a long talk with Col. Faulkner about the Battle of Groveton and described to him the positions of the troops, etc. He read me the two reports of Gens. Stuart and Trimble about the capture of Manassas Station,—giving contrary statements of the same thing. Strange indeed. Capt. Hardin, of the 31st Va., told me that at Port Republic his Regt. advanced through the wheat field to the pasture field, or near it, and that the Yankees were behind the fence there, and came up over a rise when following them. Says our Regiments on the left were sent in, seemingly, one by one. The Report is prevalent, today, that fighting is going on at Charleston. God grant that we may repulse the enemy there. Gen. Lee came over to our Hd. Qrs. in the P.M.

Thursday, April 9th. Worked at map of Port Republic. A fine day.

Friday, April 10th. Worked at map of Port Republic. After dinner Brown and I went to Fredericksburg, riding down Deep Run and then across to the Marye House,—looking at the many evidences of the hard fought field that were visible; torn trees, battered walls, broken houses. The day was very pleasent and spring-like and the grass and grain are just brightening up, the peaches reddening to blossom and the birds enlivening the scene, but the evidences of grim visaged war hang as clouds amid the brightness. Bos. went on a round with Col. Lee, the Chief Eng. and Dr. Hunter came home with him.

Saturday, April 11th. Nearly completed the map of Port Republic Battle Field and the Route to it and laid it before the Gen. who had only one change to suggest, i.e. that instead of "Valley Army," at one place on it, I should put "Army of the Valley." I had a long talk with McGuire and Pendleton. Dr. McIlhenny came back from Richmond and went on home today. I heard that the 31st and 25th Va. Regts. had been ordered to Imboden, on the mts. They were very glad to go. The 50th Va. from Kanawha Co., etc., came to fill the place of the 25th. The day has been a delightful one, the air balmy.

Sunday, April 12th. Mr. Lacy preached in the morning;—a capital sermon. The day was very pleasant, and I enjoyed it much. The prayer meeting, in the evening, was very good. The attendance at church was large and I saw a number of my old pupils. It rained late in the P.M.

Monday, April 13th. Finished the map of Port Republic and took it to the Gen. He also examined the maps of Fauquier and Stafford and was much pleased with the small one of Stafford that I made. Said he did not know when he might want 6 of them. Boswell went to Richmond and took baggage to the rear. I spent part of the day overhauling papers, etc. Quite a spring day. Wrote home at night.

Tuesday, April 14th. Spent the day fixing up papers, desk, etc., Sent my boy, Wm., home with trunk, etc. Sent wife my jars, etc., etc. The day was a very fine one, sun shone warm; I conversed with the Gen. for some time, at night, on various topics, beginning about teaching;—he said he was fond of it;—then languages came up and he asked which I liked the best, said he preferred Spanish,[38] and then gave its peculiarities of pronunciation, spelling, etc.; then we were on Eng. Gram. and the phrasing of sentences, etc. Then we got on the scenery of New river; said he lived for several years some 12 miles from the Hawk's Nest;—He now has an only living sister, Mrs. Arnold of Beverly; his only brother died young, as well as another sister—He said he had a step-brother somewhere. The Gen. received a present of a magnificent scarf, from a young Maryland lady now in La.; it had all the staple agricultural products of the South worked into it. Brown was in my tent at night and copied portions of my Journal. Smith told an anecdote of Gen. J. at Mrs. Taylor's, a few days ago. The young ladies wanted some of his hair and he said they might have some if they would get no gray hairs, they said he had no gray hairs, "Why," said he, "the soldiers call me "Old Jack." Wrote in my journal at night. There was some fighting at Kelleysville again today. Gen. Lee was over to our Hd. Qrs. today.

Wednesday, April 15th. Worked at map of the "Second Battle of Manassas, of Groveton." The Gen. sent for me several times about dates on my map of Port Republic;—wanted to know why I said we left there the 18th and why he went to Staunton in the night; was sure we started for Richmond Monday and he started at midnight, Sunday, so as not to travel Sunday; but I convinced him that we did not start until Wednesday. He said he had got it confounded with the next Sunday when he went to Richmond, from Frederick's Hall,—starting at midnight; said it showed the importance of comparing ideas. In the morning he was comparing our Engineers with the enemy's, and thought they had the best,—instancing that they found a gap in our lines at Fredericksburg and there massed their troops, and that they did the same at Groveton, and their Engineers must have found that out. He spoke of the panic one of our batteries, caused, (Latham's)[39] by running away the day after the battle of Cedar Run,—and when it left him it was not much loss. He was speaking also of the Ist Battle of Manassas and said he never knew what became of the Yankees, on his left when he charged there; also said he doubted if Kerby Smith[40] joined in the charge there as was usually related.

I went over to Maj. Harman's, late in the P.M., and we had a long talk of many things.—He told me that he made the arrangements for Gen. J. to go to Richmond on the 22nd of June; said he rode all day to overtake him and got there and found him at his devotions;—bought a horse for him and he and Harris and Mr. [?] started at about midnight and went by the "Three Chopped Road" to R. The Gen. told Harris to call him Colonel, so no one would know him. Harman says he and the Gen. had a quarrel at Port Republic.—He had reported that there were many arms on the field and the Gen. asked him to send for them—and when he reported, he said: "Gen., a good many of them look like our own arms," and he said the Gen. went into a towering passion and told him he wanted to hear nothing of that kind from him; that Shields had many of the same kind of guns, etc., etc., and at last told the Gen. that he would send in his resignation, which the Gen. opposed. But he sent it in and the Gen. sent for him and told him he was much annoyed at that time, and many others had fretted him by telling him the same thing, etc., etc., and he disapproved of the resignation. The Maj. says that he went down to the battle field of Port Republic to say to the Gen. that he had got the wagons across S. River, at Weyer's Cave, going up through Port Republic, and wished to know how far he should take them on the Brown's Gap Road; the Gen. said, to the top of the Ridge, but some of them had to go beyond, for the trains reached farther than from the Furnace to the top, and while he was talking with the Gen. he told him to go down there and tell the officer commanding a Regiment that was not far off, to take it into the fight. It was the 52nd Va.—Col. Skinner's,[41] he wanted to know how, or where, he was to take them in; but Harman said, "The Gen. says take them in," and he took them.—The Gen. was then a short distance beyond Morris' house and near Ch. Lewis' lane. Harman says that at Manassas Junction, in August, 1862, the Yankee Brigade of Gen. Taylor came up three times, in splendid order, but broke without firing. Says our artillery there was very badly managed, and that if we had kept quiet until the Yankees got close enough we might have got them all, as they evidently thought it only a cavalry raid. Said that after they broke, Gen. Jackson followed, cap in hand, hallooing "Surrender; throw [down] your arms, and surrender." He says we ought to have caught Banks after the Saturday's fight, for he was still in the rear, having been left to guard stores at Warrenton Junction.

Capt. Elhart[42] said, while I was at Harman's, that it would take over two million five hundred thousand dollars to pay off this Corps for 2 months; he had just made his estimate based on 66,000 men, present and absent, in our Corps, to be paid.

Boswell came back today—Pencils were a dollar each in Richmond. It began to rain at 11 P.M. yesterday and continued hard all day;—the streams rising considerably. Brown wrote from my journal. The Gen. sent off his Report of Port Republic. Harman says Col. S. Wounded himself at the Battle of Cold Harbor.

Thursday, April 16th. Worked at map of Manassas 2nd Battle, or Groveton; the day was somewhat cool. Boswell went down to Moss Neck. I supped at the Gen.'s; Maj. Seddon[43] was there, who commanded the Irish Battalion at Cedar Run;—he says that Winder had not got his Division posted when he was killed and that the enemy came on before Taliaferro had time even to find where the troops were.—Says the Yankees came on our left and it only reached a third of the length of the wheat field.—Says that when the Yanks were advancing through the wheat field and were within 125 yards, he ordered his men to fire and looked down the line and saw that the muskets were well leveled—and the men were perfectly cool and collected; then he looked at [the] Yankee line and not a single shot had taken effect. Though he was routed he did not lose a man that day, save one that died of heat. Says Taliaferro's Brigade had been under arms all the night before to resist a night attack, which the enemy began. He says Col. Garnett commanded the Brigade of Col. Campbell. Had a talk with Col. Faulkner about the Battle of Sharpsburg and made him a sketch from Gen. Early's Report, to make it intelligible. Pendleton says he went the next morning to carry an order and in going through a corn field he thought he had come to Lawton's men lying down in order of battle. But he found, to his surprise, that it was a whole rank of dead men that the fire of the enemy had mowed down. A. P. Hill was not under the immediate command of Gen. Jackson that day.

Friday, April 17th. Still at map of engagements about Manassas;— made a reduction of Spotsylvania at night. The enemy's gunboats came up the river yesterday and this morning the Gen. had his couriers going in every direction, and ordered all the artillery to be ready to move at a moment's notice. Boswell went to Port Royal and it is ordered to open on the gun boats tomorrow morning if they come in range where we can get our guns. Crutchfield was up to Hd. Qrs. today; he has some 3,000 men in his command, artillery; several of them have been promoted in a few days, Walker, Poague, Latimer, etc. Pendleton says he did not think Smead was at Port Republic, but the Gen. says he was, for Col. Jackson came back from taking an order during the fight and said that Col. Smead and Col. Jackson were quarreling in the midst of the fighting.

Speaking of Cross Keys; all thought it wrong to dismiss it as only part of Port Republic, as it was thought an important battle at the time, and Gen. J. sent Pendleton, during the fight, to say to Ewell, "I will keep Shields back if you can hold Fremont in check," and Ewell replied; "The worst is over now, I can manage him." Trimble wanted to make a night attack on Fremont.

In writing of Cedar Run Gen. J. says: Branch[44] and Winder went in at the same time, while it is well known that Winder's Brigade had charged the Yankees thro.' the bushy field and taken several stands of colors before Branch had passed Major's [School House] on his way to the field. The Gen. went down the river today;—a company of cavalry charged by him, with drawn sabres, and would not stop. He learned from a straggler that they had heard that the enemy had crossed at Hayfield and they were going to charge them, and tho. he had just come by there he sent Smith back to see if the enemy was there. The Yanks had two balloons up in the morning. Quite a pleasant day. The feeling of satisfaction at the news from Longstreet is general.[45] A pleasant day but a little cool. Col. Faulkner finished his reports of all Gen. J.'s battles today.

Saturday, April 18th. Worked at map of Battles about Manassas. This has been a lovely day. There was a shower at night. The enemy had up two balloons at once today. Boswell is yet down the river looking after the gunboats. Heard that John Letcher is to run for Congress against

Baldwin. I was conversing with Gen. J. and Sam Letcher, in the evening, on subsistence, and remarked that beans were the most nutricious of all substances. The Gen. said, No, rice has 95 per ct. and beans only 92, and he remarked that hog drivers from Western Va. said their hogs could go further on *honey* than any other food. I made, at night, a map of Spotsylvania reduced.

"I have fought a good fight, I have finished my work"

SUNDAY, APRIL 19TH. I got my pocket full of tracts and Testaments and went down the river to see one of my old pupils, Sam. J. Forrer,[1] who is in the guard house of the 10th Va. Regt. on a charge of desertion to the enemy;—he had written to come and counsel him. I could but remember him as a boy and the serious conversation I had with him about his stubborn will and his wayward disposition, and telling him, some 15 years ago, that I had no doubt he would come to the gallows unless he radically changed his notions of right and wrong. I had a pleasant ride down, the air balmy and vegatation rapidly advancing; the peach trees in full bloom and a few wild flowers showing themselves. My horse snuffed the fresh herbage and I let him crop it; the army horses were turned out in droves on the wide bottoms to recruit and get something besides corn. I found my young friend thoroughly cut down, deeply mortified at his situation. He told me, candidly, all about his conduct; how he came to attempt to cross the lines, after medicines, passing himself off as a British subject, and how he was arrested,. and then his attempt to escape. His case is a hard one and I can only hope he may escape death and only receive some severe punishment, which he is willing to endure. I saw his Capt. and

Col. and then went and saw some of the court which is to try him. I dined with the Corps Court, at Moss Neck, and rode back at a late hour. There was a heavy rain at night. Mr. Lacy preached to a large audience at Hd. Qrs.

Monday, April 20th. I worked on a tracing of a map of Frederick Co., Va., completing it, then unpacked a box of provisions, which my servant, William, brought to me from home today, as well as a capital letter from my wife. It rained very hard most of the day. Brown went to Guinea's as did Boswell too. The General's wife and child came today; the soldiers cheered them loudly when they saw her and him together.[2] The Gen. met his wife at the cars and took her to Mr. Yerby's; spent a short time there and then came back to his business again. We hear that Longstreet is operating successfully against Suffolk.

Tuesday, April 21st. Worked on some reductions of maps for Gen. Lee (Culpeper, Orange and Madison Cos.) which were brought over by Col. Smith of the Engrs., our Chief Eng. The day was cool. Boswell went down the river. My horse got away in the P.M. and one of our wagon horses; they were searched for in vain. I had turned them out to graze and they soon went off. The day was cool.

Wednesday, April 22nd. I started at an early hour to look for my horse, went to Moss Neck and scoured the bottoms, looking through the droves of horses grazing there, to no purpose, and had others searching too. The day was quite warm after the morning, which was cool. I worked some at map of Culpeper when I came back, and wrote some at night. It began to rain at 9 P.M.

Thursday, April 23rd. It rained hard nearly all day. I worked at map of Culpeper, etc.

Friday, April 24th. I went to look for my horse and found him in possession of a Q.M. in Semmes'[3] Brigade. It rained most of the day; part of the time very bad.

Saturday, April 25th. Worked on map of Culpeper. It was a fine day; warm and spring like.

Sunday, April 26th. We had preaching from the parable of the rich man and Lazarus, by Mr. Lacy, with a congregation of some 1,500 or 2,000, at our Hd. Qrs. Gen. Lee was present, Maj. Gen. Early also, and many other officers of rank. The day was pleasant, with a fresh breeze. The Gen. brought his wife up. She is slightly built and tolerably good looking, and somewhat gaily though modestly dressed. We had a prayer meeting in the evening.

Monday, April 27th. Worked at map of Culpeper; in the P.M., after dinner, rode with Brown to see the drill of Hay's Brigade by Gen. Hays; it was a very good one. Boswell went over to Gen. Lee's and Gen. L. told him that Hooker was intending to advance; would have done so on Friday but for the rain, and that all the enemy was this side of Potomac Creek. Gen. Lee came over to our Hd. Qrs. Boswell went away with Dr. McIlhenny for the night. Dr. M. reports the enemy in force in Fauquier Co. The day was very fine. I heard from home; they had had a hard hail storm. I wrote at night to John B. Baldwin and to young Forrer.

Tuesday, April 28th. Worked awhile at map of battle of Groveton, but the Gen. said I need not finish it but go to something else, as he did not care much about sending it; it was so difficult to fix all the positions accurately; so I worked at the map of Culpeper. Took supper at Hd. Qrs. and Mr. Lacy told two of his good anecdotes, both about Dr. McPheeters, one about his preaching three days in his overcoat because he had put on an old wornout coat, cut up, etc.,; the other about his baptizing Aunt Judy, Dr. Bott's servant, by immersion; both good. It rained some and was a little cool. Boswell came back late at night. Gen. Lee told him, several days ago, that Hooker intended to come over last Friday, but the rain prevented him;—he had moved all his forces this side of Potomac Creek.

Wednesday, April 29th.—We were told about the time we arose—, $6\frac{1}{2}$ or 7 A.M., that musketry firing had been heard and soon news came that the enemy was crossing the Rappahannock again at Bernard's, and soon the sounds of coming strife, musketry and artillery, were heard by all. The morning was misty and considerably foggy, and under cover of these the enemy crossed over, and in the skirmish that ensued, they captured a company of Louisiana troops and a Lieut-Colonel; they then commenced crossing in force, extending their line towards the mouth of the Massaponax, gaining the hill on the north side of that stream at about dark. We fired some artillery at them, soon after they came over, and did them some damage. There was some skirmishing during the day, but not much. We were concentrating our forces. Early was put on Jackson's left, reaching Deep Run with Courtney's battery there, and having his right near Hamilton's crossing; with A. P. Hill's division in his rear as a second line; D. H. Hill's division (Rodes') extended from Hamilton's Crossing to near the Massaponax, with Trimble's (Colston's) division as a second line. McClaws'[4] division extended from the foot of the hill beyond Deep Run to and into Fredericksburg, and Anderson's division was beyond there up the River. The day was mild and it cleared off about noon; the yankees had their balloons up, but it was somewhat smoky. It thundered in the P.M. and we had a smart shower, lasting an hour or so about four and a half P.M. The foliage is just opening. The peach and cherry [trees] are in full bloom and the grass is looking fresh and green; the wheat fields are also bright, the wheat some 6 inches high. The anemone, sanguinaria and Houstonia are dotting the woods and hill-sides. The plain of the Rappahannock, the former battle-field, presents a beautiful appearance; alas soon to be stained again with blood! Hooker appears to be inclined to go farther down than Burnside did. There is news of a crossing of the enemy at Kelly's Ford, so telegraphs Gen. Stuart, in some force and they may attempt to turn our position from that direction. General Jackson was at Mr. Yerby's last night and the messenger with the news of the enemy's movement went there for him; he sent Lieut-Smith to Gen. Lee, whom he found in bed, and when Smith told him he said: "I thought I heard firing, but was waiting for some one to come and tell me, and you are a good boy for telling me." When General Jackson passed along the line to inspect it the whole line cheered him. Our artillery was back at Bowling Green and was sent for by tele-graph. We had Graham's[5] and Courtney's batteries at hand. The enemy massed a heavy force behind the Pratt house and had a very large force on the other shore. They had cavalry and artillery on their left opposite the mouth of the Massaponax. Ramseur's[6] brigade is below the Massa-ponax. I worked at a map of Caroline County, after packing up, until in the P.M., then rode down and went along the line and looked at the enemy until it began to rain, when General Jackson told me I had better go back and make myself comfortable. The extra tents were all sent off. We established a hospital at Yerby's, as before. He was much opposed to it.

Thursday, April 30th. I worked at maps all day, desiring to finish the one of Culpeper County, etc. as it might be needed. The General sent for me in the P.M. and I rode down to the front, when he directed me to "Strike off eight maps embracing the region between the Rapidanne and the Rappahannock and reaching back to the Virginia Central Railroad, and one for himself extending to Stevensburg." The morning was drizzly and cool and it was misty and foggy until noon when it cleared for a time. It rained in the P.M. but cleared and was quite pleasant at night. We opened artillery on the enemy at noon and kept it up at intervals during the P.M., doing them considerable damage, causing their regiments to break. & c. They replied but feebly. The enemy has a flanking column coming down the River, having crossed at Germanna and Ely's Fords. It reached Chancellorsville to-day. The General sent me, at 9 P.M., to look for a feasible route for our troops to Salem Church, so I was riding all night. The moon shone brightly. I found our forces in motion by 3 A.M. Our loss in skirmishing &c. was quite small.

Friday, May 1st. I got back to camp at 4½ A.M. Found all packing up to move; the wagons about to be off for Guiney's Station. Mr. Lacy and General A. P. Hill's command had marched, he (L), being guide, having gotten General Jackson to go and see General Lee and get his consent to the early move. I followed on, at a later hour, with Brown, and overtook the army at Tabernacle Church, then finished maps and supplied the division Commanders. We had two skirmishes with the enemy and repulsed them and gained the summit of the hill towards Chancellorsville. Ramseur's brigade was the one principally engaged. We slept on the top of the hill where the furnace road turns off—; General Lee and his Staff sleeping at the same place. The day was quite pleasant, a genuine May day. The General left our camp about a half hour before day and reached Tabernacle Church about 8½ A.M.; General A. P. Hill going by Goodwin's and Guest's, Boswell guiding them. Smith, Johnson and Boswell came on 20 of the enemy's cavalry, at Miller's, on the Plank Road, three miles from Chancellorsville, and they, or engineers, retired to Morrison's, a half mile and reported to General Jackson, when Wright's[7] brigade came up and had a skirmish, of some 15 minutes duration, about 11-½ A.M. There was also considerable firing on General Mahone's[8] line, on the Old Turnpike, near Zoar Church. Artillery opened at 11½ from the hill to the right of the Old Turnpike and near Zoar Church. We went to assist General Anderson and General Jackson took command.

Saturday, May 2nd. The Generals were up at an early hour and had a consultation, in the pines on the top of the hill where the Catherine Furnace road turns from the Plank Road, sitting on Yankee Cracker boxes which the enemy had left there. I went down to Mr. Welford's, where General Stuart had his quarters, and ascertained the roads that led around to the enemy's rear and came back and reported to Generals Lee and Jackson, who consulted and examined the map and then started the Second Corps down by the furnace, Rodes' division in front, and went on to the Brock road, and then up it a piece and into a private road, and so on to the Plank Road and across both Plank Roads to the Old Turnpike and formed our line of battle at the [Lucket's] house and with three lines of battle fell on the enemy's rear at Talley's, at precisely 6 o'clock, and after an infantry fight on our side, of 32 minutes, the enemy using infantry and artillery, we routed them and drove them completely from the field and some three miles beyond, driving them out of two lines of entrenchments and on to some breastworks when it had become dark and by accident our men fired into each other and by that fire General Jackson was wounded, having three balls through his left arm and one through his right hand, having held up both hands to urge our men to desist.[9] The enemy had but a moment before breaking our advance and throwing it into confusion but General J. had rallied it by telling the flying men "Jackson himself calls on you to halt." The enemy took advantage of our mistake and opened a terrific volley of musketry and artillery, sweeping the roads in which our forces had become massed by the dense growth on either side and the swampy nature of the ground. Disorder reigned supreme for a few moments, the "Great Chief" being struck down; but General A. P. Hill, who had rushed to the General's side saying, "I have been trying to make the men cease firing," himself met the advance of the yankee skirmishers then formed a line of men and repulsed them, so saving General J. from capture and he was borne off in a litter by Smith and [Wilbourn].[10] One of those bearing him was struck by a shell in the furious cannonade and the General received a fall.[11] I hastened back for an ambulance and some spirits and found Dr. McGuire and sent him forward. I rode a long ways back, but could find no spirits. Mr. Lacey had left me at Tally's, at dark, and I looked for him in vain. Late at night I found my way back to the Wilderness Tavern, where General Jackson had been taken, and where he was yet in a state of stuper from the shock he had received—, not having rallied enough to have his wounds dressed. At 12, midnight, I started for General Lee's, with young Chancellor as a guide, to inform him of the state of our affairs, making a wide detour, as the enemy had penetrated our lines. I went around and struck the Catharpen road and went on and found General Lee, at his old camp, at 4 A.M., and informed him of what had occurred. Wilbourn had preceded me an hour and informed him of the General's wounds. He was much distressed and said he would rather a thousand times it had been himself. He did not wish to converse about it. I informed him of the situation of the troops and he and Colonel Long consulted and arranged for the morrow. I lay down and slept awhile. He ordered General Stuart, who had taken Jackson's command (General A. P. Hill having been struck on the leg by a shell and disabled for the time), to move around to the right and connect with the left of Anderson who was on General Lee's right and would move to the left of McLaws who was in his front, and so make a connection behind Chancellorsville which the enemy held. I spent a part of the day at General Lee's headquarters copying map, and when the enemy advanced towards the front of General Lee and made a demonstration on the rear of General Jackson's ordnance train and artillery, near the furnace, Mr. Lacy and myself went down the Catharpen road and made our way by the Brock Road to General Jackson's position in time to be present at the fight. The enemy thought we were retreating towards Richmond when they fell on our train. They were repulsed by some of the artillery that turned back, but they soon came on again and were held in check by the 23rd. Georgia and the Irish Battalion until they surrounded and captured them after an obstinate struggle, but our train escaped. After General Jackson was wounded General Hill restored order, aided by the gallant efforts of Major A. S. Pendleton, and several fierce encounters took place in the night, in all of which the enemy was repulsed. The day was quite warm and pleasant—the night clear. The trees are becoming quite green and the apple and pear trees are in full bloom. Hooker commanded in person on the yankee side. The musketry was incessant from 6 to 6½ P.M. and as heavy as I ever heard. Our loss was considerable. There was a slight shower in the P.M. and a thunder storm towards the Blue Ridge during the battle.

Sunday, May 3rd. After breakfasting with General Lee he sent me back with a message to General Stuart to press the enemy vigorously and make the junction of our wings. The enemy had withdrawn from the furnace so I went that way. Our men were capturing and bringing in the yankee pickets which had been left out. Anderson was forming his line of battle near the furnace to make the junction of the two wings, as I passed. Gen. Lee told me to tell General Stuart that he would soon come there in person. I went on around and down to near Tally's, and there rested a while, being so sleepy that I could hardly keep my eyes open. Our forces were pressing forward and fighting severely. After resting awhile I started on to look for my friend Boswell, whom I had not seen or heard of since the fight. I went to where the General was wounded and there I found him, some 20 steps in advance, by the road-side, dead, pierced through the heart by two balls and wounded in the leg. I was completely overcome, although I had expected it from the state of his mind before, expecting him to be killed in this fight. His body had been riffled of hat, glass, pistol daguerreotype, & c., but his look in death was as peaceful and pleasant as in life.—I procured an ambulance and took him to where the General was, at Wilderness Tavern, and with many tears buried him in a grave which I had dug in the family burying ground at Elwood, the home of Major J. Horace Lacey, by the side of General Jackson's arm which had been amputated and buried there. We buried him just as the moon rose, wrapped in his martial coat, Rev. B. T. Lacy making a feeling prayer. Brown, who assisted me, the two men I had employed to dig the grave, Mr. Lacy and myself were all that were present. I wept for him as for a brother; he was kind and gentle and with as few faults as most men. Peace to his memory.

We united the two wings of our army and drove the enemy, by a vigorous and bloody onset, out of his strong works at Chancellorsville and took possession of that place, the loss being very heavy on both sides. Hooker was in the Chancellor house until it was struck by a shell, he then retired to a safer place.

Brown and I slept in the yard at Elwood, on the rich and soft green carpet of its verdant slopes and our weary horses cropped the choice grass. The sight of the dead and wounded today is horrible. Warm and pleasant. A heavy dew in the morning. The woods were on fire in many places and some of the wounded must have been burnt up. Morrison[12] was sent for Mrs. Jackson.[13]

Monday, May 4th. Mr. Lacey aroused me up at an early hour to guide the ambulance with General Jackson and Colonel Crutchfield to Guiney's Station. I saddled up and we soon got off, going by the Brock Road to Todd's Tavern and then to Spotsylvania C. H. and on to Guiney Station. The General stood the ride very well. We passed crowds of wounded men going the same way, all cheerful and each one wishing himself the badly wounded one instead of General Jackson.—The day was quite pleasant but we had a thunder storm late in the evening. Our forces fell on the enemy today and drove them from Marye's Hill which they had taken from us, and drove them up the River; so we now have the old town again. We found the cavalry camp at Spotsylvania C. H. and the country full of wild rumors about the Yankee cavalry raids to Richmond, cutting our communications, etc. I found that our wagons at Guiney's had been sent away to avoid capture and were back again in alarm. Found Col. French at Guiney's, he having been on the train that was captured near Ashland. He said the enemy was at Chickahominy Bridge and there was nothing to keep them from Richmond & c. That the enemy had destroyed much of the Virginia Central Railroad and that Stoneman was behaving very well. Col. F. slept with me. General Jackson stood the ride very well. I washed and cleaned up and got some sleep. General Jackson came to Guiney's by General Lee's advice.

Tuesday, May 5th. We were roused up before day by a report that the enemy was coming—, that is—his cavalry, and the wagons were hitched up to depart; so I got on my horse and went over to see the General; found him cheerful, although he had not rested much; bade him good-by. He said he hoped to be soon in the field again and sent his regards to General Lee. I went by Mr. Alsop's and breakfasted with him, then on to near Fredericksburg and across to the plank road and thence on to General Lee's headquarters near Chancellorsville. I ascertained that he wanted the roads to the United States Ford, so went back by the furnace to get them and on to Mr. Stevens', where, in the P.M., there was a heavy thunder storm. After which I went on to Mr. Bullock's, a mile beyond Wilderness Run and learned from him about the roads, & c. Some young men came after him for a guide. We went to bed for a short time.

We fought the enemy near Salem Church yesterday. It was cool in the morning; the rain made the mud very deep. We have many thousand Yankee prisoners at Guiney's.

Wednesday, May 6th. We were up at 3 A.M. and off to camp. I found Gen. Stuart near Chancellorsville, asleep, the division of Gen. Rodes about moving to the enemy's right flank to dislodge him from his strong position between Chancellorsville and United States Ford. General Stuart sent me on to General Lee and told me to tell him he was satisfied the enemy was retreating. I found General Lee at his old camp and just dressing. He did not much credit the report of the enemy's retreat, and, after a cup of coffee, sent me back to tell General Stuart to press on the movement to our left. General Lee soon came up and he and General Stuart had a consultation, with the map, about the roads I had ascertained. General A. P. Hill soon came up and joined them. It rained nearly all of last night, hard, and most of to-day. It was soon ascertained that the enemy had retreated, leaving five lines of strong entrenchments which they had just thrown up. We followed them closely but they had availed themselves of the rain and darkness to make good their escape, and the mud, and the immense advantage secured to them by the other bank for artillery, prevented our doing them much damage, though we took a good many prisoners.

We spent most of the day near Chancellorsville. Orders were given for the forces to go back to their old camps. General Lee directed me to make a map of the battlefield, then General Stuart and then General A. P. Hill to whom I had reported. Late in the evening General A. P. Hill's wagons started back towards our old quarters. I went on and waited for them, but they did not come, so I started to go to Colonel Smith's quarters, but the rain, mud and darkness made me halt in a Miss. camp, where I was kindly entertained by the Sergeant of the 12th.,[14] and got a good night's rest. It has rained heavily and is quite cold.

Thursday, May 7th.—Went by Col. Wm. Proctor Smith's[15] and saw him about the map of the battlefield, & c., and then on to our old camp. The wagons came up and we pitched our tents as before, but General A. P. Hill is in the house of our hero and Boswell is not. Smith, Morrison, McGuire and Crutchfield are away and Mr. Lacy, it seems, does not like the same place. It is said our loss is over 10,000 and that we have 8,000 yankee prisoners. The day has been quite cool and there was some rain at night.

Friday, May 8th. It was rainy and misty in the morning but looked like clearing off in the afternoon, so I ordered my wagon hitched up and started for the battlefield, reaching to near Guest's and there encamping for the night, near where Anderson and McClaw's fought Sedgwick's[16] corps. The day was quite cool.

Saturday, May 9th. Went on to Chancellorsville and then to General Colston's[17] for a detail of men to aid in surveying. They did not come to me until late, when I ran a line from Chancellorsville to the old Furnace, late in the P.M. Had quite a visit with Hinrichs at Colston's quarters. Chichester came to my camp for the night. Stoneman[18] crossed back, day before yesterday, at Raccoon Ford. The day was a very fine one, though quite warm. Rodes was made a Major-General for his conduct. Major-General Ed. Johnson is expected here to take command of Jackson's old division.

Sunday, May 10th. I spent the day in my camp near Catharine Furnace. Too much fatigued myself and my horse to go down to church, to our old quarters, where Mr. Lacy preached (as I afterwards learned from Brown who came up in the evening) from his old text "All things work together for good." He had a large audience: General Lee and Staff were there.—Much to our grief General Jackson died today, at $3\frac{1}{2}$ P.M.; lost to his country but to himself, he has won his crown immortal and we may fondly hope he may still plead, as he pleaded here, for peace. The day has been warm and very pleasant.[19]

Monday, May 11th.—Started at an early hour to survey the battle-field of Chancellorsville. We measured the road up to Melzi Chancellor's old house—then out to the turnpike and on up to Talley's and Lucket's where our line of battle was first formed; then measured several by-roads and at last came on to Chancellorsville and there met our horses and rode back to camp. We rested a while, at noon, at Talley's and conversed some with the yankees there at the hospitals. They are still for war, though the men whose time were out during this fight were much put out because they were brought into it.—The day was very warm and we were much fatigued by our day's work, being unused to walking much.

The remains of General Jackson were taken to Richmond, to-day, [May 11th] where they were met by a large concourse of people. The bells were tolled and grief held the multitude for the hour. Mr. Wm. Boswell[20] came up to see me to-day and he Chichester and Bartlett spent the night with me.

Tuesday, May 12th. We measured out the Brock Road thence up it to the Furnace Run and then went up to Talley's and measured several lines there,—then around the long line of defences south of Chancellorsville. I had no idea the enemy was so well fortified and wonder they left their works so soon. Brown broke down about the middle of the afternoon. I worked on awhile longer but was about worn out; the heat was great and I got quite lamed from the unusual exercise of these two days. Bartlett has been assisting Chichester and he is with us tonight. The day was very warm. I came by and saw Dr. Coleman. He says the loss in Trimble's division was some 1,900 and over; showing plainly that the "old division" held its reputation. When I got back I found my horse and one wagon horse gone and the other wagon horse dead.—Processions in Richmond for Gen. J.'s remains.

Wednesday, May 13th. Spent the day looking for my horse, riding up and down fruitlessly. The day was very warm until we had a shower in the P.M. Quite a thunder storm. I heard to-day that McClellan was a spectator of the fight at Chancellorsville.[21]

Bartlett tells me that at Chantilly General Jackson put him to driving back men going out of the fight, and that he himself was urging them back. That he told one man to go back and when he delayed Jackson doubled up his bridle-rein and hit him on the head, and said, "Go back."

It is reported the General Jackson swooned after his arm was cut off and that when he revived he said clearly, "Order all the infantry to the front."—General Jackson's remains were taken, via Gordonsville, to Lynchburg. There was a procession at Lynchburg. They arrived in Lexington at 4 P.M. of the 14th. and were buried in the cemetery there on the 15th. *Thursday, May 14th.*—We measured lines all day, got quite weary. It rained some.

Friday, May 15th.—Surveyed over towards the river, then went up to the United States Ford where the yankees had a pontoon across the river over which they were carrying their wounded which General Lee had offered to them in exchange. They took over some 1,300 at this place. They also took many over at Banks' Ford and at Fredericksburg. I conversed yesterday with one of General Howard's[22] Staff. He says they were badly worsted and thought the war ought to end, but did not see how the difficulties of boundaries could be adjusted. We talked for some time. Today I read the Washington papers. They all spoke highly of General Jackson, though evidently pleased that they were rid of him. Saw the pontoon taken up; it was quite an interesting sight. The yankees would not let it remain until the ambulances were all over but ferried some of them across. They were ordered off by Hooker;[23] it was said because the time of the men was out. After seeing the pontoon removed I took another look for my horse. The day was very warm.

Saturday, May 16th.—Started the wagon towards the new camp today. I got some intimation of the whereabouts of my horses and so took Bartlett and Humphries and went after them. Found them at Todd's Tavern Post Office, where they have been all the time. Mine the mail man had ridden to carry the mail, so I had to remain all day for his return. It was quite warm and we took a sleep on the grass. Rev. Melzi Chancellor came along and told us about the advance of the Yankees and Gary's arresting him for offering him a piece of bread in his hand when he wanted something to eat, and of the conduct of his daughter, etc. Came back to camp at Guests'.

Sunday, May 17th. I went down to headquarters to preaching. Mr. Lacy preached the funeral sermon for General Jackson from the words of Paul in Timothy: "I have fought a good fight, I have finished my work, etc." A very good and feeling discourse. The audience was large, but it looked strange not to see the earnest face of General Jackson there, and to hear strange words spoken on the spot consecrated by his prayers and the services of God's house.—General Ed. Johnson was there and looking very well indeed; he was very glad to see me. I came by Colonel

Smith's after dining with Elhart; Charles Grattan accompanying me back part of the way. I heard from home; all well there.

Tuesday, May 19th. Started my wagon back to headquarters at an early hour. I went by the way of Fredericksburg, going over Marye's Hill and taking a look at the old town, sad and desolate. Our men were digging new works on Marye's Hill. The army horses were dotting all the plain below the city. Vegetation has advanced rapidly. Got to headquarters about noon and pitched my tent on the hill above the old camp and prepared to go to work. Came by Colonel Smith's; he is not well. A fine day but very cool morning.

Wednesday, May 20th. Worked at map of Chancellorsville all day. It is very warm. There is much talk about Gen. Jackson's successor.

Thursday, May 21st. Worked at map of the battlefield all day. Went over to see Gen. Lee's engineers in the evening and had quite a visit; found Chichester there. A very warm day.

Friday, May 22nd. Worked at map all day; very warm. Pendleton came back and told us about General Jackson's funeral in Lexington. He seemed much depressed.

Saturday, May 23rd. A very warm day but I worked very closely. Col. Smith came over to see me in the P.M. Praised my map much. He told me that Gen. Lee said I ought to be commissioned and wished to know why I could not be; and when told it was because Virginia had her portion, he said "I ought to be commissioned from new Virginia then." We had a pleasant chat. After dark I went over for a map from Gen. Lee and had a talk with the Old Hero. He gave me the map I desired. Pendleton came over there to see if he could be transferred to General Early, but it was of no use. All of General Jackson Staff expect to go away from here if General A. P. Hill is put in command, as he desires to have his own Staff; but it is thought Gen. Lee will not approve of their leaving.

Sunday, May 24th. Mr. Lacy preached at headquarters from Ruth's declaration to Naomi. A very touching discourse. Gen. Lee and Gen. Johnson were there. The day was very warm. The attendance at church was large and there is much religious interest awakening in the army.

Monday, May 25th. Worked all day at battle map, very warm.

Tuesday, May 26th. Worked at battle map. Gen. A. P. Hill still in command. Warm and dry.

Friday, May 29th. Worked at map of battlefield; in evening called on Hinrichs'; his man is to work for me tomorrow. Lieut-Gen. Ewell & wife came up from Richmond to-day. He is to take command of the Second Corps and Lieut.-Gen. A. P. Hill of the Third Corps. Ewell's old division, now Early's, and part of Jackson's old division, now Johnson's, turned out to meet him at the cars and gave him an enthusiastic reception. The day was quite warm.

Saturday, May 30th. I spent the day going over the battlefield of Salem Church, reconnoitering, &c. It was very warm; came by and saw Col. Smith and we had quite a chat. Brown has been appointed a Lieutenant in the Sappers and Miners regiment and so has Williamson. I got quite weary to-day.

Sunday, May 31st. Attended preaching in the morning. Mr. Lacy preached an excellent sermon on the parable of the feast to which many were invited. There was a large attendance, including Generals Lee, Ewell &c.—In the evening I went over to the Fifth Va. Regiment and supped there with my old pupils, Fisher and others. Spent a pleasant hour. They had a prayer meeting and are having quite a revival. Day warm.

Monday, June 1st. I worked part of the day on my map of the battle-field—then went to see Gen. Early and some of General Paxton's Staff to get positions of forces during the battle. General Ewell took command this morning. By request I showed him and General A. P. Hill my map. They were much pleased with it and General Ewell gave me a map that General Lee had given him, to copy. General Ewell looks feebly. There was a conference of Generals at General Lee's headquarters today. General Lee came over to our headquarters in the P.M. Quite warm. Williamson got back from the Valley on Sunday. Took my map to Hinrichs to have a copy finished.

Tuesday, June 2nd. Worked awhile copying a map for General Anderson and then we went across to Fredericksburg and looked at the enemy to see if any changes had taken place and then back. I went over in the evening to see Hinrichs; he had nearly completed my map. We had quite a long chat. The day was quite warm and it is becoming very dry; had a sprinkle at night. Some of the troops are changing camps.

Wednesday, June 3rd. I worked awhile at a map of Northeastern Virginia, then went down to the "Pratt House," below Fredericksburg and sketched the fortification built there,—then back to Hinrichs camp and aided to help finish the map of the battlefield, working until quite late. All things indicate that we will soon move. Captain Richardson came over to our quarters today and joined me in a mess. The day was quite warm; a shower in the P.M. A portion of the First Corps—General [Longstreet's] started up the river today.

Thursday, June 4th. I took the map of the Chancellorsville battlefield over to General Lee. Then visited Col. Smith's tent and procured some maps and went back and prepared some maps of routes towards Culpeper, and so busied myself the rest of the day, being often called upon for topographical information. General Rodes' division marched today, by Spotsylvania C. H. Orders have been issued to the other divisions. I saw Capt. Sam Smith over at Col. Smith's in the P.M. and took him over to see General Johnson and Lieut. Hinrichs. He says that Hooker is at Dumfries with most of his army. He worked on a map until quite late. The day was warm but it turned cool in the evening.

"But now he often wishes he had many Jacksons"

FRIDAY, JUNE 5TH.—We broke up our headquarters camp at Yerby's on the Massaponax Hills, at 8 A.M., after having been there since the battle, and rode on up to a point near Locust Grove—, one mile from there, going by the battlefield of Chancellorsville. I gave General Ewell an account of the fight as we went along; pointing out to him the localities of incidents as we passed them. He was much interested and asked many questions. Spoke of the fine positions of the enemy and was surprised they had not held them longer.—Dr. McGuire told me today that our loss in killed and wounded was 10,000 in the last fight. Early and Johnson are moving via Spotsylvania C. H. McLaws Division went along by Locust Grove to Raccoon Ford today. The day was quite warm and the roads are dry and dusty. We are all quite weary tonight.

Saturday, June 6th. We had proposed to start at daylight but a messenger came from General Lee saying that a small force of the enemy had crossed over below Fredericksburg and he requested General Ewell to halt until he could see the enemy by daylight, though he was satisfied that it was a mere feint. So we spent the day in camp until 4 P.M. when we got orders to move on, which we did and went half way to Raccoon

Ford. Had a fine shower in the afternoon which made it a little muddy.— I worked some on a map of Culpeper County and on one towards the mountains.

Sunday, June 7th. We were up at an early hour and had prayers by Mr. Lacy—, then marched on and crossed the Rapidanne at Raccoon Ford and then turned up and went to Summerville Ford where the troops were crossing, Rodes in front, who had spent the night not far from the Ford, followed by Early who had come from near Verdiersville and who was followed by Johnson's division which had encamped behind him. McLaws division of the First Corps had camped the night before near Raccoon Ford. We found Rodes well on the road and across the Ford. The troops soon recognized General Ewell and began to cheer him as had been their habit with General Jackson, thus transferring to him the ardor they felt for their old Commander. He took off his cap and rode rapidly along the line. We came on, quickly, to Culpeper C. H., getting there about 10 A.M., and there found General Lee who had come to our camp of Friday night on Saturday and crossed at Raccoon Ford today. General Longstreet was there also,—having his headquarters about a mile southwest from town. McLaws' was just coming in; he encamped on the Sperryville road. Rodes went out three miles toward Rixeyville and Early and Johnson halted on the road four miles back. We found Hood's division just coming back from towards the River and encamping near town. We took our quarters at Mr. Cooper's House, a mile and a half northeast from town. The day has been fine and bracing, the country looks beautifully, the grass being high and thick. I saw Gen. JEB Stuart.

Monday, June 8th. I went to work on a map reaching to the mountains, towards Front Royal, as Gen. Ewell told me that was the route he wished the troops to take tomorrow after they had rested and cooked rations. Early came up and went to a camp beyond McLaws', four miles towards Sperryville, and Johnson went beyond him. I worked until noon and then went over to the C. H. To get information about roads &c. Later in the evening I went to see Col. Smith and Major Clark[1] and spent a few minutes at Gen. Longstreet's headquarters. Our wagons were busy until late at night loading up commissary stores. The day has been quite pleasant. We expect to start early tomorrow.

Tuesday, June 9th. General Lee gave Gen. Ewell his choice about moving today and he concluded not to go on, so I got to work on a map of the Valley, copying one of Major Clark's, for our field of operations is to be there. Some firing was heard in the morning and soon an order

came for Gen. Ewell to move his command towards Brandy Station, as
the enemy was advancing in force. We moved rapidly down and formed
in line of battle near Brandy Station, but General Stuart succeeded in
driving them back across the River, after losing many officers and men.
He took considerable artillery. The enemy came over vigorously and fell
on some of the cavalry brigades, unawares, in the morning, and damaged
them considerably, but they rallied in [gallant] style and drove the enemy
back. We (Gen. Ewell and Staff and Gen. Lee and Staff) took a point of
observation at James Barbour's house near Brandy. It was thought the
enemy had infantry but it did not come forward. The day was quite warm.
At one time we thought the enemy's cavalry would come to our headquarters and General Ewell said we could gather into the house and defend it to the last. Rodes moved his division down to near Brandy Station and encamped near there.

Wednesday, June 10th. We remained at our headquarters near Culpeper C. H. I copied a map of the Valley. The day was very pleasant.
Rodes started towards Front Royal in the P.M., going, by the old Richmond Road to Flint Hill, as far as Hazel River. Johnson and Early took
the Sperryville turnpike.

Thursday, June 11th. We left our quarters at an early hour and went
by the Sperryville road, towards Front Royal, as far as Gaines' Cross
Roads and there encamped, near Johnson's division, which encamped last
night at Woodville. Rodes went on beyond Fling Hill and Early encamped between Little Washington and Gaines' Cross Road. Pendleton
and Gen. Ewell went to see General Lee and then came on in the carriage. The rest of us rode rapidly to Gaines' Cross Roads, 32 miles, and
there Generals Ewell, Johnson and Early discussed the plan of capturing
Winchester and Martinsburg. I was at the conference and made some suggestions as to routes, &c. which were afterwards adopted. Supped with
General Johnson. The day was very pleasant, the roads dusty but a
shower and fresh breeze improved the day. We found the grass, clover
and timothy, perfectly luxuriant, a great change from the bare fields of
Fredericksburg. The men marched well. Pickett's[2] division came to Culpeper C. H. yesterday and Longstreet moved his headquarters towards
Amissville. I worked at map of the Valley at night.

Friday, June 12th. We were roused up at 2 A.M: and I worked awhile
at a map for Gen. Rhodes. We got started at 4 A.M. and rode rapidly
through the fields and overtook Gen. Rodes, on the road between Flint
Hill and Sandy Hook, in motion, and he got into the carriage with Gen-

eral Ewell and we went on in advance of the army, crossing the Blue
Ridge at Chester's Gap and reached Front Royal, by 11 A.M., with our
advance. The passing of a pontoon train the day before had made the
people anticipate our coming and they came out everywhere to welcome
us. We crossed the rivers by the Winchester road, fording. Our pontoons
were on the shore there but Gen. Ewell said it would take too long to
put them down, so our advance waded the rivers. After we crossed
Crooked Run Gen. Jenkins[3] of the Cavalry joined us and Generals Rodes,
Early, Jenkins and Ewell had a consultation there and decided on plans;
General Rodes then moved on towards Berryville, going 5 miles to near
Stone Bridge. Gen. Johnson moved to near Cedarville and Gen. Early
encamped near the river. The day was a very fine one and we enjoyed
the transition from the Piedmont country to the Valley.

Saturday, June 13th. We started at $4\frac{1}{2}$ A.M. Johnson's division and
its Stonewall Brigade[4] being in advance, and we reached the toll-gate
by seven A.M. and the mattress show at $8\frac{1}{4}$ o'clock. Gen. Ewell went with
Johnson by the plank road. Early turned off at Nineveh to go by Newton,
at $7\frac{1}{2}$ A.M. At $8\frac{1}{2}$ we moved on, having started the enemy's picket near
the Opequon. Gen. Ewell said to Gen. Johnson: "You are the operator
now, I am only a looker on." At $9\frac{1}{2}$ there was a cavalry skirmish at Hogg
Run and the enemy's reserve picket was driven in. At $10\frac{1}{4}$ Johnson
skirmishers were thrown out, a half mile from Hogg Run, and some
skirmishing took place. Artillery opened at $11\frac{1}{2}$ and at 12 our infantry
advanced to the left of the plank road and some skirmishing took place
there; then we moved to the right and drove the enemy out of the woods
on the hill. Firing began on the Valley turnpike, near Kernstown, at the
same time; infantry and artillery quite rapid, at $12\frac{1}{2}$ P.M., the Stonewall
Brigade lying in line of battle in the hollow to the right of the road and
beyond Hogg Run—, Johnson's left in the valley of Hogg Run, to the
left of Mrs. Hamilton's $\frac{1}{4}$ mile, and reaching to the right near the Berryville Road. At 4 P.M. Early had a skirmish at the toll-gate on the Valley
turnpike. At $1\frac{1}{2}$ P.M. we opened a battery on the Front Royal road, at
the corner of the woods; a heavy cannonade took place,—the enemy being on the ridge near Hollinsworth's mill. Early had considerable skirmishing until dark—he reaching Hollinsworth's mill, the enemy holding
the hill there. We held all southwest of the town of Winchester. It began
to rain at $6\frac{1}{2}$ P.M. and rained more or less all night. Rodes took Martinsburg at sundown. We slept a mile back beyond Hogg Run.

Sunday, June 14th. Ground wet—cloudy. A few guns were fired by the enemy at 4 A.M. We rode to the front at 5 A.M. Lively skirmishing, by Early at $7\frac{1}{2}$, to the left of the Valley turnpike and on the hills in front of the Cedar Creek turnpike. Early took La. heights at 9 A.M. The enemy evacuated the hill, except skirmishers, at an early hour. At 10 A.M. a lively skirmish took place on the right. Johnson having moved to the woods on the right. At $10\frac{1}{4}$ A.M. skirmishers of the Stonewall Brigade advancing on our right towards the town and in the valley and an advance over the hill on the left. At $10\frac{3}{4}$ the battery on our left opened. At 11 a line of skirmishers on the right falling back. Very warm. At 4 P.M. skirmishing on the right. At 6 P.M. Early took the hill and at 8 P.M. advanced over it. The enemy fired several volleys after dark. We had our headquarters for the night on the top of the hill on the Front Royal Road near Bowers' house. The General and Staff witnessed the movements of the army from the hill on the Millwood Road. The firing was quite heavy. Early took [some] guns on the hill and his infantry turned them on the enemy as they fled. Early did not wait for his artillery to cease firing but moved up to the assault while the firing was [going] on, and so surprised the enemy. He made a long detour to the left. James Fulton of the Staunton Artillery, an old pupil of mine, was killed. A very warm day. Many people came out to see the fight.

Monday, June 15th. At 4 A.M. Johnson's division and a part of Early's had a fight with the retreating enemy about 4 miles below Winchester and took some 2,000 prisoners; says he took 30 with his opera glass. Milroy [escaped] after having his horse shot under him. Soon after 4 o'clock A.M. Gen. Ewell discovered the enemy's flag hauled down. Early had been ordered to the assault of the works. Gen. Ewell sent me to order Gordon⁵ to advance rapidly and take possession of property and protect it. I found him just at Fort "Jackson"—, his troops just then crossing the ravine. The Maryland troops had passed through the town and reached there before. Our victory was complete; we took 22 pieces of artillery; Gen. Rodes took 5 at Martinsburg; We also took over 300 wagons, many ambulances, &c. &c. all the baggage of Milroy's command was captured. The cavalry pursued and took many prisoners. Early had advanced his lines to storm the works at daylight but he found them abandoned. I took an order to Gordon to press on and aid Johnson. Our wagons soon came up and we moved to a camp some 3 miles from Winchester, near a pond, on the Martinsburg Road. The day was quite warm. I went to Winchester in the afternoon and looked for paper and engineering materials; visited Logan's house where Milroy had quartered. He was a great brute. The enemy escaped to Harper's Ferry, some 1,500—; we took about 6,000(?).

Tuesday, June 16th. Gen. Ewell called me, at an early hour, to go and make a map of the battlefield, so I was busy all day riding along the lines of the works of the enemy, our lines of march, &c. The enemy's lines of entrenchment were very strong. In the evening we ran up a Confederate flag, made from the U.S. flag on the staff in the main Yankee Fort and with a national salute of 13 guns we named it Fort "Jackson." General Early and Ewell were present, also many ladies who cheered the Generals. They called on Gen. Early for a speech. He said he had never been able to make a speech to one lady much less to so many. I took tea at Mrs. Kiger's. In the P.M. we moved our quarters to Mr. Boyd's, near Bunker's Hill, where we arrived late at night. Our cavalry went yesterday to Chambersburg, Pa.⁶

Wednesday, June 17th. I rode in the morning with Major A. S. Pendleton down to Gen. Rodes' headquarters, at Williamsport, and made some maps for General Rodes. Our men were destroying the canal. Early & Johnson moved towards Shepherdstown, Johnson in front. The day was very warm, the wind high and the dust flying in clouds. Gen. Rodes was in fine spirits. I spent the night at Rodes' headquarters. Our headquarters came to camp Stevens, four miles from Martinsburg towards Williamsburg.

Thursday, June 18th. I worked at a map of Maryland and Pennsylvania for General Rodes. General Ewell came down and Major Sorrell⁷ of Longstreet's Staff and with Gen. Rodes they planned the route of General Rodes and the movements of the Second Corps. The people of Maryland were much surprised at our advance. The day was quite pleasant. Late in the P.M. I rode back to our camp. It rained some in the P.M. and at night.

Friday, June 19th. We started at an early hour for Shepherdstown. Gen. Ewell went to Leetown to see Gen. Longstreet. I went on to Gen. Johnson's quarters and across the Potomac, at Shepherdstown, at the Rev. Mr. Douglass', as Gen. Ewell said Gen. Johnson might wish to consult me about routes, &c. The people of Shepherdstown were very glad to see us. Gen. Rodes advanced to Hagerstown and Gen. Early came near to Shepherdstown. Gen. Longstreet was near Charlestown and Gen. A. P. Hill near Berryville. It rained quite hard in the night and raised the river. I worked on a map for Gen. Johnson.

Saturday, June 20th. Spent the day at Mr. Douglass' very busy drawing maps. Heinrich's and Stalnaker came and drew maps also. Quite warm—; it rained some at night. Early is kept back by the high water; the enemy is still in Loudoun county.

Sunday, June 21st. Spent the day at Mr. Douglass'. Mr. Lacy preached a short sermon in the morning. I had to finish a map, by order. Early is still on the Virginia shore, Johnson at Sharpsburg, Rodes at Hagerstown and Jenkins near Chambersburg. Rain in the P.M. The river up.

Monday, June 22nd. We started at an early hour and went on to Boonsboro[8] and made some purchases there at reasonable prices. We rode through the battlefield of Sharpsburg. No traces of it left on the face of the country. We encamped three miles beyond Boonsboro, Early being near our headquarters, he having taken the wrong road; should have come by Cavetown. Johnson is near by. Rodes crossed into Pennsylvania today and went to near Greencastle. A warm pleasant day.

Tuesday, June 23rd. We started from our camp, three miles west of Boonsboro, at an early hour, and went on through Hagerstown, stopping to make some purchases. Then by way of Middleburg, crossing the Pennsylvania line, to Greencastle to General Rodes' headquarters. His infantry yesterday was the first advance of that sort into Pennsylvania. Early went by Cavetown and Waynesboro towards Gettysburg. Johnson came on behind Rodes. The people were much surprised to see us, but manifested no hostility—, [quietly] submitting to our rule. The day was quite pleasant. Judge Wilson and several others of us dined at a Penna. House. Contributions were levied at Greencastle.[9]

Wednesday, June 24th. We started from Greencastle at an early hour and went to Chambersburg, fixing our headquarters three miles beyond. We met with no opposition. We got a good dinner there, at the hotel, and purchased many valuable supplies—, levying contributions of the town. Jenkins cavalry was in advance. I procured maps, and engineering supplies and purchased some goods. The day was quite warm and the roads dusty. Gen. Rodes encamped near us, Gen. Johnson three miles back of town and Gen. Early in the gap of the South Mountain beyond Waynesboro. General Steuart took his brigade to McConnellsburg, via Mercersburg, to gather supplies. Richardson[10] went with him.

Thursday, June 25th. We spent the day in camp, 3 miles from Chambersburg. I went into town in the morning and made a few purchases. The Gen'. sent for me, while there, as he wanted maps to plan the movements of the next four days. Generals Early and Rodes came also. Early was to go to Gettysburg, York and Columbia Bridge. Worked at map part of the day. It began to rain in the afternoon. Richardson came back from McConnellsburg; the enemy fled from there at our approach; the people were much alarmed. We procured many supplies in Chambersburg. Early was at Greenwood and Friday went to Gettysburg.

Friday, June 26th. We marched, at an early hour, from our camp and came to one mile east of Shippensburg. The people looked sullen. Our cavalry is scouring the country for horses &c. The people are fearful of retribution from us, but some were disposed to joke and spoke of our being in the Union now. It rained most of last night and today. We occupied the houses of some Union people for the night, but no damage was done to anything. The land is full of everything and we have an abundance. The cherries are very fine. Our men behaved admirably. Gen. Lee wrote to Gen. Ewell that he thought the battle would come off near Fredericks City or Gettysburg.[11] Early encamped at Mummasburg.[12]

Saturday, June 27th. We spent the night on the Pine Road, one and a half miles from Shippensburg towards Carlisle, General Rodes being in front; Gen. Early operating East of South Mountain towards York;— Gen. Johnson takes the turnpike towards Carlisle, today, and Gen. Rodes the Walnut Bottom Road. Gen. Ewell and Staff accompanied Gen. Rodes. Gen. Steuart, of Johnson's Division, came back to Chambersburg from McConnellsburg. A. P. Hill and the Third Corps are near Chambersburg. It rained part of last night, and this morning, it is misty and roads quite muddy. We marched at 6 A.M., Jenkins in advance; he went on past Carlisle, meeting no opposition. We reached that place by one P.M. and took our headquarters at the United States Barracks. Rodes' Division encamped there and nearby. It is a lovely place and we enjoyed our rest there. Jenkins went 6 miles beyond Carlisle. The people were not as sullen as those at Chambersburg. The day became quite warm and pleasant. Early encamped near Berlin.

Sunday, June 28th. We spent the day at the barracks. Mr. Lacy preached there twice. Early left his Camp at Berlin and marched to York by noon and encamped there. We raised the Confederate flag, in the P.M., on the flag-staff at the Barracks, and remarks were made by Generals Rodes, Trimble, Daniels,[13] Ewell, &c. Quite an animating scene. Fine day. It rained in the P.M. Jenkins went to within 3 miles of Harrisburg. Gordon's Brigade of Early's division went to Wrightsville on the Susquehanna.

Monday, June 29th. I went to Carlisle in the morning, but the General sent after me and I made a map of Adams' county. He had ordered

Rodes to move in the afternoon towards Harrisburg. Jenkins having gone to within 3 miles of that place, but General Lee sent orders for us to move back to Gettysburg and Johnson's division started back to Chambersburg in the afternoon. Captain Johnson and Major Clark came up last night and went with Richardson down to near Harrisburg, today, to reconnoiter. Johnson and Clark came back and spent the night with me. The General was quite testy and hard to please, because disappointed, and had every one flying around. I got up in the night to answer questions and make him a map. General Jenkins shelled the works of the enemy on the south banks of the Susquehanna. It rained some in the afternoon and that night.

Tuesday, June 30th. We started at an early hour and went through Papertown; stopped awhile to examine the extensive paper mill there—, then went on across the Blue Ridge, through Peterstown, to Heidlersburg, stopping awhile on the mountain at a terrified old Dutchman's. We encamped near Heidlersburg. Early was some 3 miles off. It rained some but the day was quite pleasant.

Wednesday, July 1st. We marched towards Cashtown until we reached Middletown, having heard that the enemy was at Gettysburg. At Middletown we heard that A. P. Hill was approaching Gettysburg, from the mountains, so we turned with Rodes' Division and went on by the Middletown and Gettysburg road until within some 2 miles of Gettysburg when we turned to the right. Early came through Heidlersburg and went directly on to Gettysburg. We pressed forward and soon engaged the enemy on the hills to the west of Gettysburg. A. P. Hill attacked on our right at about the same time. At 11 A.M. firing of artillery by Hill; 11-30 infantry firing by Hill; 11-45 Rodes' line of battle advanced— Iverson being in front. We were moving in column along the crest of the hill. At 12 M. the enemy driven back and Hill advancing; 12-20 Hill's artillery brisk on the right; $2\frac{1}{2}$ P.M. Early's artillery opened on the left; $3\frac{1}{4}$ P.M. Early's infantry advanced and swept gallantly up to the town; Rodes advanced on our right and had severe fighting with the enemy on the [Emmitsburg ?] road. The enemy shelled our position on the hill and compelled us to retire; but our artillery played on them with effect just before Early advanced. The General was thrown from his horse, the horse being struck by a shell, on the head, and several were wounded near by. Early's line was thrown into some disorder by his advance and he reformed at 4 P.M. and moved into the town at 5 P.M. Heavy firing took place on our right. Rodes entered at about the same hour as Early and we followed into the town, meeting the crowd of prisoners coming back. Gen'l. Lee came up about 4½ P.M.

We supped and [slept] just in the edge of the town. We killed and wounded large numbers of the enemy and took several thousand prisoners. The complete success on our part. The pursuit was checked by the lateness of the hour and the position the enemy had secured in a cemetery. Quite warm in the P.M. and some rain in the A.M. but pleasant. We slept at Spangler's.[14] Our loss was not heavy though the enemy captured most of Iverson's Brigade.[15] We captured most of two Corps of the enemy, the 11th and [I Corps][16] Lieut. J. P. Smith came up today from taking Mrs. Jackson home.

Thursday, July 2nd. There was skirmishing going on nearly all day, a good deal of it in the town. At 4 P.M., Longstreet, having come up on the right, A. P. Hill being in the centre, and Ewell on the left, we made a vigorous attack on the enemy, although not a simultaneous one, and drove them from some of their positions; but they had strongly entrenched the hills on which they were and we did not succeed in gaining their main works. Longstreet drove the enemy some distance and captured a good [many] prisoners. Our attack on the left was repulsed with considerable loss to us, though we gained the outer works twice. General Lee was at our quarters in the A.M. and there planned the movement, though not, in my opinion, very sanguine of its success. He feared we would only take it at a great sacrifice of life. Mr. Lacy and myself, after the fight, went back to our wagons on the Fairfield road. I spent the night at Allan's (Lieut. Col. Wm. Chief of Ordnance Second Corps). A fine day, some little rain. General Ewell stayed at Spangler's.

Friday, July 3rd. A terrific cannonade took place about sunrise but with no results. We had 120 pieces of artillery on one ridge; 400 pieces were firing at the same time. Skirmishing and occassional firing was kept up until 1 P.M., When the attack was furiously renewed and we drove the enemy from their works, but our supports were not near enough and the enemy rallied and regained them. Pickett's division took the hill on the right, but Pettigrew[17] failed to sustain him. We were repulsed on all sides; only gained a little ground from the enemy who kept closely in his works and did not advance. Our loss was very great, the men fighting with desperation and great valor. Many were killed and wounded. Captain Richardson of the Engineer Corps was wounded yesterday. Stuart had a fight with the enemy on the left and whipped them. The Generals had a council at General A. P. Hill's headquarters on the Cashtown Road, about sun-down, and decided to fall back. Our wagons were parked on the hill above the Black Horse Tavern on the Fairfield Road. I met Pickett's Division, returning after the battle, that night, scattered all along the road; no officers and all protesting that they had been completely cut up. A general movement of wagons, wounded, prisoners, etc., took place to the rear, and the unmistakable signs of a retreat were plentiful. There was a general feeling of despondency in the army at our great losses, though the battle is regarded as a drawn one. We have taken some 8,000 prisoners and sent a large number of them to Carlisle today, paroling them there, though Halleck[18] refuses to acknowledge any such parole. The day was quite warm and there was a shower in the P.M. The conference of the Generals took place on the Cashtown Road one and a half miles from the Evangelical Lutheran Seminary. I went back to the wagons and worked on a map. Our line was withdrawn to the top of the hill and the General (Ewell) spent the night there. The heads of departments were summoned to prepare to move and activity prevailed most of the night. I slept in Mr. Lacy's tent.

Saturday, July 4th. I got up at 2 A.M. and went to work on a map of the country back towards Virginia. Major Harman, the Chief Q.M. of the 2nd. Corps, started, about 3 A.M., with a train of baggage and captured property for Williamsport. The General (Ewell) told him to get that train safely across the Potomac or he wanted to see his face no more. Everything is moving to the rear; our troops are in line of battle on the ridge in front of Gettysburg. Mr. Robinson[19] (S. B. of 7th La.) came to me to-day to assist in making maps and is at work. We had a tremendous thunder shower in the A.M. and took a fine sleep during it. We moved our wagons out towards Fairfield to graze the horses. The General is staying on the Cashtown Road but everything is moving on the Fairfield Road, the First Corps in the front and the Second in the rear. We spent the night on some rails, by the road side, four miles from Gettysburg. The General came up late; we piled on the rails and made a large fire; it rained most of the night and our army was passing all the time. Many wounded men were also moved back. Our loss was very heavy yesterday but we only fell back to the hills. It was quite cool.

Sunday, July 5th. General Lee came down in the A.M. and determined to fight the enemy if they came on to a place he should select. The First and Third Corps passed by and left the Second in the rear. The enemy did not come up and we moved on to Fairfield, stopping there to see General Lee. The enemy's cavalry and artillery came on and got a hill and shelled the rear of our train. We soon drove them off and came on and encamped on the ridge beyond Fairfield. Longstreet went on. The enemy's cavalry attacked our train, on the mountains, yesterday, and captured some of it, but the most of it went through and reached Williamsport this morning. We drove the enemy back and they encamped beyond Fairfield. It rained quite hard last night. Rodes is our rear guard today and encamped with us.

Monday, July 6th. We started at an early hour continuing the march; the enemy followed slowly, only advancing as we retired.[20] Early was in the rear yesterday and Rodes is to-day. It was quite misty in the morning. We moved slowly on, crossing the mountains (South or Blue Ridge) by Monterey Springs and Waterloo to Waynesboro, and there encamped. The General (Ewell) sent me to see General Lee, at Waterloo, at the foot of the mountain, to learn about the route, the location of Middleburg, &c. General Lee told me to go back quickly and tell General Ewell that we had not lost many wagons, that Imboden and the wagoners had whipped the Yankee cavalry at Wiliamsport, and tell him: "If these people keep coming on, turn back and thresh them soundly." When I told General Ewell he said: "By the blessing of Providence I will do it"; and he sent back to Rodes to fight them, but they only followed to the top of the mountain. Longstreet and A. P. Hill went to Hagerstown and Stuart and the wagoners had a fight with the Yankee cavalry there. It was quite a fine day. We got some supplies at Waynesboro.

Tuesday, July 7th. We came on through Leitersberg to near Hagerstown and encamped near the Greencastle Road, one and a half miles from Hagerstown. Rodes south of the road to Leitersberg and Early on the Greencastle Road, Johnson back near the crossing of the Antietam. It rained in the P.M. and very hard at night; bad sleeping in the mud, but all bore it patiently. General Lee has his camp some 2½ miles from Hagerstown, on the road toward Williamsport.

Wednesday, July 8th. We, General Ewell and Staff, went over to General Lee's and there found Generals Longstreet and A. P. Hill and the engineers of the several corps and thence went on a reconnoissance of a line of defense from Hagerstown towards Williamsport. We were all day in the saddle. It was quite pleasant in the P.M. We rode until dark. The enemy had a cavalry force at Boonsboro and Stuart fought them there. A fine warm day.

Thursday, July 9th. We went to General Lee's early in the morning and selected a line of defense on the left of the road, a continuation of the line selected yesterday. Generals Lee, Early, Ewell, and Hill rode with us until 12 M., then they went back to General Lee's and the rest of us (Col. Smith, Captain Howard[21] and myself) went on to the left. We took dinner at a house in that direction. A fine day; quite warm in the P.M. All quiet along the lines.

Friday, July 10th. Worked awhile at a map of the vicinity of Williamsport, then went over to General Lee's and put the ridge for defense on his map. The Lieut. Generals were all there. The enemy advanced to the line of the Antietam and we had a cannonade and some skirmishing with them. We retired to the bank of the stream. Generals Early, Rodes and Johnson moved, late in the day, to the positions selected for them on the Williamsport road. I conducted Gen. Johnson's division. We moved our headquarters to a point on the National road one and a half miles west of Hagerstown. Very warm, everything growing finely; the harvest is going on, much of the wheat being cut. We have fed and destroyed much grain.

Saturday, July 11th. I rode over the line selected by the Engineers and the Generals, in the morning, with Generals Ewell, Rodes, Early and Johnson and the positions for the troops were chosen and they were assigned to their places and put in position and commenced fortifying. The First Corps was put on the right and reached to the River (Potomac) below Falling Waters; the Third Corps came next on the left and extended to the Funkstown road; the Second Corps reached across to the National Road a mile west of Hagerstown and at night we went some 3 miles from Hagerstown towards Williamsport to a large spring. A fine day. All along our front the enemy is making movements.

Sunday, July 12th. Our line was very well fortified this morning and some skirmishing ensued during the day. The enemy is fortifying also. We were roused at an early hour expecting a fight to-day. I went down to Williamsport to see what was going on and found the ferries busy and the Quartermasters making arrangements to ford the river, so I took a party, at the request of Major Harman, and made a causeway on the Virginia shore. Had considerable trouble to get it fixed. We began crossing wagons at 3 P.M. had quite an exciting time. Had a heavy thunder shower at about 3 P.M. It also rained at night. We had our headquarters at the same place as last night. We had three ferries going, but to pass 4,000 wagons over a wide and swollen river is a serious matter. Some heavy skirmishing in the P.M.

Monday, July 13th. We were up and breakfasted at an early hour, about 4 A.M., the skirmishing beginning at about that time, and all thought we would surely have a desperate battle, but the firing soon ceased and comparative quiet reigned along the lines most of the day. There was a gradual movement of our forces to the right as the enemy was concentrating in that direction. Yesterday our Engineer troops made boats to supply the place of those we had lost, and today, by noon, the pontoon was finished at Falling Waters and the river became fordable at Williamsport, so we passed our wagons over rapidly. I went down and saw my wagon safely ferried over—then came back to our headquarters on the Williamsport Road, then went along down our line and passed over the pontoon at Falling Waters. Our wagons soon came up and I went with them to Camp Stevens, four and a half miles from Martinsburg. The train passed the pontoon quite rapidly; the artillery began to move about dark, the infantry also began to move towards the river—the cavalry taking their places along the lines. It rained throughout the day and very hard at night; all were very weary; it was quite late when we encamped; the whole Virginia shore was alive with wagons.

Tuesday, July 14th. The infantry commenced crossing the river at 1 A.M. to-day—Longstreet first crossing the pontoon and A. P. Hill behind him leaving a rear guard. Ewell's Corps waded the river at Williamsport, the water reaching up to the arm-pits of the men. It was said that we lost 8,000 pairs of shoes in crossing.[22] Everything came safely over and the cavalry crossed soon this morning. The enemy's cavalry came on and surprised some of Hill's men but suffered in consequence when they rallied. The enemy fired his artillery at our cavalry after they had crossed at Williamsport. General Ewell came up to our camp at 4 A.M. and we moved to a dry place in the woods, the camp named "Stephens" by General Jackson June 20th, 1861. The day was quite pleasant and we all dried ourselves. Johnson's division encamped near us. Rodes and Early back towards Falling Waters. General Lee went on towards Martinsburg (Gen. Jackson was at Camp Stephens until July 2nd. 1861).

Wednesday, July 15th. Orders were [given] to march at 8 A.M., but the First and Third Corps did not get by, so we did not march until in the afternoon when Johnson's division went to Darkesville, but Rodes stopped at the Big Spring, three miles from Martinsburg, and Early behind him. Longstreet and Hill went on to Bunkers Hill. We encamped, quite late, at Big Spring. I spent part of the day at Colonel Charles James Faulkner's. A fine warm day.

Thursday, July 16th. We went to Darkesville and selected a camp at

Byerley's Mill, our Corps being on the waters of Middle Creek. A fine day.

Friday, July 17th. Spent the day in camp; made a beginning of a reduction of a map of Western Virginia. An order for a large reduction of baggage was a result of a conference of the Generals yesterday, so I packed up my wagon to go [back]. All our headquarters are to go into two wagons, a necessary thing, as our wagons, ambulances and artillery extend over some 50 miles of road when on a march. Johnson's division went down to Martinsburg to tear up the railroad.

Saturday, July 18th. I went up to Winchester to see my baggage off; did not start until late; the day was very warm. I dined at Dr. McGuire's —then came down with Colonel Allan in the P.M. and supped with him at his camp.

Sunday, July 19th. Spent the day in camp; Mr. Lacy preached in the morning. I wrote some in my Journal and also wrote home. The Generals had a conference. A fine day but quite warm. Pickett got orders to occupy Snicker's Gap and went to Berryville, but the Yankees got to the gap first; he tried Ashby's Gap the same way; then he pressed on and three regiments got to Chester's Gap and one to Manassas Gap before the yankees. Pickett lost some men in crossing the river.

Monday, July 20th. We spent the day in camp, making maps, &c. Johnson sent word that the enemy had come to Hedgesville and he thought we might entrap him by going back of the North Mountain, so Early started in the P.M. to the valley of Back Creek and Rodes towards Martinsburg. The General and most of the Staff went on to Johnson's headquarters. The camp remained over night and I remained there. A fine warm day. Lieut. William G. Williamson[23] reported here, today, for engineer duty. A fine warm day. Longstreet started for Berryville.

Tuesday, July 21st. I went on to Martinsburg and found General Ewell a mile beyond but we soon heard that the enemy had left so Rodes was turned back and Johnson followed. Early came on to two miles this side of Hedgesville and encamped. We came back and slept at our old camp at Darkesville, though the wagons were sent to Winchester yesterday, A. P. Hill moving also that way. A warm day.

Wednesday, July 22nd. We came up to Winchester and encamped one mile northeast, near a branch of the Red Bud. Rodes went to Abram's Creek. Johnson encamped on the Red Bud and Early came to Bunker's Hill. A fine day. I worked at a map in the P.M.

Thursday, July 23rd. We went on towards Front Royal; Rodes went on through Front Royal and found the enemy coming through Manassas Gap and aided Wright's Brigade in giving them a handsome reception; with one division repulsing two or three corps. Johnson came on and encamped near Cedarsville, but was hurried up to aid Rodes; both finally came on up the River. Rodes' advance coming to near Asbury chapel, and we had our headquarters there. I rode in the carriage, via Middletown, to Cedarville and so on. We passed a portion of Jones' division on its way to Winchester . . . . A fine day. We lost 45 killed and wounded. Blackberries are getting ripe and are quite nice now. Our pontoon was across the River at Front Royal.

Friday, July 24th. We went on to a point three miles beyond Milford. Rodes stopped at Milford. The pontoon was taken up and removed up the Valley turnpike; everything got out of Front Royal which the enemy occupied but did not press on. I went over to Browntown and posted some pickets. The day was hot and our men suffered much.

Saturday, July 25th. We came up to Pass Run and fixed our headquarters near the Brick Church—, Rodes being just below the Sperryville Road. Johnson is encamped near the Luray and Front Royal, on Pass Run; Early spends tonight at Mt. Jackson; Longstreet and A. P. Hill are in Culpeper. We find elegant pasturage here. The day was very warm.

Sunday, July 26th. We spent the day in our camps resting; services were generally held. Mr. Lacy preached at Headquarters in the A.M. I wrote home by Lieutenant Smith; wrote in my Journal. The day very warm. Early marches to this side of Massanutton Mountain today. The enemy advanced to near Little Washington. Shower in the P.M.

Monday, July 27th. We marched at an early hour across the Blue Ridge to Sperryville and encamped two miles beyond at Mr. [?]. The day was very pleasant; the roads in a horrible condition from having been neglected so long. It rained quite hard in the P.M. Williamson went on ahead to select Camp. I read the first volume of Les Miserables of Hugo. Worked some at night. Rodes encamped near us; Johnson on Hughes River; Early crossed at Fisher's Gap (Milam's) and encamped near Criglersville. A very warm day.

Wednesday, July 29th. We moved early and went on to Madison C. H. Rodes encamped on the west bank of Robertson River and Johnson on the east bank; Early moved to the west of Madison C. H. We fixed our headquarters on the James City Road a mile east of the C. H. I finished a map of the region in which we are operating. The day was warm and pleasant.

Thursday, July 30th. I worked awhile at a map then went to Culpeper C. H., to Gen. Lee's headquarters, to see Col. William Proctor Smith,[24] Chief Engineer of the Army. Got there in the P.M. and found him away, but he came about dark. The engineers had been locating a line of defense on the south bank of the Rapidanne. Major Clark was there also. I spent the night with Col. Smith and procured the maps, etc., that I wanted. There was quite a heavy shower in the P.M. The enemy is in Fauquier County, Meade[25] being near Gatlett's, or Bealton. The day was quite pleasant. All in camp.

Friday, July 31st. Saw General Lee and talked about the roads, &c., then I came back to headquarters, via Colvin's Tavern; got there by 2 P.M. Soon after my arrival a message came that the enemy was moving towards Fredericksburg and we were ordered to move towards Orange C. H.; so we moved our headquarters to Jack's Shop; Rodes moved up to near us and Johnson followed. Early moved to the Rapidanne at Barnett's Ford. We worked quite late at night. It was very warm. Gen. Ewell's wife came up today and he went on to Liberty Mills.

Saturday, August 1st. We started quite early and went to Orange C. H. and took our camp near Mr. Shaw's, our wagons soon got up and we went to work copying the maps of Culpeper and Louisa Counties. The day was intensely hot. Johnson fixed his camp between Orange C. H., on Two Run, and Early went to near Pisgah Church[26] at the foot of Clark's Mountain. The day was intensely hot. General Ewell spent the day with his family.

Sunday, August 2nd. We were obliged to work to-day to copy the maps lent us by Col. Smith, and were very busy all day and worked late last night. It continues very hot. The enemy advanced towards Culpeper C. H. and we had a little fight with them, some of the first or third corps on our side. We had 15 killed and a number wounded and killed and wounded quite a number of the enemy.

Monday, August 3rd. We finished the maps of Culpeper and Louisa about 2 P.M. and I sent the originals to Col. Smith. The day was very hot. Gen. Ewell and Gen. Rodes rode over the line selected for defense yesterday. Gen. Ewell is away with his wife today. It is said the enemy is advancing.

Tuesday, August, 4th. I obtained permission from Gen. Ewell to go home for a day or so to get some maps, etc., and fixed up this morning and went with William (Gearing, my servant) on the cars. Gen. Lee was at our headquarters in the morning, having moved his headquarters out of Culpeper, and today he pitched them near here. Gen. Rodes also went upon the train. It was very warm. We were delayed by the down train and I did not get to Staunton until after dark—, then I got a horse of Major Bell[27] and rode home by mid-night. Was delighted to get there and found all delighted to see me after my 6 months absence. Thunder storms at night.

Wednesday, August 5th. Spent a delightful day at home; a glorious, joyous one. O! that I could spend many such. Called on several neighbors and all were glad to see me. Everything here (At Churchville and Loch Willow house) appears prosperous. A heavy rain in P.M.; quite warm.

"I spent the day in camp"

THURSDAY, AUGUST 6TH. Started back at 5 A.M. Had a hard ride to Staunton; found my boy William there and got back to Camp in the P.M. after a very hot ride. The cars were full of returning soliders. Gen. Rodes went back and we snacked together.

Friday, August 7th. Wrote some and worked at a map of routes, etc. Very warm; it rained quite hard and was very muddy at our camp.

Saturday, August 8th. Worked during A.M. on a map of routes of Second Corps from Fredericksburg, Va. to Gettysburg, Pa., and back, to accompany my report for June and July. In P.M. I went to look for a new camp. Late in P.M. we moved to the top of the hill, into Mr. Shaw's yard,—a fine place. Gen. Ewell got into a towering fashion about the move. A heavy rain in P.M. Very warm.

Sunday, August 9th. I spent the day in camp, reading. Mr. Lacy preached in Early's Division. Generals Lee, Ewell, and others, went to Orange C. H. to church. I heard today that Hood's Division is at Chancellorsville and another of Longstreet's is at Raccoon Ford. The day was very warm.

Monday, August 10th. Worked at a map of Spotsylvania and verified some other maps. The weather is very warm, almost suffocating. Mrs. Ewell and her daughter went away today.

Tuesday, August 11th. Reduced a map of Spotsylvania County which Mr. Robinson reduced again for our general map. The day was intensely hot. Maj. John Harman came back from his visit home. Our army is filling up daily and will soon be in fine condition. Drilling is going on.

Wednesday, August 12th. Worked at map of vicinity of Winchester, until P.M., then went down to General Lee's to see Col. Smith and obey an order of General Ewell's to obtain a map of our line of defense, and also see what Col. Smith wished me to do. He gave me a portion of the country to map carefully for General Lee. It was very warm and we had rain in the night. All quiet.

Thursday, August 13th. Worked in A.M. verifying a map of Orange Co. copied by Mr. Robinson. We had a heavy shower, with thunder, in A.M. In P.M. I rode up to Gen. Johnson's headquarters and saw Lieut. Hinrichs and divided the line of river given me to have mapped with him, he to come to Popular Run and Two Run. I then sketched a portion of the road near Orange C. H. Gen. Johnson told me of his route at Winchester. Quite warm part of the day. Major Pendleton went this A.M. down to Moss Neck to see his old sweetheart.[1] I approved an application of H. Von Stenicker[2] for pay, at $3 per diem, as draughtsman.

Friday, August 14th. I went down in the morning to see Col. Smith, but met him in the road, so I went on to my work. Went along the River from Barnett's Ford to Peyton's Ford and sketched the roads in the vicinity. Bathed in the river. It was very warm in the A.M. and there was a heavy rain with thunder in P.M. Mrs. Ewell came back today. We commenced fortifying our line. In the evening I went down to Gen. Lee's and got a map of Rapahannock Co.

Saturday, August 15th. Spent the day reconnoitering along the Orange and Alexandria Railroad down to Rapidanne Station. The day was quite warm and we had a hard thunder storm in the P.M.

Sunday, August 16th. Spent the day in camp. Mr. Lacy preached us an excellent sermon on "The Spirit and The Bride Say Come." The day was very warm. We had a heavy thunder storm with high wind after dark. Mr. Yarrington called to see me in the evening.

Monday, August 17th. Went on my reconnoissance. We rode over the roads to the left of the Barnett Ford road. Quite warm.

Tuesday, August 18th. Went down by Marye's and to Rapidan Station then back by Mrs. Taylor's. The day was warm. We had a discussion in

the evening about Gen. Jackson's having been recalled from Franklin by
Gen. Johnston. Pendleton said Gen. Jackson intended to fight Milroy
(at Franklin) but the smoke of the burning woods delayed him until the
enemy had had time to collect their forces at Franklin and draw some
away from Bank's in the valley, then he determined to come back and fall
on Banks before Fremont could join him. He says Gen. Jackson intended
to come back by Brock's Gap and that Gen. Jos. E. Johnston did not
order him back. Smith said he had read a letter from Gen. J. E. Johnston
to Gen. Jackson, written a few days after the battle of McDowell, in
which he told Gen. Jackson not to go too far into the mountains, but to
come back to Swift Run Gap and remember that his was only "an army
of observation." He also wrote General Jackson that he had ordered Gen.
Ewell to Richmond. Gen. Jackson sent to Gen. Ewell to come and see
him, on his way back, and Gen. Ewell came up to Mt. Solan to see Gen.
Jackson, one Sunday morning, and they had a conference there in which
Gen. Ewell showed his orders to go to Richmond. Gen. Jackson unfolded
to Gen. Ewell his idea of the condition of Banks and the advantage of
falling on him and Gen. Ewell said he would go with him if Gen. Jackson would assume the responsibility. Gen. Jackson said he would, and
Gen. Ewell went back then and moved on, and the Louisiana Brigade
came to near 10th Legion and there Gen. Ewell came to see Gen. Jackson
again and showed him preemptory orders from Gen. Johnston to come to
Richmond. Gen. Jackson put the orders in his pocket and they went on
to Winchester. Gen. Lee was at our headquarters in the P.M.

Wednesday, August 19th. Remained in camp to make a map of my
surveys. The day was quite warm but it was cool at night. Drew all day.
Mr. Lacy slept with me at night, some preachers being in his tent. Gen.
Ewell and most of his Staff went to Clark's Mountain for a picnic. Col.
Lee brought up a copy of "The Life of Stonewall Jackson," by John Esten
Cooke,[3] and we had quite a talk over it; dissenting from some things but
rather gratified at the tone of it. Received a letter from my brother. Sorry
he had not heard from me for a long time.

Thursday, August 20th. We had a heavy fog in the early morning. I
spent the day drawing a map of the vicinity of the Rapidan; worked some
18 hours. The day was quite warm. Generals Rodes and Johnson were at
our headquarters for some time. A son of Dr. Ben M. Smith was here
during the day.

Friday, August 21st. This is a fast day, proclaimed by the President
of the Confederate States,[4] and has been observed as a Sabbath in the

Camp. Mr. Lacy preached at our headquarters and nearly a thousand soldiers and many officers came to hear him. General Lee and Staff and Generals Johnson, Rodes, Ramseur,[5] Hoke,[6] and others were there. Mr. Lacy took his text from the 16th. verse of the 6th. chapter of 2nd. Kings and gave us a noble discourse in which he handled, unsparingly, our sins as an army and people, but held out that God must be on our side because we are in the right as proven by our deeds, and our enemies had shown themselves cruel and blood-thirsty. He said our army had not been defeated, but had been asked to do an impossible thing and had not done it. His allusions to General Jackson in his prayers were very fine. After the sermon there was to Virginia an exchange of salutations among those present. General Lee, I noticed, spoke to each lady there and to all the children. The day has been very warm. After sermon Dr. Coleman, of Johnson's Division, conversed with a group of us for sometime and we spoke of Cooke's Life of Jackson which had just come out, and also of Dr. Dabney's sermon on him, from which he read some extracts, but said the finest tribute he had ever heard was from a Mrs. Neal, at Yerby's, near Hamilton's Crossing. She had been very attentive to our wounded there during the battle of December 13th., flying about, in her mob cap, and ministering food, prepared by herself, mingled with tears when overcome by feeling. He had not seen her again until after the battle of Chancellorsville. When he called to thank her for her kindness and assistance while he had his hospital there before. Their conversation turned to General Jackson, when she said her opinion of him had entirely changed after his family came there and she saw the stern warrior unbend himself and fondle his child and talk artlessly to it, and how deeply and fondly he loved his wife, coming there, often late at night and going away before day in the morning; and that she admired him so that she got to thinking of the efforts the Yankees would make to capture him if they knew of his lodging, totally unguarded; and that one night she thought of it until she could restrain herself no longer and she rushed up to his room and said: "General; why don't you bring a guard with you here at night and have them go with you in the morning? You have them and it is not right for you to expose yourself thus. Your life does not belong to you, you belong to the country." He smiled and she proceeded. "After this war is over and we have achieved our independence, I don't care how soon you die," (and here she covered up her face and wept bitterly while telling it to Dr. Coleman) "for *this* world has no honor commensurate with your merits."

Dr. McGuire spoke of a remark by General Jackson, made near Charlestown, expressing a desire to live on account of his family, but not for himself, for he was satisfied that if he died he would go to Heaven.[7] Mr. Lacy spoke of the baptismal scene, at Mr. Yerby's, when he baptized Julia Laura, daughter of General Jackson. The day has been very warm. I wrote to my brother at night.

Saturday, August 22nd. I went to Barnett's Ford and to Hidens' Hill to examine some roads. Verified a map of Rappahannock County in the morning. General Early and the Louisiana Brigade had a fuss about his saying they were all a pack of thieves. General Ewell received a game cock and a Sumatra hen. I worked at a map until late at night. We had a tomato supper. Dr. McGuire, Smith and myself. Everything quiet. The commissary issues green corn and an abundance of everything.

I asked Dr. McGuire what there was in the tale about General Jackson's standing guard at Manassas while his brigade slept. He said it was true in this way:—"We left Winchester to go to Manassas one day at 1 P.M. and reached Paris, 18 miles distant, by 1 A.M. the next day. The men being unaccustomed to march were very weary. Most of the Staff (Pendleton, Ned Lee[8] and Jones) all except McGuire, went to a Hotel at once and left the General and Doctor by the road, where the General turned in his men to encamp. They got off their horses and sat on the fence. The Dr. asked him if he intended to put out any guards.—"No, said he, for the men are very weary and are to march at dawn. I will wait here myself and put the artillery in camp and see to things." The Dr. observed that he was very sleepy and he proposed to watch and turn Capt. Pendleton's artillery in, by the old church on Piles, where he wanted it. So the General laid down on some hay and slept and McGuire fell asleep also, but was awakened by the rumbling of the cannon. The next morning they went on towards the depot and got to where the roads forked, one going on the other to the depot. The General left McGuire there to turn the wagons and artillery one way and the men the other; he then went on, but soon came back and asked if the staff had come up, and when told they had not he said; "Well, when they come up, label them and send them on."

He also said that during the battle of Manassas Gen. Jackson was wounded and some one told him (Dr. McGuire) and he was much alarmed, being at his hospital, just below the Lewis House. While they were talking the General came up, and hearing what they said, smiled and held up his hand, the left, which had one finger shattered, saying:

"I am not much hurt" and when Dr. McGuire was going to leave some patients to come to him, he said: "Do not leave the others to come to me. Attend to them first." When the Dr. added—"There are plenty here to attend to them"—the Gen. said: "Then you may dress mine, as I wish to go back to the field." The surgeons around advised that the finger be cut off. Dr. McGuire dissenting, said: "General, I expect you had better have it cut off as these gentlemen advise." "But what do you think of it said the General?" "Why I think it can be saved." He replied—"Then you do what you think best." While McGuire was bandaging the wound some one said—"There comes the President." Mr. Davis came riding down the hill, at break-neck speed, on a rawboned horse. General Jackson jumped up and swinging his cap said: "Three cheers for the President," at the top of his voice and with great enthusiasm. Shortly after this he said to Dr. McGuire—"If they will give me 10,000 men, I will go to Washington to-night."

Sunday, August 23rd. Mr. Lacy preached a short sermon, at 9 A.M., to a few besides the Staff. It was earnest and good. I spent the day in camp. Generals Johnson and Rodes were over here for awhile. The news from Charleston looks as though we would have to evacuate Sumter. The day was very warm. Elliot Johnson came back. Early and the Louisiana Brigade had some trouble.[9]

Monday, August 24th. I finished the map of my survey in the morning—, then went to see Hinrichs. who has nearly completed his, then came back and went to General Lee's and procured from Major Clark a map of King William County to reduce. Mr. Robinson is reducing, or rather copying, my map. Last night was quite pleasant, but it was very warm during the day and we had a thunder storm at $7\frac{1}{2}$ P.M. I received, yesterday, a copy of John Esten Cooke's Life of Jackson, presented by the author. General Lee went to Richmond.

Tuesday, August 25th. I worked at the reduction of King William; Mr. Robinson copying Culpeper County. The day was quite warm and showery; it rained hard in the P.M. and at night. Pendleton went to Richmond. Some excitement about a raid on Staunton. Wrote report at night.

Wednesday, August 26th. Worked at reduction of King William; Mr. Robinson at copying Culpeper. In the P.M. all the Staff went to a review of Rodes', Ramseur's and Daniels' brigades. It was very fine. The soldiers presented a very fine appearance. It was quite cool last night.

Thursday, August 27th. I finished the reduction of King William; Mr. R. still at Culpeper. Last night was very cool and so was part of the day. General Ewell went to a review of Rodes' other Brigades. Pendleton came to me for General Jackson's cap, saying Mrs. Jackson wanted it. I refused to give it to him unless Mrs. Jackson requested it in writing, knowing the circumstances as to its coming into my possession. He told of [Frederick] Volcks' having all General Jackson's clothes, boots, etc., to aid in forming a complete statue. He said that in making the bust from the cast he had made the nose Roman, as Boteler and others insisted, but he called in Mrs. Jackson and she at once detected the fault and he corrected it to suit her ideas. In the evening I had a long talk with J. P. Smith about General Jackson and what his friends said. He told me of a long article, by General F. H. Smith which he had prepared to read to the Cadets, in which he spoke of General Jackson's early life, hard manual labor, etc., and his getting him appointed to the command at Harper's Ferry, &c. Saying he had all this from papers in his possession alone. One night he came to where Mrs. Jackson was and read it to her and some others. When he ended there was a long silence. General Smith then asked if it met with her approbation, adding that it was all established by documents. She replied "It is correct in the main, but afterwards she told General Smith she would like to correct many things in it, one especially about his working so hard, though no disgrace. He had never been hearty and when young could not endure hard labor."[10]

Capt. Johnson (Elliot of Md.) spoke of an interview at Harper's Ferry between General Jackson and the Supt. of Transportation of the Baltimore and Ohio Railroad in the early part of the war. Benj. F. Butler,[11] who was commanding at Baltimore, sent this Supt. to Jackson to propose to him that if he, Jackson, would let [beef] come over his end of the road, he, Butler, would let groceries go over his. General Jackson said to him—"You took good care to get all your stock on your end of the road; did you not?" "Of course I did, as was my duty, regardless of my opinions." "Very well; tell Gen. Butler we can do as well without raisins and almonds as he can without beef." To the amazement of the Agent, asking if he had anything more to say, and upon replying that he had not, General Jackson bade him good-morning.

Captain Johnson also said that on the first day of the battle at Groveton (2nd Manassas), while following up an advancing line of battle, General Jackson saw some stragglers—, when he fiercely called out to them—"Clear out, you cowards." "Go to the woods and hide yourselves." "Never show your faces again."

Friday, August 28th. I rode up to see Hinrichs and met him coming down with his report, so I came back and chatted a while with him and with Mr. Yarrington, the correspondent of the Richmond Dispatch, then wrote out my report of the operations of June and July and of the marches of the Second Corps. In the P.M. took my report and map, list of maps, map of part of Orange County and Hinrich's report, to Col. William Proctor Smith; found him in good humor and got maps of Hanover and Henrico Counties. Col. Smith and I rode over to Ramseur's drill and he came on to our headquarters. The day was quite cool in the morning. Last night cold. General Lee still away. General Ewell went to a review of Johnson's Brigade.

Saturday, August 29th. I worked all day reducing the map of part of Orange County by Lieut. Hinrich's. It was quite cool. All were away to a review. General Early came to our camp, at night, and brought his report of the operations of his Division from Fredericksburg to Gettysburg and back to Orange C. H. We had a long talk about the battle of Fredericksburg and he spoke of sending in the brigades of his command, one after another, as he heard of the eruption of the enemy and without waiting for orders. We also conversed about Sharpsburg and the coming up of McLaws, etc. I read Les Miserables (Cosette). Picnic at General Johnson's. Rained during the day.

Sunday, August 30th. Mr. Lacy gave us a short sermon, at 9 A.M., to our few at headquarters; then all scattered to different churches. I remained in camp in the forenoon but in the afternoon went to Gen. Johnson's headquarters and heard Mr. Lacy preach there, to a very large audience, on the nice seats prepared there, from "Jesus of Nazareth Passes by."—I wrote home, read some &c. In the evening McGuire, Pendleton, Smith and myself had a long talk on matrimony. The day was quite cool. I supped with Dr. Black. General Ewell spoke in the morning of the anecdote Gov. Smith[12] told of him at Lynchburg, and said it was one of the biggest lies that ever was told. I received a letter from home.

Monday, August 31st. I finished the reduction of Hinrich's map and looked over the one of Hanover County which Robinson had just copied. Most of the day was cool. A review of some of the brigades of Johnson's division took place and to-night they are dancing on the lawn at our headquarters. Everything is quiet; General Lee still in Richmond. There is a wild rumor that part of this army is to go to Tennessee.[13]

Tuesday, September 1st. I took my map to Colonel Smith, in the morning, and got some more maps; came back and took some maps to Hinrichs to reduce; he came to our quarters for a time. The day pleasant, the nights cool.

Wednesday, September 2nd. Copied Brown's Valley Map part of the day. Col. Smith came for me to go and look at the line of defense and at part of my work about which there was some dispute. I vindicated my map by the ground. We rode to Col. Alexander's and spent an hour there. Early's review took place today. There was a dense fog in the morning but the day was pleasant. I wrote to John Esten Cooke. Robinson is copying a map of Richmond and vicinity.

Thursday, September 3rd. Worked at a tracing of the Valley. Day quite pleasant. Robinson at same map. Some troops were sent to Richmond.

Friday, September 4th. Worked at tracing of map of the Valley—Robinson as before. Dr. R. L. Dabney came up today to obtain materials for his life of Jackson and we had a long talk on various topics about him.[14] A fine day. Drew my pay for July and August—$280.

Saturday, September 5th. I completed my tracing of map of Valley; Robinson at same map. Quite a fine day, fall like. Received a long letter from my brother. At night we had a long talk about Jackson and Dr. McGuire related many things about him to Dr. Dabney. The conversation was very interesting and brought many good things to light. Rev. Mr. Rice came to day and Mr. Lacy slept with me.

Sunday, September 6th. Dr. Dabney gave us a short morning discourse, then I went to the Presbyterian Church and heard a good sermon on "Faith." Read in the afternoon and at night. Had a long talk with Col. Ned Lee, Pendleton, etc. A fine day. General Lee sent up after a lot of sailors to go to Charleston.[15] In the evening Dr. Dabney and Lieut. Smith went to Dr. Grinnan's to spend the night.

Monday, September 7th. I started at an early hour and rode to the battle field of Cedar Run, by the way of Barnett's Ford, passing over the same ground we went over the year before and recalling the scenes of that eventful period. I rode to where we stopped at Mrs. Petty's, then to the top of the hill where we had our camp, and thence, by the way of Mr. Garnett's, along Ewell's route on the slope of Cedar Mountain to the house of Dr. Slaughter; then came down near Mrs. Brandt's ("Brandywine") across to Mrs. Crittenden's, then to the corner of the woods and there met Gen. Early, Gen. W. E. Jones, Dr. Dabney, Major Pitzer[16] and Dr. Grinnan, and we rode back across the field and General Early showed me the position of his brigade; where the 12th. Ga. was; where Thomas's Brigade was on the right of the Cedars; and where Brown[17] and DeMent[18] had their batteries. Gen. Early spoke of the enemy's rapid advance when our battery was run out. At night Col. Ned Lee told me about meeting General Early at night and General Early's saying; "What regiment is that?" Col. Lee answered—"The Stonewall Brigade, and asked what regiment is that; and was replied to: "I am General Early and his brigade." This was in the corn-field.

We took dinner at Mrs. Major's and she told us of the plunderings of the Yankees and how she had once saved her box of valuables from them by sitting on it about the time of the battle. After we left, Sigel, Banks, and three other Yankee Generals came there for breakfast. Mr. M. spoke of the first shot we fired at the Yankees from the top of the hill, and the enemy shots that fell near the house, which was built by Col. Phil. Slaughter[19] of the Revolution. After dinner I went back to near Cedar Run church with the rest of the company, when they went on back, and I, after sketching awhile, went on to Culpeper Court House, to the headquarters of Major-General J. E. B. Stuart and there spent the night quite pleasantly. We conversed about many things connected with the Pennsylvania campaign. Stuart said he had been much blamed by those that knew nothing about it.[20] The day was quite warm. I have not been well; was much disposed to dysentery during the day. It is quite dry.

Tuesday, September 8th. I started back at an early hour, going by Cedar Run to examine the route to the battle field and the location of Hudson's Mill, where General Trimble was stopped by a mill pond. Found no obstacle there that he could not have overcome. I then went on to camp, by way of Rapidan Station, quite indisposed and almost unable to ride. Got to camp and went to bed. Had Dr. McGuire administer some medicine and sent in for a furlough. The day was quite pleasant. General Early had a party at the Cedar Run battlefield fixing up the graves of our fallen. The hogs had been rooting there. I found that Rev. John Pinkerton had been to see me in my absence, but had left.

Wednesday, September 9th. I spent the day on my bed, quite sick, awaiting my furlough and preparing to go home tomorrow. Dr. Dabney copied my map of Chancellorsville. There was a fine review of the Second Corps by Gen. Lee; said to have been a grand affair. The day was very pleasant.

Thursday, September 10th. I got my leave of absence and started home, on the cars, at 10 A.M. Dr. Black aiding me to get off, as did also the others; all very kind. Mr. Robinson accompanied me to Gordonsville. I got to Staunton very well and felt much relieved to get home. Started my servant with my horses. The day was very pleasant. The country quite dry.

Friday, September 11th. Dr. Wilson came and saw me and gave me some active medicine. I am quite weak and suffer. Dr. W. came over in the P.M. Quite warm [and] dry (at home at "Loch Willow" near Churchville, Augusta County).

Saturday, September 12th. Dr. Wilson came to see me today and in the afternoon Dr. Robert S. Hamilton. It began to rain last night and rained part of the day. I am as yet no better and suffer much.

Sunday, September 13th. Rained some today and quite hard tonight. Dr. Hamilton came to see me and several of the neighbors called.

Monday, September 14th. Was confined to my bed all day and suffered a good deal. Fine weather.

Tuesday, September 15th. Still prostrate, though getting a little better under Dr. Hamilton's care.

Wednesday, September 16th. Passed an uncomfortable day, have considerable medicine to take but can easily endure it. Afflictions are necessary to enable us to appreciate the blessings we usually enjoy.

Thursday, September 17th. Began to rain about 9 A.M. and rained all day.

Friday, September 18th. Mrs. Chesley Kinney and my niece, Miss Allie Rounds, came over today from Striblings Springs. It rained until 9 A.M., then cleared off. I am better today.

Saturday, September 19th. It is quite cool to-day. I am somewhat better. My wife went to Staunton. I spent the day on the lounge by the fireside.

Sunday, September 20th. We had a frost this morning. My wife is quite sick with rheumatism. I feel much better and to-day sat up for some time. It was quite pleasant.

Monday, September 21st. I walked out in the yard and looked after a good many things; feel much better and ate quite a hearty dinner. Got a long letter from Mr. Robinson. The day has been very pleasant and I have enjoyed the air much, my wife is still quite sick.

Tuesday, September 22nd. After stirring about some at home, I went over to Churchville and spent most of the day there—going up to see

Captain F. F. Sterrett, who is very sick. In the afternoon heard Col. John B. Baldwin speak on the subject of "Home defense." His argument was in reference to the duties of the people at home to the families of soldiers. There was a frost this morning; the day was cool but the sun shone brightly. We heard that Bragg had whipped Rosecrans[21] and that fighting was going on on the Rapidan. Dr. Hamilton spoke of spending two nights at the house of Mrs. Arnold, the sister of General T. J. Jackson, in Beverly. He thought her a superior woman. She read him an affectionate letter she had received from General Jackson, just after the capture of the City of Mexico, in 1847. Mr. Arnold was one of the wealthiest men in Randolph County and a man of literary taste.[22]

Wednesday, September 23rd. Spent most of the day at home, but went over to Christian Bear's for dinner. The day was very pleasant, though there was a frost in the morning. We hear good news from Bragg's army and hope for something decisive there. I received a letter from Captain Richardson, from Long Island, New York, where he is a prisoner. He is longing to get back.

Thursday, September 24th. A white frost followed by a very fine warm day. The farmers are busy cutting up their corn and the yield is very good. I went in the morning to see my wife's cornfield and had a long talk with Mr. Knowles, who is much out with the course of many citizens.

Friday, September 25th. Spent most of the day at home; am recruiting [improving] slowly. Went to Mr. Dudley's in the afternoon. Hard frost and some ice. The news of Bragg's great victory at Chickamauga comes in slowly; the intelligence is cheering.[23]

Saturday, September 26th. I rode to Staunton, but was much wearied by my trip; dined with Major Bell and spent a while in the office of the Topographical Engineers who are surveying and making a map of the Shenandoah Valley. The day was warm though we had a heavy white frost. I read General Imboden's report of his march.

Sunday, September 27th. Spent the day at home not feeling very well. Read some and slept some. Frost and ice in the morning.

Monday, September 28th. Went to Staunton; Court day; a large crowd there and buying, selling going on at a great rate. Senator Wigfall,[24] of Texas, and "Extra Billy" Smith[25] spoke to the people on the War, their duties, &c. &c. I saw many of my old acquaintances. The day was very warm and pleasant. My brother's wife came over to-day. Got an extension of my furlough, for 10 days yesterday.

Wednesday, September 30th. Spent the morning at home and in the afternoon went down to Mt. Solon and spent the night at Major John Marshall McCue's. Had quite a long chat with Rev. John Pinkerton. A fine day but cool.

Thursday, October 1st. I rode on to Bridgewater, by way of David Garber's, where I went to see Richard Gibbons, my old Irish servant. He was rejoiced to see me and agreed to come and live with us next year. At Bridgewater a sale was going on, of personal property, at which fabulous prices were obtaine . Breakfast plates brought $5 each—pillows $15— cows $300, &c. I dined at Mrs. Brown's, then came back to Mr. Daniel Forrer's, at Mossy Creek, where I stopped awhile, when it began to rain, so I concluded to spend the night there. Found S. Jacob Forrer there, who had just returned from Gettysburg where he had been [taken] prisoner. There were several soldiers, for the night, there, and also R. P. Eubank and wife, and I had quite a visit with my old pupils of 15 years ago. It rained very hard in the night and was quite cool.

Friday, October 2nd. It rained very hard most of the day; the streams rose rapidly and were much swollen and the wind was quite high, but the ground needs the rain badly and all things are much refreshed by the timely showers. We visited, ate apples, peaches and grapes, of which they have plenty, and had a good dinner. Late in the afternoon it slackened some and I went on home; found my wife anxiously looking for me.

Saturday, October 3rd. Went to Staunton to hear from the army and do some business. Took to Lieut. P. W. O. Korner[26] a number of maps to use in his survey of Augusta County. The day was very fine and warm and everything is growing; it seemed like spring. Found my drawing table finished &c.

Sunday, October 4th. I started my servant, William Gearing, [back] to camp, to go today as far as his wife's home, at John Hamilton's on Christian's Creek. I went to church. Rev. R. C. Walker preached a very good sermon. I had a talk with Mr. Wooster about his conduct. The day was a fine one; frost in the morning.

Monday, October 5th. I spent the day packing up and getting ready to go to camp; found much trouble in getting a conveyance, but finally got Cyrus to work for Christian Bear and he agreed to take me. The day was quite warm. Rev. R. C. Walker called to see me for a few minutes.

Tuesday, October 6th. I went to Staunton, starting at 3 A.M. Very reluctant to leave home, so many cares devolving on my wife. Mr. Bear took me in, Cyrus going along. Left Staunton at $7\frac{1}{4}$ A.M. and arrived at

Orange C. H. by 2 P.M. Found Major Allen on board. I went to Major Harman's for the night, but accepted Mr. Shaw's invitation and went to his house. The army is down the river, some 12 miles. The day was quite warm. Mr. H. D. Whitcomb, the Supt. of the Va. Central Railroad, was on the train and we conversed on many topics. He said the army was certainly going to move soon. . . .[27]

Tuesday, October 20th. Spent the day in Camp verifying a map of Culpeper County and was much fatigued from being over the table all day, as I have not been used to it for some time. Our camp is near F. W. Brown's in a damp place. The day has been very pleasant. We hear that Stuart has been fighting the enemy at New Baltimore. In the [evening] Lieut. J. P. Smith and myself rode over with General Ewell to look at Mrs. Taylor's house for headquarters. We found it much injured and the fine furniture destroyed by the Yankees. General Ewell talked about General Jackson; asked if he was ambitious &c. &c. Generals Lee and Ewell went to Kelley's Farm in the morning.

Wednesday, October 21st. I went up to Freeman's Ford sketching the road; heard the enemy was at Warrenton and so came back. Our army is engaged in fortifying the north bank of the Rappahannock at the Railroad bridge. A very fine day—quite warm. When I got back found the camp moved to Mrs. Taylor's and went and got a room and fixed up a good deal.

{Thursday,} October 22nd. Spent the day in camp verifying maps of Culpeper and King and Queen Counties. In the evening I rode to Brandy Station and saw Major John A. Harman and Major W. J. Hawks, and called on the Misses Wise. The day was a very fine one. Our wagons were hauling away railroad iron and we had some skirmishing with the enemy. I wrote home. We heard of Imboden's success in the valley.[28]

Friday, October 23rd. Went down to the Rappahannock in the morning and saw a skirmish with the enemy, then went up to Beverly's Ford and sketched the road and river, and then went to look for my horses among the cavalry. Had a long ride and got back quite late; went by General Lee's. Lieut. R. K. Meade came here to-day. It began to [rain] some at 2 P.M. and is raining quite hard at 9 P.M.

Saturday, October 24th. Spent the day in office on work at maps. It rained part of the day and was quite unpleasant.

Sunday, October 25th. I remained at "Berry Hill" all day, reading, &c. It was a cool fine day. Wrote several letters to [friends] in the evening.

Monday, October 26th. I verified maps and worked all day, as also did Robinson and Harmot. After dinner Robinson and I went over to Brandy Station and I called at the Misses Wise and heard from home. We skirmished with the enemy on the other side of the Rappahannock and were [hauling] away railroad iron.

Tuesday, October 27th. Spent the day in camp verifying maps; verified maps of Orange and Culpeper. Hard frost in the morning followed by a fine day.

Wednesday, October 28th. General Ewell called for maps to accompany his reports, so I prepared a map of the second battle of Winchester and had Robinson make a copy for the General. Hard frost in the morning; fine day.

Thursday, October 29th. Spent the day on map of the 2nd. battle of Winchester to accompany the General's report; worked closely. Went to Colonel Smith's in the P.M. and got map of Greene County; called at Mrs. Wise's to bid them good-by and wrote home and sent my wife $40. —Fine day. Frost in the A.M. Returned map to Colonel Smith.

Friday, October 30th. Made map of battlefield of Gettysburg to accompany General Ewell's report. Worked hard all day and was very weary; went to bed early. General Johnson was at our headquarters and said he never wanted to go up the hill at Gettysburg. The day was hazy, threatening rain.

{Saturday,} October 31st. Finished map of battle of Gettysburg and Mr. Robinson commenced making a copy of it. [Harmot] finished his part of the map of the N. Va. After dinner I went to Brandy, after a bucket of butter my wife had sent me. Saw Major Harman, who is quite sick. The day quite cool; it rained last night and this morning but cleared off finely. Col. Willis came to me at night for maps of part of the Valley, etc.

Sunday, November 1st. Smith and I went up to Culpeper C. H. and heard a sermon from the Rev. Mr. Cole, at his house, on "John the Baptist." We called at Dr. Slaughter's for a while—then came back by way of Brandy Station, where we took dinner with Major Hawks, and then to camp by night. Very fine day, warm, pleasant.

Monday, November 2nd. Finished the three maps to accompany General Ewell's report—; then began putting on paper my notes in Fauquier County. A fine warm day. Heard from home; all quite well.

Tuesday, November 3rd. Worked at map of Fauquier most of the day. Helped Gen. Ewell fix his crutch. Went over to Brandy after dinner and drew my pay for September and October. A very warm day for the [season] like spring. Robinson preparing a map for the General.

Wednesday, November 4th. Worked very closely at map of Fauquier. Robinson reducing Rappahannock. At night I looked over some reports. The day has been delightful. Carroll came back today.

Thursday, November 5th. Went over to a [cavalry] review had by General J. E. B. Stuart near Brandy Station[29] and looked for my horse. The day was very fine, though windy, and the review of some 6,000 cavalry, on an extensive plain, was a very fine one. The charge was quite amusing and animating. There was a large turnout of infantrymen and officers and a number of ladies, among them, Mrs. General John B. Gordon. General Ewell and Staff went up.

Friday, November 6th. Worked at map of Fauquier; sent Major Hawks a map of Culpeper County; fixed the maps to General Ewell's report of the Pennsylvania Campaign. A fine day, but windy.

Saturday, November 7th. Finished putting 'on paper my reconnoissance of Fauquier; Mr. Robinson finished the map of the Rappahannock region, which I gave Gen. Ewell; Mr. R. then traced a map of Culpeper. It was reported in the morning that the Yankees were advancing and soon they appeared, in [force] at Kelley's Ford, with several batteries, and opened on the small force Gen. Rodes had out, on picket, with only short range artillery; they drove it away and crossed the river. A portion of his men fought to the last, until surrounded and forced to give up; by that time he got his division into line and drove back the advance of the enemy and then halted in his old camp. Gen. Johnson was sent from his camp, near Brandy, to Rodes' aid and formed on his right. In the meantime the enemy had advanced, in force, on Rappahannock Station, where General Early had Hoke's and Hays'[30] Brigades, on picket, across the river, on the east side, in a work built to guard the end of the pontoon bridge. The enemy formed a line of battle, after skirmishing until near dark, and behind each regiment put others in column of companies, and thus formed, advanced rapidly and passed over and got possession of the work on our right and cut off our men from the bridge, and most of those, after a bloody fight, were compelled to surrender, though many of them got away by swimming the river. Some even clubbed their muskets and fought. Gen. Early destroyed the bridge so the enemy could not cross at once. The error seems to have been, partly, in the construction of works that could be so easily passed over; and it is said they had several dead points that our fire could not reach, and that they were dug partly under the hill and so the enemy were able to get on the hill above them, unperceived. Some of the men say the enemy came in the form of a wedge and forced the work. Be it as it may, they took 1,300 prisoners from us and compelled us to leave the bridge. Orders then came to fall back to between Mt. Pony and a point on the Orange & Alexandria Railroad, 3 miles from Brandy Station towards Culpeper C. H. I was sent after Gen. Johnson to guide him to and fix him in position; so, at about 11 P.M., after spending the evening chatting with Dr. Rosser, who came to spend the night with me, I went down to near the river (Rappahannock) where Johnson had formed his line of battle, or was forming it, and brought him up by our quarters and through the woods to his position, which we reached before day and then the men rested.

Sunday, November 8th. Col. W. Proctor Smith was at the position we were directed to when we got there, looking at the ground. As soon as day came, I went over and looked over the ground of Gen. Rodes' [division] on the right, with Gen. Rodes, and then came back and helped Gen. Johnson select his line, next on the left; Early extended on towards the railway, and then A. P. Hill. The wagons were ordered across the Rapidan. I selected a crossing and had a ford and foot bridge made; then our men fortified the line and there we spent the day, the cavalry fighting at the front. About dark we started for Raccoon Ford. Rodes in the advance followed by Johnson; Early came by Somerville Ford. General Ewell came on in his carriage. I rode ahead with Pendleton & Carroll and we came on to Hon. Jere Morton's[31] ("Morton Hall") and got there about half-past 9 P.M. Tired and hungry; got some corn-bread and milk. The day was fine. The troops crossed over Rapidan River. We slept on the floor at "Morton Hall"—Dr. Black with us.

Monday, November 9th. Our wagons came up during the day and we got something to eat and I fixed up a room for myself, upstairs, at Morton Hall. The day was quite fine.

Tuesday, November 10th. Went up in the ambulance to Orange C. H.; called on Major Hawks and saw Captain A. M. Garber, Q.M., about a wagon. Thought of going to Orange C. H. to find a room, but the place was too full. The day quite chilly. The troops are getting into camps along the Rapidan from Germanna Ford up to Liberty Mills.

Wednesday, November 11th. Moved down stairs to give Gen. Ewell a room for his wife who came to our camp yesterday. We worked at maps. Mr. Robinson copying of Greene County and I looked over, to verify it, the map of Northern Virginia. We had some flurries of snow.

Thursday, November 12th. Employed same as yesterday. A fine day.

Friday, November 13th. There are some signs of a move,—it being reported that the enemy is moving towards Fredericksburg.—General Early sent over for a map of the surrounding country, as he is really in command,—General Ewell's leg being in such a condition that he is unable to attend to business. Mr. Robinson copied a map for Col. Pendleton and I fixed up one for General Early. Dr. Hunter McGuire, Medical Director, got back to camp. A very fine day.

Saturday, November 14th. I worked at a reduction of a map of Spotsylvania County; Mr. Robinson copied Orange County for Gen. Jubal A. Early and then parts of Caroline and Spotsylvania Counties for General Robert E. Rodes. A very fine day; it rained in the evening and thundered and lightninged. Hugh McGuire, brother of Dr. McGuire, came to our quarters in the afternoon. The enemy has become quiet again. A very dark night.

Sunday, November 15th. We had barely finished [breakfast] this morning when a rapid discharge of artillery started us from our quiet and set us to packing up, at once, in hot haste as we are so near the river. There was hurrying to and fro. General Early took command of the Corps and General Ewell arranged to go away, as his leg is in such a bad condition that he cannot command. We were soon packed up and troops were hurried forward toward Raccoon Ford and Morton's Ford to which we went down. It turned out to be only an advance of some Yankee cavalry that had been quickly repulsed—; so we came back to our old quarters at Morton Hall and had the [wagons] brought back. General R. E. Lee came down; there were ten Generals present. General Ewell unpacked and spent the night here. The troops were sent back to the old camps. A white frost—, a very fine day and rain at night.

Monday, November 16th. We went to work again, Robinson reducing Greene County and I Spotsylvania. General Ewell after much hesitation, with wife and stepdaughter and step-son, (Major Campbell Brown),[32] went to Orange C. H., accompanied by Dr. McGuire, leaving General Early in command, who today moved over to our headquarters. Col. A. S. Pendleton, A.A.G., got a letter, at 8 P.M. in the evening, I suppose from his betrothed, Miss Corbin, which affected him much. He sat down to write—, then ordered his horse and started off at once, we suppose for Moss Neck.[33] General Early was out on the lines all day. A fine day, a little cool. Rev. B. Tucker Lacy came back yesterday.

Tuesday, November 17th. I worked at a map of Spotsylvania County and Robinson one of Greene County, after making a tracing of part of Orange for General Early. Col. W. P. Smith came in, late in the afternoon, and I gave him some dinner. A very fine day, but cool. I sent my wife $100, by Carroll, and wrote to her.

Wednesday, November 18th. I worked at map of Spotsylvania and verified one of Greene, Robinson reduced Greene to the 1-160,000th. scale. I copied General Jackson's letters, from the official letterbook of the Corps-Headquarters, at night. All very quiet. Col. Pendleton got back by 8 o'clock this morning, having ridden 90 miles in 48 hours, and, I suppose, satisfied his lady love, as he is in a good humor. I sent to Captain Grant for a map of Albemarle County, but he is using it. A fine day but the air is chilly and there is a halo around the moon. Hon. Jere Morton went away yesterday.

Thursday, November 19th. Verified two copies of a map of Greene County. A fine day.

Friday, November 20th. Went up to General Lee's quarters for a map of Albemarle County, but they were using it and so I did not get it. The day was pleasant but bracing. I enjoyed my ride much. Mr. Robinson is reducing Louisa County.

Saturday, November 21st. I worked at a map of Spotsylvania County and Mr. Robinson continued at one of Louisa County. Col. Smith and Captain Fitzhugh came to our quarters. I sent and got map of Albemarle County. It was a dark rainy day.

Sunday November 22nd. I went and heard Mr. Lacy preach to the prisoners in the guard house. A very good sermon. I enjoyed the fine, warm sunshine. Read some and in the evening wrote home. President Davis came to Orange C. H., yesterday, and was at church there, to-day, with General Lee.

Monday, November 23rd. I worked at a map of Spotsylvania County and Robinson at copying Albemarle. It rained some and was a gloomy day. Rev. H. White came up to see Mr. Lacy. Lieut. J. P. Smith is sick in my room. I copied Jackson letters at night.[34]

Tuesday, November 24th. I worked at map of Spotsylvania County and Robinson at one of Albermarle. It has rained, more or less, all day so the review of the Second Corps, by the President, did not come off, as appointed for to-day, and the President went back to Richmond. It rained some at night.

Wednesday, November 25th. I worked on map of Spotsylvania County and Robinson on a reduction of Albemarle. The day has been cool, threatening snow. Some little rain late in the P.M. There was a report in the morning that the enemy was crossing cavalry at Ellis' Ford and moving towards Ely's Ford, and late at night General Lee sent word that the enemy was moving and orders came for some of our troops to move down the river early tomorrow. Captain Wilbourn, our Chief Signal Officer, says they have broken up their cavalry camp near Culpeper Court House. Gen. Hoke dined with General Early to-day. General Early and his personal staff gave Mr. Lacy $50—for religious purposes. I wrote until quite late at night. Paid Smith $100—towards paying for my horse.

Thursday, November 26th. I worked at a map of Spotsylvania part of the day. The enemy made demonstrations and crossed at Mine (Culpeper) and Jacob's fords in the P.M. We packed up to move. Bad news from Bragg at night. He was defeated at Chattanooga.[35] Ground frozen in the morning and air frosty, the day clear.

Friday, November 27th. We took breakfast at 4 A.M. and General Early and the Staff started for Verdiersville, going by Zoar Church along a line of our troops and to the old turnpike, and so on to [Verdiersville] by Salem Church. We met Gen. R. E. Lee at Verdiersville—, also Generals J. E. B. Stuart and A. P. Hill—then came back and advanced our line towards Locust Grove, Hays by the old turnpike, Rodes by the Office Road, and Johnson by the Raccoon Ford road. We found the enemy and cannonading began about noon; the infantry advanced and commenced skirmishing soon after. I came back, with Robinson, to Cube's old house and made a map for Col. J. Thompson Brown.[36] The morning was very cold and the ground was frozen hard and was slippery. A lunar halo last night. It got warmer but was cool and cloudy all the day. Skirmishing with the enemy, at Locust Grove, was kept up until quite late. We put up our tents and encamped near Captain Rowe's house, but were soon ordered further back to make room for a line of defences, so we went back to Salem church and there spent the night. General Early came in very late. We lost some 500 wounded and 60 killed in the fight Gen. Johnson had near Locust Grove. It looks like rain.

Saturday, November 28th. We got up about daylight. It soon became misty and then rain followed, very hard, off and on, until 2 P.M. They brought Johnson's wounded to Salem church but soon took them further back. Our line was formed along the west side of Mine Run by the Gold Mine to the plank road to Cube's, to near Col. Rowe's and then to near Zoar Church. The enemy advanced in the morning but we soon repulsed them; skirmishing occasionally during the day. I made a map of Orange County for Major Walter Taylor,[37] General Lee's A.A.G., then also one of Spotsylvania; made a map for Col. J. Thompson Brown. The day has been very damp and cool. We have our camp on the old Turnpike a mile from Col. Rowe's. I wrote a letter home and also one to Major H. M. Bell.

Sunday, Nov. 29th. We rose at dawn, had breakfast and packed up— then went to the front where our men were on a new line, which they had fortified, making it very strong. I sketched the line. Gen. Ewell came back in the P.M. The enemy only made a slight demonstration on our right. The morning was windy and raw; a little rain, then warmer and cold again at night.

Monday, Nov. 30th. We were up quite early but were about through breakfast when the enemy opened art'y, at 8 o'clock, quite furiously— keeping it up, at intervals, all day, but not doing much damage. There was some skirmishing and we had several killed and a number wounded. The day has been very chilly; a keen biting wind, tho. clear most of the day. Mr. R. and I made maps of the surrounding country, at Mrs. Bledsoe's. We came to the same camp, just above the saw-mill and about 1 mile from Capt. Rowe's.

Tuesday, Dec. 1st. The morning was very cold, the ground frozen hard, but it was calm;—the wind afterwards rose and it became quite cold, but mellowed some as the day advanced. There were no movements made along the lines on either side, no firing; the enemy withdrew his pickets from our left in the P.M.. There are signs of a move among our troops. Gen. Early stays in command, by request of Gen. Lee. Gen. Ewell remains here. Gen. Early spends the night near the breastworks. We have our quarters at the same place as last night. R. and I made a map of Orange and Spotsylvania which I sent to Gen. Early.

Wednesday, Dec. 2nd. We were up at dawn and sent our baggage to the old Turnpike and we went to the front, but nothing was to be seen of the Yankees. Soon a negro came across the lines and said they had retreated across the river. We immediately followed with the 2nd. Corps, going down the old Turnpike and a road nearer the river; but they were too fast for us and most of them got safely over the river, tho', we took some 300. They had begun to move yesterday and were going all night. They committed all manner of depredations and brutalities on the people they passed by. We went to near Germanna, then came back to the house of Mr. Davis, near the breastworks. The troops started back towards their old camps. The day was a very fine one, white frost followed by a thaw. Stout and Reeves spent the night with us.

Thursday, Dec. 3rd. We slept longer this morning than for some days, but started at 8 A.M. and went back to our old quarters at the Morton House, where Gen. Fitz. Lee has had his quarters since we left. We found the place much abused. I took my old room. Gen. Early is still here. Gen. Ewell wrote to Gen. Lee about his taking command. I wrote home at night. The day has been very pleasant and warm. No movement of the enemy.

Friday, Dec. 4th. I got out my maps and worked at Spotsylvania Co., and Mr. R. at Albemarle. Gen. Ewell rec'd. notice, from Gen. Lee, to assume command and he wrote to Gen. Early expressing his thanks for his able management of the Corps. The day was cool but pleasant. Brown dined with us yesterday. Mr. Lacy joined our mess today.

Saturday, Dec. 5th. I spent the day verifying a map of Albemarle Co. and Robinson at Louisa. Gen. Early went back to his Div. today. There came a report that the Yankee cav. had come to Locust Grove again, but it turned out not to be so. The day was quite chilly, threatening a storm.

Sunday, Dec. 6th. I spent the day at Hd. Qrs., reading various books. The day was chilly. Mr. Lacy preached at the La. Brigade; Pendleton and McGuire went to Orange C. H.

Monday, Dec. 7th. I finished verifying the map of Albemarle Co., then took it up to Col. Smith. Got 4 yds of linen;—could not get maps;—dined there,—a very poor dinner of meat and bread;—then afterwards, with Maj. Allen, came home after dark. A fine breezy day. Gen. Lee has his Hd. Qrs. near the foot of Jack's Mt. on the old Turnpike. R. is reducing Hanover Co. and Louisa Co.

Tuesday, Dec. 8th. I prepared a map of part of the Valley for Col. Willis of the 12th Georgia; he is going there; also worked a while on Spotsylvania. Capt. Fitzhugh brought down a new map of Spotsylvania and R. went to copying it. Col. S. also sent me a map of N.E. Va. Chilly day—hard frosts—cold nights.

Wednesday, Dec. 9th. Worked at Spotsylvania and Caroline Co's, reducing; Robinson copying Spotsylvania. Read the President's message at night. Like most of his views. Gen. Lee went to Richmond today.

Quite chilly; a hard frost. Rec'd. an order from Col. Smith to survey the Route of enemy's position, etc., in the late movement; also to locate our works.

Thursday, Dec. 10th. I worked awhile, in the morning, on a map to accompany Report of Gen. Lee on our late line, then at a map of Spotsylvania, Louisa and Orange, parts of, for the reconnoissance Pendleton and I are to go on tomorrow to find camps for winter. This was appointed by Gen. Lee for a day of fasting and prayer with the people of Ga. Mr. Lacy preached at two places. The day was very chilly. Capt. Blackford sent to ask for a map of Spotsylvania for Gen. Stuart. We got provisions today. R. is copying Spotsylvania.

Friday, Dec. 11th. This is the anniversary of the opening of the Battle of [Fredericksburg]. Pendleton and myself started for Louisa Co.,; went first to Gen. Lee's and saw Maj. Taylor about our destination and where we were to look for camps, then went, by the Brock Road, to Brock's Bridge, Clayton's Store and Mansfield, to Mr. Mansfield's. It was quite cold, threatening a storm. We met Crutchfield going to our Qurs. We rode over 30 miles.

Saturday, Dec. 12th. We paid $4. for our supper, lodging and breakfast and $4 each; got off at an early hour, having had a pleasant night, and went over the country between the branches of Contrary Cr., then went on to Frederick's Hall, where Mr. N. W. Harris invited us to his house. We visited his tobacco factory and then went to his house where we were hospitably entertained. A Lieut. Williams was there. Miss Flora Harris was quite entertaining to Pendleton. It rained some during the day and very hard during the night.

Sunday, Dec. 13th. We started back to camp, went by New Bridge and Herd's Store, got back after dark; a long and hard ride. It cleared off in the morning and was a very warm and fine day, spring like.

Monday, Dec. 14th. Worked at correcting Orange and Spotsylvania. The day was quite pleasant. R. at Louisa Co.

Tuesday, Dec. 15th. I worked at map of Spotsylvania and Orange. R. at Louisa. The day was bracing. Gen. Early went to the Valley, Pendleton accompanied him, to meet the enemy advancing towards Staunton.

Wednesday, Dec. 16th. McGuire went off to the Valley. I got up early and went to sketch our line at Zoar Ch. The day was quite cold. I spent the day riding along the lines.

Thursday, Dec. 17th. Spent the day working at reduction of Orange Co., ruled Washington Co., Md. R. began reduction of McDowell's map of N.E. Va. It rained last night and has sleeted and rained most of the day; quite cold, warmer at night. Mr. Morton was in our room, at night, for some time.

Friday, Dec. 18th. Was busy at my map, etc., all day; packed up my trunk and sent baggage to Orange C. H. tomorrow. Day quite cold.

"Alas we are fast passing away!"

SATURDAY, DEC. 19TH. I went up to Orange C. H. today, got my furlough approved, drew my pay and made sundry arrangements. Saw Col. Smith and got orders for maps of lines of battles, etc. A fine day, but cold.

Sunday, Dec. 20th. I came up to Orange C. H. in the P.M., with Wm., took dinner with Maj. Harman and spent the night with Capt. Garber. It was intensely cold. Rode's Div. moved up to nearer Orange C. H.

Monday, Dec. 21st. I came up to Staunton on the cars; sent William on horseback; spent the night at Maj. Bell's; Saw McGuire at Gordonsville. The raiders of Averell,[1] etc., are all going back, our men after them. Early passed through Harrisonburg today. A fine cold day.

Tuesday, Dec. 22nd. I went out home on a Q.M. horse; found all well and very glad to see me. A fine day, threatening snow.

Wednesday, Dec. 23rd. I went to Staunton, met my horses, transacted some business, came home and sold my roan mare, for $600., to Mr. Geeding. Wife and self called at H. Bear's at night; he had just got back from pursuing the Yankees as one of the home guard. There was a little snow in the morning, mts. white, but it got clear and cold. People are gathering ice.

Thursday, Dec. 24th. I went to Mossy Creek to see Richard; c'd. not get him to come up now. Took dinner at Mr. Forrer's; got home just after dark. A cold windy day.

Friday, Dec. 25th. I went to Staunton in the morning to see about servants, then came back to E. Geeding's to dinner, where we had quite a party, my family including Allie and C. Bear's family. We came home at dark and I went over to H. Bear's, whose son Sandy died today. It was very pleasant. There were many servants in town and but little hiring.

Saturday, Dec. 26th. I went to town to see about servants; got back late; a fine day.

Sunday, Dec. 27th. Spent the day at home; it rained more or less all day. Mr. Forrer took dinner with us; weather mild.

Monday, Dec. 28th. I went to Staunton to hire servant, hired one of Poe. It rained part of the day; the waters are up; saw many old friends.

Tuesday, Dec. 29th. I went to Capt. Sterrett's, in the morning, to see about servts., then got my horse and went to a sale at Silling's; came home and drew maps awhile. Allie came back; a fine day, warm but muddy and damp.

Wednesday, Dec. 30th. Spent the day at home, at work at map of Orange Co. Mrs. Wise called here at night; quite cold.

Thursday, Dec. 31st. Worked at map of position on Mine Run. A Pleasant day.

Friday, Jan. 1st., 1864. Went to Staunton; the day was pleasant in the morning but it turned intensely cold and windy. There were a great many people in Staunton, buying and selling serv'ts. It froze very hard. Mrs. Wise called.

Saturday, Jan. 2nd. Spent most of the day at home, drawing maps;— sent off map of position on Mine Run to Col. Smith. The day was quite cold. We went to Capt. Sterrett's at night; had a pleasant visit. It froze hard.

Sunday, Jan. 3rd. I went to church. It was quite cold. Allie came back today. Mr. Walker preached.

Monday, Jan. 4th. Allie went to Staunton with Wm. Sterrett. It began to snow in A.M. and snowed all day. I worked copying a map of Penna. Got letters from camp.

Tuesday, Jan. 5th. In obedience to orders from Col. Smith I made a map of our position in Culpeper Co., which I sent to him today, then worked at a map of our position in Washington Co., Md. It rained some last night. We went to Sieg's on a visit at night—a fine day.

Wednesday, Jan. 6th. Finished map of battle of Williamsport and position of July 11th. A fine day, cloudy. Made envelopes at night.

Thursday, Jan. 7th. Worked copying map of Pa. A fine day. They are getting ice 5 inches thick.

Friday, Jan. 8th. Spent the day copying map of Pa. Cold and clear.

Saturday, Jan. 9th. Went to Staunton. Sent in some books; the day was quite cold. I begged some socks, etc., for the La. Brigade.

Sunday, Jan. 10th. Wife and self went to Union, to church. Mr. W. gave us a very good sermon; said he c'd not go to the army. I talked to the people some about giving to the La. Brigade. Clear and cold.

Monday, Jan. 11th. Worked at map of Pa., and went to Steven's in the evening; had a pleasant visit. Clear and cold.

Tuesday, Jan. 12th. Went around to look after business. A fine day. Some of the young folks came in at night.

Thursday, Jan. 14th. Went to Staunton on way to army. Shall spend the night at Rev. Davis'. Gen. Early is in town and goes down tomorrow. The troops are encamped near by. A very fine day; warm.

Friday, Jan. 15th. Went on over to Orange C. H. Spent the night there with Mr. Lacy. Dr. Hamilton went down with me. A very fine, warm day; mud deep at Orange.

Saturday, Jan. 16th. Gen. Early told me I was to go back to the Valley to reconnoitre for defences. He went to camp by Gen. Lee's and got orders; took Dr. H. to the camp of the 52nd. Got to Hd. Qrs. in P.M., had quite a pleasant visit, with all parties, until late. A fine, warm day; mud deep.

Sunday, Jan. 17th. Spent the day at Hd. Qrs., reading, etc. It was quite pleasant.

Monday, Jan. 18th. It began to rain about midnight and kept it up most of today, and, it being mild, the frost came out of the ground and it became very muddy. I loaded up and went to Orange C. H., going by Hinrich's, and Col. Smith's, and Gen. Lee's. Got my orders, etc. Spent the night with Dr. Hegy.

Tuesday, Jan. 19th. Atkinson and myself came up to Staunton on the cars. R. and Wm. went on the horses. We did not get to Staunton until 2 A.M. of Wednesday; the stock of the rail road is in bad condition. The day was chilly and windy.

Wednesday, Jan. 20th. We spent last night at the American; board $5. a day. Today I got an office for $35. a month and we moved into it. Heard my wife was very sick and went home at night. A very fine day.

Thursday, Jan. 21st. Went to Staunton in the morning. R. and Wm. got there too. Went to work making tracings of map for my reconnoissance; got my orders from Gen. Early last night; telegram in the morning. Fine warm day.

Friday, Jan. 22nd. Worked all day preparing for trip, then called on Koerner in P.M. The day was very pleasant; warm.

Saturday, Jan. 23rd. Worked at maps, etc., until 3 P.M., then Mr. Robinson and myself went out home; had a pleasant ride; the day was warm; found all well; heard the sad news of the death of my sister Jenny. Alas we are fast passing away!

Sunday, Jan. 24th. Spent most of the day at home; wrote to Nelson. We had a very pleasant day; rode back to Staunton in the evening and I went to Pres. ch. and heard Mr. Stuart preach. Warm.

Monday, Jan. 25th. I started, quite early, for the mts.; went to Buffalo Gap, then examined the North Mt., sketching the roads to Summerdean. Spent the night at R. B. Dunlap's. The day was very warm, farmers ploughing.

Tuesday, Jan. 26th. Crossed the mt., by Pond Gap, to Elizabeth Furnace, then back by Dunlap's and Pond Gap to Summerdean. Spent the night at Dr. G. Baylor's; very warm, frost coming out of ground.

Wednesday, Jan. 27th. Went along N. Mt.; took dinner at Mr. Walker's; crossed Kelso's Gap to McCutchen's. Warm haze at night.

Thursday, Jan. 28th. Went on to near Goshen, then to California Furnace up Bratton's Run, down Dunlap's Cr. to the Cow Pasture and then to Clifton Forge, to Kayser's, and there spent the night. It froze quite hard last night; warm day.

Friday, Jan. 29th. Went up Jackson's River to Covington, then up to the mouth of Falling Sp. Br. and spent the night at Mann's. A fine day; frost in the morning; had an adventure at the mouth of Indian Draft. Officers from Covington came after me.

Saturday, Jan. 30th. Went across river and down to Indian Draft, then across towards Callahan's, back to mts., down the river to Kincaid's. Got my dinner by being picked up; then came by the Jackson Road to Cedar Cr., to Mr. Williams'; frost at night. It rained in P.M., but not hard until night. Sugar making going on; mild weather.

Sunday, Jan. 31st. Went to Healing Sps., then to Hot, Warm and Bath Alum; called to see Col. Jackson, but he was away; got some of Averell's maps. Dense fog in the morning; fine day.

Monday, Feb. 1st. Some rain last night. I went on to old Millboro', through the rain; stopped there to dinner, then went on through Goshen and across the mt. to Sterrett's, in Rockbridge; the rain ceased in P.M. & it got warm.

Tuesday, Feb. 2nd. Went on, via Esteline Furnace and Pond Gap, to Staunton; got there at 4 P.M.; found business going on well; sketched the ride from Rockbridge to Pond Gap—a fine day.

Wednesday, Feb. 3rd. Got supplies, etc., for my men and fixed up to go again; then went home in P.M.;—the evening was quite cool, some snow fell.

Thursday, Feb. 4th. Went through Jenning's Gap and met my guide, Mr. Williams, and went on thro' Deerfield to Glendy's, near Cloverdale. Sketched the road from Deerfield to Glendy's. The day was cool, but pleasant.

Friday, Feb. 5th. Went on to Scottstown and across to the Cow Pasture River and up to Williamsville, then back to J. S. Crawford's;—cool but pleasant.

Saturday, Feb. 6th. Went to Green Valley and back to Scottstown,— but the rain compelled me to go back to Crawford's;—it rained most of the P.M.;—snow on the mts.

Sunday, Feb. 7th. Spent the day at Crawford's; the mts. and ground were quite white in morning;—day quite cool.

Monday, Feb. 8th. Got an early start and went by the Back road to the Bath Alum Sps., then back by the river road and across to Green Valley by the Indian Draft Road.;—quite cool—but pleasant.

Tuesday, Feb. 9th. Went over to Millboro' by Pig Run Road and back by Indian Draft Road, and over to Crawford's; air chilly, but the sun shone brightly.

Wednesday, Feb. 10th. Went up to Williamsville and then through, near the Red Holes, to Warm Sps.;—saw Col. Wm. L. Jackson.[2] Day cold, tho'. the sun shone.

Thursday, Feb. 11th. Went on to Nall's (Noel's ?) and up towards Huntersville, to Bradley's;—very cold morning,—suddenly turned warm.

Friday, Feb. 12th. Went up Back Creek to Capt. Wade's;—a long ride;—day quite pleasant;—part of Wm. L. Jackson's command was there over night;—windy.

Saturday, Feb. 13th. Kept on up Back Creek to Rockman's;—part of day quite cool. Road very rough.

Sunday, Feb. 14th. Went by Galltown to Jackson's River and down it to Mike Wise's and there spent the night;—fine day, windy, cool in P.M.

Monday, Feb. 15th. Went on down the river to Cleek's Mill;—it then began to snow, so I went on to Warm Sps. and Bath Alum. Spent the night at Bath Alum on my way home. It snowed, steadily, from about 10 A.M. the rest of the day.

Tuesday, Feb. 16th. It cleared off last night, but snowed again this morning. I rode to Millboro in the storm; got grain for my horse and sent him to Dickinson's, then went on to Staunton on the cars. It was intensely cold.

Wednesday, Feb. 17th. Making a map of Imboden's route to Pa., by order of Col. Smith;—a cold and windy day.

Thursday, Feb. 18th. Spent the day in my office, at Staunton, making a map of battle by Bristoe, by order of Col. Smith. Went home at night; —it was a very cold day. Gave information to Lt. [?], signal officer going to the mts.

Friday, Feb. 19th. Went back to Staunton in A.M., very cold. Saw Gen. Early and got order to make a map of route he had been in the mts.

Saturday, Feb. 20th. Worked putting some of my notes together;— quite cold, but moderated some.

Sunday, Feb. 21st. Worked all day and until past midnight on map for Gen. Early. A fine day. Sent to Col. Smith "Battle of Bristoe," "Imboden's Route to Pa.," "Reconnoissance in Fauquier Co.,"[3] by Lt. Harris.[4]

Monday, Feb. 22nd. Took Gen. Early's map to him at 1 P.M. and got order to continue my reconnoissance. Saw many of my neighbors. Mr. Forrer called on me at night and Lt. Schley of the Signal Corps.

Tuesday, Feb. 23rd. Went up to Millboro' on cars, then on wagon to Millboro Sps', with Lt. Schley and Maj. Parrish—; the day was quite warm. Sent horse up by boy.

Wednesday, Feb. 24th. Went down the Cow Pasture and to Clifton Forge and then to Rich Patch;— day windy and somewhat cool.

Thursday, Feb. 25th. Went to Covington, then to Callahan's and up Dunlap's Cr. to Stack's. A warm and pleasant day.

Friday, Feb. 26th. Went up to Sweet Sps. and then over to Pott's Cr., to Swin's. It snowed some in the morning and was quite cold, but got warm in P.M.

Saturday, Feb. 27th. Crossed mt. to Scott's and then on to New Castle and beyond to Dorsey's;—fine warm day.

Sunday, Feb. 28th. Went up Craig's Cr. and over towards Salem, to Garst's. Fine warm day.

Monday, Feb. 29th. Went to Salem and down to the Depot, then back and on to Fincastle. It was somewhat cool in A.M. and began to rain at about 4 P.M.; got muddy.

Tuesday, March 1st. Went on to Buchanan and on 10 miles beyond. It rained steadily most of the day and got very muddy.

Wednesday, March 2nd. Went to Lexington and on to Brownsburg, sketched the road. It was quite pleasant. I spent the night at Capt. Curry's.

Thursday, March 3rd. Went on to Staunton, via Middlebrook; sketched the road. Fine day.

Friday, March, 4th. Spent the day in Staunton. Went home late in P.M. Wife quite sick. A pleasant day. Lt. Brown is here.

Saturday, March 5th. Spent the day at home fixing up my notes. Mr. Sieg called to see me and we had a long talk about the Brownsburg affair. A fine day, but cool.

Sunday, March 6th. Spent the day at home;—had an exciting time with Jordan,—the wretch went to Staunton late in P.M. Saw Capt. Howard at night. Pleasant.

Monday, March 7th. Spent the day in Staunton;—late in P.M. went over to Buffalo Gap with Howard and Rogers;—cool, threatening a storm.

Tuesday, March 8th. It began to rain in the night and is at it this morning. Spent the night at Buffalo Gap. There has been some excitement the past week owing to the attempt of the Yankees to get to Richmond, but all is again quiet.[5] Went towards Staunton; found it was not going to rain, so turned back and crossed Shenandoah Mt. The day became quite pleasant. Talked about Milroy at night and his battle at McDowell. They said he had been there over 2 months;—his hair white, beard yellow;—he had started his command, on Monday, for Staunton, and some 5,000 got to Shaw's Ford.—He was at McDowell when the fighting began at Rogers', hurried over to stop his men on Shenandoah Mt., but they got over before he got there, etc., etc.

Wednesday, March 9th. Went down Cow Pasture and up Shaw's Fork across to McDowell and down Bull Pasture to McClungs;—a fine warm day,—froze hard last night, white frost.

Thursday, March 10th. Spent the day at McClung's. It rained nearly all day. Inked my notes and read some.

Friday, March 11th. Spent day at McClung's. It rained, off and on, all day,—quite mild.

Saturday, March 12th. Went down to Williamsville and back to

McClung's by the Valley Road. It was quite pleasant, but became cool,—roads bad.

Sunday, March 13th. Spent the day at McClung's, reading, etc. There was a little snow over night—afterwards it cleared off.

Monday, March 14th. Went across the mt. to Cow Pasure river, then back and up to Stuart's. The day became quite cold and it snowed a little.

Tuesday, March 15th. Went up to McDowell, then up Crab Run and spent the night with Mr. Miely;—ate warm sugar,—the day was quite cold and it snowed some.

Wednesday, March 16th. Went home today, 32 miles. It was quite cold riding,—found my wife quite sick.

Thursday, March 17th. Went to town to see my men and get some work, then back home,—got some milder, but is still quite cold.

Friday, March 18th. Spent the day at home, at work copying map of Pa. Cold—my wife quite sick;—went to Heizer's after dinner.

Saturday, March 19th. Worked at map of Pa.;—quite cold. Went to Arnold's sale, in P.M., for a while. Worked at map until midnight. Pleasant day.

Sunday, March 20th. Spent the day at home with my wife, but went to Mr. Walker in P.M., at Churchville. Mild.

Monday, March 21st. Worked at Pa. map and map of West Virginia. Air chilly.

Tuesday, March 22nd. It snowed more than half the day and was very cold. I worked at Pa. and West Va.

Wednesday, March 23rd. Worked at maps until evening, then went into town; roads no better. It thawed some,—snow 4 inches deep, chilly.

Thursday, March 24th. Worked putting my notes together,—called on Koerner in evening. Capt. Wilbourn spent the night with me. Day chilly, but warm in P.M.

Friday, March 25th. Worked putting notes together. Oltmanns' copying Pa., Robinson reducing Frederick Co., Md. It has rained and snowed nearly all day,—5 inches of snow fell, not very cold.

Saturday, March 26th. Worked platting my notes, Oltmanns at Pa. map, R. copying Koerner's S.W. Va. map. Cloudy.

Sunday, March 27th. Very fine day. I went over home and spent the day and came back in P.M. My wife is getting better. It was quite warm.

Monday, March 28th. A fine day, but a little chilly. Worked at map of mts., R. copying K.'s map. Olts., finished copying Pa. map. Saw many people today at court. Maj. McCue spends the night with me.

Tuesday, March 29th. Copied notes on Mt. Map. Olts. copied R.R. map. I wrote names on Pa. map and on Koerner's map. It rained and snowed all day. Not very cold. Got a cord of wood.

Wednesday, March 30th. Worked at Map of Western Va. O. copying R.R. Map. R. writing names on Pa. Map. Pleasant day, but cool.

Thursday, March 31st. Making map of Western Va. O. finished R.R. Map and worked at Shenandoah River, copied Valley Map at Koerner's after 4 P.M. R. at Pa. Map. [Wilbourn] went to mts. Cool and cloudy. Sent letter to mother.

Friday, April 1st., 1864. Worked at map of Western Va. O. made tracing of Augusta Co. R. writing names on Pa. map. Pleasant day.

Saturday, April 2nd. Worked at map of Western Va. R. writing names on Pa. O. reducing Shenandoah. Some rain. I went home in P.M. Snow covers mts.

Sunday, April 3. Spent the day at home, had a pleasant visit. A fine day. Came back to Stn. in P.M.

Monday, April 4th. Began reduction of Western Va. to 1/160,000 scale. R. writing names on Pa., finished. O. reducing Shenandoah. Snow and rain all day. Maj. McCue spent the night here.

Tuesday, April 5th. Worked on Western Va. map, O. on Rockbridge, R. reducing Augusta. I looked over reduction of Shenandoah River at night. It snowed and rained some.

Wednesday, April 6th. Worked on Western Va., O. on Rockbridge, and copying Rockingham, R. reducing Rockbridge. A fine day.

Thursday, April 7th. Worked at Western Va. Went home in P.M.;— a fine day,—rained some in A.M.

Friday, April 8th. Fast day. I went with my wife to church, in Churchville;—the day was very solemnly observed. It was a fine day. I went on to town late in the day. It rained at night.

Sat. Ap. 9th. Worked at map. It rained very hard last night and today and the streams are quite high. R. and O. copying maps, etc.

Sunday, April 10th. I went down to camp today, in company with Rogers, went to Brown's for the night. The rivers are very high. It rained some today;—went to ch. at night.

Monday, April 11th. Went first to Gen. Lee's and saw him;—had a few minutes conversation about the times;—he said he wanted every man to his post, that we had hard work to do this year, but by the blessing of Providence he hoped it would turn out well. Said he knew the enemy had not as large a force as they had last year,—though it was said they were coming with large forces in every direction; said he was glad to see me back and was pleased that I had been able to attend to duty and yet be often at home. I went by Clark's Mt. to Gen. Ewell's; dined with Gen. E.; he was pleased to see me;—had quite a visit and returned to Brown's. A fine drying day.

Tuesday, April 12th. Came back to Staunton. Saw Gen. Stuart on the cars. All the ladies were leaving camp, by order of Gen. Lee;—the parting was quite affecting. Some rain during the day.

Wednesday, April 13th. Worked at map and at verifying maps of Washington Co., etc.

Thursday, April 14th. Worked verifying maps; R. copying Wn. Va., etc. A fine day. I went home in the evening;—fixing for camp. Fine day.

Friday, April 15th. Worked copying map of S.W., etc., and packed up. Sent Oltmanns to Koerner's. It rained in P.M.

Saturday, April 16th. Finished packing up and started Robinson and Billy with the horses to camp. It rained in A.M. Sent baggage home. Rain in A.M., but it cleared off.

Sunday, April 17th. Spent the day in Staunton;—went to [Presbyterian church] twice. Cool day—wrote home.

Monday, April 18th. Came back to camp on R.R.;—found my horses at the Depot and got to Hd. Qrs. at dark. A fine day.

Tuesday, April 19th. Went up to Orange C. H. to look for some of my baggage. Robinson at S.W. Va. Map.—Oltmanns copying Culpeper, etc. A fine day, but air still cool.

Wednesday, April 20th. Spent the day at Hd. Qrs., at work at map of Valley of Va. Pleasant but cool. R. and O. at same.

Thursday, April 21st. Worked at map of Wn. Va. A fine day, somewhat milder—all quiet—wrote home at night.

Friday, April 22nd. Worked at map of Valley. R. reduced Berkeley Co. and Oltmanns copying S.W. Va. A fine day,—cool and a sprinkle in P.M. Mrs. Ewell went away today.

Saturday, April 23rd. I went up to Orange C. H. to get some acc'ts. paid and get some maps;—saw our new Eng. commander, Maj. Gen. M. L. Smith.[7] Saw Hinrichs. The day was a very fine one, warm and spring like.

Sunday, April 24th. Remained in camp. The Rev. Mr. Garland preached at Hd. Qrs. on the "Final Judgment." Read some at Leigh Hunt and the Bible—Listened to a mocking bird. It began to rain at dark. The enemy's cavalry crossed at Ely's Ford. Burwell came.

Monday, April 25th. It rained all last night, a warm spring rain. I worked at a map of the Valley. R. reduced Frederick Co., Md., and O. copying map of Wn. Va. A very fine day. Gen. and Col. Smith dined here.

Tuesday, April 26th. All at work, as yesterday;—the day was warm, —turned cool in the evening. Wrote to Prufer and wife at night. Gen. Early arrested by Gen. Ewell.[8]

Wednesday, April 27th. Worked at 1/160,000 Map. O. copying 2nd copy of Mts. map. R. reducing Loudoun and [Fredericksburg]. A fine day; cool at night.

Thursday, April 28th. Reduced map of Frederick Co., Va. R. finished copying Loudoun Co. and began Franklin, Pa. and O. at 2nd copy of Mt. map. Cool but pleasant day. Gen. Pendleton here in P.M.

Friday, April 29th. Engaged on map of Fred. Co., Va. R. reducing Franklin Co., Pa. and O. copying, on linen, S.W. Va. A fine day, leaves coming out finely, cherries and peaches in full bloom.

Saturday, April 30th. Worked on map of Fauquier, etc., R. on Franklin Co. Pa., and Oltmanns copying mts. map. Quite cool day.

Sunday May 1st, 1864. Went to Orange C. H. to church with Col. Pendleton. Took dinner with Col. Allan, Chief of Ordnance. Heard, on our return, that the enemy was moving towards the front, and that Burnside and his Corps had arrived at the Rappahannock. Wrote home at night. A fine warm day. The leaves are just coming out and the cherries and peach trees are in full bloom.

Monday, May 2nd. Worked at map of E. Va., extending it to Washington; Robinson putting names on Wn. Va. map and Oltmanns copying E. Va. Pleasant day; a wind storm and some rain in the evening; snow on the Mts. Heard from home.

Tuesday, May 3rd. Worked reducing Fairfax and Prince William. R. & O. as yesterday. Cool day. Wrote to Maj. Bell and Kemper.

"We spent the day in front of Washington"

THE WILDERNESS, 1864, CAMPAIGN.[1]

Wednesday, May 4th. Worked at map of Western Va. as also did Mr. Robinson; Oltmanns copied Photograph Map. A fine day. The Yankees crossed the river, in the morning, at Elley's. The 2nd Corps moved across to the "Old Turnpike," except a portion of Early's Division. The Gen. left; all except Mr. Robinson and myself; we spent most of the night at our old Hd. Qrs. I remained to receive and give orders.

Thursday, May 5th. Went over to Locust Grove at 3½ A.M.; found Gen. Ewell gone to the front, where the road to Spotswood's leaves "Old Turnpike." We drove the enemy past this point from Locust Grove and skirmished some with them. In the evening they made an attack on us and partially broke our line, but we rallied and drove them back with great slaughter. I went to Gen. Lee's twice, and examined our line of battle; scouted some on the right. Gen. Lee was near Parker's Store, some 8 miles from us. The day was quite warm. Gen. Lee was some 3 miles beyond Parker's Store.

Friday, May 6th. We had our Hd. Qrs. at Locust Grove last night. Got up at 3 A.M. this morning. The enemy advanced upon our lines at daylight and came to within some 40 yards. We discomfited them, completely, from behind some temporary breastworks, and drove them away with much slaughter. Hill also attacked them on the right of the road, with success. We were skirmishing with them, more or less, all day. I carried orders, reconnoitered the lines, etc. The day was intensely warm. We made an attack on them at dark, with Gordon's Brigade,[2] and drove them off the ridge on the road from Dempser's to Germana, killing and capturing many. We took the Brigadiers, Seymour[3] and Shaler.[4] They slept at our Hd. Qrs. The day was intensely warm. Gen. Lee fought the enemy on the Plank road, with Hill's and Longstreet's Corps, and drove them with much slaughter. I carried orders and sketched portions of the field.

Saturday, May 7th. We skirmished some with the enemy, collected arms and buried the dead, etc. The enemy got a large supply train over last night and has been moving towards Fredericksburg. We heard of the movement on Richmond. I had Oltmanns and Robinson making maps of vicinity of Richmond all night. I carried some orders and sketched some parts of the battlefield. In the evening we commenced moving to the right. The enemy going on down the river. A warm day and very dusty. We buried about 1,500 Yankees today and collected many arms.

Sunday, May 8th. We marched on down towards *Spotsylvania C. H.*, Longstreet's Corps, under Anderson being in advance. The enemy moved down by the Plank Road and came on to near Spotsylvania C. H., where our cavalry fought them back until they had to give way; just then Anderson's advance came up and he joined in and drove the enemy back. We had skirmishes with them at various points, the two lines being only a few miles apart. I was sent by Gen. Ewell to take our wagons to Shady Grove Church. The train went to Lebanon church. We spent part of the day at Shady Grove and late in the P.M. went to near the old Block-house. The day was intensely warm and dust deep. The trees are just getting fully out; the apples and peaches in full bloom. Lee spent the night near us. We had several hundred wounded and took some prisoners.

Monday, May 9th. We got our troops into position on the S. side of the [Nye] River and fortified our line; had some skirmishing with the enemy. Early came up, during the day, with Hill's Corps, halting near the old Block-house. Stuart had a fight with the enemy near Massaponax church, (cavalry), but the force of the enemy was so large they forced a passage and went on to Hanover Junction, Stuart following after them. The day was very warm. I got my men and worked all day at Dr. Hick's,

Von Steinaker helping, copying maps of vicinity of Richmond, etc. Late in the P.M. went down to the front; some heavy skirmishing. We moved our Hd. Qrs. to the road near the battle field, sleeping in the open air. Attended the burial of A. Hanna, one of my old pupils.

Tuesday, May 10th. The enemy attacked our lines in several places, today, at 4 P.M., making desperate efforts to break them. They succeeded at one point, near the Harris house, and carried a portion of the line, but we repulsed them and gained our works again. They continued to make desperate attacks on various parts of our lines, but with no better success. Capt. Turner,[5] of our Staff, was badly wounded. The attack was hardest late in the P.M. I worked at maps, in the field, near Frazier's. We moved our wagons to that point. Late in the P.M. Early moved to our left and drove the enemy back across the river, to which they had advanced, driving in the small force we had there. Early drove them back handsomely and captured some. There was some fighting on our right. The day was very warm. We had fortified our line and it is considered quite strong. It is very dusty. The enemy is in our front and vigorous skirmishing is going on. Mr. Hewson,[6] the special correspondent of the London Herald, is staying with me; a genial gentleman and a great friend of the Confederacy. Col. Boteler spent part of the day with us. Some wounded were brought in.

Wednesday, May 11th. Today was comparatively quiet; some firing and skirmishing. I rode up to Gen. Lee's and sent a map to Gen. Imboden, then rode down to the front, when, Gen. Lee sent me to the front to reconnoitre the enemy's left. I found them in three lines of battle and exposed to a flank movement. I reported and Gen. Lee sent me after Gen. Early to come from our left and attack the enemy, with Wilcox's[7] and Heth's[8] Divisions, which were on our right; but I could not find him as he was out examining his position, on our left, where he had Anderson's Division fortifying. It was reported that the enemy was moving there; but no fighting took place. We moved, for the night, to the forks of the road. It began to rain in the P.M.

Thursday, May 12th. We moved our wagons up to the forks of the road last night and slept there, the Gen. coming up. It rained during the night, with thunder, and there was a dense fog this morning. At 4 A.M. the enemy massed and advanced on our center, with a tremendous force, and broke it for the moment, capturing some 20 pieces of artillery that were just coming into position, having been withdrawn during the night; the idea having gained ground that the enemy was withdrawing,

—so the artillery had been sent away. Gen. Johnson sent for it in the night, but it came too late. Many of Johnson's Division were captured, Gen. J. among them, and many were killed. The scene was terrific, for several hours, before we regained the line of works we had in the rear of our front line. We drove the enemy out of most of them; they only held a salient. We got up reinforcements and drove them back and successfully resisted all their attacks, which were incessant from 4 A.M. to 1 P.M.; then came a little lull and the fight was renewed until 4 P.M. The panic at one time was fearful, and nearly the whole of Johnson's Division came pouring back to the rear, and many of them were captured; but Gordon and some others filled up the gap and received the shock of the enemy's attack and broke them every time. It rained very hard a good portion of the day, with thunder and lightning, but it made no difference in the fighting and the musketry and artillery were incessant. We lost many valuable lives. I spent the day, with many others of the staff, rallying and sending in again the broken fragments of Johnson's Division and giving orders in reference to wounded, etc., in the vicinity of the battle ground. Grant was foiled in the purpose he had in view and sullenly kept up his artillery firing. We made some movements on our right and drove the enemy back. Our troops rested on their arms for the night. It became quite muddy. The General remained at the front.

Friday, May 13th. We spent the night near Frazier's. It rained much. I spent the day in camp, copying maps. Turner was taken away today to Richmond. The Gen. and Pendleton remained at the lines. There was some skirmishing and firing of artillery during the day, but comparative quiet reigned. We moved back our line and made it shorter, the enemy occupying the old line. It has become very muddy and we are working the roads to our rear. I wrote home by Turner.

Saturday, May 14th. We spent last night on the hill near Frazier's, with our wagons; the General remained at the front. The enemy made an attack on our line during the night, but were repulsed. It rained much last night and today, with thunder and lightning. Skirmishing was kept up most of the day. At 3 P.M. the enemy made some attacks, but accomplished nothing. We were copying maps all day. I looked over a map of Spotsylvania. Some heavy showers today and the roads were very muddy. Johnson's Division was, today, consolidated into two Brigades and put, temporarily into Early's Division, it had 1,500 muskets. Late in the P.M. I went down to the front and saw the General. The enemy had moved away from the left of our line and we moved our two Brigades and drove them from our right, capturing some. Gen. Lee issued an order to the troops recounting our victories in the West, the courage of troops, and calling on them to still resist. I sent a map of the country towards Richmond to the General and returned Gen. Rodes' maps to him.

Sunday, May 15th. It has been quite quiet today, only a few shots of artillery fired. We were copying maps all day. It rained some last night and we had a heavy shower in the P.M. I heard, yesterday, of the death of my friend, Gen. J. E. B. Stuart.[9] A great loss, surely, to the Confederacy. He was a noble man, a true soldier. The roads are very deep.

Monday, May 16th. I spent the day riding over the lines and sketching them, collecting information for a map of the battle. Saw many dead Yankees. The enemy occupies only a small portion of our front, i.e. that of the 2nd Corps. It was quiet most of the day; some skirmishing and shelling during the P.M., amounting to but little. There was quite a shower in the P.M. It began on the right and moved to the left, omitting a portion of the center. We are moving our forces towards the right.

Tuesday, May 17th. I collected information for map of Battle field, on our left. Rode over the long lines of Yankee fortifications. The day was very warm. There was no fighting, only very slight skirmishing. Late in the P.M. Gen. Ewell moved Rodes' Division to our left and found the enemy in force behind breastworks; fired one volley and fell back. We got good news from Richmond. I was [quite] sick at night.

Wednesday, May 18th. There was a shower last night. The enemy made an attack on our lines, at $4\frac{1}{2}$ A.M., with a heavy column. We received them with a heavy cannonade and musketry fire. It was cloudy in the A.M. The trees are in full foliage. The attack was made on Gen. Gordon and lasted but a short time; he repulsed it handsomely. The cannonading was quite severe. We recovered another portion of the works that we previously lost. I took a line up to the [Potomac] and being quite sick spent the rest of the day in camp. We changed our camp to near the Old C. H. Mr. Hewson, the special correspondent of the London Herald, left us this morning. We had a very heavy shower at noon today. The weather is quite pleasant. The Yanks captured, say that the 21st Corps, under Gen. Augur,[10] came up to Grant yesterday.

Thursday, May 19th. I spent most of the day in camp copying maps; had all at work copying reductions of portions of Va. In the P.M. our Corps was ordered to the right, near the Po., but the order was countermanded and we made an attack on the enemy's right and gained some success. The attack was made about 5 P.M. I went out and sketched some of our line and part of the enemy's. Got a letter from home this P.M. The enemy abandoned their works in front of the 2nd Corps last night and went across the [Nye.] They admit a loss of 2,000 in their attack of yesterday and say they intended to assault our works, but the men would not come up. We found the enemy in full force on our left and lost, in all, nearly 500.

Friday, May 20th. A very fine day and no rain. Everything quiet; not a cannon fired and hardly a musket. We collected arms and got in our wounded, etc. I collected information for a map. The Gen. ordered another map of Spotsylvania and I worked at it for a time.

Saturday, May 21st. Our Corps moved, at an early hour, to the right of the army, towards the Telegraph Road and south of the Po., to meet a supposed corresponding move of the enemy. We also moved our Hd. Qrs. from near the Old C. H. to near Stuart's, So. of the Po.; then soon moved to Beazly's gate, by Bush's Road. About noon word came that the enemy was moving towards Hanover Junction, so we started down the Telegraph Road as hard as we could. Hoke's Brigade came up and it was made our rear guard. The Gen. sent me after the ambulances and Ordnance wagons and I had a long ride and great difficulty in getting them into the road in front of the rear guard; accomplished it by 10 P.M., then, on a jaded horse, found my way to camp at Kickinson's Mill. The Corps all encamped near there. The enemy attacked a portion of Pickett's Division at Milford Station; he repulsed them. There was cavalry skirmishing at various points. The day was very pleasant and mild, also the night. We marched until 11 P.M.

Sunday, May 22nd. We started on, at an early hour, and crossed the North Anna at the Telegraph Bridge, 2 miles from Hanover Junction, and having crossed moved our Corps to near the Junction. Early is again in command of his Division. Rodes was in the rear today. The rest of the army crossed higher up and the trains went by Chilesburg. The movement was well made. The cavalry fought some near Chesterfield Station. A fine day, but warm and dusty. We got into camp, at Hanover Junction, by 1 P.M. and went to work on maps of vicinity. The enemy followed up closely.

Monday, May 23rd. We spent the day in camp, making maps of country towards Richmond, R. and O. and Von S. A very warm day. The 2nd Corps was put in position in front of and to the right of Hanover Junction. Anderson's, the 1st, to the left and Hill's, the 3rd, towards Verdon, on our left. We were joined by Pickett's and Breckinridge's

Divisions.[11] Later in the P.M. the enemy advanced to Jericho's Ford and drove Hill away and crossed two Corps. He fought them with one Division but allowed them to press him back and then form a line, N. & S. and came across the Va. Central R.R., towards Little River. They also came on and took a small breastwork on the N. side of the N. Anna. The impression prevailed that the enemy would press Hill, so Pickett's Division and the 2nd Corps were ordered up the road, after dark, to support him; but finally went into bivouac along the R.R. The General sent for all his staff and there was a consultation of Gens. Lee, Ewell, Anderson, and others, under a large oak, near Mrs. Miller's, about a line, etc. I proposed the line of the Va. Central R.R. and gave reasons for it, and was ordered to go with Gen. Smith and the Eng.'s to examine a line. We rode all night and selected a line. The 1st. Corps moved to its line and fortified and the 2nd was held in reserve. A warm, dusty day.

Tuesday, May 24th. I went out with the General on the line and spent the day there. We went up to Gen. Hill's quarters and remained a part of the day there, awaiting developments, etc. Gens. Lee and Ewell and part of the staff breakfasted with Gen. Anderson. I ate a snack with Gen. Lee in the P.M. It was very warm and dusty today. Our camp was moved to Anderson's, on the Telegraph Road. I supped with Maj. Harmon who is "blue" enough. We had a heavy shower just before dark.

Wednesday, May 25th. Spent the day in camp, making maps. Moved up to the front in the P.M. We have sent everything away from Hanover Junction. The enemy has crossed the river and is strongly entrenched on this side. The 2nd Corps is on the right, the 1st in the center, and the 3rd on the left, forming an arc, the centre advanced some 300 yards from Hanover Junction and the right very near Little River, on the Va. C. R.R., and the left across Little River, above Verdun. Only a little skirmishing during the day. We had a hard wind and a moderate shower about daybreak. Quite warm.

Thursday, May 26th. We had a very hard rain shortly after sunrise, with thunder. Worked at maps all day. We had showers. There was some skirmishing and the enemy advanced a line of battle on our right, which Rodes' skirmishers drove back. Quite pleasant.

Friday, May 27th. It was ascertained, at an early hour, that the enemy had left the front of the 2nd Corps recrossed the N. Anna, burning the bridge behind them, and that only a small force was in front of the 1st and 2nd Corps. Gen. Lee at once ordered a forward move, down the

R.R., towards Richmond. Gen. Breckinridge went down the R., F. & P. R.R., the 2nd Corps, under Gen. Early, (Gen. Ewell very sick) went down the Central R.R., by the way of the Merry Oaks, where we crossed to Hughes X Roads, and near there spent the night. The enemy was reported crossing at Hanover Town, in the A.M. We took our wagons, via Ashland, and Merry Oaks, to Satterwhite's. Gen. Ewell was sick. We tried to work during the day, but did not stay long enough in one place, but at night we worked all night, at Satterwhite's, and finished 3 maps. It was very warm and showery during the day.

Saturday, May 28th. We started at 3 A.M. and went by Atlee's Station and Shady Grove Church to Hundley's Corner, placing our Corps along the road from and on the crest of the Totapotomay Creek. I corrected maps of the road and examined the country some, and slept at Hundley's Corner. Gen. Early is in command of the Corps. There was a hard cavalry fight at Enon Church; ours drove the enemy until they brought up reinforcements of infantry when we had to fall back. The enemy did not follow. It was quite warm and rained in the P.M. We went to Mechanicsville to camp. We had a grand vegetable supper and slept soundly, 5 miles from Richmond, the army 8 miles.

Sunday, May 29th. We copied maps of the country N.E. of Richmond and I took one to Gen. A. P. Hill and corrected some of the roads. Gave a map to Gen. Butler,[12] of S.C., of the cavalry, also one to Gen. Ramseur,[13] comd'g. Early's Division. All quiet. The enemy moving to the right, slowly. The day quite warm.

Monday, May 30th. We moved camp to Col. Richardson's. Gen Ewell still somewhat unwell. Copied map of Hanover, 1/160,000, and made one of vicinity of Richmond. We moved to the right in the P.M. and had quite a hard fight; drove the enemy to their works when they repulsed us from them; they were masked. We lost a good many. Col. Willis is mortally wounded. The fight was near Bethesda Church. The day was very warm. I went to Gen. Smith's in the evening.

Tuesday, May 31st. I went into Richmond and went to see Col. Baldwin, and attend to some other business. The day was very warm. Hoke's Division came out and joined our Corps and had some fighting on the Old Church Road. Col. Willis, of the 12th Ga., died today; he was one of the noblest spirits in the army; "I am no more afraid to die than I was to go into the battle," said he just before expiring.

Wednesday, June 1st. Spent the day in camp correcting and copying a map of part of Hanover Co. and Oltmanns copied some of the Photograph map. Robinson went to Richmond. Col. Tyler, Mr. Hewson and others, came out to see us and dined with us. Late in the evening Dr. Coleman and myself went out towards Cold Harbor and witnessed the fighting there, on the right of our line, where we had, in the morning, driven the enemy away from a position that we wanted and which they all day attempted to retake. The assault of the enemy was very heavy on McLaw's Division, of the Ist Corps, and on part of Hoke's Division. Haygood's Brigade,[14] of new S.C. troops, broke and ran and the enemy gained some of our works, but we soon drove them back. The day was intensely warm and very dusty.

Thursday, June 2nd. I spent most of the day in camp; rode out along the line in the morning and took two maps to Gen. Early, who was at Hunter's House, near the Old Church Road. Hill's Corps moved up to Hundley's Corner and somewhat past, and the 2nd Corps, under Early, moved to the right and rested between the two roads and to the right of the Old Church Road. Gordon was north of the Old Church Road, Rodes on the left. Breckinridge's Division moved round to our right, last night, and there was some skirmishing there all day. About 5 P.M. the 2nd Corps and part of the 3rd made an attack on the enemy and captured several hundred prisoners. The day was quite pleasant. It began to rain late in the P.M. I sent Wm. to Richmond and Mr. Hewson sent us out some delicacies.

Friday, June 3rd. I finished a map for Gen. Rodes and took it to him; made a sketch of the line occupied by our Corps before the advance, and sketched the surrounding country. There was active skirmishing all along the line and a hot artillery duel, on the left, in which Poague's Battalion, of the 3rd Corps, suffered much. Heth was on the left of our line. Late in the P.M. the Yankees made a grand attack on our lines in front of Gaines' Mill, Anderson, but were repulsed with much loss. The cannon-ade was very hard and terrific. We had a good many casualties. Lt. Long was killed. There were several showers during the day and it was quite cool at night.

Saturday, June 4th. Sketched the lines towards the Totapotomay; work at map in P.M. O. and R. copying 1/80,000 maps. The day was cool and pleasant. We fell back last night, to our former line, but held the other with skirmishers. Heth moved to Gaines' Mill, to the right of our line. It began to rain at 4 P.M. There was a heavy attack on our right, about dark, heavy cannonade, also an attack on the 2nd Corps at 9 P.M. Sent Wm. to Richmond and got some cherries, etc. Rodes is on our left, passing Hundley's Corner. Gen. Early had his Hd. Qrs. at Hunter's today.

Sunday, June 5th. Gen. Early received notice of his appointment as Lt. Gen. (Temporary) and ordered our wagons over to the Nance house where we spent the rest of the day. I went down to the front for a time. A warm day.

Monday, June 6th. We moved our wagons over to the Starke house. The enemy left the front of the 2nd Corps last night and we followed them up today, to Gilman's Mill; had some skirmishing. I sketched the lines and roads in that direction. A very warm day. We encamped in the edge of the woods near the Starke House.

Tuesday, June 7th. Gen. Lee sent for me to make a sketch of our line of battle. I got as far as New Cold Harbor, had some warm work, owing to the constant skirmishing that was going on. The day was very warm. Our Corps is in reserve this P.M. We moved out in the morning on the flank of the enemy and had some skirmishing. Camp at same place.

Wednesday, June 8th. Went down to Turkey Hill and sketched the line up to New Cold Harbor. A very warm day. Some artillery fighting took place. Heard that the enemy was in Augusta Co. We moved our quarters to the Starke House.

Thursday, June 9th. Gen. Smith sent for me to sketch line near McGhee House for a fort; made a tracing of my sketch of battle line and took to Gen. Lee, then spent the rest of the day along the lines, in many dangerous places, but was Providentially spared. Skirmishing all day, but no results. Got orders to make a survey at night, so was at the Steuart House until midnight. Warm day. Hd. Qrs. at Dr. Curtis'.

Friday, June 10th. Gen. Smith sent for me to accompany him to sketch positions and we went to the McGhee House and the Steuart House and made sketches for forts. Talked awhile with Gens. Davis[15] and Finnegan.[16] It was very unpleasant working through the trenches. The day was very warm. At night I went with Col. Talcott[17] and his Eng. Regt. to the road near Cold Harbor and showed him the outlines of the fort he had to construct, etc. Got to camp at 11 P.M.

Saturday, June 11th. Went in the morning with Maj. S. Johnson and showed him the position for the fort at the McGhee House. The day was very warm. Sketched the road back from New Cold Harbor to Dr. Curtis'. Bad news from the Valley, but Breckinridge will be on hand today. Skirmishing only. Cavalry fight on North Anna.

Sunday, June 12th. Spent the day in camp as we expected to move. Gen. Early sent for Heads of Departments and Major Generals. Jacksonian silence observed.[18] Mr. Lacy was in camp. Last night was quite cool. A fine day. Skirmishing as usual. Our Corps in reserve near Dr. Curtis'. Hd. Qrs. at same place.

Monday, June 13th. The sending for Heads of Departments yesterday convinced all that an important movement was on hand and we found it realized when we started, at 3 A.M., today. Our whole Corps, under command of Lt. Gen. Early, for some distant expedition. Rodes' Division moved in front. We started from our camp, a mile W. of Gaines' Mill, and went via Mechanicsville and Meadow Bridge to the Brooke Turnpike, then up the Plank Road to Goodall's Tavern where we turned down the Old Mt. Road and went to the banks of the South Anna, near Auburn Mills, where we encamped. Hd. Qrs. at Chewning's, ½ mile from the mill. Morning cool, but the day was warm and roads dusty. I went via Richmond and got supplies from the Eng. Bureau. The enemy crossed at the Long Bridge on the Chickahominy and there was some fighting there. We marched 25 miles.

Tuesday, June 14th. Started at sunrise, Ramseur in advance, crossed S. Anna, via St. Peter's Church and into Mt. Road again, which we followed to 3 miles beyond Gardiner's X Roads. Hd. Qrs. near Goodwin's. Warm. Roads dusty. Our wagons moved by parallel roads S.W. of us. The troops march well and are in fine spirits. Corrected map of Louisa Co. as we went along.

Wednesday, June 15th. Marched at sunrise, Gordon in advance; passed through Louisa C. H. and by Trevillians, where a cavalry fight took place a few days ago, and on to Valentine's Mill, in the Green Springs neighborhood. Hd Qrs. at West's. Very warm. Roads dusty. I rode in ambulance not being well.

Thursday, June 16th. We marched at sunrise, Rodes in front, via Mechanicsville, to Charlottsville. The Corps encamped N.E. of the Rivanna, from Shadwell back. Hd. Qrs. were on Carr's Hill near the University.[19] I rode in the ambulance; pleasant, not quite so much dust. Heard that Breckinridge had gone to Lynchburg.

Friday, June 17th. The General had us up by 2 A.M. to start to Lynchburg. We went to the cars and waited until after sunrise before Ramseur's and Gordon's Divisions got on the cars; then we went on to Lynchburg; got there by 1 P.M., and the troops marched out by the Salem Road, some 3 miles, and in front of the Militia, and Breckinridge's force. Rodes marched to North Garden Depot and the artillery moved on by the Lynchburg road. It was very hot and dusty. The enemy is some 3 miles off. I got maps, tho. not well, and make copies of the vicinity.

Saturday, June 18th. The General was up by 2 A.M. and went to the front. I spent most of the day in an office, in Lynchburg, making maps of vicinity; furnished copies to each Maj. Gen. Rode to the front in the P.M. Some skirmishing by Ramseur and Gordon. Very warm. Rodes' Division came up. Gens. Ramseur and Elsey[20] reported. Our troops in line of battle 3 miles in front of Lynchburg. Rodes went into line on the Forest Road.

Sunday, June 19th. The enemy retreated last night and this morning we followed them, Ramseur in advance, along the Salem Road. Went to Liberty, 25 miles; had some skirmishing with the rear and took some prisoners. The skirmish occurred near Liberty. I rode out to take map to Gen. Rodes and found the army gone; rode 6 miles, then came back to Lynchburg and gave orders to Robinson and [rode] on to within 3 miles of Liberty, but was too sick to go on, so spent the night at Dr. Mitchell's and was very kindly treated. Rodes went by the Forest Road; Cavalry went by the Forest Road. A warm day, dusty and dry. The troops march well; enemy destroyed the R.R.

Monday, June 20th. We marched on after Hunter to Buford's Gap, close in his rear; had some skirmishing; got to Buford's by noon, Gordon in front followed by Rodes, Ramseur and Breckinridge. Ransom and his cavalry went by the Peaks Gap to Buchanan and thence to Salem. Very dusty, not as warm as yesterday. The enemy made a show of resistance at the Gap and we formed to flank them, Gordon on the left and Rodes on the right, but the movement was so slow that night came on and nothing was accomplished and we spent the night in the Gap; the enemy's rear on the top of the mt. The night was quite cool. Gilmor went on mt. to the left.

Tuesday, June 21st. Owing to mistake in the delivery of orders our troops did not get underway until long after sunrise; Rodes was in advance. We found the enemy gone; we followed to Big Lick, then we turned off, across the country, and went to Mason's Gap, hoping to strike the enemy before they all got through; but we were too late. The cavalry got there early in the day and gained some advantages and got a number of pieces of artillery, wagons, etc. Imboden crossed the mt. to the left of Buford's Gap, and got in the rear of and followed up the enemy. Ramseur followed Rodes. We went to the Hanging Rock and later in the day to Botetourt Springs. The enemy got into the mts. and Imboden followed. We are encamped along the Salem Turnpike. Very warm day.

Wednesday, June 22nd. We spent the day in camp, the troops resting, washing, etc. Ramseur moved to the Springs; our cavalry is still after the enemy. I wrote home by Capt. Sterrett. Fine, warm day.

Thursday, June 23rd. We moved at dawn, Ramseur in front and went to Buchanan by the McAdam Road. Most of Ramseur's Division crossed the James; Gordon encamped near Waskey's Mill; Breckinridge was in the rear. I went by Mt. Union Church to Fincastle, (where I met the General) looking after the enemy, who went towards Craig Co. The day was very warm. We spent the night at Mrs. Boyd's, at Buchanan. Cherries are in their prime.

Friday, June 24th. We moved early, Ramseur in advance; went towards Lexington. The General and some others went by the Natural Bridge and at Tom's Brook and Rodes at Pugh's Run. We had a shower in the P.M. Hd. Qrs. at Kendrick's.

Saturday, July 2nd. We rode on to Winchester, stopping at Middletown for breakfast; got to Winchester by 11 A.M. and camped at McDonald's Spring. Gordon came to Abram's Creek; Ramseur to Bartonsville. The day was quite warm, but modified by the showers of yesterday. The people of Winchester were so glad to see us and as loyal as ever.

Sunday, July 3rd. We marched to Leetown, via Brucetown and Smithfield, and camped at the old General Lee place; Ramseur came with us; Rodes to Smithfield and Gordon and Breckinridge went to Martinsburg and took that place, with little difficulty, with some prisoners and many stores, and encamped towards Shepherdstown. The cavalry fought with the enemy near Leetown and drove them through Kearneysville. We had a number (30) killed and wounded. The cavalry encamped between Leetown and Kearneysville. The day was very warm.

Monday, July 4th. We went to Halltown, via Gibson's, Flowing Spring and Brown's. Ramseur's Division and Rodes' came to Charlestown by the Turnpike, and on to Halltown, and we drove the enemy back from Halltown to Harper's Ferry and took Boliver with Rodes' and Ramseur's skirmishers. We spent the day on Boliver Heights, skirmishing with the enemy who fired their heavy artillery at us all day, doing but little damage. At night they evacuated Harper's Ferry and we went in, getting many stores. Hd. Qrs. at Brown's. Warm and dry. We breakfasted at Maj. Hawks' in the A.M.

Tuesday, July 5th. We rode to Bolivar in the morning; the enemy evacuated Harper's Ferry and crossed to the Maryland Heights. We spent some time at Bolivar, then went to Halltown and on to Shephardstown. Gordon marched from near Duffield's Depot to Boteler's Ford and crossed the Potomac and went down to Antietam Furnace and encamped. Vaughan went to Sharpsburg. Ramseur and Rodes spent the day at Harper's Ferry. Warm and dusty. We rode over to Antietam Furnace and burned canal boats, etc. Hd. Qrs. at Bedinger's.

Wednesday, July 6th. We had our camp near Shepherdstown last night; today we crossed the Potomac and went to Sharpsburg; camped near there, in an orchard. Gordon marched down the river to near Maryland Heights. Rodes and Ramseur crossed to near Sharpsburg. The cavalry went to Boonsboro. I made a map of part of Maryland for Maj. Harman, Chief Q.M. of the army, & of parts of Maryland and Virginia. Warm day.

Thursday, July 7th. We spent the day at Sharpsburg. Made a map of parts of Maryland for Col. Pendleton. The day was intensely warm. We had quite a row in camp, caused by a plentiful supply of lemon punch. The General went down to Maryland Heights and Gordon's Division had some fighting there and drove the enemy to within 600 yards of "Fort Duncan," or "Round Hill." Breckinridge and Rodes were in Pleasant Valley, near Rohresville; Ramseur near Sharpsburg. Our cavalry went to near Frederick City; fighting some near Middletown, Md., then burned up the stores there and came to Sharpsburg. Maj. McCue came to see me yesterday and spent the night with me.

Friday, July 8th. Ramseur marched through Boonsboro and on to Catoctin Mt., 5 miles from Frederick City; Breckinridge (Gordon in front) marched by Fox's Gap, from Rohresville, through Middletown. Rodes crossed the S. Mt., by Crampton Gap, to near Jefferson. We had our Hd. Qrs at the western foot of Catoctin Mt. Warm and very dusty. Gen. Gordon showed us the battle field of South Mountain where D. H. Hill commanded.

Saturday, July 9th. We went on to Frederick City, the enemy falling back towards Monocacy Junction. We had some skirmishing and artillery practice before we reached the river. The enemy resisted our passage most of the day, but McCausland dashed over on their left and gained an important position, and Gordon followed with his Division and flanked them, and drove them off in gallant style; at about 1½ o'clock P.M. Ramseur advanced on them in front and engaged them there and across the river. Rodes marched out on the Baltimore Road and engaged a small force there and drove it across the river. The rout was complete. We crossed over and had Hd. Qrs. near the Junction and moved nearly everything across the river; pursued the enemy two miles beyond the river. A levy of $200,000 was collected from Frederick City today. I dined, with several, in the city. The day was intensely warm and very dusty. Robinson made a map for Breckinridge.

Sunday, July 10th. I made a sketch of the Monocacy Battle Field, then followed the army through Urbana towards Washington; went to Summit Point, 1 mile from Gaithersburg, where we encamped. The enemy fled towards Baltimore. Breckinridge's Corps was in advance; Ramseur brought up the rear. Our cavalry, yesterday, started towards Baltimore and the R.R. north of it. The day was very warm and dusty. We found many friends.

Monday, July 11th. Moved at an early hour towards Washington; Rodes in advance. We went to Silver Spring, in the edge of the D.C., and advanced to near the fortifications. Gen. Early told some of the troops, as we passed them, that he would take them into Washington that day, but they were so exhausted by the intense heat and dust that he made no decided attack; only skirmished some. McCausland's Cavalry Brigade[21] advanced by the Georgetown Road, and Johnson's went towards Baltimore. Mosby[22] came towards the Chain Bridge. We had our Hd. Qrs. at Riggs'. I got some maps from Frank Blair's[23] House, by order of the Lt. General.

Tuesday, July 12th. We spent the day in front of Washington;[24] had some skirmishing; especially late in the P.M. by Rodes; we also had a cavalry skirmish on the Georgetown Road. Gilmor was near Baltimore and at the Gunpowder River. Johnson's Brigade came back. Our trains started back at dark and we followed on at 11 P.M., by the same route we came, getting to Rockville at daylight, continuing the march through Danestown to Dawsonville, where we halted for a time. The day was quite warm, but we had a shower in the P.M. Ramseur in the rear, Breckinridge in advance.

Wednesday, July 13th. We got to Dawsonville about noon and rested at Seneca Church until sundown. The enemy followed our cavalry and Jackson repulsed them at Rockville. The day was quite pleasant. Our troops marched well. We got many horses and cattle.

Thursday, July 14th. We marched on, last night, to the river, by Poolesville, to White's Ford, and bivouaced there about midnight (Breckinridge in advance), and our trains closed up. At an early hour we commenced crossing the river and went on to the Big Spring and took up our quarters there. Some of the troops are on Limestone Creek. We got to camp about noon; warm and dusty. It has been quite dry in Loudoun Co.

Friday, July 15th. We spent the day in camp at the Big Spring. I made a map of the routes of the army during the expedition; had Robinson and Oltmanns copying maps of the Potomac Border. I got George Hanger to take my horses home and also sent bundle to wife. Our ordnance train, prisoners, horses, cattle, etc., went on to Ashby's Gap, via Upperville, starting in the night. The day was very warm. The enemy made some demonstrations along the river and stampeded our wagons at Waterford.

Saturday, July 16th. We started at an early hour for Snicker's Gap, Gordon in front, followed by Wharton,[25] then the train, then Rodes and Ramseur. The Yankee cavalry, from Hillsboro, fell on our train at Purcellville and captured and destroyed some 30 wagons before Rodes got up, but we soon drove them off and took a piece of artillery and killed and captured several. We crossed the Mt. and encamped on the W. side. Breckinridge crossed the river. Rodes encamped on the Mt. and Ramseur in the Gap and on the S. slope; McCausland followed the ordnance train to Ashby's Gap. Jackson preceded us and crossed the Shenandoah and Johnson followed on our right flank. Pleasant breeze, but warm and dusty.

Sunday, July 17th. We crossed the Shenandoah and went to Berryville and encamped near there, on the Charlestown Road. Breckinridge remained near the ferry and Rodes went to Rock's Ford; Ramseur on the Charlestown Road near the Co. line; Jackson towards Charlestown, Imboden to Millwood, and Johnson to [?]. I sketched the road up to Berryville and spent the rest of the day quiet in camp. Very warm and dusty.

Monday, July 18th. Sketched the roads E. of Berryville, dined at Wm. T. Allen's. I had not seen him for 17 years. Rode all day, came back and found camp moved to Winchester Road, 1½ miles from B., and a brisk fight going on at Rock's Ford and Castleman's Ferry. The enemy crossed at Dr. McCormick's and Rodes drove them back. Gordon fought at Castleman's. Our cavalry fought them yesterday and today crossing the Mt. Our wagons were all moved towards Winchester. We did not get to bed until quite late. Hot and dusty.

Tuesday, July 19th. I sketched the turnpike to Winchester; dined with W. Allen, and sketched the old road back to camp, at Russell's old Tavern. The enemy crossed at Berry's Ferry, where Imboden gallantly repulsed them. They also advanced from Martinsburg and were held in check by Jackson. Our trains, etc., were started back, some by Winchester and some by Millwood and White Post, to Newtown. Ramseur marched to Winchester and towards Bunker's Hill; and on the 20th had a fight with the enemy at Rutherford's Tavern, in which he was defeated and lost 4 pieces of artillery.

Wednesday, July 20th. We started at 2 A.M. by the Salem Church Road to Saratoga, there rested awhile and then went on to White Post and Newtown, near which we encamped. Judge Wilson and myself came ahead. I sketched the road from the Tollgate to Newtown. Skirmishing towards Martinsburg. Hot and dusty; showers in the P.M., and thunder, cooling the air. Breckinridge marched by Millwood and Cedarville to Middletown. Ramseur covered the removal of our wounded from Winchester. Ramseur lost 4 pieces of artillery and 400 men; a disgraceful affair. Rodes came through White Post and on to Newtown and encamped there. Ramseur camped at Kernstown. Hd. Qrs. near Newtown. Hot and dusty; rain in some places.

Thursday, July 21st. Rode over roads to the north of the Valley pike. Our trains were moved back to Fisher's Hill. The army moved to the vicinity of Middletown and Cedar Creek. We had our Hd. Qrs. on the bank of Cedar Creek. The day was quite pleasant.

Friday, July 22nd. I sketched the roads N. of Strasburg. Ramseur moved to the Capon Grade, one mile N. of Strasburg. Rodes went to Fisher's Mill. Breckinridge remained on Hupp's Hill, near Strasburg. A fine day, cool and pleasant. Hd. Qrs. at Kendrick's.

Saturday, July 23rd. Sketched roads N.W. of Strasburg, came by Rodes' Hd. Qrs. All quiet. The cavalry had a skirmish at Newtown and drove the enemy to Kernstown. Fine day.

Sunday, July 24th. We started at dawn for Winchester, Breckinridge in front, followed by Ramseur and Rodes. (Gordon in front) Vaughan's Cavalry[26] to Bunker's Hill; Jackson on the "Middle," Imboden on the "Back" Road. Drove in enemy's pickets at Bartonsville. Cavalry engaged them, near Kernstown, at 10 A.M. Infantry soon advanced. Wharton was advanced on the right of pike and Gordon advanced, by the left flank, on the left. I conducted Ramseur from Bartonsville to the Middle Road, and he formed across it at Mrs. Massie's. Jackson fought awhile near Kernstown and then moved to Opequon W. of Sandy Ridge. The enemy advanced and we drove them back. Wharton struck them on the left flank; they retreated in confusion and we pursued; they attempted to make a stand at Winchester, but it was very feeble and we pushed on through. Rodes flanked to the Front Royal Road to cut off the cavalry, but they took to the fields and escaped. Rodes followed on the right of the pike and got into it below Winchester and followed to Stephenson's, giving a vigorous pursuit, marching over 30 miles. The cavalry pursued until in the night. Gordon went across the Red Bud and Ramseur came up to it. The enemy began to burn wagons at Winchester and kept it up to Bunker's hill; burnt over 70 and 12 caissons. Very dusty and warm. Hd. Qrs. at Town Spring, Winchester.[27]

Monday, July 25th. We remained in Winchester until 4 P.M., then went to Bunker's Hill and encamped at Boyd's. I got drawing boards fixed up; got chairs, etc. Rodes marched to Bunker's Hill, in advance, followed by Ramseur and Breckinridge. Oltmanns copied Valley Map for Gen. Rodes, Robinson at reduction of Adams Co., Pa. It began to rain about 2 A.M. and rained splendidly until 11 A.M.; cooled the air and did much good. Men in fine spirits. Cavalry followed enemy to Martinsburg and had skirmish there. Very pleasant.

Tuesday, July 26th. We went to Martinsburg and encamped near there; the enemy crossed the river. Rodes and Ramseur encamped on Dry Run. Breckinridge at Tuscarora. Cavalry went to opposite Williamsport. Hd. Qrs. in Col. Faulkner's yard; against his will. Fine day.

Wednesday, July 27th. We moved our camp into the field and Robinson and Oltmanns made maps. I rode to the Mt. and sketched the road. Troops are destroying the B.&O. R.R. Warm day.

Thursday, July 28th. Spent the day in camp, making a route map of campaign. Oltmanns finished a map of parts of Virginia and Maryland, which I sent to Gen. McCausland; also made and sent Gen Rodes a map of Lower Valley; also made a copy of map of N.E. Virginia, 4 miles to the inch, and Robinson put in the names. The cavalry started to Pa. (Green went along) in the night. Very warm.

Friday, July 29th. We went down to Willamsport, Rodes in advance, followed by Ramseur; drove in the enemy's pickets and made a demonstration as far as Hagerstown, while the cavalry crossed higher up and went on into Pa. We got some stores in Williamsport and spent most of the day there, then crossed and encamped on the Hill south of the river. Very warm day. Robinson reducing Adams Co. and Oltmanns at Valley map.

Saturday, July 30th. We left our camp at daylight and came back to Martinsburg. I guided Ramseur by Hammond's Mill. Very warm. Breckinridge remained at Martinsburg yesterday. Came back to old camps.

Sunday, July 31st. We marched, at dawn, to Bunker's Hill and encamped in Gen. Jackson's camp of 1862. Ramseur encamped near us, Rodes S.E. and Breckinridge at Darkesville. Got to camp early and rested. Warm day.

Monday, Aug. 1st. I rode up to Newtown, sketching a back road and spent the night at Vaucluse in company with Lt. Koerner. Intensely warm. All quiet in camp.

Tuesday, Aug. 2nd. Rode back by Parkins' Mill and the Old Front Royal Road to Winchester, then to camp. All quiet. We heard of the mine of Petersburg. Robinson made a Valley map and Oltmanns one of N.E. Virginia. Showers in places. Very warm. Yankees have gone across the river. Mosby at the R.R. at Adamstown on the 29th; he came to our camp tonight.

Wednesday, Aug. 3rd. I sent maps to Breckinridge and Ramseur, then rode up to Winchester and sketched a portion of the road. Dined with Allen, who got orders to move his train. A fine breezy day.

"The Yankees got whipped and we got scared"

THURSDAY, AUGUST 4.¹ We started at sunrise and went to Shepherdstown via Leetown. Breckinridge went the same way. Rodes and Ramseur went by Martinsburg to near Hainesville. Headquarters at Mrs. Bedinger's. Pleasant.

Friday, August 5. We crossed the river to Sharpsburg and had engagement with Cole's² cavalry and drove them away, and then encamped near there. General Early and myself rode over part of the battlefield of Sharpsburg, and I sketched, by his order, the position of his brigade there. General Ransom³ accompanied us. Rodes and Ramseur encamped at Clagget's Mill. A warm day.

Saturday, August 6. We marched to Tilghmauton and the crossroads beyond Hagerstown, and then went to Williamsport and encamped on the Virginia side. We found Rodes and Ramseur near Saint James' College. The general went to Saint James' College and paroled Doctor Kerfoot and Professor Coit for the return of Doctor Boyd, of Winchester, to his home in three weeks. He talked to Doctor Kerfoot for some time. It began to rain very early in the morning and rained most of the forenoon, then cleared off finely. We dined at Williamsport. Breckinridge encamped opposite Williamsport. Rodes and Ramseur went to near Hammond's Mill. The Yankees have a force at Harper's Ferry.

Sunday, August 7. We started at an early hour and went to Martinsburg and spent most of the day at Ed. Pendleton's, and in the P.M. went on to Bunker Hill. Breckinridge came to Darkesville and Rodes and Ramseur to Bunker Hill. General Pegram[4] reported for duty. Quite warm.

Monday, August 8. Worked at map of the battle of Monocacy all day. Quite warm. Enemy reported coming up from Harper's Ferry.

Tuesday, August 9. Spent day in camp at Bunker Hill making map of battle of Monocacy. Robinson reducing Adams County and Oltmanns copying map of District of Columbia. Lieutenant Koerner came to see me in P.M. about details &c. Warm.

Wednesday, August 10. We moved at an early hour to Stephenson's Depot, Breckinridge in advance, and then by Jordan Springs to the Red Rub and Abraham's Creek, where Breckinridge encamped. Rodes marched to the right of the road at Stephenson's and encamped. Ramseur marched yesterday to Winchester to meet a reported advance of Averell from Romney. We got the details of the rout of our cavalry at Moorefield. It was a disgraceful affair. We lost some 400 men and 4 pieces of artillery. We had headquarters near Burgess', a mile from Winchester on the Berryville road. Dined at Wall's. Warm day. Enemy made demonstrations on the Millwood, Berryville, and Martinsburg roads in the P.M., and were easily repulsed.

Thursday, August 11. Appearances indicating a general attack by a large force, we this morning formed a line of battle covering the approaches east and southeast of Winchester; Breckinridge covering the Berryville and Millwood roads, Ramseur the Front Royal road, and Rodes the Martinsburg road. Everything was moved from Winchester and we had a skirmish on the Millwood road. About noon I guided Gordon across the country, by a route I had selected in the A.M., to the pike near Kernstown and took him to a position south of Newtown. The rest of the army followed, and we had a brisk skirmish, about dark, on the road to the Double Toll-Gate from Newtown. We drove the enemy back and encamped near Newtown. Headquarters at Chrisman's. Very warm. Bryan's[5] and Lowry's[6] batteries, on the Millwood road, were engaged some.

Friday, August 12. We marched at an early hour and went across Cedar Creek and formed a line of battle. The Yankees came on and formed on the north side of the creek, and we had some skirmishing but no general engagement. In the evening we fell back to Fisher's Hill and took up our headquarters at Funkhouser's. I spent the day reconnoitering and carrying orders, and at night took Colonel Jackson and his cavalry to the Middle Road and posted them for pickets. Got to camp at midnight. Very warm.

Saturday, August 13. We selected a line of battle on Fisher's Hill, Wharton on the right of the pike, Gordon to the top of the hill beyond the railroad, Ramseur from Gordon to the top of the hill beyond the Middle road, and Rodes half a mile beyond the Middle road with strong pickets across the Valley to the Back Road; cavalry in front, McCausland at the foot of Three Top Mountain, Jackson on the Middle road and Johnson on the Back road. We spent the day on the lines. The troops fortified them. Very warm.

Sunday, August 14. We spent the day on the lines, staying under a tree by the roadside. Had a little skirmishing with the enemy. Most of them remained on the north side of Cedar Creek. Our signal men were driven off the point of Three Top Mountain, but Captain Keller[7] and his sharpshooters drove the Yankees off and killed 2 and captured 3.

Monday, August 15. Spent the day on the lines and at Breckinridge's headquarters. In the P.M. we drove the enemy back to Cedar Creek Hill and found them in the same position. A very warm day. It rained late in the P.M. and at night. Major Jones spent the night with me. General Lomax[8] came to-day.

Tuesday, August 16. Sketched the country between the river and Massanutten Mountain and along the foot of Fisher's Hill. Quite warm. Fitz Lee came to see General Early, his cavalry being at Front Royal. Anderson had a fight with the Yankee cavalry at Guard Hill, in which he got the worst of it.

Wednesday, August 17. We found the enemy gone this morning and the smoke rising from all parts of the Lower Valley from the burning of barns and hay and wheat stacks by the retreating Yankees. We followed, Gordon in advance; then Wharton, Ramseur, and Rodes. McCausland went down the Valley pike, Jackson on the Middle, and Johnson on the Back roads. We did not get up with the enemy until we reached Kernstown; there drove in the skirmishers, and found the cavalry posted on Bowers' Hill. I took Forsberg's[9] small brigade to the Middle road and threw them out to the left and drove the enemy from the hills in front and to the left of Bell's, Johnson's cavalry being there on our left; then reported, and Wharton's division was sent there. I put it in line to advance against Bower's Hill. Then saw it go in and take the hill. Ramseur's sharpshooters advanced at the same time. I watched the left of the line and the advance of Johnson's cavalry, then reported to General Early after dark. Gordon crossed from Kernstown to the Front Royal road and came into Winchester from that way. We lost some killed and wounded, and inflicted some loss on the enemy and drove them through the town. We got the town just after dark. We encamped at Pritchard's, near Kernstown. We took 200 prisoners. The day was pleasant and cloudy; part of it very hot. Anderson marched up to the Opequon.

Thursday, August 18. We moved our camp to the yard of Mrs. Wood, near the Town Spring, at Winchester. Rodes moved out a mile or so on the Berryville road, Ramseur on the Martinsburg road, and Gordon and Wharton remained on Abraham's Creek, near Hollingsworth's Mill. General Anderson came up with Kershaw's[10] division and Fitz Lee's cavalry and encamped near the Opequon, on the Front Royal and Millwood roads. It rained most of last night and half of today quite steadily. Oltmanns finished a map of the Valley, which I sent to General Lomax, and corrected some maps.

Friday, August 19. We moved at an early hour to Bunker Hill, Ramseur in advance, followed by Rodes and Breckinridge. All encamped in the vicinity of Bunker Hill. Anderson and Fitz Lee remained at Winchester. Lomax and his cavalry went to vicinity of Martinsburg and held the line of the Opequon all along. A fine day. Slight showers. Cool evening. Lomax went to Martinsburg and Shepherdstown.

Saturday, August 20. We spent the day in camp. I corrected some maps. Oltmanns copied part of battle of Monocacy and Robinson copied a Valley map. It rained and misted most of the day. We had some skirmishing with the enemy along the Opequon. Camps as yesterday.

Sunday, August 21. We moved toward Charlestown at an early hour. Drove the enemy from the Opequon. Met their infantry skirmishers at Aldridge's about 9.30 A.M. Rodes was in front and threw out his skirmishers and drove the enemy to the vicinity of Charlestown. Ramseur was put on his right and advanced to near the Summit Point road. Anderson came by the old Winchester and Charlestown road and Fitz Lee by the Berryville road. They had some fighting near Summit Point. We advanced by Smithfield. It threatened rain some, but cleared off by noon. Lomax, with Vaughn, Johnson, and Jackson, advanced by Leetown and then toward Charlestown. McCausland came on in our front and went toward Summit Point with part of his force from Smithfield. Gordon was put on the right and Wharton on the left of pike in reserve. We skirmished with the enemy during the P.M. and used some artillery. They made some advances, but were repulsed. We encamped some two and a half miles from Charlestown. A fine day. I reconnoitered positions, &c.

Monday, August 22. We advanced at an early hour and found the enemy gone, leaving only cavalry behind. We soon drove them off, and three miles beyond Charlestown. Anderson and Fitz Lee came to vicinity of Charlestown, and our cavalry was thrown out toward Shepherdstown and toward the Shenandoah. It rained very hard for several hours in the P.M. I dined at Mr. Strider's. Robinson copied map for General Kershaw in P.M. and night. Headquarters near Davenport's.

Tuesday, August 23. The army remained in front of Charlestown. Made some few movements to thwart moves of the enemy, moving more to the left. I sketched the portion of country that we fought over on Sunday. There was a dense fog in the morning, but it cleared off and became quite warm. Headquarters at Davenport's.

Wednesday, August 24. Still at same place. Enemy drove in our pickets toward Harper's Ferry and created some stir, which was soon quelled. Quiet the rest of the day. I rode over to Rock's Ford on the Shenandoah, to view the country. Dined with Major Adams at Osborne's. Very warm day.

Thursday, August 25. We started at an early hour for Shepherdstown, via Leetown, Wharton in front, followed by Gordon, Rodes, and Ramseur. Fitz Lee went by Smithfield to Leetown and Lomax collected his at the same place, and all went on to Martinsburg and Williamsport. We met the enemy's cavalry advance about one mile and a half from Leetown and had quite a heavy skirmish with them. Wharton's division was thrown out and engaged, most of it on the left of the road. Gordon was moved to the right and Rodes to the left. We soon drove the enemy off, with considerable loss on both sides. They made another stand near Shepherdstown on the Charlestown road, which Gordon repulsed with Terry's[11] brigade on the left, then York[12] and Evans[13] on the right. Quite a lively skirmish ensued, in which Gordon was wounded in the head, but he gallantly dashed on, the blood streaming over him. We finally drove the Yankee cavalry in every direction, and encamped at night near Shepherdstown. Headquarters at Boteler's house. A stampede of ambulances when the firing began came near causing a stampede of Wharton's division. We lost a good many. The Yanks had started on a raid and had three days' rations with them. Very warm. The cavalry is opposite Williamsport to-night.

Friday, August 26. We spent about half the day at Shepherdstown, then marched back to Leetown, Ramseur in advance, followed by Rodes, Gordon and Wharton. Our cavalry came to the vicinity of Shepherdstown, having found the enemy in force to oppose their passage at Williamsport. They had an artillery duel in the morning, Anderson had a fight near Charlestown in the P.M. Headquarters in the orchard at the old General Lee house. Colonel Boteler spends the night with me. Robinson and Oltmanns worked awhile at maps. Fine day. Windy and some rain at night.

Saturday, August 27. We continued our march back to our old camp at Bunker Hill. Rodes went by Dandridge's and the Sulphur Springs, the rest by Smithfield. Ramseur followed by Gordon and Wharton. Anderson came from Charlestown by Smithfield, and went on to Stephenson's. Pleasant, but quite cool in the P.M. We also found the cavalry falling back, but General Early ordered McCausland back to Charlestown, and he went beyond toward Harper's Ferry. Fitz Lee and Lomax remained near Shepherdstown.

Sunday, August 28. We spent the day in camp at Bunker Hill, and had preaching in some of the divisions. The enemy's cavalry advanced on ours, and we had some fighting near Smithfield, especially Harry Gilmor, but our cavalry retired, Lomax toward Bunker Hill, and Fitz Lee toward Brucetown. The enemy occupied Smithfield, burning three houses there. Some infantry marched toward the Opequon, but was not engaged. The day was quite cool. Robinson made a map for General Wickham.[14]

Monday, August 29. The enemy's cavalry advanced this morning and drove ours across the Opequon. Ramseur was marched out by the turnpike and advanced to drive them back. Gordon moved by a road to the right to turn the enemy's left flank. The artillery was also advanced. After some brisk cannonading across the creek, and skirmishing, we drove the enemy through Smithfield and two miles and a half beyond, then returned to our old camps again. Rodes held the road toward Martinsburg. We lost 10 killed and 75 wounded. Late in the P.M. our cavalry was again driven across the Opequon by the enemy. I went to General Anderson in the morning to apprise him of the situation, then came back and witnessed most of the advance. Pleasant day. Cool in the morning and evening. Robinson and Oltmanns worked at maps. I sent Green's baggage to Winchester.

Tuesday, August 30. Spent the day in camp, not feeling very well, but worked some at maps. Robinson and Oltmanns copying maps of the Valley. Fine day; cool night; all quiet.

Wednesday, August 31. I sketched the road to the Opequon and back. The Yankee cavalry made some advances toward Winchester. Came to the Opequon. Anderson moved back to near Winchester. Our cavalry was moved to meet them, but they went back in the P.M. and the usual quiet prevailed. Fine day; cool at night. Rodes' division went to Martinsburg and back.

Thursday, September 1. I rode up to Winchester in the A.M. and brought back some dispatches for General Early. Oltmanns copied map of the Valley. Robinson finished reducing Adams County, Pa. A very fine day.

Friday, September 2. Dispatches came in the morning stating that the enemy was moving toward Berryville in force. So we moved across the country toward Stone's Chapel by Fry's Ford, Gordon in advance, followed by Wharton and Ramseur. We got nearly to Stone Chapel when Vaughn's brigade of our cavalry got stampeded at Bunker Hill and ran away, leaving the wagons and Johnson's brigade to take care of themselves. A few hundred cavalry took fourteen wagons and some men and compelled us to turn back. Rodes had been left near Stephenson's. He turned back and drove the enemy nearly to Bunker Hill. We turned back through Brucetown, Ramseur in advance, and encamped between Brucetown and Stephenson's. Our wagons went from Stephenson's nearly to Summit Point ahead of the army, but all got back safely to Stephenson's about midnight. The enemy retired and Fitz Lee reported that the enemy had gone to City Point. Anderson and Fitz Lee moved toward Berryville.

Saturday, September 3. The enemy's cavalry appeared at White Post this morning threatening to come to Newtown. Fitz. Lee moved toward Newtown and Anderson toward Berryville. He met the enemy near there in the P.M. and drove them from a line of works with small loss. The cannonading kept up until 9 P.M. Rodes started in the morning for Bunker Hill, to be followed by the rest of the corps; but he alone went on and had a skirmish with the enemy there after the cavalry fight, in which Harry Gilmor was wounded. Ramseur remained in camp guarding some roads. At night Gordon moved to Winchester, his men in high spirits. It rained in the night; began just about dark. I went to Winchester to attend to some business. [Quite an amusing scene occurred between

Judge Dan Wilson's servant, Addison, himself and Dr. Coleman, about fighting for one's country when the Judge and the Doctor ran away from a shell.]

Sunday, September 4. We were roused up very early to go to Berryville, Ramseur in front, followed by Wharton and Rodes (Gordon remained at Winchester). We found Anderson in line of battle in front of Berryville and joined on to his left. He was skirmishing some with the enemy. Their cavalry soon passed back from Millwood. We marched to find the enemy's right flank. Went as far as Sidney Allen's. Found them well fortified, so skirmished with them until night and then withdrew to a line parallel with the Winchester and Berryville roads, and there spent the night. Headquarters at Russell's. A fine day. It rained some at night.

Monday, September 5. We remained in front of Berryville until 2 P.M., then withdrew and returned to Stephenson's Depot by the way of the Burnt Factory, Jordan Springs, &c. Rodes was in front, followed by Wharton and Ramseur. Anderson moved back to Winchester in the morning. Our cavalry had a skirmish with the enemy below Stephenson's and was falling back when Rodes' advance came there, just before dark, and threw out a brigade to the right of the pike and advanced rapidly and drove Averell's cavalry some three miles, inflicting some damage. It rained very hard late in the P.M. and also after dark. Headquarters at Mrs. Stephenson's.

Tuesday, September 6. We spent the day in camp, and it rained and misted most of the time. I corrected maps and wrote some letters. Gave Colonel Smith a map of the northeast part of Virginia.

Wednesday, September 7. I rode over a back road to Winchester on the left of the pike and back by one on the right and sketched them. A fine, clear day. Enemy's cavalry made a demonstration near Brucetown; also near the Yellow House on the Martinsburg road, and also on the Millwood and Front Royal roads not far from Winchester, and were repulsed at all points. The general went to Winchester.

Thursday, September 8. I went to Newton to-day to see Lieutenant Koerner. Met him and we went to Major Jones' and spent the night. It rained most of the day; began at 10 A.M. We changed camp and went back to Mrs. Stephenson's.

Friday, September 9. It cleared off and we had a fine day. Koerner and myself came back to camp, then went over to Breckinridge's and fixed to have his engineer company go and aid in the survey of the country. The enemy came to the Opequon and burned some mills. Wharton went to meet them.

Saturday, September 10. We moved down to Bunker Hill, Rodes in front, followed by Ramseur. Some of Lomax's brigade preceded us. We had a very fine rain in the morning, with thunder and lightning. We marched through. Our infantry marched just beyond Darkesville. Our cavalry drove the Yankees through Martinsburg after the infantry had started them from Darkesville. There were only two brigades of cavalry this side of the Opequon. All the enemy went south of that stream. We came back to our old camp at Bunker Hill. Ramseur and Rodes came there. Lomax remained at Darkesville. The day became pleasant.

Sunday, September 11. It began to rain about 11 P.M. last night and rained very hard until 7 this morning, with thunder and vivid lightning. The infantry moved back to Stephenson's to-day. I went with Captain Wilbourn by the Back road to our old camp at Stephenson's. The cavalry remained at Darkesville. There were several hard showers during the day, accompanied by thunder and lightning. We dined at Mr. Abbott's.

Monday, September 12. Spent the day in camp preparing to go to Staunton. All quiet. A fine day; showery. Cool mornings and evenings. Major Jones dined with us.

Tuesday, September 13. I left for home. Went to the engineer camp, seven miles southwest of Strasburg, and spent the night. There was heavy cannonading near Brucetown road. We broke up camp at Stephenson's at 2 P.M. The general spent the day at Carpenter's[15] battery on the left of the road near the Opequon. We skirmished across the creek. Carpenter had 2 guns disabled, 3 men killed, and 5 wounded. Gordon on the left, Ramseur on the right. Enemy left. Headquarters at the same place at night.

Wednesday, September 14. I rode as far as Mr. Cowan's, near Tenth Legion. It rained very hard most of the day. Cold and chilly. Colonel Boteler left for Winchester. Anderson took his division away to Culpeper Court-House via Front Royal.

Thursday, September 15. Went on home by way of Mossy Creek. Dined at Mr. Craun's and called at Major McCue's. A fine, cool day. The people are busy sowing grain. Grass is growing finely. Oltmanns made copy of map of Virginia. Lieutenant Boyd came to headquarters to report to Lieutenant Koerner.

Friday, September 16. Went to Staunton by the way of E. Geeding's. Looked some for supplies. Got maps and sent some down to camp. A fine day. Cool in evening. Lieutenant Koerner sent Boyd and Chichester to the west of Winchester to survey.

Saturday, September 17. Rode around among my neighbors to buy supplies for the year. Had some difficulty, but got along well. Fine, bracing day. They had dinner in camp at 1 P.M. and two day's rations were ordered, and moved at 3 P.M. to Bunker Hill, Gordon in advance, preceded by Jackson and followed by Rodes. Camped at Bunker Hill.

Sunday, September 18. I spent the day at home, as it portended rain and rained some in the A.M. Henry Sieg and others called to see me. Fine day. At 3 A.M. Gordon marched for Martinsburg. Cavalry met enemy's pickets at Big Spring and drove them through town of Martinsburg. Two brigades of Gordon went to the left of Martinsburg, and one (York's) to the right. Destroyed Tuscarora bridge, took 21 men and horses, 5 wagon loads of coal, and 5 coils of telegraph wire. Left at 4 P.M. and came back to Bunker Hill; headquarters at Stephenson's. Rodes came to Stephenson's. Grant said to be at Harper's Ferry.

Monday, September 19. I started back to camp by the way of Staunton. Passed through Harrisonburg, where there was a large crowd at court. Came to Big Spring and spent the night at Lincoln's. Fine, warm day. Enemy came on by the Berryville road and Ramseur engaged them three miles from Winchester, at right angles to the road, from 3 A.M. Lomax, Johnson, and Jackson on the right. Rodes came up at 10 A.M. and formed on Ramseur's left, and Gordon came about noon and formed on Rodes' left. Wharton came up and fought along the Martinsburg road to Gordon's rear. He drove the enemy's cavalry back several times. The infantry fighting became heavy about noon. General Rodes was killed between 1 and 2 P.M.[16] Enemy advanced several times. Were repulsed with very great loss. The Yankee cavalry made a dash on our left at 1 P.M. and were driven back, but at 4 P.M. they turned our left and fell on our rear and made our men give way in great confusion, coming to the suburbs of Winchester. Then Gordon's line gave way and we were compelled to retreat about sundown. This was effected with little loss. The enemy's cavalry came on to Kernstown, but were checked by Ramseur. We fell back to Newtown, Gordon in front and Ramseur in the rear. Camped about midnight. We took 400 prisoners and inflicted a loss of 8,000 or 10,000 on the enemy. Our loss about 1,500. Fine day. Chilly night.

Tuesday, September 20. Started early for camp. When I got to New Market heard that we had had a disastrous battle and General Rodes had been killed, and at Rude's Hill I met his body. A severe loss, his men along the road lamenting it deeply. Soon met trains of ambulances, and troops of wounded and stragglers filled the road all the way to Fisher's Hill, where I found the army in its old position. Our losses were heavy yesterday. A fine, warm day. The army came to Fisher's Hill at daylight. Ramseur was put in command of Rodes' division and Pegram of Early's division, which Ramseur has been commanding this summer. We lost 3 pieces of artillery at Winchester. Rodes is much lamented by the army. Wharton is now on the right of the turnpike, then Gordon across to the Middle road, then Pegram and Ramseur, with Lomax on the left, on the Back road, except McCausland's brigade, which is across the river opposite Strasburg. Wickham, of Fitz Lee's division of cavalry, fell back to Front Royal. Only one division of the enemy's cavalry followed us. The enemy came to Strasburg. Headquarters at Fisher's Hill.

Wednesday, September 21. We spent the day in line of battle and fixing our works. The enemy's infantry in front and cavalry on the left made some demonstrations. Late in the P.M. they drove in our skirmish line on the Middle road, and got a hill there which they fortified. Wickham had to fall back to Milford. Breckinridge and staff left to-day. I watched the movements of the enemy. A fine, warm day. We had some artillery fighting.

Thursday, September 22. The enemy advanced a line of battle in front at an early hour, and engaged our skirmishers, but did not push forward much. At 9:30 A.M. they engaged our skirmishers quite earnestly, and, at 1 P.M., advanced several lines of battle in front of Ramseur, but did not come far, and only drove in our skirmish line. At 4:30 P.M. they drove in the skirmishers in front of Gordon and opened a lively artillery duel. At the same time a flanking force that had come on our left, near the North Mountain, advanced and drove away the cavalry and moved on the left flank of our infantry—rather beyond it. The brigade there (Battle's)[17] was ordered to move to the left, and the whole line was ordered to extend that way, moving along the line of the breastworks. But the enemy attacking just then (5.30 P.M.) the second brigade from the left, instead of marching by the line of works, was marched across an angle by its commander. The enemy seeing this movement rushed over the works, and the brigade fled in confusion, thus letting the enemy into the rear of Early's division, as well as of Gordon's and the rest of Rodes'; our whole line gave way toward the right, offering little or no resistance, and the enemy came on and occupied our line.

General Early and staff were near by, and I with others went after Wharton, to [the right], but it was too late. Our whole line had retreated before he got on the turnpike. The enemy opened a furious cannonade on him. Our men came back in a perfect rout, and so rapidly that the enemy was crossing the railroad before the head of the column got into the pike, even. It was then getting dark. I hastened back to try and stop the mass of fugitives on the top of the hill near Mount Prospect. General Gordon, General Pegram, and Colonel Pendleton with others came up. Colonel Pendleton and myself had gotten a few men to stop near a fence, there, and also two pieces of artillery, which were opened on the enemy. By the combined efforts of all a few men were induced to stop. The artillery was opened on the woods where the enemy was advancing and it checked them for the moment, but most of our men went on, officers and all, at breakneck speed. Wharton came along parallel to the pike and on the left, and kept some of his men together. He checked the enemy some, and a rear guard was formed from his division which made a stand at Tom's Brook, and gave the enemy a volley which made them desist from pursuit. Battle's brigade moved to the left and came out intact. Colonel Pendleton was mortally wounded soon after we made a stand on the hill.[18] The rout of wagons, caissons, limbers, artillery, and flying men was fearful as the stream swept down the pike toward Woodstock, as many thought the enemy's cavalry was aiming to get there by the Middle road and cut us off. I became alarmed for the bridges, lest they should be broken and stop the retreat, so I hastened along as best I could and checked the speed of the train, which was fairly flying. I finally got to the head of the train at Hawkinstown and advised Major Harman to park beyond Mount Jackson. Then I went to the river, beyond Mount Jackson, and got Captain Hart,[19] of the Engineer Company, to put out guards and stop the fugitives, a duty which he and Lieutenant Boyd[20] nobly performed. I then laid down and slept two hours and fed my horse. I got there about 1 A.M. A fine warm day. We lost some eighteen pieces of artillery and about 600 or 800 men.

Friday, September 23. The troops marched all night. The enemy only came to Tom's Brook. We got to Mount Jackson at an early hour. All the wagons got there safely, except a few that were overturned. They were this morning all sent across the river to Rude's Hill. We spent the day in line of battle. Wharton on the left and Ramseur on the right, in front of Mount Jackson, just beyond the hospitals, and Gordon and Pegram between Mount Jackson and the river. The enemy's cavalry came up and threw a few shells, but no advance was made. After dark we came across the river. We had our headquarters just back of Rude's Hill and all spent the night near there. Some rain; cool.

Saturday, September 24. We formed a line of battle on Rude's Hill in the morning, Wharton on the left and Ramseur on the right, in front, and Pegram on the right and Gordon on the left, in the rear, and remained there until noon. The enemy came on and threw a few shells and began to move up the opposite side of the river on our left flank. We then fell back to near New Market, then gradually, in line of battle and by the flank, skirmishing and using artillery, to Tenth Legion Church, where we formed a line and kept the enemy at bay until after dark. The enemy drove our cavalry rapidly on the Back and Middle roads. Wickham brought his cavalry across the Massanutten to New Market and then went back and up the Luray Valley. The enemy followed him closely. I took orders to Major Harman about the wagons, and then aided in getting them off the pike and onto the Keezletown road. After dark the infantry retired to Flook's, eight miles from Tenth Legion, on the Keezletown road, getting there about midnight, Ramseur in front, followed by Gordon, Wharton, and Pegram. I remained and posted Jackson's cavalry brigade. Our cavalry was driven in great confusion nearly to Harrisonburg. We rested at the wagons at Flook's until the moon rose. A fine day. Cool in P.M. and some rain.

Sunday, September 25. We started the wagons on toward Port Republic at 1 A.M. At daylight the army came on, Pegram in rear, by Peal's Cross-Roads, Meyerhoeffer's Store, &c. Wharton preceded Pegram. I came to Port Republic to guide the head of the train. It went on to Brown's Gap. Harman and Allen were with me. I rode on to Staunton to look after my map box. Got there by noon. Found much excitement. They were evacuating the place. I dined at Major Harman's. Got back to camp by 10 P.M., having ridden forty miles to-day. A fine warm day. The enemy did not follow. Their cavalry came to Harrisonburg. We got our whole command into Brown's Gap, except the cavalry. Left them north of the South River. Headquarters at Mount Vernon Furnace.

Monday, September 26. Kershaw's division came up from Swift Run Gap. Joined us about noon. The Yankee artillery fired a few shots at it as it turned off at Lewis' to come to Brown's Gap, and a few cavalry went down the river to attack his trains. Kershaw got some men and artillery in position and gave them a warm reception. The Yankee cavalry drove ours across the river and came up to our lines. Pegram's division was marched out on the Cave road, and skirmished some with them near the angle of the road, and repulsed several charges of their cavalry, using artillery. The enemy also advanced on the turnpike, and Ramseur drove them back from there. Wharton moved out in rear of Ramseur, and Gordon in rear of Pegram. I showed Kershaw the way up, and carried some orders. Oltmanns copied a map of the Valley. A fine, warm day. Enemy reported up South River, and Wickham moved to near Patterson's, on South River. My horse was killed by a bullet in the Yankee charge.

Tuesday, September 27. Wickham crossed the river at Patterson's, and Gordon followed him with artillery, &c. Ramseur followed Gordon. We attacked the Yankee cavalry encamped near Weyer's Cave and drove them away from between Middle and South Rivers, and also from the vicinity of Port Republic, giving them some help with our artillery as they went toward Harrisonburg. Pegram pushed forward and crossed at the cave, and then went toward Port Republic. Kershaw held the front of Brown's Gap. Wharton followed Pegram. We surprised the Yankees, but an untimely opening of artillery advised them of our approach. We brought our camp to opposite Weyer's Cave. The army (except Kershaw, who remained at the Furnace) encamped between the rivers. I suggested the routes of the army and guided movements. Pleasant day.

Wednesday, September 28. We started at an early hour to go to Waynesborough, but a report of an attack on Pegram's pickets turned us back for a time. Then we had to wait for Kershaw's train to pass by. Then a misunderstanding of orders caused delay at Mount Meridian. The train went up South River and crossed at Patterson's Ford, Ramseur in front. Pegram, followed by Wharton, went by the Waynesborough road from Mount Meridian. Five miles from Waynesborough Wharton took the River road and Pegram kept on to Dogtown. I guided Kershaw by Mount Meridian to New Hope. A mile beyond New Hope we took the Waynesborough road. We encountered the enemy's cavalry pickets near the Hermitage, five miles from Waynesborough, and drove them rapidly forward. Pegram drove them to Dogtown by dark, and attacked them there just after dark and drove them toward Fishersville and encamped where they had had their camp on the Staunton road. Gordon followed Kershaw. All encamped in the vicinity of Waynesborough at a late hour. Headquarters at Gallagher's. A fine day. Some rain in P.M.

Thursday, September 29. We moved our camp to the southwest of Waynesborough and spent the day cleaning up. I rode around the lines with the general in the A.M. The enemy went toward Mossy Creek at a rapid rate. They made the night light with burning barns, hay stacks, &c., during the day and night. I went to the tunnel in the morning to see if any damage had been done there; also examined the track of the railroad and got the pioneers and engineer troops at work on the bridge across South River, which the enemy had burned. Showery day. Rained hard at night. Quite warm.

Friday, September 30. We spent the day at Waynesborough. It rained and misted in the morning, but got quite pleasant in the P.M. The Yankees went to Bridgewater yesterday. Our cavalry went up to Staunton and put pickets out to Middle River. A great deal of burning going on to-night toward Rockingham—mills, barns, &c.

Saturday, October 1. We moved to near Mount Sidney. I guided Gordon, Kershaw, and Pegram by the road from Waynesborough to the Willow Pump and took them three miles beyond Mount Sidney on the Valley turnpike. Ramseur and Wharton went by the Mount Meridian road, then to New Hope, and thence to Mount Sidney. Three miles from Mount Sidney, near the river, then encamped. Our cavalry pickets were moved to Pleasant Grove Church and some cavalry went to Centerville. It misted and rained all day quite hard, and was cold and unpleasant. Hard marching. I stopped at Mr. Guy's a few moments. Headquarters at the angle of the Valley pike and Keezletown road.

Sunday, October 2. We spent the day in camp. The enemy pushed up on the pike and drove in our pickets. The "Stonewall" Brigade marched out and drove the enemy across the river at Mount Crawford. Had some skirmishing and some artillery firing. We got 2,000 bushels of wheat from Grattan's mill. The cavalry had some fighting at Bridgewater. Sent Robinson to my house and let William go home. I went and heard Mr. Bowman preach. A fine, warm day.

Monday, October 3. Spent the day in camp. Army quiet, save some skirmishing with Yankee cavalry along North River. It misted and rained during the day and rained hard at night. General Rosser came yesterday, and to-day reconnoitered the front. The enemy holds the line of North River. Sent map of Southeastern Virginia to General R. E. Lee.

Tuesday, October 4. Spent the day in camp. Oltmanns went to Staunton. Robinson copied map of Valley. It cleared off and was a fine day. All quiet. Rosser's cavalry encamped near Staunton; came from Lynchburg and Richmond. The enemy burned barns, &c., at night.

Wednesday, October 5. Spent the day in camp drawing—Robinson reducing Pennsylvania maps, Oltmanns copying Valley map. Gordon moved camp to vicinity of Naked Creek. Rosser moved to Landes' Mill, on road from Stone Church to Mossy Creek. Cars ran to Smith's to-day, two miles and a half from Staunton. We have rebuilt the bridges over South River and Christian's Creek. About two miles of track are to be relaid. Enemy still near Harrisonburg. The general rode along the lines to-day. Fine day. Lieutenant Boyd dined with us.

Thursday, October 6. The enemy left Harrisonburg last night. We followed early this morning [with] our cavalry. The infantry started at 11 A.M. Gordon, in front, went a mile beyond Harrisonburg. Kershaw, Pegram, Wharton, the artillery, and Ramseur followed. All encamped near Harrisonburg, all around it. Our headquarters about two miles southwest. Lomax went to Peale's Cross-Roads, Rosser to near Timberville. The enemy did a vast amount of damage in Rockingham. A good many Dunkers left the county and went with the Yankees. They burned some of the houses they deserted. Rosser fell on Averell's (Custer's)[21] cavalry at Brock's Gap and routed it. A very fine day. I directed the repair of the telegraph line and put Chichester in charge of the party. Got it to Mount Crawford to-day. Cool in evening. It rained some.

Friday, October 7. We moved on as far as New Market. Got there at an early hour. The troops came on in good time, Pegram in advance. He encamped near the river on the Timberville road, Gordon and Ramseur on the Forestville road. Headquarters near town. Dined at Doctor Strayer's. Our cavalry went to Stony Creek, driving the enemy's with loss. Quite cool.

Saturday, October 8. We remained in camp. It hailed and snowed some and was quite windy and cold. Rosser on the Back road drove the enemy's cavalry to near Round Hill, encamping at Tom's Brook, and Lomax did the same on the pike. Worked some, but it was too cold to do much.

Sunday, October 9. We spent the day in camp until about 4 P.M., when a stampede of the cavalry came rushing back as far as New Market, and Ramseur and Kershaw were marched to Rude's Hill to meet any further advance of the enemy, but they only came to Mount Jackson. The Yanks moved on Rosser on the Back road, at Fisher's Hill, and drove him back, capturing 5 pieces of artillery and some wagons, then turned on Lomax, on the pike, and drove him to Mount Jackson, and took 3 pieces of artillery. Rosser rallied and drove the enemy back and established his pickets at Stony Creek. Lomax fought stubbornly at Woodstock.

We came back to camp late in the evening. It was very chilly all day. Mr. Landstreet preached in the A.M.

Monday, October 10. We spent the day in camp. I started parties to fix the telegraph from Harrisonburg to New Market. Had Robinson copy Yankee map of battle of Winchester and reducing Pennsylvania maps. Oltmanns copying map of Georgia. Very heavy frost. Pretty day. Cavalry on Stony Creek. Church at night.

Tuesday, October 11. Troops remained in camp. A lovely day. I looked after telegraph. Had two parties at work—Gordon's and Ramseur's pioneers. Took Kershaw's pioneers late in the day and went and built a bridge over the river at Mount Jackson for infantry. Lomax's division went to Page Valley late in the P.M. [I wrote home and to Allie and Ed. Palmer].

Wednesday, October 12. We marched at sunrise, Ramseur in front, followed by Gordon, Kershaw, and Pegram. Ramseur encamped southwest of Narrow Passage, and Gordon and Kershaw between there and Woodstock, and Wharton—. Headquarters two miles southwest of Woodstock. The cavalry on the Back road came from Timberville to Columbia Furnace. Lomax's old brigade preceded us and went beyond Woodstock to Pugh's Run. Cool. Some rain in P.M. and at night.

Thursday, October 13. Moved on at 6 A.M., Gordon in advance. Got to Hupp's Hill by 10 A.M. and moved Gordon's division into the woods on the left of the pike, concealed from the enemy, and got the other divisions in line under the brow of the hill. Only showed a few cavalry and some artillery. The enemy was encamped north of Cedar Creek. We opened the artillery on one of their camps and made them run off and leave it. We opened first on a brigade on picket near Hite's house and scattered them. The flight from the camp was a perfect stampede. Then a column of Yankees came down from Hite's house to the bridge across the bottom. We played on them and scattered them some. They crossed the bridge and formed at right angles to the pike and advanced. Conner's brigade, of Kershaw's division, was advanced on the right of the pike to meet them. They moved forward in fine style and driving the enemy back, the artillery playing on the enemy at the same time. We also suffered some from the Yankee artillery. Gordon's and Whartons' skirmishers also advanced on the left, and we drove the enemy in confusion across the creek, advancing to Stickley's house, where we were exposed to the fire of their batteries. Wharton was formed on Gordon's left. Ramseur came up in rear of Kershaw. Rosser advanced to Cedar

Creek on the Back road. Lomax's old brigade, Payne commanding, was our advance on the pike. Lomax's division came down Luray Valley. The day was windy and quite cool. We moved back to Fisher's Hill late in the P.M. Headquarters at Funkhouser's. General Conner[22] was badly wounded. We took 65 prisoners, and killed and wounded a good many. Our loss, 22 killed and 160 wounded.

Friday, October 14. We spent the day on Fisher's Hill. Enemy's cavalry came this side of Strasburg, and we sent out Gordon's and Wharton's skirmishers and drove them back to Hupp's Hill. No loss. Wharton was put on the right of Fisher's Hill, then Kershaw, Gordon, Pegram, and Ramseur to the left, and Rosser on the Back road. Lomax came to near Front Royal yesterday and drove the enemy's pickets to Guard Hill. The force of the enemy that had been destroying at Front Royal went toward Winchester. A pleasant day.

Saturday, October 15. We spent the day at Fisher's Hill. Some of our skirmishers went to Hupp's Hill. Enemy on north bank of Cedar Creek fortifying. We rode along the lines some. Windy and cool.

Sunday, October 16. All quiet. Yanks fortifying. We went on Round Hill in the morning and looked at them. Then Colonel Allan, General Pegram, and myself rode down the Back road to Lebanon Church, then back by the Middle road. A few Yanks had been there and left. Pleasant. Made and sent Rosser a map of country.

Monday, October 17. The troops were marched out a mile or so in front of Tumbling Run in the A.M., as Rosser's brigade of cavalry, with Grimes' brigade[23] of infantry behind it, went yesterday to surprise a Yankee camp near Petticoat Gap, and was to come back this A.M. The Yankee camp had been moved, but they captured a picket of 50 men. He went by Snarr's Store and back of North Mountain. Ramseur held the left of the line on the Back road, Pegram advanced on the Middle road, Kershaw to the right of the Middle road, Gordon on the ridge west of the pike, and Wharton held the right. General Pegram reconnoitered some in his front toward Cedar Creek in the P.M., and General Gordon, General Evans, myself, by direction of General Early, went to the end of Three Top Mountain and examined the position of the enemy around Belle Grove with reference to an attack. I made a map of the position, and General Gordon and myself fixed upon a plan of attack to suggest to General Early, which we discussed fully as we came back. General Gordon was to propose it to General Early. We had an arduous journey, and it was after dark when we got back. I supped with General Gordon.

Reported the state of things to General Early when I got back. A fine day.[24]

Tuesday, October 18. General Pegram came up to report to General Early, urging a movement by the line he had examined. I told him General Gordon had a plan to propose, and stated the substance of it to General Early and showed him the map, as I did not wish his judgment to be forestalled by General Pegram. Soon all the division commanders, General Gordon, Pegram, Ramseur, Wharton, Rosser, and Kershaw, and Colonel Carter,[25] of the artillery, and Payne,[26] of the cavalry, came and there was a conference at headquarters at Round Hill. General Early decided to go by the route recommended by General Gordon and myself, and decided on a plan of attack to which all agreed. General Gordon, in command of the Second Corps (Gordon's, Ramseur's, and Pegram's divisions), was to cross the river at Fisher's Hill and go round the end of the mountain and cross again at Bowman's Mill near the mouth of Cedar Creek, and cross and advance over the front of the enemy's line of breastworks. Wharton, followed by the artillery, was to go along the turnpike to Hupp's Hill and cross after the others and press up the pike. Rosser was to cross Cedar Creek at Mohamy's Mill and engage the Yankee Cavalry. Payne was to precede Gordon and try to capture Sheridan[27] at Belle Grove. This plan having been decided on, Generals Gordon, Ramseur, and myself went to examine the route around the mountain, going almost to Water Lick. General Pegram went to the top of the mountain. We selected a route; got back late in the P.M., when I took the pioneers of Rodes' division and went over the route and made bridges and cut out trees, &c. Got back after dark, expecting to meet the column, but found the generals waiting for General Pegram, who had gone to General Early to report some new works that he thought he had discovered from the mountain on the enemy's left, and he rather opposed the movement, but General Early held firm; said he saw no occasion to change his plans, and General Gordon started at 8 P.M. We slept until midnight, then started along the turnpike, Kershaw and Wharton having gone before. The general found some stragglers who had been after whisky, and stopped and poured it out as we passed. A fine day. Cool at night.

Wednesday, October 19. We went through Strasburg and took Kershaw to his position on the top of the hill above Bowman's Mill. He was there by 5 A.M. Wharton was also in position on Hupp's Hill. The hour fixed for Rosser, then Gordon, and then Kershaw to attack. Page and myself examined the route ahead, and I urged the moving of Kershaw nearer. A light mist hung over the creek and river. Soon we heard Rosser driving in the pickets on the left, then Gordon on the right, then Kershaw advanced across Cedar Creek in gallant style, and in almost a moment he was going up the hill and over the breastworks. A few flashes of musketry, a few shots of artillery, and he had the works, guns and all, surprising the enemy, though they had sounded the reveille in many parts of their camps before we attacked. Then, in conjunction with Gordon, Kershaw swept over the Eighth and Nineteenth Corps and drove them in wild confusion across Meadow Run, upon the Sixth Corps and through Middletown, Colonel Payne at the same time charging their train, &c., along the pike and helping the confusion and capturing wagons, &c. Wharton and the artillery came up and helped across Cedar Creek. Our troops then formed and drove them from their camps northwest of Meadow Run to the ridge in front of Middletown, where the Sixth Corps made a stand and drove Wharton and Pegram back. Then we had the artillery brought up to near Middletown and massed it on them and drove them from the ridge. The fog concealed the enemy some time. The vigorous use of the artillery and advance of the infantry drove the enemy beyond Middletown, and by 10 A.M. we had formed a new line, extending through Middletown at right angles to the pike and along the Cedarville road on the right and the Furnace road on the left. Gordon was on the left, near Stickley's; then Kershaw came across the ridge; then Ramseur down the slope to Meadow Run; Pegram from that up to the turnpike; Wharton to right with Wofford's brigade,[28] of Kershaw's division, on his right at the angle of the Cedarville and Buckton roads; then Payne's cavalry extending to the woods. Rosser had driven the enemy by the Grove road and was to the left and in advance. We lay there some time, using some artillery on the right and left and advancing our skirmishers a little, but making no decided move. We skirmished with the cavalry on the right and they charged our lines several times, but were repulsed. Thus we lay until 4 P.M., making a few efforts to get off the immense captures we had made of artillery and everything else. We had some twenty-three guns. The enemy having had time to rally, had collected in rear of the large body of woods in our front and formed a line of battle and advanced at 4:30 P.M., obliquely to the left, and struck our left, or rather between the two brigades on the left, where the line was weak and it gave way with little resistance, and was followed by all the rest of the line toward the left, and soon everything was in full retreat toward Cedar Creek. The artillery nobly fell back fighting and kept the enemy in check, and everything was getting off well, when Rosser, having fallen back, the Yankee cavalry crossed by Hite's old mill and came up to Stickley's and fell on our train and artillery just after dark, on Hupp's Hill, and dashed along, killing horses and turning over ambulances, caissons, &c., as there was nothing to defend them and we had no organized force to go after them. Only a few Yankee cavalry did it all. They came as far as Spangler's Mill, and there tore up a bridge which had been broken and impeded our train, but had been repaired and we were passing over it. The general and staff got to Fisher's Hill and tried to rally the men. We succeeded in getting many of them into camp, but could get none to go back and recapture the wagons, &c., at Strasburg. Colonel Brown got eight or ten to go on guard at the stone bridge. We got 1,300 prisoners off safely. The general was very much prostrated when he learned the extent of our disaster and started the wagons for the rear, and sent for Rosser to come and cover the retreat. He sent me to Edenburg to stop the stragglers. Thus was one of the most brilliant victories of the war turned into one of the most disgraceful defeats, and all owing to the delay in pressing the enemy after we got to Middletown; as General Early said, "The Yankees got whipped and we got scared." I got to Edenburg and put the engineer troops on guard at the bridge to stop fugitives. A very fine day. Cool at night. I spent the day with the general; carried orders, &c. We had many narrow escapes. We were frequently fired at and much exposed. Colonel Godwin[29] was wounded in the neck. General Ramseur was killed.[30] Payne had 326 men and took 399 prisoners (Payne).

Thursday, October 20. Our wagons came to New Market, and, starting at daylight, the infantry came there also, most of the men having sorted themselves and order been somewhat restored. All took their former camps. Captain Shorter,[31] engineer officer, came up to-day. It was quite windy and cool. The Yankee cavalry followed ours slowly to Edenburg.

Friday, October 21. Spent the day in camp. Made a sketch of the battle for General Early to send to General Lee. Oltmanns copying map of Georgia. Fine day, but cool. Enemy at Strasburg and Cedar Creek.

Saturday, October 22. I started on the stage for Richmond at 7 A.M. to bear dispatches to General Lee. Got to Staunton after dark. Spent the night at M. G. Harman's. Had quite a long chat with Andrew Hunter. Quite cool.

Sunday, October 23. Went to Richmond on the cars. Many of the reserves were going down and I met some coming to the Valley District. A fine day, but cool. I went to General Lawton's to get a horse to go to General Lee's at Chaffin's. Took tea with General Lawton and had a long chat. Got a horse and went to General Lee's, six miles. Got there at 11 P.M. Saw General Lee and we had a long talk about matters in the Valley, commanding generals, etc. I spent the night there. General Early told me not to tell General Lee that we ought to have advanced in the morning at Middletown, for, said he, we ought to have done so.

Monday, October 24. I went down to see General Ewell at the Chaffin house; found him in a fine humor. We rode out along the line of works and to Fort Gilmer. Saw Fort Harrison and the Yankee lines. Came back and conversed awhile with General Lee, then went up to Richmond. Transacted some business at the Engineer Bureau. Went to the Spotswood and found my old friend Colonel Heck there. Called on Col. Nat. Tyler in the evening and went home with him and spent a pleasant hour or so. A fine day.

Tuesday, October 25. Went to Staunton on the cars and then got a horse and rode home. Got there at midnight and spent a few delightful hours with my family. [Read Schele's Philology, for pastime, today.] Fine bracing day. All quiet at the army.

Wednesday, October 26. Started for Staunton at 5 A.M., then went on to New Market on the stage. Found all quiet, save that the cavalry of Sheridan had been fighting Lomax at Milford, and he had repulsed all their attacks. Cool day. Some rain at night. Rosser's brigade went to Luray in the night.

Thursday, October 27. Spent day in camp writing, correcting maps, &c. Pleasant. All quiet. The enemy's cavalry reported to have left our front. It began to rain about dark and rained most of the night.

Friday, October 28. Spent day in camp making sketch of the battle of Rutherford's farm. All quiet. Cool. Papers abusing General Early roundly.

Saturday, October 29. Making map of battle of Castlemen's Ferry. Robinson copying Valley map and Oltmanns map of Georgia. Fine October day. Generals in consultation. A contention between Generals Gordon and Early about the battle of Cedar Creek, &c.

Sunday, October 30. Went to church. Warm. Quiet.

Monday, October 31. I rode to the division headquarters to get information for battle maps. Robinson copying Valley map and Oltmanns battle of Chattanooga. Sent to Engineer Bureau a map of Georgia. Cool day. Let William go home.

Tuesday, November 1. Made map of battle of Berryville and position of army next day. We worked in a shop. All quiet. Quite cool. Robinson finished a copy of Valley map, and began map of Southeastern Virginia for Engineer Bureau. Oltmanns copying battle of Chattanooga. General Early came to camp in the evening and chatted until quite late with Doctor McGuire and myself; an interesting dish of discourse. Forrer called.

Wednesday, November 2. Employed as yesterday. It rained nearly all day. Quite cool and unpleasant. Fixed stove in my tent.

Thursday, November 3. Engaged as yesterday, except I began a map of the battle of Belle Grove. It rained and misted all day.

Friday, November 4. Engaged as yesterday, at Belle Grove, Chattanooga, and Southeastern Virginia. Some rain. Quite cool.

Saturday, November 5. Ditto as to work. Windy and cool. Froze quite hard. Army filling up rapidly. Much in want of small arms.

Sunday, November 6. [Went to church twice. Wrote home last night. Quite a revival in progress.] Fine day. Bracing air.

Monday, November 7. Engaged as before. It misted and rained, most of the day. Captain Shorter came over in the evening.

Tuesday, November 8. At same work. Oltmanns finished map of Chattanooga and began map of Virginia; fifteen miles to one inch. Fine day; showery.

Wednesday, November 9. In the P.M. got orders from General Early to have the foot bridge over river at Mount Jackson repaired; so went and had Captain Hart go and see to it late in the P.M. Marching orders were issued at quite a late hour. It rained some; turned quite warm.

Thursday, November 10. We marched down the Valley at sunrise, Kershaw in front, followed by Pegram, Grimes (who commands Rodes' division since Ramseur's death), Gordon, and Wharton. The artillery followed Kershaw. Two divisions encamped beyond Woodstock; the others this side. Headquarters on the Burner's Springs road, a mile from Woodstock. Marched twenty-two miles. The troops marched well. Rosser went to Fairview; Lomax to Front Royal. Fine day; mild in A.M., but chilly wind in P.M.

Friday, November 11. Marched at 6 A.M., Pegram in front, Kershaw in rear; rest as before; artillery third in order. Found enemy's pickets at Middletown; drove them to Newtown. Payne's brigade in our advance. We formed a line near Chrisman's Springs; found the enemy intrenched at Newtown. Headquarters near Vaucluse. Rosser on the Middle road northwest of Newtown, on our left; Lomax on our right, from Cedarville to near Newtown. Pegram is on the right, near the road to the factory; then Gordon to the pike; then Grimes to top of Jones' Hill; then Wharton and Kershaw to the left. I sketched the left of the Yankee position at battle of Cedar Creek. Rosser and Lomax were at headquarters at night. Enemy's infantry camps near Kernstown and Bartonsville. Had details of ten from each division made for an army pioneer party, and put Lieutenant Flood[32] in charge of it. A bracing day; clear and cool.

Saturday, November 12. We were roused up at an early hour; took breakfast, and prepared for a fight. The army was, part of it, in line of battle last night, and held the same position to-day. We formed in rear of the stream that runs from Chrisman's Spring on the right of the pike, then across Jones' Hill on the left. Kershaw, Wharton, and Grimes on the left, and Gordon and Pegram on the right of the road. We had some skirmishing, but no general engagement. On the Back road Custer drove back a portion of Rosser's brigade as far as Cedar Creek. He brought up his other brigade and Payne went to him, and they routed the Yankees in turn and scattered them far and wide, saber in hand. We remained in line until about dark, then fell back to Fisher's Hill, getting to camp at a very late hour. The day was raw and cold. Late in the P.M. the Yankee cavalry fell on McCausland's brigade at Cedarville. He repulsed two attacks, and then thinking they were gone he halted to feed, but they came on and caught him unprepared and drove him across the river and through Front Royal, capturing two pieces of artillery. I finished sketching the battle-field of Cedar Creek; found it quite cold and raw; Oltmanns went with me. Camp at Round Hill.

Sunday, November 13. We moved back at daylight up the Valley, Grimes, Gordon, Wharton, Kershaw, and Pegram. The army encamped on Pence's hill, on the south bank of Stony Creek, the artillery going to near Hawkinstown. The calvary came to the vicinity of Edenburg. Headquarters went on to New Market. Intensely cold, windy and snow flying. The mountains and hills white.

Monday, November 14. We spent the day resting, fixing up camp, &c. Col. William Proctor Smith came up day before yesterday as chief engineer of the Army of Valley District. It was milder to-day, but still raw and cold. The army came on up, Gordon, Wharton, Kershaw, Grimes, and Pegram, the artillery in front. Captain Hart with his company and Lieutenant Flood and the pioneers were ordered to encamp near headquarters and report to the chief engineer.

Tuesday, November 15. Moved into a house and began new map of battle of Cedar Creek; Robinson, at Southeast Virginia, and Oltmanns, at Eastern Virginia, for Engineer Bureau. Kershaw started up the Valley for Richmond. It was quite cold and rained some. Wrote memoranda of Army of Valley District for Colonel Boteler or Hon. Mr. Goode.[33]

Wednesday, November 16. [The day of National thanksgiving. Mr. Lacy preached from Exodus XIV—15, "Go forward." A capital sermon. There was a good audience, the Gen. attended]. It was a fine day. In the P.M. Colonels Smith and Allan and myself rode to the top of the mountain on the Luray road. [Enjoyed ride much.] Sent off document to Colonel Boteler, showing that to this date we had marched, since the opening of the campaign, 1,670 miles, and had seventy-five battles and skirmishes.

Thursday, November 17. Worked at battle of Cedar Creek; Robinson finished Southeast Virginia and worked on Franklin County, Pa. Oltmanns at Small Virginia. Misty and rainy. Pegram moved up to Big Spring. Hinrichs called to see us.

Friday, November 18. Spent day as yesterday. It rained and misted all day.

Saturday, November 19. Drawing map of battle of Cedar Creek. Oltmanns' copying map of Eastern Virginia. Robinson reducing Franklin County, Pa. It snowed in the morning and rained and misted until about noon.

Sunday, November 20. [Attended sacramental meeting in the Lutheran Church. Rev. Mr. Kline, the Pastor, preached and administered the sacrament.] The day was chilly and misty. Captain Page came back from Richmond.

Monday, November 21. All engaged as before. It rained and misted all day. Got orders at dark to go to-morrow with Major Harman to select camps for winter quarters for the troops in Augusta County.

Tuesday, November 22. We were up by 5 A.M. I took breakfast with Major Harman, and we were far on our way by sunrise. Colonel Allan accompanied us. We stopped a short time at Mrs. Grattan's, but pressed on and reached Major Harman's, near Staunton, by 4 P.M., forty-three miles. The air was very chilly and the ground in places white with snow. The enemy's cavalry, two divisions, encamped at Woodstock last night, and to-day it came on up as far as Rude's Hill. We marched three divisions of infantry down to meet them, Gordon's, Wharton's, and Grimes', from their camps three and four miles southwest of New Market. Grimes, Gordon, and Wharton in order. We took a line on the top of the hill—on the left of the road—on the right, and—in reserve in the rear of the others. A regiment of cavalry and—pieces of artillery. The enemy came boldly up to near the hill, when we opened on them and sent them back in great disorder, inflicting considerable loss. Our infantry skirmishers pursued to Hawkinstown and the cavalry to below Edenburg. A brigade of our cavalry pursued. All came back to the old camps at night. Marched twenty-five miles.

Wednesday, November 23. Major Harman, Colonel Allan, and myself went toward Waynesborough to look for winter quarters for the troops. Colonel Allan soon found a camp for his ordnance train and left us, and we spent the day riding through woods, &c. We selected a set of camps near Fisherville and returned to Major Harman's by 5 P.M. The day was chilly. Rode thirty miles.

Thursday, November 24. We rode toward Christian's Creek and selected some camps there if it should be desired to encamp some troops there. [Called awhile at Davis Bell's and then rode up to Staunton. I transacted some business there and then at 1 P.M. started home where I arrived at 4 P.M., unexpected, and spent a very pleasant evening. Mr. H. Seig came up.] The engineer troops passed through Staunton on their way to Lexington. The day was quite pleasant. Rode twenty miles.

Friday, November 25. Started back to camp at 7 A.M. Stopped a few moments at Mr. Forrer's. Got to Harrisonburg by 12:30 P.M., where met Major Harman. We got to camp by 6 P.M., and reported to the general. We were very tired. The day was warm and pleasant. Cool late in the P.M. Cosby's[34] brigade of cavalry passed me at Bridgewater on its way to Tennessee. Rode forty-three miles.

Saturday, November 26. Spent day in my room working on map of battle of Cedar Creek. Robinson is reducing Cumberland County, Pa. Oltmanns copying Western Virginia. Day cool, and it rained in P.M. and at night. Rosser started.

Sunday, November 27. [Went to church twice. Mr. Bell gave an exposition in the P.M. Mr. Kline preached in the A.M.] The day was chilly, though very pleasant in the A.M. General Early was considerably excited by habeas corpus writs for soldiers from Judge Thompson.

Monday, November 28. Spent day in camp. Finished battle of Cedar Creek and worked at battle of Kearneysville. Oltmanns finished Western

Virginia; Robinson made map of Harper's Ferry. Mild day; fog in morning.

Tuesday, November 29. I sketched the road to Mount Jackson, and got position at Rude's Hill. A fine, warm day; summer-like. Heard that Rosser had captured a gun at Moorefield and gone on toward Cumberland.

Wednesday, November 30. Spent the day in camp making map of the engagement at Rude's Hill. Oltmanns copying battle of Chattanooga. Robinson made maps for Colonel Smith's monthly report, showing position of army, pickets, &c. A fine, pleasant day. We heard of General Rosser's capture of New Creek; 800 prisoners, 8 pieces of artillery, &c. [This is my 36th brithday; how rapidly the years glide away! God grant that they may not have been spent in vain.] I drew my pay for November, $833.33⅓, under new appointment. [$10,000 a year and allowances]

Thursday, December 1. Finished my map of the engagement at Rude's Hill. Visited General Gordon's camp. Got information of positions, &c., from General Wharton, Major Peyton,[35] &c. Oltmanns copying Chattanooga. Robinson is sick. Colonel Smith went to Luray Valley. Fine, warm day.

Friday, December 2. Worked at map of battle of Charlestown. Oltmanns finished map of battle of Chattanooga. Robinson is sick. Rosser got back to-day with flags, &c. Major Peyton called to see me to-day. Colonel Smith got back. It began to rain about noon. Somewhat cool.

Saturday, December 3. Finished map of battle of Charlestown. Oltmanns began yesterday a reduction of the map of Northeastern Virginia and part of Maryland and Pennsylvania. Robinson is sick. A pleasant day. The Yankee prisoners were brought in.

Sunday, December 4. Spent day in camp. [Went to church in A.M. and read in P.M.] A fine, warm day.

Monday, December 5. Finished map of action at Kearneysville and worked at battle of Harper's Ferry. Robinson finished off several battle maps and outlined some. Oltmanns at reduction. A hard white frost and day chilly. Mr. Lacy spent some time with us.

Tuesday, December 6. Finished map of Harper's Ferry and worked some on one of Fort Duncan. Robinson made a copy of Rude's Hill; Oltmanns at reduction of Northeastern Virginia. Gordon's division changed camp and moved up toward Staunton; also Pegram. A pleasant day; little rain in A.M.

Wednesday, December 7. I began map of fight at Smithfield. Robinson copied Cedar Creek. Oltmanns at reduction of Northeastern Virginia. Wickham's brigade went from Mount Jackson to Timberville.

Thursday, December 8. Finished Smithfield and began map of New Creek. Robinson finished copy of Cedar Creek. Oltmanns at reduction. Finished copying my journal at night. It is reported that Gordon's and Pegram's divisions went to Richmond from Staunton last night. A big battle is expected at Richmond. The Sixth Corps of Sheridan's army[36] has gone there, and it is reported to-day that more of his men have gone.

Friday, December 9. Finished map of vicinity of New Creek and corrected map of Northeastern Virginia. Robinson made map of vicinity of Lynchburg. Oltmanns at reduction of Northeastern Virginia. The day was very cold, chilly; it began to snow after dark. General Lee sent word that Grant had sent off two corps of his army. Heavy cannonading said to be heard toward Richmond. Gordon and Pegram got to Waynesborough Wednesday night and went on to Richmond. There were a good many deserters in Pegram's division—the conscripts that lately came in. Made list of maps I had furnished at night.

Saturday, December 10. It snowed all last night and for some time to-day; the snow is about ten inches deep. I began another map of the battle of Cedar Creek, after correcting a map for Robinson to copy of Rosser's route. Oltmanns at reduction. Quite cold.

Sunday, December 11. [Went to church and heard Dr. Dabney on the text, "How long halt ye between two opinions"? An excellent argument. Mr. Lacy came to my room at night & we had a long talk.] The day was cold and chilly; it rained a little and snowed a little.

Monday, December 12. Worked at Cedar Creek. Robinson copying Monocacy. Oltmanns at reduction. A very cold day; wind sharp and biting. It froze very hard last night. [Mr. Lacy spent the day in our room.]

Tuesday, December 13. Robinson finished Monocacy. Oltmanns at reduction, I at Cedar Creek. Cool day; looks like storm. [Wrote to my wife, S. Howell Brown, and Gen. Ewell.]

Wednesday, December 14. Worked at Cedar Creek. Robinson at map of vicinity of Washington; Oltmanns at reduction. Some rain that froze early in the A.M.; mild day. Grimes' division left for Richmond.

Thursday, December 15. Spent the day finishing some maps for Colonel Smith. Robinson was very sick and we sent him to the hospital.

Oltmanns worked at reduction awhile and then packed up. Mild day; thawed some.

Friday, December 16. We started from New Market about 11 A.M. Wharton's division started by daylight and went to near Mount Crawford. Rosser's division went on toward Swoope's and Lomax's to Swift Run Gap. We rode on to Harrisonburg and spent the night there. It thawed all day. Warm south wind. [I spent the night at Joseph Andrews'.]

Saturday, December 17. I rode on quite early to show General Wharton his camp. Turned off at the Willow Pump and went by the Barren Ridge road to the Waynesborough road; showed his inspector the camp and then went to John Hamilton's for the night. It continued to thaw and most of the snow left. General Early came to Staunton. Wharton went out two miles toward Waynesborough. It rained some in the P.M. and at night.

Sunday, December 18. I rode back to Staunton to see General Early, then came back to Fishersville, where the wagons came, and went to look for a camp. It rained most of the day and the mud got quite deep. We spent the night in the woods near Fishersville. The general did not come from Staunton.

Monday, December 19. I obtained quarters near Fishersville and moved to them. Wharton's division came two miles this side of Staunton night before last and encamped, and to-day came on to camps near Fishersville. The general came down late in the P.M. and went to Mrs. McCue's. We went to Staunton on the cars again, owing to report of enemy coming up the Valley—at Woodstock to-night. Two divisions of their cavalry crossed the Blue Ridge at Chester Gap. Mild day.

Tuesday, December 20. We started back down the Valley this morning to meet the advance of the enemy. Rosser, who moved to Swoope's Sunday, went in advance. I guided Wharton across by Major Harman's into the pike and we went on to Naked Creek, where we spent the night. Had our quarters in the church. Rosser went to Harrisonburg and the enemy came to Lacey's Springs, a division of cavalry. Most of the snow gone, but the day was quite chilly and before midnight a severe storm began of sleet, hail, and snow.

Wednesday, December 21. We marched on at daylight in the midst of a blinding storm, cold and biting, but most of the men in a good humor, though in no plight for a battle. Rosser moved at dawn and attacked the enemy just as they were saddling up. Routed their first and second brigades, capturing 35 prisoners and getting their wagons and ambulances, but they rallied on their third brigade and he had to fall back and they got their wagons back, but at once retreated down the Valley. The infantry was halted at the Big Spring on the pike three miles southwest of Harrisonburg, and went into camp. Rosser did not get all his men up in time for his attack. We got to Harrisonburg about noon. The storm ceased at noon. It was quite warm for a short time. It was very slippery on the pike. The general stays in Harrisonburg. I had J. Arthur Wilson detailed for topographical duty.

Thursday, December 22. The day was windy and quite cold. [Spent the day at home; made some calls and attended to some business. William cut wood.] Wharton marched back to near Staunton. Payne's and Wickham's brigades came to near Staunton.

Friday, December 23. In P.M. went to Staunton and down to quarters at Fishersville; air keen and cold, but clear. Roads very icy. Wharton's division (two brigades) took the cars and went across mountain (Blue Ridge); one brigade went to old camp.

Saturday, December 24. Went to Fishersville, then back and up to Staunton, and Mr. Oltmanns and Colonels Smith and Allen went home with me to a Christmas dinner, and we had a very pleasant evening. Robinson came out yesterday. A fine day. It thawed some. The Yankees came near to Gordonsville and were repulsed there.

Sunday, December 25. Colonels Smith and Allan went back to Staunton to-day. [I went to Union to church]. A fine day, quite pleasant and thawed some.

Monday, December 26. I rode to Staunton. Was there awhile and then came back and examined the location for a bridge over Middle River. Lieutenant Flood and party came out there to-day. It was warm. The sun shone brightly and most of the snow was melted.

Tuesday, December 27. I rode to Staunton in the A.M., and after looking after business there awhile, I went on to Fishersville; dined at our quarters, then went to see General Early and got a furlough until January 3, then went back to Major Harman's. It was very muddy. Quite warm; rain at night. Troops back in camp near Fishersville.

Wednesday, December 28. Spent part of the day in Staunton looking for servants, &c., then rode home, stopping to see Lieutenant Flood, who is building a bridge at Middle River. There was a heavy fog and mist in the morning; then rain in the P.M., and at night quite hard. Very muddy.

Thursday, December 29. Spent the day at home. Worked at map of

Kernstown. It thawed some. Snowed last night. Froze at night. Robinson engaged at Lynchburg. [James Arthur Wilson went to Conrad's Store after his baggage.]

Friday, December 30. Spent the day at home. Worked at vicinity of Winchester. Robinson at Lynchburg map. It was quite chilly.

Saturday, December 31. Spent some time at battle map of Kernstown, and Robinson at Lynchburg. Snow in the morning; quite cold.

"Many of the soldiers have reached home"

SUNDAY, JAN. 1ST, 1865. Spent the day at home, reading, etc. It was very cold, but clear. [Addenda. On the 1st of Jan.,1865, Lomax's Division of Cavalry was located; one Brigade at Bartonsville, one Brigade at Liberty Mills, one Brigade at Stanardsville. Three Regiments on picket. Hd. Qrs. at Barboursville. The outer line of pickets began at Creglersville on the left, then, via Madison C. H., to Locust Dale. Interior reserves at Culpeper C. H. Videttes at fords of Rappahannock.]

Monday, Jan. 2nd. Went to Staunton to hire servants but did not get one as they were hired only for grain and at very high rates, men bringing 100 bush. of corn or wheat. The day was quite cold in the A.M., but became pleasant. Gen. Early has gone to Richmond. Bought William Gearing.[1]

Tuesday, Jan. 3rd. Went over to see the bridge at the river, which the pioneers nearly completed today, then H. Seig and myself went to Staunton where I hired a servant woman, of Mrs. Opie, for $50. in specie or its equivalent. Came back and hunted wagons to haul wood tomorrow. A fine morning but it began to snow about noon and snowed all the rest of the day.

251

Wednesday, Jan. 4th. Spent the day at home looking after hauling wood, etc.; had 4 men of Pioneer Party to cut and a team from them and Dr. Wilson's and Dudley's teams; got 2 loads of wood from Dudley's and 12 from Hizer's woods. Cold in morning, but became pleasant. Robinson copying battle maps.

Thursday, Jan. 5th. I went up to Swoope's Depot to see Gen. Rosser, found him at Col. Baylor's. Got from him positions of cavalry in fights, etc. of fall, dined with him and then returned home. Munford with Wickham's Brigade came from Midway to Swoope's today. He came by the Parkersburg road to Staunton the same day we went to Harrisonburg after Custer, then crossed to Ivy Depot, back to Greenwood, then to Rockfish and across Tye River Gap. Rosser's pickets are still at Stony Creek and he has a squadron in Pocahontas Co. It thawed and froze, alternately, today.

Friday, Jan. 6th. Spent the morning at home looking after things generally. After dinner self and servant rode to camp, to Fisherville. It began to rain last night and rained quite steadily all day; the streams are rising rapidly and the snow is nearly gone, but the frost has not yet left the ground. Gen. Early came back yesterday. Robinson is copying battle maps at my house.

Saturday, Jan. 7th. Worked at map of Rosser's fight at Lacy's Sps. Oltmanns at reduction. James Arthur Wilson began work today by copying map of Rockbridge. A fine bracing day, thawed some in A.M. and froze in P.M. and at night; clear.

Sunday, Jan. 8th. Spent most of the day in my room. Went to church in the P.M., heard a grandiloquent sermon. "It froze hard last night, thawed some today." Had quite a chat with McGuire about his pet Clerk, darkey, and ambulance driver.

Monday, Jan. 9th. Orders came to move camp to Staunton and this morning the General and all moved up. I went to look for rooms; had much trouble. Ground frozen hard in the morning; thawed and rained in P.M. Robinson came back to camp. W. and O. at maps.

Tuesday, Jan. 10th. It rained all last night, and most of the day quite hard. Ground still frozen some, but very muddy. Got rooms at Arnall's for $50. a month. It cleared off about sundown.

Wednesday, Jan. 11th. Worked at Rosser's fight at Lacy's Springs and at Hanging Rock. Oltmanns at reduction. Robinson at copy of Lynchburg. Wilson finished Rockbridge. It froze very hard and the day was quite bracing; thawed some in P.M. Gen. Rosser attacked and captured garrison at Beverly this morning, before day, and took 585 prisoners of the 8th and 34th O.V.I. Col. Cook[2] lost his leg, Comd'g. Paynes brigade. Snow from 6 to 18 inches deep on Cheat and Alleghany.

Thursday, Jan. 12th. Finished map of battle of Hanging Rock and Wilson began copy of map of Western Virginia for Rosser. Col. Smith sent to Lexington. Quite Cold.

Friday, Jan. 13th. All engaged as usual, cool day.

Saturday, Jan. 14th. Worked at Battles of Wilderness. Wilson copying Western Virginia. Oltmanns at reduction. Robinson copying Hanging Rock. Wilson and myself went home after dinner and spent a pleasant evening with my family. "Little snow in the A.M., air quite bracing. Rosser at Greenbriar Bridge."

Sunday, Jan. 15th. Went to Union to church, had a good sermon, on Paul's conversion, from Mr. Walker (Rev. Robert C. Walker, Pastor of Union Church). A fine day, quite mild; robins singing. Went to Churchville in P.M. to hear Mr. Davis, but he did not come. Spent a pleasant evening at home.

Monday, Jan. 16th. Came to camp early in the morning and worked at Wilderness battles. Robinson copying Hanging Rock. Oltmanns and Wilson at same as before. Maj. Harry Gilmer came to see the General at night; he is now in command in Hardy Co. Gen. Early seems to think we have hard times ahead of us, the supply of grain is so small.

Tuesday, Jan. 17th. Finished Wilderness map and began one of Spotsylvania Battles. Oltmanns reducing Adams Co. Wilson finished map of Part of Western Virginia, for Gen. Rosser, and began Map of Part of Pa. for Maj. Gilmor. Robinson finishing Map of Hanging Rock, tracing part of Spotsylvania, etc. I read "Joseph and his Court"[3] at night. Day bracing; flurries of snow. Rosser himself reported and gave account of his Beverly campaign.

Wednesday, Jan. 18th. Worked at Spotsylvania, etc. Oltmanns finished Adams and began York. Wilson at Pa. Robinson helped Col. Smith to make his "Property Return." I sent to Eng. Bureau, etc., for maps last night. Echols'[4] Brigade going to Dublin Depot; McCausland's Brigade came to Fishersville and he to Hd. Qrs. on way to Alleghany and Greenbrier, the 14th to go to Weldon. Cold day, air chilly. Wrote to Rosser at night and enclosed map.

Thursday, Jan. 19th. All engaged as yesterday except Robinson who began map of Wilderness Battle. The Cavalry of Lomax's Division is on its way westward to subsist. McCausland was here at night and gave me details of the campaign in regard to his Brigade. A fine bracing day.

Friday, Jan. 20th. Wilson finished Map of Part of Pa., R. also copy of Wilderness. Oltmanns at York, I at Spotsylvania. Jackson's cavalry went through, westward. Fine bracing day. Read Joseph II at night. (Mulbach's)

Saturday, Jan. 21st. I finished Spotsylvania and began Lomax's Gordonsville fight. Robinson finished map of 1st Day in Wilderness. Oltmanns at York. Wilson at map of Western Virginia for Lomax. It sleeted and froze all day; cold, trees loaded with ice. I went home in P.M.

Sunday, Jan. 22nd. Spent the day at home except in P.M., went to church in Churchville. Mr. Walker preached. It misted some but thawed most of the day. Very muddy. Enemy captured picket, at Edinburg, which was retaken.

Monday, Jan. 23rd. Returned to Staunton early; worked at Gordonsville and Liberty Mills, completed them. Robinson at Spotsylvania. Oltmanns and Wilson as before. It rained quite hard most of the day, froze at night. Robinson copying Report to Eng. Bureau.

Tuesday, Jan. 24th. Made maps for actions at Hedgesville, Martinsburg and Hanover Junction. Robinson copying Spotsylvania. Oltmanns York, Wilson Western Virginia. Dr. McGuire gave us a lecture on Anatomy of the eyes in the evening, very good. It froze nearly all day and was quite cold.

Wednesday, Jan. 25th. Corrected map of Western Virginia, office copy. Robinson finished Battles of Spotsylvania for Gen. Ewell. Wilson finished Western Virginia for Gen. Lomax and Oltmanns at York. Quite cool and bracing. Wrote to Nelson and Gen. Lawton. Finished Report at night.

Thursday, Jan. 26th. Made Map of Routes of 2nd Corps in May, for Gen. Ewell. Wilson began second copy of Western Virginia. Oltmanns at York. Robinson copied actions at Liberty Mills and Gordonsville. Rosser came and gave details of Beverly affair, at night, and got from Munford actions of his Brigade during campaign. Day very raw and cold. Dined with Gen. Early.

Saturday, Jan. 28th. I made map of Rosser's Beverly affair and the route to the same. Robinson copied them. Wilson at Western Virginia. Oltmanns at York. A very cold and windy day. I went home in the P.M.

Sunday, Jan. 29th. Went to Union to church; sacramental meeting. Mr. Junkin preached and at night at Churchville. Mild and pleasant.

Monday, Jan. 30th. Attended trial of Col. Munford and gave evidence;[5] Finished Route Map to Beverly and made map of action at Milford at night. Very cold and frosty morning, but the day was very pleasant. Mr. Myers came to town with me. I hired a boy of Mrs. Opie, for $75. Confed., in advance, for the balance of the year. Much agitation about peace.

Tuesday, Jan. 31st. Finished map of action at Milford and made map of Position of Army the 1st day of Feb. 1865. Oltmanns not well, finished York. Wilson finished Western Virginia. Robinson copying maps for Col. Smith. A very fine day, warm, thawed; the ice has been 10 inches thick. Gen. Wharton spent night with me.

Wednesday, Feb. 1st. Completed the map showing the present position, etc., of the army and made Map of McCausland's Expedition to Chambersburg, Pa. At night made map of action at Guard Hill. Oltmanns finished York Co., Pa. Wilson copying King George Co., Va. Robinson copying maps for Col. Wm. Pr. Smith's Report for January. Col. Thos. Carter came up to say good bye; he and two battalions of artillery go to Richmond tomorrow. A fine warm day. Nelly came to see me; Allen and Wm. Reen dined here.

Thursday, Feb. 2nd. Reduced map of Tygart's Valley. Oltmanns reducing Cumberland, Co. Pa. Wilson at King George. Robinson copying for Col. Wm. P. Smith. Fine day, somewhat cool.

Friday, Feb. 3rd. Reduced Tygart's Valley; at night wrote twelve pages of report to Chief Engineer of Army of Northern Virginia of operations of the Army of the Valley District, 1864. Some rain.

Saturday, Feb. 4th. I went home in the P.M. Very mild and pleasant; thawed most of the day. Wrote six pages of report at night. Servant girl came back from Opie's.

Sunday, Feb. 5th. Spent the day at home, reading, etc. Called at Mr. Sieg's in P.M. and Myers called to see me. The wind was quite high last night and it froze hard; was quite cool today.

Monday, Feb. 6th. Returned to Staunton, quite early, and made route map. We heard of the return of the so-called Peace Commissioners,[6] with no results. No one seems disappointed. Quite cold in the morning; day became pleasant but was chilly. Wrote ten pages of report at night.

Tuesday, Feb. 7th. Worked at Route Map; Robinson was finishing up maps for Gen. R. S. Ewell, and Wilson tracing maps of routes, etc., for me; Oltmanns reducing Cumberland Co., Pa. It began to snow before day and snowed, quite steadily, all day. Finished my report of Thirty pages and sent it off. Snow about 8 inches deep; no cars.

Wednesday, Feb. 8th. Employed on maps for Report. Sent Gen. R. S. Ewell six maps to accompany his report. Wilson traced maps for me; Oltmanns finished reducing Cumberland Co., Pa. Payne's Brigade yesterday got orders to cross the Mt. from Lexington. We heard of the defeat of the 2nd Corps below Petersburg and Gen. Pegram's death.⁷ Fitz. Lee leaves tomorrow. A fine day; cooler towards night. Robinson finished Gen. R. S. Ewell's map.

Thursday, Feb. 9th. Made map of Route of 2nd Corps from Hanover Junction to Gaines' Mill. Robinson copying map of Wilderness. Wilson tracing outlines for me and began N.W. Va. Oltmanns finished Cumberland Co., Pa. A fine day; thawed a little; good sleighing. Robinson and Wilson went to Churchville in P.M.

Friday, Feb. 10th. Engaged on map of Battles in Hanover Co., Va. Oltmanns finished Loudoun Co., Va. Mr. Junkin spends the night with me. Fine day; thawed some. I was at Opie's in P.M.

Saturday, Feb. 11th. My wife came in early this morning and we went on the cars to Charlottesville and then to Rockfish Depot where my brother met us and we went on to his house, in Buckingham Co., Va. The morning was quite cold, but the day was pleasant. We had a cold ride. Oltmanns began copying Howard Co., Md.

Sunday, Feb. 12th. Spent the day at my brother's; called at Mr. Mosely's in the evening; cold and windy; ground covered with snow 6 inches deep and crusted.

Monday, Feb. 13th. Came to Howardsville and dined at Dr. Young's, then Nelson brought us to Mr. Brown's, where we spent the night. The day was pleasant and it thawed some, but it became very cold in the evening.

Tuesday, Feb. 14th. We started quite early for the Depot; came to Charlottesville where we had to wait several hours, then came on and got to Staunton about dark. Intensely cold morning, but pleasant day; thawed some. Nelson came over with us.

Wednesday, Feb. 15th. My wife and brother went home in the morning. I worked at Battles near Richmond. Oltmanns finished reducing Howard Co., Md. It snowed very hard in the A.M., then rained and thawed, very sloppy.

Thursday, Feb. 16th. Engaged as yesterday. Oltmanns began Anne Arundel Co., Md. Robinson and Wilson came back and Robinson copied map of Routes; Wilson at Western Va. Thawed considerable.

Friday, Feb. 17th. Same as yesterday; also Oltmanns and Wilson.

Robinson copied Route Map from Hanover Junction to Gaines' Mill. It rained nearly all day. I sent William out home. Not very cold.

Saturday, Feb. 18th. Finished map of positions in Hanover Co., Va. Robinson copied Route from Gaines' Mill to Staunton; others as before. I went home in the evening. A fine, warm day; thawed rapidly. We heard of the fate of Columbia, S.C.[8]

Sunday, Feb. 19th. Spent the day at home with my brother; then came to Staunton with him late in the P.M. Fine day; thawed some.

Monday, Feb. 20. Nelson left on the cars. I worked at map of Fisher's Hill; Robinson copied Route from Staunton to Washington; others as before. Very fine day; cool morning. Heard of the fate of Charleston, S.C.[9] Part of army hospital went to Richmond.

Tuesday, Feb. 21st. Finished map of Fisher's Hill; Robinson copied three small maps; Oltmanns began copying Fauquier Co., Va. for Engineer Bureau. Wrote in journal at night. A very pleasant day. Sent William home in P.M.

Wednesday, Feb. 22nd. Worked at map of Winchester; Oltmanns copying Fauquier Co., Va. and Wilson Western Virginia. Robinson copied Cavalry Fight at Milford. The Churchville Cavalry started for Petersburg. The day was quite pleasant. It began to rain about 4 P.M. and rained very hard. Read Life of Philip II and wrote, at night.

Thursday, Feb. 23rd. Engaged as on 22nd. I looked over the reports of the battle of Belle Grove at night. It rained and misted all day; foggy in the P.M.; very muddy.

Friday, Feb. 24th. I put positions on battle of Cedar Creek, from the "Reports," then worked at "Winchester No. 3." Oltmanns Yankee survey; Robinson battle map and Wilson at Western Virginia. Maj. Gens. Kelly[10] and Crook[11] were brought here by McNeil's[12] men; boldly captured, from their beds, at Cumberland, Md., last Tuesday morning; from the very midst of an army of 5,000 men. Cloudy, but temperate.

Saturday, Feb. 25th. Finished Map of Battle of Winchester; corrected Map of Part of E. Va., copied from U.S. Surveys, for Engineer Bureau. Oltmanns reducing Fairfax Co., Va.; Robinson copying Spotsylvania battles and Wilson at Western Virginia. It rained quite hard a good deal of the day and was very muddy. I went home late in the P.M. The enemy is reported preparing to advance.

Sunday, Feb. 26th. I spent the day at home. It was quite warm and the snow melted rapidly, raising the streams, which got very high. It rained very hard during the night. Several young ladies were kept at our house by the high water. The R.R. bridge over Christian's Creek washed away.

Monday, Feb. 27th. I came back to Staunton via West View, the river being too high to ford. It was very muddy. A fine day. I looked over some maps for Bureau; others engaged as on Saturday. [There] was a meeting of Citizens, at the C. H., addressed by J. R. Tucker, A. H. H. Stuart, and others, and a large subscription of supplies and money for the government was made. Enthusiastic meeting.[13]

Tuesday, February 28th. We worked awhile when orders came to "Pack up," as the enemy is advancing; came to Mt. Jackson last night. Said to be Hancock with 20,000 men. So we packed up and spent the day on the Streets. Much excitement in Staunton.—Moving stores, etc. Late at night the enemy reported near Harrisonburg. A pleasant day. Major B. H. Green came back from a Yankee prison, day before yesterday, and is with us now. Col. Smith was at the railroad bridge and finished it today. Sent off maps of E. Va. to Engineer Bureau. Dick left us.

Wednesday, March 1st. Orders were issued yesterday for Breakfast at daylight and be ready to move at sunrise, but it was nearly noon before our baggage all got off and the last train did not leave until half past four P.M. The General and staff left at a quarter before four. Everything was removed from Staunton. The enemy came on from Harrisonburg, rapidly, driving the squad of cavalry that we had before them and capturing many refugee wagons etc. The enemy came across Middle river and encamped. Their advance at the "Poague Farm." Some of their pickets came into Staunton in the night, it was reported. We went to Waynesboro; sent our wagons across the river. My servant, William, got drunk in Staunton and got out of the way and I left Staunton without him, and did not know of his whereabouts until I got to Waynesboro, so I rode back in the night, very dark and mud very damp, to John Hamilton's, and got my servant and horse and came back about 2 A.M. of the 2nd, and slept awhile at a refugee camp, as I could not find my own. Our infantry picketed the road at Fishersville, but spent the night in its own camp. General Rosser had but few men; 20 or 30, to watch the enemy's movements. Pleasant but chilly.

Thursday, March 2nd. Wharton's Division was put on line of battle, at an early hour, at Waynesboro. The left at the edge of the woods, northwest of town, and the right at the barn back of Gallagher's, with two pieces of artillery on the right, one just in rear and near the railroad and one more to the right on the river road. After the enemy advanced four pieces were taken to the left wing and disposed along it. The enemy came on very early and drove in our pickets and destroyed the railroad bridge over Christian's creek; it was then reported that they had gone back and the troops were ordered to the woods to make fires to protect themselves from the cold sleet, which was constantly falling; but before the order could be sent news came that they were advancing in force and the General and staff went on the hill, on the N.E. of the railroad, about 2 P.M. The enemy came on and formed a line of battle about a mile in front of Waynesboro and on the right of the road, deploying skirmishers along our front and to the left. We opened artillery on them, especially on our left, and did them some damage, compelling them to fall back and break their line, and it seemed, from appearances through the sleet, that they were falling back; but about 3 P.M. they massed and moving through the woods turned our left flank, which made a feeble resistance and gave way, followed by the giving way of the whole line and one of the most terrible panics and stampedes I have ever seen. There was a perfect rout along the road up the mountain, and the enemy (all of the force being cavalry and mounted infantry) dashed rapidly forward into the swarm of flying men, wagons, etc., and pursued over the mountain of Rockfish Gap, capturing over a thousand prisoners and all the artillery and trains. No artillery had been posted on the other side of the river, as I had suggested to Gen. Long,[14] so there was nothing to check the enemy. The mud was very deep and it rained and sleeted all day and became very foggy. The whole army was captured, or scattered, and we had no cavalry to aid us, as it was back towards Lexington. The General committed an unpardonable error in posting so small a force with a swollen river in its rear and with its flank wholly exposed. The left having an interval of $\frac{1}{8}$ of a mile between it and the river and with a body of woods that concealed every movement that might be made. The only precaution taken was to have boards put on the railroad bridge, for a foot bridge, in the morning. The only other crossing was a foot bridge, by the road side, two or three feet wide. Nothing was done to cover a retreat. I had just gone to the fire to warm when the stampede began. I went to the stable and got my horse and rode rapidly across the river, expecting to find artillery on the hill there and by its aid rally the men who were crossing by the railroad bridge; but, to my surprise, there was none there, and the situation, as I turned and saw it, convinced me that all was lost, especially when I saw general officers rush by me in the headlong stampede; so I rode rapidly on towards my wagon and got my saddle bags and reports and had my servant mounting his horse, when the enemy came and commenced firing and compelled me to go on. I went up the mountain at a gallop; the road full of fugatives and the foe yelling "Stop! Stop! Stop!" behind, and firing constantly. I left the road near Lipscomb's and took to the right, into the woods, was soon joined by another man on horseback and shortly after by Antrim, of Waynesboro, and we kept on along the mountain side and finally went to the top, and, just before dark, reached B. F. W. Harlan's, where we spent the night. The enemy crossed a large force during the night and went on towards Charlottesville. We had very hard work getting through the woods. The trees were loaded down with sleet and the ground covered with snow. A portion of the enemy encamped at Waynesboro.

Friday, March 3rd. The fog and rain continued all night, but it ceased before noon. The enemy kept on crossing the mountain. Robinson came up in the morning, having been out all night. I spent the day at Harlan's, going out in the P.M. and looking at the situation. Saw the enemy's pontoon train, etc., cross the mountain. The enemy took about 1100 prisoners, which they marched to Hamilton's shop today. Gen. Early spent last night at Jarman's Gap and today went to Whitehall. The whole army scattered. The enemy passed towards Charlottesville.

Saturday, March 4th. Mr. Antrim and myself went out early and found the enemy gone, so we went on to Waynesboro, through the wreck of our train, etc. Crossed South river, which was quite high; dined at Antrim's and then I went on to John Hamilton's, near Fishersville. Could hardly get through, the mud was so deep. The enemy left many of the captured wagons and four pieces of artillery, of the six they captured, stuck in the mud. It was a fine day. Col. Wm. A. Harman was killed at Waynesboro. The enemy did a great deal of damage. Rosser encamped at Middle river.

Sunday, March 5th. I went on to Staunton, quite early, and then up to Buffalo Gap, to Gen. W. L. Jackson,[15] and got him to send cavalry to aid Gen. Rosser in recapturing our men who went down the Valley guarded by about 900 men. He sent a regiment (Arnett's)[16] and Imboden's Brigade, under Col. G. W. Smith, which went down the Warm Springs Road. The cavalry only got here today. Rosser, with a few men, is following the enemy down the Valley. A fine day. Cool in P.M. The prisoners encamped at Cline's Mill yesterday. Rosser fought the enemy at Harrisonburg and went to Melrose.

Monday, March 6th. Col. G. W. Smith and staff came, late last night, and spent the night with us. He went on, early, to join his Brigade, which came to Parnassus, during the night, from McDowell. Col. Arnett's regiment spent the night at Churchville and went on also, today, to Harrisonburg. I spent the day at home, fixing up after the losses at Waynesboro. Bought a horse of Robert Knowles for $1,000; blind in one eye, J. A. Wilson came home yesterday also. The country is full of rumors and all unsettled. A very fine warm day. Rosser went to Rude's Hill.

Tuesday, March 7th. James Arthur Wilson and myself started to go to Lynchburg, after going to Greenwood to see about my maps; went via Staunton and saw Maj. H. M. Bell, then to Fishersville and got my servant William and on towards Waynesboro; heard, but did not believe it, that the enemy had pickets at Rockfish Gap, so turned to the right and spent the night at Gibson's. A very fine day. Met Robinson (S. B.) & Jesse going to my house. Rosser attacked enemy, at 10 A.M., at Rudes's Hill, had three companies over river.

Wednesday, March 8th. We went to Stuart's Mill and crossed South River, then by a path to the Howardsville Road and then along the top of the Ridge to Rockfish Gap and thence to Greenwood; did not find any maps there, so we took our snack and fed and then went up to Jarman's Gap for the night. It was quite pleasant until 3 P.M. when it began to rain. The Yankees went to Charlottesville and thence towards Lynchburg.

Thursday, March 9th. Went down to South River but could not cross, so went up and crossed at Waynesboro, dined at Antrim's and then went on to Staunton, where I found Gen. Rosser. Spent the night there. A fine day. Heard that the enemy was at Tye River.

Friday, March 10th. Spent the day in Staunton, went to church and heard Dr. Sparrow, this being Fast Day appointed by the President.[17] In the evening I went to John Harman's. A fine day. Imboden's Brigade came to Staunton.

Saturday, March 11th. Gen. Rosser started, at 7 A.M., towards Lexington went three miles beyond Midway; had about 500 men. Went to Fishersville to see about my servant and then went on and joined Gen. Rosser at Bell's, beyond Midway. It froze quite hard last night, but the day was fine.

Sunday, March 12th. Started at sunrise, and crossed the Blue Ridge at Tye River Gap and went by Massie's Mills and Fleetwood and halted to feed at Hubbard's. A very fine day, froze some last night. Enemy reported returning to Scottsville. After resting until dark we went on to Lovingston and three miles beyond, to Mrs. Harris', where we put up at midnight.

Monday, March 13th. We started by 8 A.M., by the "Old Stage Road," and crossed Rockfish River to Col. Heiskell's and then turned across, by by-roads, to the Brooksville and Scottsville Road, at Mrs. [?], three miles from Scottsville; there we fed and then went on, through Scottsville, where the Yankees did a great deal of damage, to Mrs. Sprinkle's five miles down the river road. A fine pleasant day; roads very muddy. We marched until 10 P.M.

Tuesday, March 14th. We started at 8 A.M., rode twenty miles, to Columbia, where we rested three hours and fed, then went on to Hodensville eighteen miles, where we rested, for the night, at 11 P.M. The Yankees did a great deal of damage at Columbia. A fine day.

Wednesday, March 15th. We started at 8 A.M. and went to Thompson's Cross Roads, then to Poague's Mill, and via Salem Church to the Louisa Road and down it to Goodall's Tavern and then to Ashland, where we stopped at 11 P.M. The enemy was driven from Ashland about dark. It rained some but was pleasant.

Thursday, March 16th. We spent last night at Ashland and Gen. Rosser moved on today towards Hanover C. H. I came on to Richmond with dispatches for Gen. Lee; attended to some business at the Bureau, etc. Went to Gen. Ewell's for quarters. Found Gen. Early in Richmond. A very fine day.

Friday, March 17th. Spent the day in Richmond getting my business arranged. Saw Maj. Campbell about maps, etc. Got Gen. Gilmer[18] to send Eng. troops to R.R. Spent the night at Col. Nat. Tyler's. Very fine day. Gen. Early went to see Gen. Lee.

Saturday, March 18th. Spent the day in Richmond. Went to Maj. Campbell's, also saw Gen. Gilmer about the publication of my map. A fine day. Trees leafing out. Spring weather. Spent the night at Gen. Ewell's. Gen. Early came back.

Sunday, March 19th. Remained in Richmond, went to Dr. M. D. Hoge's church and heard Dr. Burrows in the morning and Dr. Reade at night. Called to see Mrs. Hudson (Emily Link). Gen. Early informed me that we were all to go to the Valley again. He spent the day at Worsham's. What a man! A very fine day. A large lot of returned prisoners came up.

Monday, March 20th. I started Wilson and William with the horses back to the Valley, with Maj. Rogers, etc. I finished my business and got my boxes to go to Petersburg, but the drayman carried them to the wrong depot and I missed the train, so spent the night with Oltmanns. Fine weather, cool nights.

Tuesday, March 21st. Started for Petersburg at 6 A.M., got there about 10 and spent the day at Gen. Jno. B. Gordon's, Grimes', and Walker's Hd. Qrs., getting information for my report of the campaign of 1864. It rained a good deal during the day and was cool. I spent the night with Capt. Hinrich's at Walker's Hd. Qrs. The 2nd Corps is in the breastworks in front of Petersburg and the Division Commanders all have quarters in Petersburg. Gen. Early went to Lynchburg yesterday.

Wednesday, March 22nd. Left Petersburg, at 6 A.M., for Lynchburg by the Southside R.R.; a very rough one. We did not reach Lynchburg until 8 P.M., then we tried to get transportation, but could find no officer. The canal to Lexington is broken, so we will have to go via Salem. Gen. Early left Lynchburg, in the P.M. of today for Abingdon. Pleasant, but cool. The cars are full of our returned prisoners.

Thursday, March 23rd. Got transportation and left Lynchburg for Salem at 8 A.M.; reached Salem by 2 P.M., and found Maj. A. W. Pitzer leaving on the cars to join Gen. Jubal A. Early. Capt. S. J. C. Moore and myself went to Pitzer's for the night. A very fine day. Enemy reported advancing from East Tennessee.

Friday, March 24th. We went to Salem in the morning and got a wagon and four mules and rations and in the P.M. started for Staunton; went 11 miles, to Cloverdale Mills, and encamped at Langhorn's. Fine day.

Saturday, March 25th. Started at 6 A.M. and went, via Buchanan, to Flaherty's, six miles beyond; got our own supper, because refused a lodging at Flaherty's, then went to Barger's for the night. Fine day.

Sunday, March 26th. We continued our journey, via the Natural Bridge, to Lexington; found the road very rough and some deep mudholes. I spent the night at Rev. W. H. Ruffner's. Maj. Kyle[19] joins us from here. Fine day.

Monday, March 27th. We went to Ballard Smith's, three miles beyond Midway, Fine day, roads better.

Tuesday, March 28th. We reached Staunton about 2 P.M., the stage being only a half day ahead of us. Lt. Flood and party got there in the P.M. After looking up my horses, seeing to my baggage, etc., I went on home; got there about dark. Found Wm. L. Jackson's and John D. Imboden's brigades near Churchville. They reached there Monday from Hanover Junction. Fine day, quite warm.

Wednesday, March 29th. I spent the day at home; had a boil on my arm. Attended funeral of old Capt. Sterrett. A very fine day. Robinson and Wilson went to town.

Thursday, March 30. It rained quite hard last night and was showery all day today; grass and all things growing finely. I came to Staunton and got rooms at the Virginia Hotel. Gen. Lomax was ordered to take command of the Valley District today. Robinson made map of Rude's Hill, Rosser's affair, and Wilson finished Western Virginia. I did not do much. There was a fight on Hatcher's Run.

Friday, March 31st. I corrected some maps. Robinson made second map of Rude's Hill and Wilson copying vicinity of Lynchburg. A pleasant day but cool. Lomax moved to the country.

Saturday, April 1st. I spent the day assorting my maps and putting all things in good order. Robinson ruled the map of the Valley for reduction and a sheet for the same, Wilson copying vicinity of Lynchburg. I went home in the P.M. Fine day.

Sunday, April 2nd. I spent the day at home; rode to Staunton in the P.M. Col. Wm. P. Smith, Capt. Morgan, R. Winsboro and Mam. Thomas Shumate dined with us. A very fine day.

Monday, April 3rd. Spent the day fixing up, etc. Robinson and Wilson engaged as on Saturday. At an early hour a report got out that Richmond had been evacuated[20] and then one that the Yankees were coming up the Valley; gloom pervaded the whole community and some made preparations for moving away. Gen. L. L. Lomax came to town and ordered the impressment of teams to haul bacon, etc., to Lexington. No definite information could be gotten from Richmond. News came up the Valley that 300 Federal cavalry came to Woodstock yesterday. A fine day; shower after dark. Col. Chas. F. O'Farrall attacked enemy in camp at Hawkinstown and routed them.

Tuesday, April 4th. Spent day getting transportation, etc., to move away. Town full of rumors. Richmond has certainly been given up and Lee has gone towards Danville. Robinson reducing Valley map, Wilson copying vicinity of Lynchburg. I corrected Valley map some. Fine day.

Wednesday, April 5th. Wilson as yesterday. I corrected Valley map. Robinson reducing Roanoke Co., Va. The enemy is again advancing up the Valley, encamped last night at Fisher's Hill and came today to Maurertown; our cavalry skirmishing with them. I went home in the

P.M. and spent the night. Started Robinson, with my maps, to Lynchburg. A fine day, but cloudy.

Thursday, April 6th. I came back to Staunton at an early hour. The enemy is still advancing up the Valley, also said to be at Christiansburg. Our trains from Richmond going towards Lynchburg; enemy at Goochland C. H.

It rained quite hard last night and this A.M. We spent the day in Staunton. Late in the P.M. it was reported that the enemy had gone back down the Valley. Fine day.

Friday, April 7th. Lomax's Division started towards Lexington yesterday, in the P.M., and went some ten miles, and today it went through Lexington and to the mouth of Buffalo Creek. I accompanied it; supped at Col. John T. L. Preston's. We marched until 10 P.M. Gen. Lomax went ten miles farther, to the "Rope Ferry." Fine day. Country full of rumors and much excited.

Saturday, April 8th. We continued the march today, by the "Amherst Road," to Lynchburg; got there after dark. Gen. L. L. Lomax reached there about 2 P.M. The citizens had determined to surrender the place and were much excited at the near approach of the enemy from the W., only a few hundred, but Gen. L. L. Lomax soon restored confidence and got convalescents, etc., into the trenches; but he soon found that only a small force was coming from the West and that it had retired, so he put his cavalry out towards Farmville, as reports came of disaster to Gen. Lee's Army, which was at Appomattox Station. We travelled 36 miles. Fine day. Peaches, apples, etc., in full bloom.

Sunday, April 9th. We rode around the city to see its defences and went also to the cavalry camp, three miles down the river. News came rapidly that our army lost most of its trains and artillery yesterday and that there was a fight this morning and the army had surrendered.[21] It was confirmed late in the day and sadness and gloom pervaded the entire community. Gens. Thos. L. Rosser and Thos. T. Munford came in, late in the day, and the town was full of fugitives. Cool part of the day. I went out to Gen. Wm. L. Jackson's camp for the night.

Monday, April 10th. We marched, at 6 A.M., towards Danville, via Campbell C. H. The command went to Pannel's Bridge. Gen. Lomax went by the "Ward Road"; the train and artillery started yesterday; I crossed to it from Campbell C. H. and went across Ward's Bridge and four miles beyond to McDaniel's. Saw Gen. Thos. L. Rosser in the road going to Danville, to see Gen. R. E. Lee, who was said to have gone down there the day before. It rained a good deal of the day. Rode 30 miles. The country is full of fugitives from the surrender.[22]

Tuesday, April 11th. We rode to seven miles beyond Pittsylvania C. H. towards Danville. The Division came by Chalk Level to a few miles beyond the C. H. It misted in the morning, cool in A.M., warm in the P.M. Vegetation quite forward. Majs. Howard[23] and Rowland[24] and myself spent the night at a Dr. Hutchins'.

Wednesday, April 12th. We went to the Division camp at [?] Meeting House; there heard positively that Gen. Lee had surrendered himself. A good portion of the Division went off last night and Col. Nelson[25] today disbanded his artillery, leaving everything at Pittsylvania C. H. I soon ascertained that the Virginia troops had all determined to go home, and that the surrender of Gen. R. E. Lee had caused nearly everyone to give up all hopes for the Confederacy. Though many had escaped without being paroled, only now and then one had a gun, a complete demoralization had taken place. Gen. Thos. L. Rosser saw the Secretary of War[26] at Danville and today passed through Pittsylvania C. H. towards Lynchburg, where he disbanded his Division on Monday last. Gen. L. L. Lomax went to Danville to see the Secretary of War. The Division melted away during the day and but few were left to follow Gen. W. L. Jackson when he turned back towards the Valley. Maj. Conway Howard and myself went to the C. H., dined at Judge Gilmer's and then in company with Col. Nelson and others went to Berger's Store and two miles beyond, towards Toler's Ferry. Nearly every house was full of soldiers going home and we had much trouble in finding quarters. Fine day, but rained most of the evening and night. Skulkers and deserters are coming out of their holes.

Thursday, April 13th. We started early, crossed the Staunton river, much swollen, at Toler's Ferry; fed at Mr. Leftwich's and went on through Liberty to Nichol's, on the Peak Road, 34 miles. Fine day; the full springtide of growth; vegetation much advanced, fully six weeks earlier than last year. Some Federal cavalry at Lynchburg; country getting quite quiet. The paroled men are getting home. We wish to find the wagons to get our baggage.

Friday, April 14th. We started quite early and went by the "Peaks Gap" to Buchanan, working our way through the blockade made against Sheridan in March; found everything gone from Buchanan, so went towards Salem, as far as "Blue Ridge Tavern," then went home with Mr. Obenchain for the night. Fine spring day. Apples and peaches, etc., in full bloom in the Valley; rode 36 miles. Heard that Echols had disbanded his force at Wytheville, save a few cavalry with which he had started for the Trans-Mississippi Department, via Kentucky. It rained some late in the P.M.

Saturday, April 15th. I spent the day at Mr. Obenchain's, suffering from a boil on my left breast. Maj. Conway Howard went to the turnpike to ascertain where the train was. It was quite cool and rained most of the day.

Sunday, April 16th. We went to Buchanan, met Mr. S. B. Robinson there and found where the train had gone to, and where the property had been distributed. Maj. Conway Howard went back towards Salem and Robinson and myself on to Lexington, got there about dark and put up with the Rev. W. H. Ruffner. Pleasant day. Roads muddy. Gen. Wm. L. Jackson's and Gen. L. L. Lomax's Division disbanded at Buchanan yesterday until the 1st of May.

Monday, April 17th. We spent the morning in Lexington arranging some business. Saw Col. Geo. W. Smith and Gen. W. N. Pendleton. Heard many particulars about the surrender of Gen. R. E. Lee's Army. The disposition is general to submit to the Federal Government in consideration of the mild policy proposed by Lincoln; especially if there be no truth in the many rumors of French recognition and armed intervention. Hancock, in command of Federal force in the Lower Valley, invites all the stragglers, etc., of the Army of Northern Virginia to come and be paroled on the same terms as those were that were captured at Appomattox C. H., saying they may remain undisturbed at home. Many are disposed to go and seek this parole. We rode on to Brownsburg and spent the night with Dr. Morrison. Pleasant day. Rode 14 miles.

Tuesday, April 18th. Went on home, via Summerdean, where we dined at R. B. Dunlap's; got home about dark. The "Soldiers Aid Society of Churchville" had just adjourned as I got there. Many of the soldiers have reached home. Found all well at home, not expecting me, thinking I had gone on South. The minds of soldiers much exercised as to what course to pursue. Lincoln's propositions for Virginia to come back as she was, etc., etc., have worked a revolution in sentiment.[27] Pleasant day. Rode 32 miles.

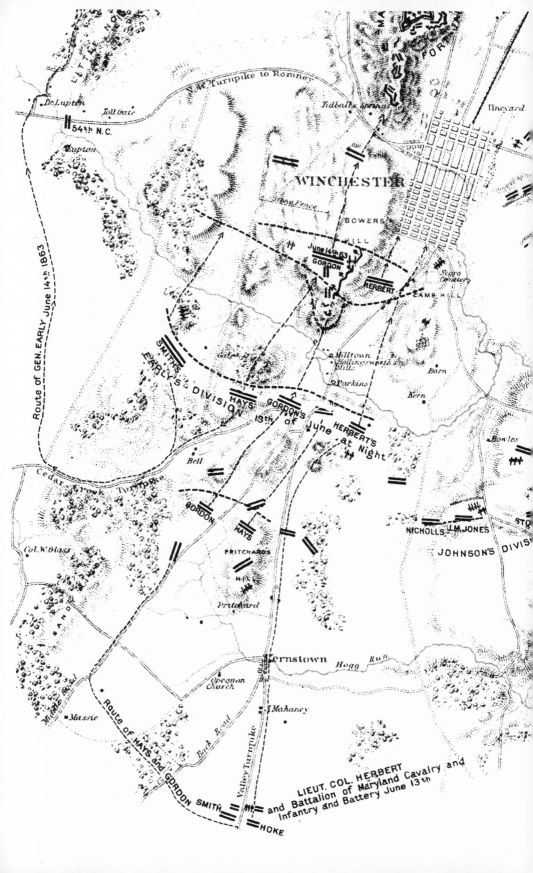

Route of GEN. EARLY June 14th 1863

New Turnpike to Romney

Dr.Lupton
Toll Gate
54th N.C.
Lupton

Tidballs Springs

Vineyard

WINCHESTER

Shawl Fence

BOWERS HILL

June 14th 63

GORDON

HERBERT

Negro Cemetery

CAMP HILL

SMITH'S DIVISION

EARLY'S DIVISION

Milltown

Hollingsworth Mill

Parkins

Barn

Bern

HAYS

GORDON'S

13th of June

HERBERT'S at Night

Bowles

Cedar Creek Turnpike

Bell

GORDON

HAYS

PRITCHARDS HILL

Pritchard

NICHOLLS

J.M. JONES

JOHNSON'S DIVIS

STO

Col. W. Glass

Massie

Route of HAYS and GORDON SMITH

Kernstown

Hogg Run

Opequon Church

Mahaney

Buck Road

Valley Turnpike

HOKE

LIEUT. COL. HERBERT
and Battalion of Maryland Cavalry and
Infantry and Battery June 13th

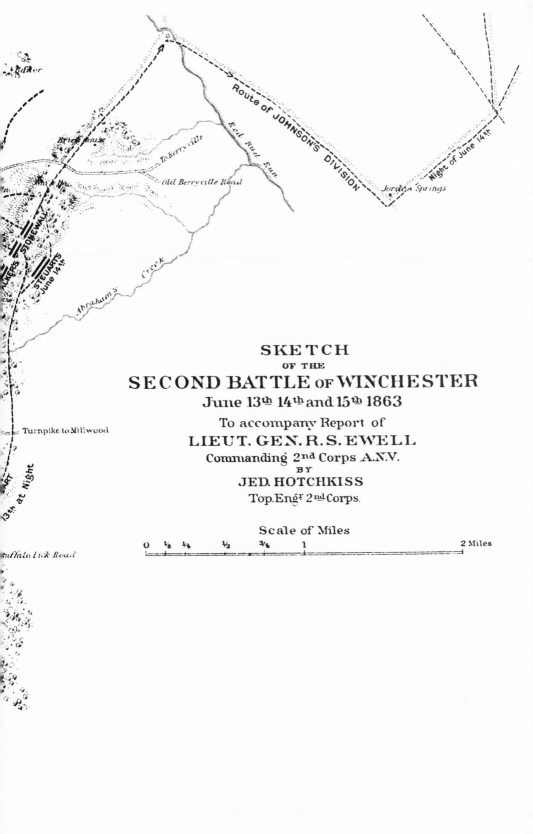

SKETCH
OF THE
SECOND BATTLE OF WINCHESTER
June 13th 14th and 15th 1863
To accompany Report of
LIEUT. GEN. R. S. EWELL
Commanding 2nd Corps A.N.V.
BY
JED. HOTCHKISS
Top. Engr 2nd Corps.

Scale of Miles

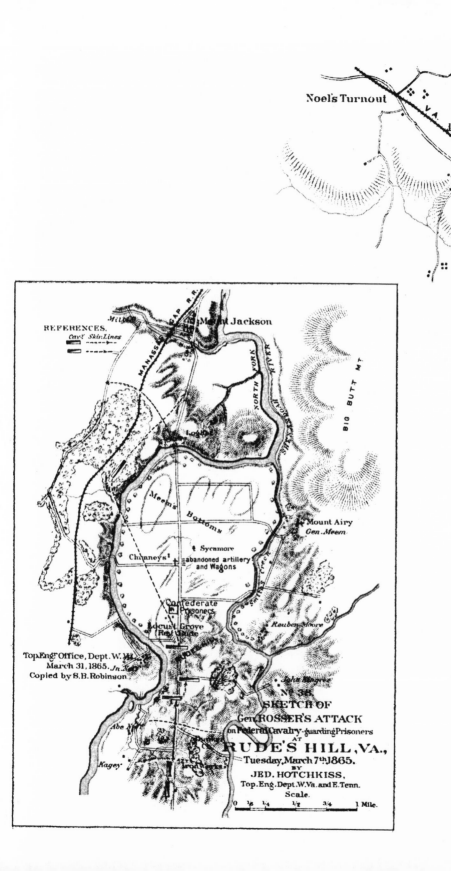

Noel's Turnout

Matthews

VA. CENTRAL

Lowry

Southern

REFERENCES.
Cav.ᵈ Skin.Lines

Mil....

Mount Jackson

MANASSAS GAP R.R.

NORTH FORK RIVER

Log D.

BIG BUTT MT.

Meem's Bottoms

Mount Airy
Gen.Meem

Sycamore

Chimneys

abandoned artillery
and Wagons

Confederate
Prisoners

Reuben Moore

Locust Grove
R.R. Store

Top.Engʳ Office, Dept.W.Va.
March 31, 1865. Jn ?
Copied by S.B.Robinson

NORTH

Abe N....

Kagey

John Moore

Nᵒ 3B
SKETCH OF
Genˡ ROSSER'S ATTACK
on Federal Cavalry guarding Prisoners
AT
RUDE'S HILL, VA.,
Tuesday, March 7ᵗʰ 1865.
BY
JED. HOTCHKISS,
Top.Eng. Dept.W.Va. and E.Tenn.
Scale.

0   ⅛   ¼   ½   ¾   1 Mile.

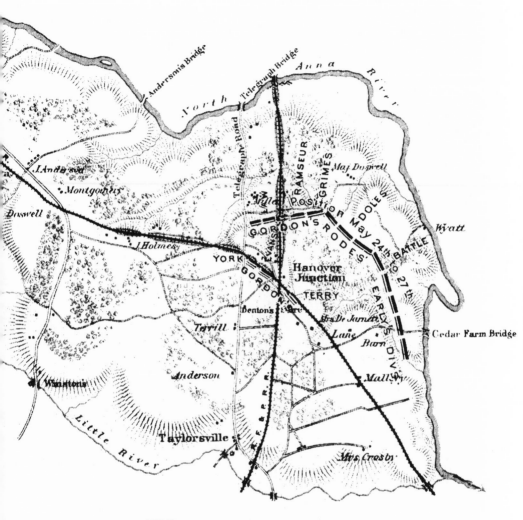

Nº 6.

MAP,
FROM
Maj. A.H. CAMPBELL'S Surveys,
SHOWING
POSITION OF 2ᴰ CORPS, A.N.VA.,
AT
HANOVER JUNCTION, VA.
May 22ᵈ to May 27ᵗʰ,
1864.
to accompany Report of
JED. HOTCHKISS, Top. Eng. A.N.V.

Scale: $\frac{1}{40,000}$

0 1/8 1/4 1/2 3/4 1 Mile.

REFERENCE
Confederate ——

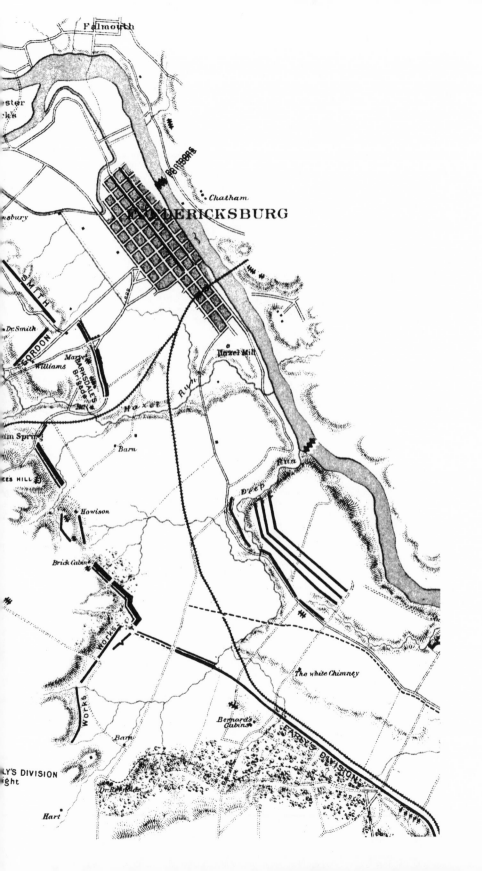

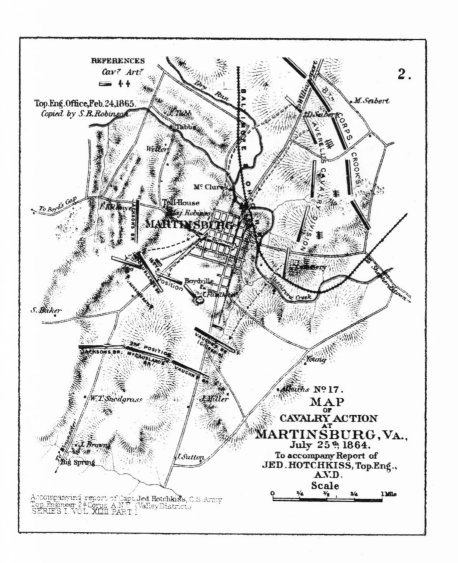

2.

REFERENCES
Cav? Art?

Top.Eng.Office,Feb.24,1865.
Copied by S.R.Robinson

To Boyd's Gap

MARTINSBURG

Toll House
Maj. Robinson
Mc.Clure
J.Tish
J.Tabb
Weller

M.Seibert
Wm.Seibert
8th CORPS CROOK'S
AVERELL'S CAVALRY DIVISION

Position
Boydville
F. Richmeyer

S. Baker

Cemetery
Hoke Creek

To Sheperdstown

JACKSON'S BR.
McCAUSLAND'S BR.
VAUGHN BR.
2ND POSITION
VAUGHN BR.
Gilmer
Young

W.T. Snodgrass
J. Miller

Bourns N° 17.
MAP
OF
CAVALRY ACTION
AT
MARTINSBURG, VA.,
July 25th, 1864.
To accompany Report of
JED. HOTCHKISS, Top.Eng.,
A.V.D.
Scale

J. Brown
Big Spring
J. Sutton

0   ¼   ½   ¾   1 Mile

Accompanying report of Capt. Jed. Hotchkiss, C.S. Army
Top. Engineer 2d Corps. A.N.V. (Valley District.)
SERIES I. VOL. XLIII PART I.

Payn
Forest
Barksdale
Moo
edorah
Butter's

No 9.
MAP
OF
ENGAGEMENT
NEAR
LYNCHBURG, VA.
Saturday, June 18th, 1864,
FROM
Maj. A.H. CAMPBELL'S Surveys,
to accompany Report of
JED. HOTCHKISS, Top. Eng.,
A.V.D.

Scale 40,000

0   1/10   1/4   1/2   3/4   1 Mile

Top. Engr Office, A.V.D, January, 1865.

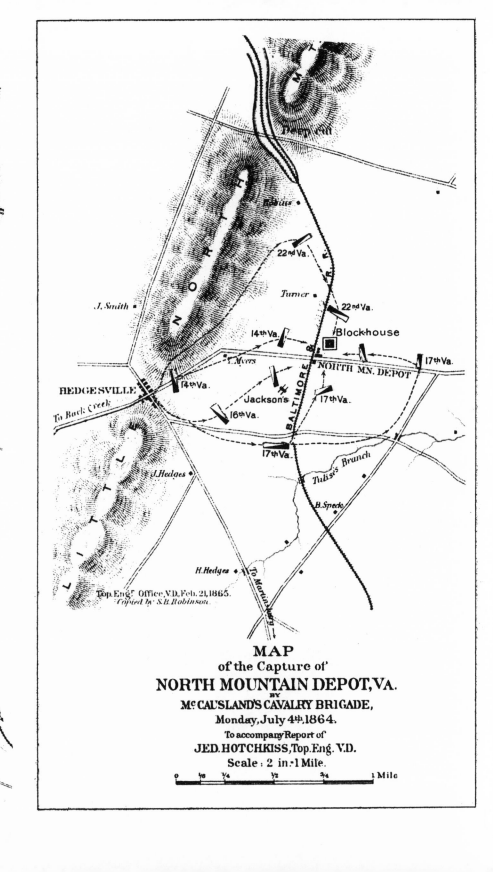

MAP
of the Capture of
NORTH MOUNTAIN DEPOT, VA.
BY
Mc CAUSLAND'S CAVALRY BRIGADE,
Monday, July 4th, 1864.
To accompany Report of
JED. HOTCHKISS, Top. Eng. V.D.
Scale : 2 in.–1 Mile.

0   ⅛   ¼   ½   ¾   1 Mile

Scale

0   ⅛ ¼   ½   ¾   1   2 Miles

Scale 1-40,000.

Nº 29.

SKETCH
OF THE
BATTLE
OF
BELLE GROVE
OR
CEDAR CREEK,
Wednesday, October 19th 1864.
Prepared to accompany Report of
LIEUT. GEN. J. A. EARLY,
Commanding A.V.D.
BY
JED. HOTCHKISS,
Top. Eng. A.V.D.

Top. Engineer Office, A.V. Dist.
Dec., 1864.

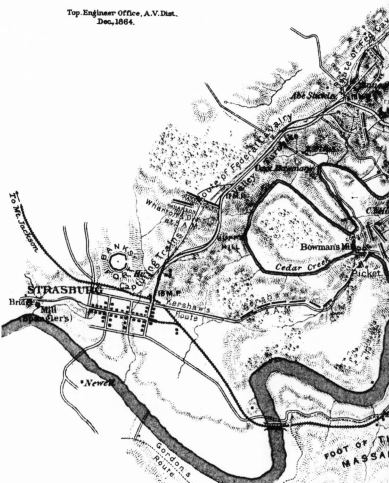

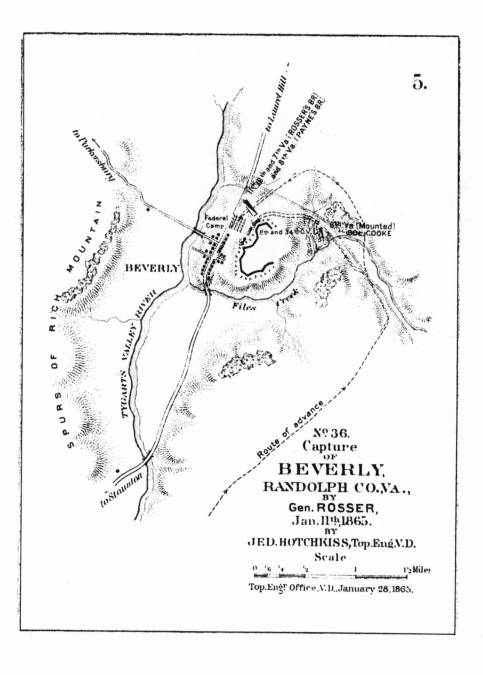

to Laurel Hill

to Parkersburg

to 11th and 7th Va (ROSSER'S BR)
and 8th Va (PAYNES BR)

Federal
Camp

8th and 3d W.O.V.I.

8th Va (Mounted)
COL. COOKE

M O U N T A I N

BEVERLY

S P U R S   O F   R I C H

TYGART'S VALLEY RIVER

Files Creek

to Staunton

Route of advance

Nº 36.
Capture
OF
BEVERLY,
RANDOLPH CO.,VA.,
BY
Gen. **ROSSER,**
Jan. 11th 1865.
BY
JED. HOTCHKISS, Top.Eng.V.D.
Scale

0   ⅛   ¼   ½   1   1½ Miles

Top. Engʳ Office, V.D., January 28, 1865.

Nº 3.

SKETCH
OF THE
BATTLE OF THE WILDERNESS.
POSITION OF 2d CORPS,
A.N.Va.,
Friday, May 6th, 1864.
To accompany Report of
JED. HOTCHKISS, Top. Eng. 2d Corps.
Scale 40,000.

0   ⅛   ¼   ½   ¾   1 Mile

Top. Engr Office, A.V.D., Feb. 13, 1863.
Copied by S.B. Robinson.

REFERENCES.

Inf. Art. Fortns

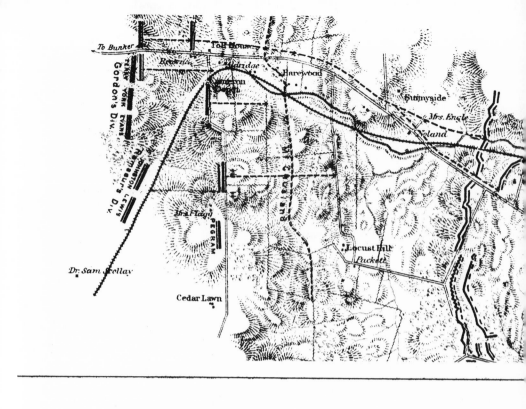

To Bunker
Toll House
Red Hill
Aldridge
Harewood
Sunnyside
Cameron
Mrs. Engle
Noland
TERRY YORK
Gordon's Div.
EVAN
Ramseur's Lewis
Richmond
Gordon's Div.
Mt. Custard
Mrs. Flag
PEGRAM
Locust Hill
Puckett
Dr. Sam Rollay
Cedar Lawn

POSITION
HELD BY THE
1ST DIVISION 3RD CORPS
AFTER HAVING REPULSED THE ENEMY
December 13, 1862.
Drawn by direction of
Brig. Gen. D.B. BIRNEY
Commanding Division

Scale
0   250   500   750   1000 Yards

open plain
by enemy's

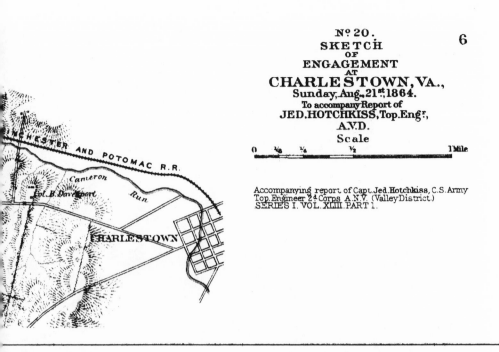

N⁰ 20.
SKETCH
OF
ENGAGEMENT
AT
CHARLESTOWN, VA.,
Sunday, Aug. 21ˢᵗ, 1864.
To accompany Report of
JED. HOTCHKISS, Top. Engʳ,
A.V.D.
Scale

```
0    ⅛    ¼         ½                    1 Mile
```

Accompanying report of Capt. Jed. Hotchkiss, C.S. Army
Top. Engineer 2ᵈ Corps A.N.V. (Valley District.)
SERIES I. VOL. XLIII. PART 1.

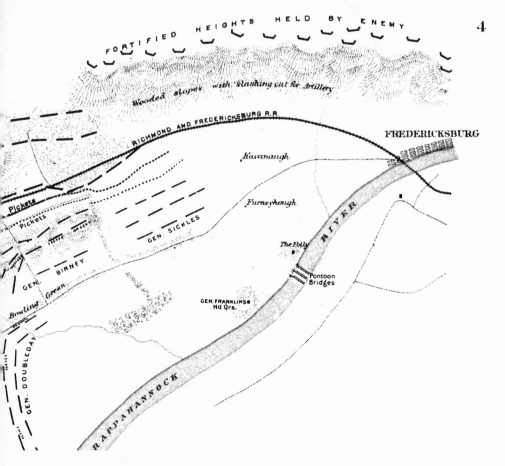

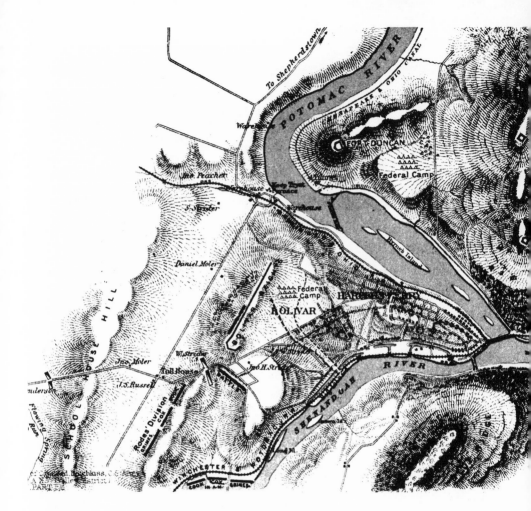

Nᵒ 12.

MAP
OF
ENGAGEMENT
AT
HARPER'S FERRY. VA.,

July 4ᵗʰ, 1864.

To accompany Report of

JED. HOTCHKISS, Top. Eng.

A.V.D.

Scale

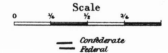

| 0 | ¼ | ½ | ¾ |

——— *Confederate*
——— *Federal*

Top. Engineer Office, A.V. Dist.,
Jan. 14, 1865.

Notes

INTRODUCTION

1. Douglas Southall Freeman, *The South to Posterity: An Introduction to the Writing of Confederate History* (New York, 1951), pp. 102-3.

2. Mrs. R. E. Christian to the editor, December 31, 1959.

3. Charles Hotchkiss Osterhout to the editor, January 14, 1960.

4. Ibid.

5. Charles Hotchkiss Osterhout, "A Johnny Reb from Windsor, New York," *Courier Magazine* (January 1955), p. 20.

6. Ibid., pp. 20-21.

7. Mrs. R. E. Christian to the editor, December 21, 1959.

8. Osterhout, "Johnny Reb," p. 21.

9. *Staunton Daily News*, January 19, 1899.

10. Charles Hotchkiss Osterhout to the editor, January 14, 1960.

11. John W. Wayland, *Stonewall Jackson's Way: Route, Method, Achievement* (Staunton, Va., 1940), p. 104.

12. Mrs. R. E. Christian to the editor, December 21, 1959.

13. *Staunton Daily News*, February 28, 1908.

14. Mrs. R. E. Christian to the editor, December 21, 1959.

15. Nellie Hotchkiss Holmes to Ellen H. Christian, March 19, 1930.

16. Osterhout, "Johnny Reb," p. 21.

17. Financial statement of Loch Willow Academy, Hotchkiss Papers, Library of Congress.

18. Osterhout, "Johnny Reb," p. 21.

19. James L. Nichols, "Confederate Map Supply," *Military Engineer* 46 (January 7, 1954): 28.

20. James L. Nichols, *Confederate Engineers* (Tuscaloosa, Ala., 1957), p. 81; Hotchkiss to Jonathan M. Heck, January 18, 1862.

21. This undated claim is in the Hotchkiss Papers.

22. Hotchkiss to Sara Hotchkiss, July 17, 1861, Hotchkiss Papers, Library of Congress.

23. Hotchkiss to Sara Hotchkiss, August 3, 1861, Hotchkiss Papers, Library of Congress.

24. D. Leadbetter to Hotchkiss, October 29, 1861, Hotchkiss Papers, Library of Congress.

25. Hotchkiss Journal, introduction to March, 1862.

26. Hotchkiss Journal, March 17, 1862.

27. Hotchkiss Journal, March 24, 1862.

28. Hotchkiss Journal, March 26, 1862.

29. Frank E. Vandiver, *Mighty Stonewall* (New York, 1957), p. 311.

30. G. F. R. Henderson, *Stonewall Jackson and the American Civil War*, American ed. (New York, 1937), p. 346.

31. Hotchkiss to Sara Hotchkiss, July 27, 1862, Hotchkiss Papers, Library of Congress.

32. Douglas Southall Freeman, *Lee's Lieutenants: A Study in Command*, 3 vols. (New York, 1944), 2:319, 346.

33. From a deposition signed by Hotchkiss on May 18, 1893, Hotchkiss Papers, Library of Congress. See also Hotchkiss Journal, December 10, 1862; Wayland, *Stonewall Jackson's Way*, p. 186.

34. Hotchkiss to T. J. Jackson, February 3, 1863, Hotchkiss Papers, Library of Congress.

35. Hotchkiss Journal, February 10, 1863.

36. Tax Receipt, Hotchkiss Papers, Library of Congress.

37. Bond signed by Beer, Hotchkiss Papers, Library of Congress.

38. Hotchkiss to Sara Hotchkiss, February 20, 1863, Hotchkiss Papers, Library of Congress.

39. Hotchkiss Journal, February 27, 1863.

40. Hotchkiss to Sara Hotchkiss, March 27, 1863, Hotchkiss Papers, Library of Congress.

41. Hotchkiss to Sara Hotchkiss, April 2, 1863, Hotchkiss Papers, Library of Congress.

42. Hotchkiss to Sara Hotchkiss, March 1, 1863, Hotchkiss Papers, Library of Congress.

43. Samuel Forrer to Mrs. Anne M. Howison, March 1, 1908, Hotchkiss Papers, Mrs. R. E. Christian estate.

44. Hotchkiss to Sara Hotchkiss, April 24, 1863, Hotchkiss Papers, Library of Congress.

45. Hotchkiss to Sara Hotchkiss, May 19, 1863, Hotchkiss Papers, Library of Congress. Hotchkiss Journal, May 2, 1863. See also A. C. Hamlin, *The Battle of Chancellorsville* (Bangor, Maine, 1896), p. 107.

46. Hotchkiss Journal, May 3, 1863.

47. Hunter H. McGuire and George L. Christian, *The Confederate Cause and Conduct in the War between the States* (Richmond, 1907), pp. 224-25. See also Hotchkiss Journal, May 4, 1863.

48. Hotchkiss to Sara Hotchkiss, May 10, 1863, Hotchkiss Papers, Library of Congress.

49. Ibid.

50. Hotchkiss to Sara Hotchkiss, May 19, 1863, Hotchkiss Papers, Library of Congress.

51. Ibid.

52. Henderson, *Stonewall Jackson*, p. 706.

53. Hotchkiss to Sara Hotchkiss, May 19, 1863, Hotchkiss Papers, Library of Congress.

54. Hotchkiss to Sara Hotchkiss, July 14, 1863, Hotchkiss Papers, Library of Congress.

55. Hotchkiss to Sara Hotchkiss, August 20, 1863, Hotchkiss Papers, Library of Congress.

56. Hotchkiss to Sara Hotchkiss, September 6, 1863, Hotchkiss Papers, Library of Congress.

57. Hotchkiss to Sara Hotchkiss, August 15, 1863, Hotchkiss Papers, Library of Congress.

58. Hotchkiss Journal, September 8-25, 1863.

59. S. Bassett French to Hotchkiss, September 28, 1868, Hotchkiss Papers, Library of Congress.

60. James Power Smith to Hotchkiss, September 29, 1863, Hotchkiss Papers, Library of Congress.

61. Wayland, *Stonewall Jackson's Way*, p. 186.

62. Hotchkiss to Nelson H. Hotchkiss, October 25, 1863.

63. This request, dated December 20, 1863, is in the Hotchkiss Papers, Library of Congress.

64. Hotchkiss to Nelson H. Hotchkiss, January 14, 1864, Hotchkiss Papers, Library of Congress; Hotchkiss Journal, December 22, 1863–January 15, 1864.

65. Hotchkiss to Jubal Early, January 20, 1864; Hotchkiss to Early, January 21, 1864; G. Campbell Brown to Hotchkiss, January 18, 1864, Hotchkiss Papers, Library of Congress.

66. Hotchkiss to Nelson H. Hotchkiss, January 24, 1864; Hotchkiss to Sara Hotchkiss, April 17, 1864, Hotchkiss Papers, Library of Congress. The prescription was for "1 Grain of Arsenic, 1 Grain of Morphine, Kresote enough to make a paste of it, then put a piece the size of a pins head in the cavity & confine it there with a little wax or cotton."

67. Hotchkiss to Sara Hotchkiss, May 1, 1864, Hotchkiss Papers, Library of Congress.

68. Hotchkiss to Sara Hotchkiss, July 15, 1864, Hotchkiss Papers, Library of Congress; Hotchkiss Journal, July, 1864.

69. Millard Kessler Bushong, *Old Jube: A Biography of General Jubal A. Early* (Boyce, Va., 1955), pp. 252, 266; John B. Gordon, *Reminiscences of the Civil War* (New York, 1903), pp. 333, 335.

70. Hotchkiss Journal, November 30, 1864.

71. Hotchkiss to Sara Hotchkiss, November 8, 1864; Hotchkiss to Nelson H. Hotchkiss, December 30, 1864, Hotchkiss Papers, Library of Congress.

72. Hotchkiss to Sara Hotchkiss, February 28, 1868, Hotchkiss Papers, Library of Congress.

73. Jedediah Hotchkiss, *Virginia*, vol. 3 of Clement A. Evans, ed., *Confederate Military History*, 12 vols. (Atlanta, 1899), pp. 543-44 (hereafter cited as *CMH*).

74. Hotchkiss Journal, April 23, 1865.

75. This parole, dated May 1, 1865, is in the Hotchkiss Papers, Library of Congress.

76. Hotchkiss Journal, May 8–June 20, 1865.

77. William Allan to Hotchkiss, July 4, 1865, Hotchkiss Papers, Library of Congress.

78. Hotchkiss Journal, July 18, 1865.

79. Hotchkiss Journal, August 4, 1865.

80. Hotchkiss Journal, September 5, 1865.

81. *Staunton Daily News*, January 19, 1899.

82. Hotchkiss Journal, October 16, 1865.

83. Hotchkiss Journal, October 23, 1865.

84. Jubal A. Early to Hotchkiss, October 25, 1865, Hotchkiss Papers, Library of Congress.

85. Hotchkiss Journal, December 2, 1865.

86. T. L. Rosser to Hotchkiss, January 31, 1866, Hotchkiss Papers, Library of Congress.

87. Festus P. Summers, ed., *A Borderland Confederate: The Diary of William L. Wilson* (Pittsburgh, 1962), p. 110.

88. N. J. Watkins, ed., *The Pine and the Palm* (Baltimore, 1873), pp. 13, 23, 28.

89. *Welsh* (W. Va.), *Daily News*, June 3, 1958.

90. Hotchkiss to Anne Hotchkiss, December 10, 1872, Hotchkiss Papers, Mrs. R. E. Christian estate.

91. Ibid.

92. Hotchkiss to Sara Hotchkiss, January 30, 1873, Hotchkiss Papers, Mrs. R. E. Christian estate.

93. Nellis H. Holmes to Anne H. Howison, August 20, 1874; Hotchkiss to Sara Hotchkiss, November 22, 1874, Hotchkiss Papers, Mrs. R. E. Christian estate.

94. Edwin Erle Sparks, *National Development, 1877-1885*, vol. 23 of A. B. Hart, ed., *The American Nation: A History*, 28 vols. (New York, 1904-18), p. 34.

95. Jedediah Hotchkiss and William Rogers, *Virginia: A Geographical and Political Summary* (Richmond, 1876), preface.

96. Julia Davis, *The Shenandoah* (New York, 1945), pp. 296-97.

97. *Welsh* (W. Va.) *Daily News*, June 3, 1958.

98. Jay Luvass, *The Military Legacy of the Civil War: The European Inheritance* (Chicago, 1959), p. 175; Freeman, *The South to Posterity*, p. 161.

99. Henderson to Hotchkiss, October 13, 1895, Hotchkiss Papers, Library of Congress; and quoted in Luvass, *Military Legacy of the Civil War*, p. 173.

100. These letters are in the Thomas T. Munford Papers, Duke University.

101. *CMH*, 3:viii-ix.

102. Osterhout, "Johnny Reb," p. 23.

103. Hotchkiss to T. T. Munford, December 1, 1898, Munford Papers.

104. Mrs. R. E. Christian to the editor, December 21, 1959, Hotchkiss Papers, Mrs. R. E. Christian estate.

CHAPTER ONE

1. Much of the material in this first chapter appears to be overlapping. It includes letters and marginal glosses which Hotchkiss apparently wrote or rewrote at a later and more leisurely time. It was arranged in this form by him, and is presented here because it contains much valuable information that only he was in a position to give, such as the personal and fresh impressions of Jackson's staff members. This of course removes the work from the diary class *per se*, but increases its value as a journal, or, as Hotchkiss termed it, "Memoranda."

2. General Thomas Jonathan ("Stonewall") Jackson (January 21, 1824–May 10, 1863) was born at Clarksburg, Virginia. He was reared in the home of an uncle, Cummins E. Jackson, following the death of his parents. Jackson entered West Point in July, 1842. Admittedly a slow student, he rose steadily to graduate seventeenth in a class of fifty-nine. Upon graduation he served in the Mexican War and advanced to brevet-major. In February, 1852, he resigned his commission to accept a professorship of natural and experimental philosophy and artillery tactics at the Virginia Military Institute at Lexington, Virginia. A poor teacher, he busied himself with the Presbyterian church, travel, and family life. On August 4, 1853, he married Elinor Junkin, daughter of the Reverend George Junkin, a Presbyterian minister and president of Washington College. Within fourteen months she was dead. Jackson then married Mary Anna Morrison, the daughter of a Presbyterian minister, on July 16, 1857. He was still on the V.M.I. faculty when Virginia seceded. He entered the service and rose rapidly to corps command. Capable of both independent and subordinate command, he was the perfect complement to Robert E. Lee. His Valley

Campaign of 1862 was a model of 'military mobility. Jackson was wounded at the Battle of Chancellorsville on May 2, 1863. He died on May 10 of pneumonia. The three best biographies are G. F. R. Henderson, *Stonewall Jackson and the American Civil War*, American ed. (New York, 1937); Frank E. Vandiver, *Mighty Stonewall* (New York, 1957); and Lenoir Chambers, *Stonewall Jackson* (New York, 1959). See also *Dictionary of American Biography*, 22 vols. (New York, 1928-1937), 2: 111-12 (hereafter cited as *DAB*) S. V. Jackson, Thomas Jonathan; George W. Cullum, *Biographical Register of the Officers and Graduates of the U.S. Military Academy, at West Point, New York, from Its Establishment, March 16, 1802, to the Army Reorganization of 1866-67*, 2 vols. (New York, 1868), 1:343-44 (hereafter cited as Cullum, *Biog. Register*).

3. Harpers Ferry Armory had been a federal depository prior to the war. It was also the scene of John Brown's raid. See R. U. Johnson and C. C. ·Buel, eds., *Battles and Leaders of the Civil War*, 2d ed., 4 vols. (New York, 1956), 1:116-17 (hereafter cited as *Battles and Leaders*).

4. The Rockingham Rebellion occurred in Rockingham County, Virginia, when a militia group refused to allow themselves to be mustered into the Confederate service. Force had to be used to restore order. Vandiver, *Mighty Stonewall*, p. 217.

5. Colonel William Thomas Poague (December 10, 1835–September 8, 1914) was born near Falling Spring Church, Rockbridge County, Virginia. Poague trained for the law and entered the war late. He enlisted in the Rockbridge Artillery, and at war's end had risen to battalion command. Following the war he served as treasurer of V.M.I. In 1903 he wrote an account of his service in the Rockbridge Artillery. See Poague, *Gunner with Stonewall* (Jackson, Tenn., 1907).

6. General Richard Brooke Garnett, a native of Virginia, was born in 1819. Graduated from West Point in 1841, he served in the Seminole War and on the Texas frontier. On May 17, 1861,· he resigned from the U.S. Army to join the Confederate service. Garnett succeeded Jackson in command of the First Brigade, but Jackson soon arrested him for retiring from the field at Kernstown (March 23, 1862). Garnett was reassigned and fell at the Battle of Gettysburg, July 3, 1863. See the *National Cyclopedia of American Biography* (New York, 1898-1959), 2:109 (hereafter cited as *NCAB*); Cullum, *Biog. Register*, 2:25; Ezra J. Warner, *Generals in Gray: Lives of the Confederate Commanders* (Baton Rouge, 1959), p. 99.

7. James C. Cochran was later colonel of the Fourteenth Virginia Cavalry.

8. Captain James Keith Boswell, another friend of Hotchkiss's, was Jackson's chief of engineers. It was Boswell who secured Hotchkiss's appointment to Jackson's staff. Repeatedly mentioned in Jackson's reports for meritorious service and bravery, Boswell was killed with his chief at Chancellorsville on May 2, 1863. See Henry Kyd Douglas, *I Rode with Stonewall* (Chapel Hill, 1940), p. 222; Vandiver, *Mighty Stonewall*, pp. 478-83; *War of the Rebellion: A Compilation of the Official Records of the Union and Confederate Armies*, 70 vols. in 127 (Washington, 1880-1901), ser. 1, vol. 12, pt. 1, pp. 383, 473, 709, 716 (hereafter cited as *Official Records*). For Hotchkiss's description of Boswell see journal entry for April 4, 1862.

9. General Turner Ashby (October 23, 1828–June 6, 1862) was born at "Rose Bank," near Markham, Fauquier County, Virginia. He was educated by private tutors and at Major Ambler's school. When Virginia seceded, Ashby organized a mounted group, which in June, 1861, became part of the Seventh Virginia Cavalry. Serving as chief of cavalry, Ashby was with Jackson in the Valley Campaign of 1862. He was mortally wounded in a rear guard action near Harrisonburg, Virginia. See *DAB*, s.v. Ashby, Turner, *CMH*, 3:577-79; Warner, *Generals in Gray*, pp. 13-14. A recent biography is Frank Cunningham, *Knight of the Confederacy: General Turner Ashby* (San Antonio, 1960); a shorter appraisal is Charles L. Dufour, *Nine Men in Gray* (Baton Rouge, 1963), pp. 40-73.

10. Hotchkiss refers to Alexander Keith Johnston, *The Physical Atlas* (Edinburg, 1850). This work dealt with the distribution of natural phenomena, geology, hydrography, and meteorology.

11. Former Loch Willow students, they were the sons of Thomas Maslin, a friend of Hotchkiss.

12. Hotchkiss here refers to deserters, a major hindrance to the effectiveness of the army. See Douglas S. Freeman, *Lee's Lieutenants: A Study in Command,* 3 vols. (New York, 1944), 3:217-19, 634-44; Bell I. Wiley, *The Life of Johnny Reb: The Common Soldier of the Confederacy* (New York, 1943), pp. 135-50, 220-29; Charles H. Wesley, *The Collapse of the Confederacy* (Washington, 1930), pp. 74-104; Bessie Martion, *Desertion of Alabama Troops from the Confederate Army* (New York, 1932).

13. General James Shields (May 12, 1806–June 1, 1879) was born in Altmore, County Tyrone, Ireland. He came to the United States in 1826 and settled in Kaskaskia, Illinois. In 1836 he was elected to the state legislature, and seven years later was appointed to the state supreme court. In the Mexican War he served as brigadier general of volunteers. Moving first to Minnesota and then to California, Shields settled down to operate a small mine at Mazatlan, Mexico. On August 19, 1861, Lincoln appointed him brigadier general of volunteers with command in the Shenandoah Valley, where he opposed General T. J. Jackson. Shields resigned from the army in March, 1863. Following the war he served in the Senate and traveled as a lecturer. *DAB,* s.v. Shields, James. See also W. H. Condon, *The Life of Major-General James Shields* (Chicago, 1900).

14. Colonel Alexander Swift ("Sandie") Pendleton (September 28, 1840–September 23, 1864) was born near Alexandria, Virginia. He was educated at Washington College and the University of Virginia. Volunteering early in the war, Pendleton served on Jackson's staff until May, 1863. Following Jackson's death Pendleton served under General Richard S. Ewell and General Jubal A. Early. Pendleton and Hotchkiss were good friends, frequently sharing lodging and food. Pendleton married Kate Corbin, sister of Richard Corbin, owner of Moss Neck, where Jackson had winter quarters in 1863. Perhaps Jackson's favorite junior officer, Sandie was wounded mortally at Fisher's Hill, Virginia, on September 22, 1864. For a recent biography see W. G. Bean, *Stonewall's Man: Sandie Pendleton* (Chapel Hill, 1959); and index to Vandiver, *Mighty Stonewall,* Chambers, *Stonewall Jackson,* and Freeman, *Lee's Lieutenants.*

15. General Ambrose Powell Hill (November 9, 1825–April 2, 1865) was born at Culpeper, Virginia. He was graduated fifteenth in the class of 1847 at West Point. He resigned his commission on March 1, 1861, to accept a position in the Confederate army, and by February, 1862, had become a brigadier general. Serving first with James Longstreet and then with Jackson, Hill was unable to get along with either. When the Army of Northern Virginia was reorganized in 1863, Hill was given command of the newly created Third Corps. He was fatally wounded at Petersburg, Virginia. See *DAB,* s.v. Hill, Ambrose Powell; William P. Snow, *Lee and His Generals* (New York, 1867), pp. 395-404; *CMH,* 3:697-98; and a biography, William W. Hassler, *A. P. Hill: Lee's Forgotten General* (Richmond, 1957). See also Cullum, *Biog. Register,* 2:189.

16. General Richard Stoddert Ewell (February 8, 1817–January 25, 1872) was born in Georgetown, D.C. He was graduated from West Point in 1841 and served in the Mexican War. Ewell resigned his commission on May 7, 1861, to accept a colonelcy in the Confederate army. He rose rapidly to division command under Jackson, and obtained a major general's commission in October, 1861. A wound sustained at Groveton in August, 1861, caused the loss of a leg, but he was back in service by May, 1863, when he succeeded Jackson in command of the Second Corps. Following the fight at Spotsylvania Court House, Ewell was unable to resume field command and was placed in charge of the defenses of Richmond. After the surrender Ewell was arrested and detained for four years at Fort Warren, Massachusetts. Upon his release he retired to his farm near Spring Hill, Tennessee. See *DAB,* s.v. Ewell, Richard Stoddert; Cullum, *Biog. Register,* 1:602; Snow, *Lee and His Generals;* and

two works by Percy G. Hamlin, *Old Bald Head* (Strasburg, Va., 1940), and *The Making of a Soldier* (Richmond, 1935).

17. General Jubal Anderson Early (November 3, 1816–March 2, 1894) was born in Franklin County, Virginia. He was graduated from West Point in 1837, but resigned from the service in 1838 to practice law in Rocky Mount, Virginia. In 1841 he was elected to the state legislature. Early began Confederate service as colonel of the Twenty-fourth Virginia Infantry and had risen by the war's end to lieutenant general and command of the Second Corps of Lee's army. Following the war he was a party to various schemes to create a new confederacy, but finally returned to practice law in Lynchburg, Virginia. See *DAB*, s.v. Early, Jubal Anderson; Cullum, *Biog. Register*, 1:529; for Early's own story, see Jubal A. Early, *War Memoirs: Autobiographical Sketch and Narrative of the War between the States*, ed. Frank E. Vandiver, Civil War Centennial Series (Bloomington, Ind., 1960); see also Millard Kessler Bushong, *Old Jube: A Biography of General Jubal A. Early* (Boyce, Va., 1955).

18. Colonel Robert L. Doyle.

19. John Letcher (March 29, 1813–January 26, 1884) was born at Lexington, Virginia. A graduate of Washington College, in 1839 he established a law practice in Lexington. He served in Congress from 1851 until 1859, when he resigned to accept the governorship of Virginia. Letcher opposed secession until Lincoln called for volunteers to suppress the rebellion. Following the war, he returned to Lexington and his law practice. See *DAB*, s.v. Letcher, John. See also *John Letcher of Virginia: The Story of Virginia's Civil War Governor* (Southern Historical Publications, 11 [University, Ala., 1966]).

20. General Edward ("Allegheny") Johnson (April 16, 1816–March 2, 1873) was born at Salisburg, Chesterfield County, Virginia. He was graduated from West Point in 1838 and served in the Seminole and Mexican wars. For his gallantry in Mexico he was voted a sword by the Virginia legislature. On June 10, 1861, Johnson resigned from the U.S. Army to accept a colonelcy in the Twelfth Georgia Volunteers. On December 11, 1861, he was appointed brigadier general, and finally in February, 1863, he received his promotion to major general. He was wounded in the fight at McDowell, Virginia, on May 8, 1862, and was twice captured by the enemy. After the war Johnson farmed in Chesterfield County. See *DAB*, s.v. Johnson, Edward; *CMH*, 3:611-12; and Cullum, *Biog. Register*, 1:972-73.

21. For a scholarly appraisal of the part played by engineers in the Civil War see James L. Nichols, *Confederate Engineers* (Tuscaloosa, Ala., 1957).

22. For General Jackson's report, see *Official Records*, ser. 1, vol. 12, pt. 1, pp. 379-84.

23. Edmund Pendleton.

24. Hunter Holmes McGuire (October 11, 1835–September 19, 1900) was born in Winchester, Virginia. He was educated at the University of Pennsylvania and at Jefferson Medical College in Philadelphia. In May, 1861, he was made medical director of the Army of the Shenandoah under Jackson. Thereafter he served as chief surgeon of Jackson's commands. McGuire was later medical director of the Army of Northern Virginia. Following the war he was on the faculty of the Virginia Medical College. See *DAB*, s.v. McGuire, Hunter Holmes; and Hunter H. McGuire and George L. Christian, *The Confederate Cause and Conduct in the War between the States* (Richmond, 1907).

25. Probably a slave. Hotchkiss frequently speaks of Allen in his correspondence.

26. Nelson Hotchkiss was a brother of Jedediah Hotchkiss. He came to Virginia to be associated with Jed in the Loch Willow Academy, handling the commissary and farming duties of the firm. Following the war he was a traveling agent with the Chesapeake and Ohio Railroad.

27. General William Booth Taliaferro (December 28, 1822–February 27, 1898) was born at "Belleville," Gloucester County, Virginia. In 1841 he was graduated from the College of William and Mary, and began legal studies at Harvard. From 1850 until 1853 he served in the House of Delegates. Taliaferro served under Jack-

son with distinction and sustained a wound at Groveton. The only mark on an otherwise excellent record was his attempt in the winter of 1861-62 to go over Jackson's authority to acquire better winter quarters. In February, 1863, he was transferred to Savannah and then to Charleston. Following the war he served in the legislature (1874-79), and was a judge of the Gloucester County Court (1891-97). *DAB*, s.v. Taliaferro, William Booth; *CMH*, 3:670-74; and Warner, *Generals in Gray*, pp. 297-98.

28. General Henry A. Wise, a former governor of Virginia, was a brigadier general in the Confederate army. At the head of the Wise Legion, he fought in western Virginia in 1861 under Robert E. Lee. For the report of the activities at Roanoke, see *Official Records*, ser. 1, vol. 9, p. 116.

29. Hotchkiss errs in genealogy. "Sandie" Pendleton was the son of William Nelson Pendleton, Episcopal minister and general of artillery in the Confederate army. Sandie was a great-grandson of Colonel Edmund Pendleton, Continental Army. See Bean, *Sandie Pendleton*, pp. 3-4.

30. Colonel Henry Kyd Douglas (September 29, 1840–December 18, 1903) was born near Shepherdstown, Virginia. He attended Franklin and Marshall College, in Lancaster, Pennsylvania, and after graduation in 1858 entered law school. When the war began, Douglas was in Saint Louis practicing law. He returned to Virginia and enlisted as a private in Company "B," Second Virginia Infantry. Soon receiving a commission, he served on Jackson's staff until December 29, 1862, when he assumed company command in the Stonewall Brigade. Douglas was severely wounded at Gettysburg. Returning to the army in March, 1864, he served until the surrender at Appomattox Court House as a brigade commander under Lee. Following the war, Douglas practiced law in Winchester, Virginia, and Hagerstown, Maryland. Douglas's book, *I Rode with Stonewall*, is an excellent Jackson source. In addition to the biographical material in the text, Fletcher Greene has an excellent sketch of Douglas, pp. 351-58. See Henry Kyd Douglas, *I Rode with Stonewall* (Chapel Hill, 1940); *DAB*, s.v. Douglas, Henry Kyd.

31. Lieutenant Richard Kidder Meade served on Jackson's staff as ordnance officer during the Valley Campaign. He was graduated second in the class of 1857 from West Point. He saw service under James Longstreet as major of engineers and under William B. Taliaferro as adjutant general. Meade died at Petersburg, Virginia, in July, 1862. See Douglas, *I Rode with Stonewall*, 363n; and Cullum, *Biog. Register*, 2:448.

32. Major General William Wing Loring (December 4, 1818–December 30, 1886) was born in Wilmington, North Carolina. He studied law at Georgetown College and practiced in Florida. He entered the army to serve in the Mexican War and following that conflict decided to remain in the service. When the Civil War began, he resigned his commission in the United States Army late in May, and on May 21 was appointed brigadier general in the Confederate service. He served under Stonewall Jackson in the Shenandoah Valley, and under Joseph E. Johnston and John B. Hood in the Army of Tennessee. A bachelor, Loring decided to remain a soldier following the war, and he joined the service of the Khedive of Egypt. See *DAB*, s.v. Loring, William Wing; Warner, *Generals in Gray*, pp. 193-94.

CHAPTER TWO

1. For an exciting account of Ashby's escape, see Henry Kyd Douglas, *I Rode with Stonewall* (Chapel Hill, 1940), p. 41.

2. General Louis Blenker.

3. Captain George F. Sheetz. Hotchkiss frequently misspells this name.

4. Lieutenant J. H. Lionberger.

5. A macadamized road was a thoroughfare constructed by the system invented by John Loudon McAdam. The process consisted of compacting into a solid mass a layer of small, broken stones.

6. Turner Ashby was a gallant soldier but a poor disciplinarian. For an account

of Jackson's efforts to correct this defect in his cavalry commander, see Douglas S. Freeman, *Lee's Lieutenants: A Study in Command* (New York, 1944), 1:337-41; Frank E. Vandiver, *Mighty Stonewall* (New York, 1957), pp. 214-16.

7. The Tenth Virginia Infantry was originally commanded by Colonel Simeon B. Gibbons. It was later commanded by Colonel Edward T. H. Warren.

8. Hotchkiss was instrumental in the establishment of Mossy Creek Academy. He had been in Mossy Creek as a private instructor since 1847 in the home of Daniel Forrer. At the insistence of Forrer and Colonel John Marshall McCue, a building committee for the Mossy Creek Academy met on August 26, 1852, and selected Hotchkiss superintendent of building and principal of the academy. See *Staunton* (Va.) *Daily News*, January 19, 1899; John W. Wayland, *Stonewall Jackson's Way: Route, Method, Achievement* (Staunton, Va., 1940), p. 104.

9. Probably the home of Captain J. Samuel Harnsberger, who served for a time as special aide on Jackson's staff.

10. Reverend Major Robert Lewis Dabney (March 5, 1820–January 3, 1898) was born in Louisa County, Virginia. He attended Hampden-Sydney College, the University of Virginia, and the Union Theological Seminary before becoming the minister at Tinkling Spring Church. From 1853 until 1883 he was on the faculty of the Union Theological Seminary. In 1861, he became a chaplain in the Confederate army and in 1862 was appointed to Jackson's staff with the rank of major. Dabney and Jackson were old friends, and the minister joined the staff with the idea of carrying on his religious duties. From 1883 until 1894 he taught philosophy at the University of Texas. He died in Victoria, Texas. For further reference, see *DAB*, s.v. Dabney, Robert Lewis; T. C. Johnson, *Life and Letters of Robert Lewis Dabney* (Richmond, 1903). Dabney wrote a biography of Jackson. *Life and Campaigns of Lieutenant-General Thomas J. Jackson* (New York, 1866).

11. This is a further reference to the discipline problems of Ashby's command. His troops had become demoralized; they were scattered and incompetently commanded by subordinates. Jackson decided to divide the command to restore discipline. The result of the meeting between Ashby and Jackson was the "detaining" of the reassigned cavalry to Ashby, and he withdrew his resignation.

12. General William Starke Rosecrans (September 6, 1816–March 11, 1898) was born in Kingston Township, Delaware County, Ohio. Graduated from West Point in 1842, he was assigned to that post as an instructor in engineering for four years. When General John Pope was transferred to the east, Rosecrans succeeded to the command of the western army and opposed General Braxton Bragg at the battles of Murfreesboro and Chickamauga. As a result of his defeat, Rosecrans was relieved from active duty. A good recent biography of Rosecrans is William Mathias Lamers, *The Edge of Glory: A Biography of General William S. Rosecrans, U.S.A.* (New York, 1961). See also *DAB*, s.v. Rosecrans, William S.; Kenneth P. Williams, *Lincoln Finds a General*, 5 vols. (New York, 1949-59), 1:104, 107, 133; 2:465, 472, 478, 544-54, 760-65; Rosecrans, "The Battle of Corinth," *Battles and Leaders*, 2:737-60, and 3:633, 638; and Cullum, *Biog. Register*, 2:42-43.

13. General George Brinton McClellan (December 3, 1826–October 29, 1885) was born in Philadelphia. He was graduated second in the class of 1846 at West Point and assigned to the engineers. Following service under Scott in the Mexican War, McClellan returned to West Point as an instructor. In 1855 he went to Europe as a military observer of the campaigns in the Crimea. In 1857 he resigned from the army to accept a position with the Illinois Central Railroad, and by 1860 was president of that company. On May 3, 1861, McClellan was appointed major general and given command of the Department of Ohio. Following McDowell's defeat at the Battle of First Manassas (Bull Run), he assumed command of the District of the Potomac, and finally became general in chief when Winfield Scott retired in November, 1861. McClellan failed to take Richmond, and his army was recalled to Washington. In the Battle of Second Manassas, he saw most of his troops transferred to Pope. After the battle he was called on to reorganize the army, and he opposed

Lee at the Battle of Sharpsburg, or Antietam. Beloved by his troops, "Little Mac" was overly cautious and hesitant. In 1864, McClellan was nominated for the presidency by the Democratic Party. See *DAB*, s.v. McClellan, George Brinton; Cullum, *Biog. Register*, 2:140-41; Hamilton J. Eckenrode, *George B. McClellan: The Man Who Saved the Union* (Chapel Hill, 1941); Warren W. Hassler, *General George B. McClellan: Shield of the Union* (Baton Rouge, 1957); George B. McClellan, *McClellan's Own Story* (New York, 1887).

14. McClellan was expected to win victories. His slow pace after assuming command caused President Lincoln to order a campaign to begin no later than February 22, 1862. The result was the abortive Peninsula Campaign. Using Fort Monroe as a base of operations, McClellan planned to advance up the Peninsula between the York and James rivers toward Richmond. Slowed by his own overly cautious nature and the tricky tactics of General John Bankhead Magruder, McClellan delayed long enough to allow General Joseph E. Johnston's force to move to the area. McClellan's train advanced to near Richmond but suffered a check at the Battle of Seven Pines. In this action, Joseph E. Johnston was wounded, and General Robert E. Lee was appointed to succeed him. For accounts of the campaign, see Freeman, *Lee's Lieutenants*, 1:137-245; Gustavas W. Smith, *The Battle of Seven Pines* (New York, 1891); J. J. Marks, *The Peninsula Campaign in Virginia* (Philadelphia, 1864); Joseph E. Johnston, *Narrative of Military Operations*, ed. Frank E. Vandiver (Bloomington, Ind., 1959), pp. 87-146. For a later account, see Warren W. Hassler, *Commanders of the Army of the Potomac* (Baton Rouge, 1962).

15. Probably Major John A. Harman, Jackson's quartermaster.

16. Confederate General Mansfield Lovell lost New Orleans in April, 1862, to an attacking force led by Admiral David G. Farragut and General Benjamin F. Butler. Their combined forces were before the city for four days. See John Fiske, *The Mississippi Valley in the Civil War* (New York, 1900), pp. 101-32; and more recently, Charles L. Dufour, *The Night the War Was Lost* (New York, 1960).

17. "Lewiston," the estate of General Samuel Lewis, was located two miles east of Port Republic. Hotchkiss and Jackson frequently stopped there. See Freeman, *Lee's Lieutenants*, 1:438.

18. Hotchkiss means that those who were advancing on foot were preceded by mounted sentinels. From their elevated position, the videttes would be able to signal danger when the enemy was sighted.

19. General Nathaniel Prentiss Banks (January 30, 1816–September 1, 1894) was born at Waltham, Massachusetts. In 1849 he began a long political career by gaining election to the state legislature. Within the next few years he served as congressman and governor. On May 16, 1861, he was commissioned general of volunteers and assigned to the Department of the Shenandoah, where he unsuccessfully opposed General T. J. Jackson. Transferred to the West, Banks led the ill-fated Red River expedition of 1864 in an attempt to reestablish Federal control in Texas. Following the war, he served in Congress, in the Massachusetts Senate, and as U.S. marshal of that state. See *DAB*, s.v. Banks, Nathaniel P.; Frederick H. Harrington, *Fighting Politician: Major General N. P. Banks* (Philadelphia, 1948). For critical appraisals of Banks's generalship, see Hassler, *Commanders of the Army of the Potomac*; John D. Winters, *The Civil War in Louisiana* (Baton Rouge, 1963).

20. "Little Sorrel" or "Fancy" was Jackson's favorite horse. Jackson acquired the animal while at Harpers Ferry in April, 1861. He was one of a dozen horses taken from captured railroad cars en route to Washington. "Little Sorrel" was described by Kyd Douglas as "a plebeian looking beast . . . ; stocky, and well made, round-barreled, close coupled, good shoulders, excellent legs and feet, not fourteen hands high, of boundless endurance . . . a natural pacer with little action and no style." (Douglas, *I Rode with Stonewall*, p. 206). The horse was once stolen, and when erroneously reported killed was the object of genuine sorrow throughout the army. When "Little Sorrel" died in 1887, he was thought to be thirty-five years old. See Douglas, *I Rode with Stonewall*, pp. 206-7; for an interesting discussion of

Jackson's mounts, see James Power Smith, *With Stonewall Jackson in the Army of Northern Virginia* (Richmond, 1920), Southern Historical Society, *Papers*, 43:96-99.

21. The home of John F. Lewis was located three miles from Port Republic. It was known as Lewis House. See Freeman, *Lee's Lieutenants*, 1:65-66; Douglas, *I Rode with Stonewall*, p. 85.

22. "Madison Hall," the home of Dr. George W. Kemper, Sr., was actually south of Port Republic. See Freeman, *Lee's Lieutenants*, 1:436.

23. Forty-second Virginia Regiment, Colonel J. M. Patton commanding.

24. Colonel Charles A. Ronald, Fourth Virginia Infantry.

25. Mechum River Station, Virginia.

26. Brown's Gap, Virginia.

27. Later General Robert Doak Lilley.

CHAPTER THREE

1. Colonel Jonathan N. Heck commanded the Twenty-fifth Virginia Infantry. For an account of the affair at Rich Mountain, in western Virginia on July 11, 1862, see Douglas S. Freeman, *Lee's Lieutenants: A Study in Command*, 3 vols. (New York, 1944), 1:27-37. Hotchkiss played a prominent part in the action by leading an assault on the mountain. For Heck's report, see *Official Records*, ser. 1, vol. 2, pp. 254-59. For Hotchkiss's report, see ibid., pp. 261-69.

2. John Wilson.

3. General Charles Sidney Winder (October 18, 1829–August 9, 1862) was born in Talbot City, Maryland. Winder was graduated from West Point in July, 1850, and resigned his commission on April 1, 1861, to enter the Confederate service. Winder was colonel of the Sixth South Carolina Infantry, and in March, 1862, he was promoted and placed in command of the "Stonewall Brigade." He was mortally wounded at the Battle of Cedar Mountain, August 9, 1862. *NCAB*, 5:514; Ezra T. Warner, *Generals in Gray: Lives of the Confederate Commanders* (Baton Rouge, 1959), pp. 339-40; Cullum, *Biog. Register*, 2:267-68.

4. The battle here described is that of McDowell, fought on May 8, 1862. Jackson defeated the forces of Generals Robert H. Milroy and Robert C. Schenck in the first action of the Valley Campaign. The battle lasted for four hours with small losses on both sides. Johnson's ankle wound prevented his return to service for over a year. For interesting accounts of the battle see William Allan, *Stonewall Jackson's Campaign in the Shenandoah Valley of Virginia* (London, 1912), pp. 85-100; Henry Kyd Douglas, *I Rode with Stonewall* (Chapel Hill, 1940), p. 49. Incidents of the battle are discussed below by Hotchkiss.

5. Colonel Elisha F. Keen.

6. Colonel William C. Scott.

7. Colonel George A. Smith.

8. Colonel Alexander G. Taliaferro.

9. Colonel Samuel V. Fulkerson.

10. General Robert Huston Milroy (June 11, 1816–March 29, 1890) was born in Washington County, Indiana. In 1843 he was graduated from Norwich University, in Vermont. He settled down to a law practice in Delphi, Indiana. When the war began, he organized a company of Indiana Volunteers but was soon appointed a brigadier general (September 3, 1862). Promoted to major general on November 29, 1862, he commanded the Second Division, Eighth Corps, in western Virginia. After the war Milroy was a trustee of the Wabash and Erie Canal and from 1872 until 1888 was engaged in Indian affairs in Washington State. *DAB*, s.v. Milroy, Robert Huston; *Battles and Leaders*, 2:279, 285-86.

11. This estimate is too generous. In Allan, *Stonewall Jackson's Campaign*, pp. 243-44, the battle figures are given as follows: Confederate—total strength about "6,000, total loss, 461"; Federal—total strength "about 2,500, total loss, 256."

12. Stapleton Crutchfield, Jackson's chief of artillery, was a graduate of V.M.I. He was captured at Port Republic but escaped and rejoined the army. Losing a leg

at the Battle of Chancellorsville, Crutchfield taught at V.M.I. until he was recalled to service in 1864, to help defend Richmond. He earned his brigadier generalcy early in 1865, and was killed at Sayler's Creek in early April of that year. See Douglas, *I Rode with Stonewall*, p. 87; W. G. Bean, *Stonewall's Man: Sandie Pendleton* (Chapel Hill, 1959), pp. 61-63.

13. Possibly Alfred H. Jackson of Lewis County, Virginia, a relative of General T. J. Jackson and formerly a member of his staff. He was wounded at Cedar Mountain (August, 1862) and died in Lexington one year later. See Bean, *Sandie Pendleton*, p. 50.

14. Captain Franklin F. Sterrett commanded a company of "Churchville" cavalry. See *Official Records*, ser. 1, vol. 5, p. 225. After the war Sterrett married Alansa Rounds, Hotchkiss's niece.

15. Captain C. R. Mason was an acting quartermaster. His more important work was as director of Negro laborers in the speedy construction of strong, rough bridges. See *Official Records*, ser. 1, vol. 13, pt. 1, pp. 718-19; Freeman, *Lee's Lieutenants*, 1:561.

16. Probably General Lorenzo Thomas, who served as adjutant general until March 23, 1863. See *Battles and Leaders*, 1:5.

17. Probably Captain H. M. Bell.

18. The correct date is Wednesday, May 14, 1862.

19. General Francis Henry Smith (October 18, 1812–March 21, 1890) was for fifty years superintendent of the Virginia Military Institute. His general's rank was in the Virginia militia. A graduate of West Point, in 1840 he assumed the position in Lexington that was to be his life's work. Smith went to the Confederate army with the cadet corps, but returned to Lexington when the school reopened. *DAB*, s.v. Smith, Francis Henry; Lyon Gardiner Tyler, ed., *Encyclopedia of ·Virginia Biography*, 5 vols. (New York, 1915), 3:203-4.

20. The *Merrimac* fell into Confederate hands when the Norfolk Navy Yard was evacuated. Although the ship had been scuttled, it was raised and armored with iron plate. Captained by Franklin Buchanan and renamed the *Virginia*, the vessel sailed down the Elizabeth River to attack the Federal blockading squadron at Hampton Roads. On March 8, 1862, the ironclad defeated the U.S.S. *Cumberland* and the U.S.S. *Congress*, but sustained the loss of its captain, who was severely wounded. Buchanan was succeeded by Lieutenant Catesby R. Jones. When the *Virginia* again challenged the Federals on the following day, it was confronted by the *Monitor*, an ironclad vessel designed by John Ericsson. Commanded by Lieutenant John L. Worden, the *Monitor* successfully defended the Federal fleet. Worden was partially blinded by a shell fragment and withdrew to shallow water. The *Virginia* withdrew at approximately the same time. The two vessels never fought again and were both soon destroyed. The *Monitor* went down in a storm on December 31, 1862. The *Virginia* was at Norfolk when the city was reoccupied on May 10, 1862. The iron plate made it unseaworthy; and when a portion of the armor was removed, the ship was indefensible. As it was unable to make the passage up the James, its commander, Josiah Tattnall, had the ship burned. The South was sorely disappointed, and Tattnall was court-martialed for his action. Although he was vindicated by the court, the South found it hard to forgive him. For further reference, see *Battles and Leaders*, 1: 692-750, 2:264-68; James Phinney Baxter, *The Introduction of the Ironclad Warship* (Cambridge,·1933); H. A. Trexler, *The Confederate Ironclad "Virginia"* (*"Merrimac"*) (Chicago, 1938); R. W. Daly, *How the Merrimac Won: The Strategic Story of the C.S.S. Virginia* (New York, 1957); Philip Van Doren Stern, *The Confederate Navy: A Pictorial History* (New York, 1962), pp. 80-89.

21. Hotchkiss refers to General George Hume ("Maryland") Steuart. Born on August 24, 1828, Steuart was educated at West Point. He was graduated thirty-seventh in the class of 1848. He resigned on April 29, 1861, to accept a captaincy in the Confederate service. He was appointed colonel of the First Maryland, and in March, 1862, was promoted to brigadier general. Wounded at Cross Keys in the

Valley Campaign, he was soon back on active service. Following the war Steuart retired to his farm in Anne Arundel County, Maryland. He died in South River, Maryland, November 22, 1903. *CMH*, 2:167-69; Cullum, *Biog. Register*, 2:225-26; and Warner, *Generals in Gray*, pp. 290-91.

22. Dr. Harvey Black was Hunter H. McGuire's regular assistant. Bean, *Sandie Pendleton*, p. 72.

23. Colonel Philip Daum.

24. Probably Captain G. W. Myers.

25. Hotchkiss is probably referring to James Power Smith, a member of Jackson's staff. Presumably Hotchkiss is offering information provided by Smith, a young staff member with whom Hotchkiss was well acquainted; after the war they became especially good friends. Smith published an account of his service with Jackson. See James Power Smith, *With Stonewall Jackson in the Army of Northern Virginia* (Richmond, 1920), Southern Historical Society, *Papers*, vol. 43.

26. General Thomas Taylor Munford was born in Richmond, Virginia, in 1831. He was graduated from V.M.I. in 1852 and was engaged in agriculture until the outbreak of the war. Entering the army on May 8, 1861, he joined the Thirteenth Virginia Mounted Infantry. Munford served with distinction at First Manassas and Gettysburg, and commanded the cavalry under Wade Hampton at war's end. Following the war he returned to agricultural pursuits. *CMH*, 3:639-41; *Encyclopedia of Virginia Biography*, 3:77-78.

27. Captains George F. Sheetz, John Fletcher, and George A. Baxter. See *Official Records*, ser. 1, vol. 12, pt. 1, pp. 702-3.

28. Hotchkiss probably refers to Alexander S. ("Sandie") Pendleton, who provided this intelligence.

29. Hotchkiss at this point omitted entries for the period from May 25 through May 29, 1862.

30. This report is included in the general reports of operations in the Shenandoah Valley, *Official Records*, ser. 1, vol. 12, pt. 1, and included here by the author at a later date. Major Wells J. Hawks's report may be found in ibid., pp. 20-21.

31. Jackson relieved Steuart of his command for this refusal, although actual charges were never filed. Freeman, *Lee's Lieutenants*, 1:477-79.

32. General Rufus King and General O. C. Ord.

33. This affair ended with Conner's resignation from the army. Freeman, *Lee's Lieutenants*, 1:479.

34. General John Charles Fremont (January 21, 1813–July 13, 1890) was born in Savannah, Georgia. He was famous for western explorations, especially in California. In 1856 Fremont became the first presidential candidate of the Republican party. Lincoln appointed him a major general in command of the Department of the West when the war began. He was shifted to the Valley when he prematurely authorized the emancipation of the Negroes in Missouri. Defeated by Jackson in the Valley, he requested to be relieved. Personally brave, Fremont never demonstrated much capacity as a general. After the war he was territorial governor of Arizona. See Allen Nevins, *Fremont: The West's Greatest Adventurer* (New York, 1928); John C. Fremont, *Memoirs of My Life* (New York, 1887).

35. Major Jacob R. Braithwaite. This information has been provided in a marginal note by Hotchkiss. See also *Official Records*, ser. 1, vol. 42, pt. 1, p. 1191.

36. Hotchkiss probably means Cacapon road.

37. In a marginal note the legal landlord is identified as a Mr. Walton.

38. Colonel Richard H. Cunningham, Jr., from Culpeper, Virginia. See Freeman, *Lee's Lieutenants*, 1:84n, 418.

39. Edenburg, Virginia.

40. The home of John Strayer, located in New Market, Virginia, at the crossroads of the Valley Turnpike and the Luray Road. See John W. Wayland, *Stonewall Jackson's Way: Route, Method, Achievement* (Staunton, Va., 1940), pp. 112-14. This establishment later became the Lee-Jackson Hotel.

41. Percy Wyndham (1833-1879), a British soldier of fortune, was the son of Colonel Charles Wyndham of the British army. In his long career, Wyndham served in the French army, the French navy, the British army, the Italian army, and the American army as commander of the First New Jersey Cavalry, and later he commanded the army of the King of Burma. He was killed in 1879 when a balloon which he had constructed fell in Royal Lake in Rangoon. (Henry Kyd Douglas, *I Rode with Stonewall* [Chapel Hill, N.C., 1940], pp. 79, 363-64). A curious incident accompanied Wyndham's capture. As he was being conducted to Jackson, Major Roberdeau Wheat hailed Wyndham. They had been friends when fighting under Garibaldi in Italy. Freeman, *Lee's Lieutenants*, 1:332-33.

42. The death of General Turner Ashby was a hard blow for Jackson, who was very close to his cavalry commander. For the effect of Ashby's death on the country, see Frank E. Vandiver, *Mighty Stonewall* (New York, 1957), pp. 272-73; Freeman, *Lee's Lieutenants*, 1:433-34; Wayland, *Stonewall Jackson's Way*, pp. 142-45; Douglas, *I Rode with Stonewall*, pp. 80-83; and his biography, Frank Cunningham, *Knight of the Confederacy: General Turner Ashby* (San Antonio, 1960).

43. Major James McDowell Carrington. See Freeman, *Lee's Lieutenants*, 1:442-43.

44. Lieutenant Edward Willis was Jackson's assistant chief of artillery. He advanced to colonel and was killed May 30, 1864, at the Battle of Cold Harbor. Bean, *Sandie Pendleton*, p. 200.

45. The two men were able to escape when Jackson brought up artillery to dislodge the Federal force. See Bean, *Sandie Pendleton*, pp. 61-62, and Freeman, *Lee's Lieutenants*, 1:439-43.

46. Major A. R. Courtney commanded the Richmond "Courtney" Battery.

47. Hotchkiss errs in his reference to Fulkerson's command. That officer commanded the Thirty-seventh Virginia Infantry. Douglas, *I Rode with Stonewall*, pp. 85-86, has a good account of this action.

48. Colonel Carnot Posey.

49. Probably William W. Kirkland.

50. General Isaac Ridgeway Trimble (May 15, 1802–January 2, 1888) was born in Culpeper County, Virginia. A graduate of West Point (1822) he entered the service of Virginia as a colonel of engineers. Appointed brigadier general on August 9, 1861, Trimble served in Ewell's division. He was wounded at Gettysburg and taken prisoner. He was held in prisons at Johnson's Island and Fort Warren until virtually the end of the war. See *DAB*, s.v. Trimble, Isaac Ridgeway; *CMH*, 2:159-62; Cullum, *Biog. Register*, 1:228.

51. General Richard Taylor (January 27, 1826–April 2, 1879), the only son of Zachary Taylor, was born at "Springfields" near Louisville, Kentucky. He studied in Europe but was graduated from Yale in 1845. Taylor established "Fashion," a sugar plantation in St. Charles Parish, Louisiana. When the war began, he joined a Louisiana infantry regiment and on October 21, 1861, was made a brigadier general. Serving with Jackson in the Valley, he earned his promotion and independent command of the District of West Louisiana. He defeated Banks in the Red River expedition. Following the war Taylor traveled widely. See *DAB*, s.v. Taylor, Richard; *Battles and Leaders*, see Index; and Richard Taylor, *Destruction and Reconstruction* (New York, 1879), an account of Taylor's wartime activities.

52. General William B. Taliaferro.

53. Lee was sending some of the best troops in the Army of Northern Virginia. In command of the reinforcements was General William H. C. Whiting. In addition to Whiting's brigade, there came also General John B. Hood's brigade and Wade Hampton's Legion. See Freeman, *Lee's Lieutenants*, 1:468.

54. Buckhorn Tavern.

55. James Duncan (September 29, 1811–July 3, 1849) was born at Cornwall, New York. He was graduated from West Point in 1834 and saw service on the frontier. Promoted to captain in 1845, Duncan rendered conspicuous service in the Mex-

ican War in the battles of Palo Alto, Resaca de la Palma, Monterrey, Cerro Gordo, and Molino del Rey, and in the assault of Chapultepec and the capture of Mexico City. Following the Mexican War he became inspector general of the army. Duncan died in Mobile, Alabama. See Cullum, *Biog. Register*, 1:446-47; *NCAB*, 11:519.

CHAPTER FOUR

1. Hotchkiss was detached from Jackson's main force and put to making maps. It is obvious, however, that his real interest was not on the drawing board, for he gave the headquarters location for each day.

2. The Battle of Cold Harbor was fought on June 27, 1862. For a discussion of the action, see Henry Kyd Douglas, *I Rode with Stonewall* (Chapel Hill, N.C., 1940), pp. 95-105; Douglas S. Freeman, *Lee's Lieutenants: A Study in Command*, 3 vols. (New York, 1944), 1:503-37.

3. Alexander H. H. Stuart, whose home was in Staunton, Virginia. See John W. Wayland, *Stonewall Jackson's Way: Route, Method, Achievement* (Staunton, Va., 1940), p. 94.

4. The Battle of Malvern Hill was fought on July 1, 1862, and ended unhappily for Lee's troops, who were repulsed by the forces of McClellan. Neither side could claim a clear victory. See Douglas, *I Rode with Stonewall*, pp. 106-16; Freeman, *Lee's Lieutenants*, 1:588-604.

5. Probably Captain Benjamin F. Winfield.

6. Hotchkiss probably means General Richard Brooke Garnett.

7. Captain David P. Curry was cited for bravery at the Battle of Rich Mountain. He was wounded in the action. *Official Records*, ser. 1, vol. 2, p. 259.

8. General John Daniel Imboden (February 16, 1823–August 15, 1895) was born near Staunton, Virginia. He attended Washington College and practiced law in Staunton. Imboden organized the Staunton Artillery and fought in the Battle of First Manassas. He commanded the First Partisan Rangers in the Battles of Cross Keys and Port Republic. Promoted to brigadier general in 1863, Imboden made a raid into western Virginia to destroy the Baltimore and Ohio Railroad. Following the war, he practiced law in Richmond. See Ezra T. Warner, *Generals in Gray: Lives of the Confederate Commanders* (Baton Rouge, 1959), p. 147; *DAB*, s.v. Imboden, John Daniel; *CMH*, 3:608-11; and for articles by Imboden, Index to *Battles and Leaders*.

9. Hotchkiss's marginal note identified Miss Bell's escort as Captain Edmund Bayley, whom she later married.

10. General Beverly Holcombe Robertson, a native of Virginia, was graduated from West Point in 1849. He served on the frontier until August, 1861, when he accepted a commission as colonel in the Virginia cavalry. In June, 1862, Robertson succeeded Ashby as Jackson's cavalry commander, but soon returned to serve under Stuart. After the Battle of Gettysburg he commanded the Second District of South Carolina. Following the war, Robertson was engaged in the insurance business in Washington. See *CMH*, 3:656-59; Cullum, *Biog. Register*, 2:243-44; Warner, *Generals in Gray*, pp. 259-60.

11. Frederickshall, Virginia, is located twenty-six miles from Gordonsville on the Virginia Central Railroad. Nathaniel Harris made his home there. Freeman, *Lee's Lieutenants*, 1:492.

12. Reverend D. B. Ewing. For an account of Jackson's stay with the Ewing family see Frank E. Vandiver, *Mighty Stonewall* (New York, 1957), p. 333.

13. Captain R. E. Wilbourn was with Jackson when he was wounded at Chancellorsville. Wilbourn was the officer who stopped Jackson's runaway horse and helped the general to the ground. For further discussion of this incident see Vandiver, *Mighty Stonewall*, pp. 477-83; Douglas, *I Rode with Stonewall*, p. 222.

14. Virginia Central Railroad.

15. Todds Tavern, Virginia.

16. Alexander Robinson Boteler (May 16, 1815–May 8, 1892) was born in Shepherdstown, Virginia. He was graduated from Princeton College in 1835. Boteler

was elected by the American Party to the United States Congress in 1858, and he served until March 3, 1861. It was Boteler who proposed the resolution which resulted in the formation of the Committee of Thirty-three, a group which tried to avert war by compromise. He was elected to the Confederate Congress from the Winchester district. Boteler was a volunteer aide on Jackson's staff. See *Biographical Directory of the American Congress, 1774-1949* (Washington, 1950), p. 869 (hereafter cited as *Biog. Dir. Amer. Cong.*); Douglas, *I Rode with Stonewall*, pp. 24, 380.

17. General Alexander Robert Lawton (November 4, 1818–July 2, 1896) was born in Beaufort District, South Carolina. He was graduated from West Point in 1839 and from the Harvard Law School in 1842. Settling in Savannah, Georgia, to practice law, he was for a time president of the Augusta and Savannah Railroad (1849-54), member of the Georgia House of Representatives (1855-56), and of the state Senate (1860). An ardent secessionist, he organized a Georgia brigade and in June, 1862, was transferred to Jackson's command in the Valley. Lawton succeeded Ewell when that officer was wounded at the Battle of Second Manassas, and was himself wounded at the Battle of Sharpsburg. In August, 1863, he was appointed to the post of quartermaster general. Following the war Lawton practiced law and was active in Georgia politics, running unsuccessfully for the U.S. Senate in 1880. In 1882 he was elected president of the American Bar Association, and he served as minister to Austria from 1887 until 1889. See *DAB*, s.v. Lawton, Alexander Robert; *CMH*, 1:618-19; Cullum, *Biog. Register*, 1:580; Warner, *Generals in Gray*, p. 175.

18. Reverend Joseph C. Stiles was a Presbyterian minister who promoted a revival in Jackson's army. Prior to the war he had served Grace Church in Richmond and the Mercer Street Church in New York City. When the war began, he returned to the South and at the age of seventy became a chaplain in Ewell's division. He lived until 1875. Vandiver, *Mighty Stonewall*, p. 416; Douglas, *I Rode with Stonewall*, pp. 197, 370.

19. Lord Charles Cornwallis.

20. General Nathanael Greene.

21. Probably Colonel Jonathan Bowie Magruder.

22. Colonel Asher Waterman Harman.

23. Thomas Snead.

24. Elisha Franklin Paxton (March 4, 1828–May 3, 1863) was born in Rockbridge County, Virginia. He was graduated from Washington College in 1845, from Yale in 1847, and in 1849 from the University of Virginia, where he studied law. Paxton's first command was as lieutenant of the Rockbridge Rifles. In the spring of 1862 he joined Jackson's staff and became his adjutant general and chief of staff with the rank of major. In November, 1862, he was promoted to brigadier general and given command of the Stonewall Brigade. He was killed at the Battle of Chancellorsville, May 3, 1863. *CMH*, 3:644-45; Warner, *Generals in Gray*, pp. 229-30.

25. Colonel James W. Jackson.

26. For further reference to the Battle of Cedar Mountain, see Douglas, *I Rode with Stonewall*, pp. 120-218; Vandiver, *Mighty Stonewall*, pp. 337-44; *CMH*, 3: 304-14; and Index to *Official Records*.

27. General James Ewell Brown Stuart (February 6, 1833–May 12, 1864) was born at "Laurel Hill," Patrick County, Virginia. He was graduated from West Point thirteenth in the class of 1852. Until the war Stuart saw service on the frontier, and as aide to Colonel Robert E. Lee in the expedition that captured John Brown at Harpers Ferry. He entered the Confederate service on May 24, 1861, with the rank of captain, and by September he was promoted to brigadier general. Stuart rose to great heights as a cavalry leader with his famous ride around McClellan's army, but serious errors such as the ill-advised independent action prior to the Battle of Gettysburg proved detrimental to his overall effectiveness as a soldier. Stuart's personal characteristics were such as to make him a hero. Courageous, gay, he wore his decorated uniform, crowned by a large plume in his hat, with the attitude of a cavalier. He was five feet ten inches in height and his face was framed by a reddish beard.

Douglas Freeman (*Lee's Lieutenants*, 1:xix) said: "About 'Jeb' Stuart there always is jingle and loudness." Stuart was mortally wounded at the Battle of Yellow Tavern, May 11, 1864. For short sketches on Stuart, see *DAB*, s.v. Stuart, James Ewell Brown; Warner, *Generals in Gray*, pp. 296-97; *CMH*, 3:667-70; Cullum, *Biog. Register*, 2:375; Freeman, *Lee's Lieutenants*, 1:283. For full biography, see Henry B. McClellan, *The Life and Campaigns of Major General J. E. B. Stuart* (Boston, 1885); Burke Davis, *Jeb Stuart: The Last Cavalier* (New York, 1957); J. W. Thomason, *Jeb Stuart* (Chicago, 1953); J. Lunt, *Jeb Stuart: Cavalier of the Confederacy* (New York, 1961). See also Heros von Borcke, *Memoirs of the Confederate War for Independence* (New York, 1938).

28. General Franz Sigel (November 18, 1824–August 21, 1902) was born in Sinsheim, Baden, Germany. A graduate of Karlsruhe Military Academy, he came to the United States in 1852. Sigel was an educator in Saint Louis when the war began. He organized the Third Missouri Infantry. In March, 1862, he was appointed major general of volunteers commanding the First Corps of Pope's army. In 1864 Sigel opposed Early in the famous raid on Washington. *DAB*, s.v. Sigel, Franz.

29. General James ("Pete") Longstreet (January 8, 1827–January 2, 1904) was born in Edgefield District, South Carolina. Graduated from West Point in 1842, he saw service on the frontier and in Mexico. Longstreet entered the Confederate service as a brigadier general on June 17, 1861. In October, 1862, he was appointed lieutenant general. Longstreet fought in the principal battles of the eastern theater and on one occasion was detached for duty in the West. He was wounded at the Wilderness on May 6, 1864, but was back for duty when the war ended. Longstreet settled in New Orleans, became a Republican, and through his friendship with U. S. Grant became, in 1880, the minister to Turkey. See Warner, *Generals in Gray*, pp. 192-93; for Longstreet's own story, see James Longstreet, *From Manassas to Appomattox: Memoirs of the Civil War in America* (Bloomington, Ind., 1960). For biographies see Donald B. Sanger and Thomas R. Hay, *James Longstreet: I. Soldier; II. Politician, Officeholder, and Writer* (Baton Rouge, 1952); also Hamilton J. Eckenrode and Bryan Conrad, *James Longstreet: Lee's War Horse* (Chapel Hill, 1936), and Nash Kerr Burger and J. K. Batterworth, *South of Appomattox* (New York, 1959).

30. General Robert Atkinson Pryor (July 19, 1828–March 14, 1919) was born near Petersburg, Virginia. He was graduated first in the class of 1845 at Hampden-Sydney College and attended the University of Virginia law school. In 1859 he was appointed to a vacancy in the House of Representatives; he was reelected in 1860. Entering the Confederate army as colonel of the Third Virginia Infantry, Pryor was soon promoted to brigadier general. In November, 1864, he was captured and held until virtually the end of the war. He lived the remainder of his life in New York as a lawyer and as judge of the state supreme court. See Warner, *Generals in Gray*, 247-48; *CMH*, 3:654-55.

31. Major, later Colonel W. M. Barbour.

32. William G. Williamson was a member of the Confederate Corps of Engineers and served briefly on Jackson's staff. He was graduated from Washington College in 1859. See W. G. Bean, *Stonewall's Man: Sandie Pendleton* (Chapel Hill, N.C., 1959), p. 146.

33. Catlett's Station, Virginia, is located near Cedar Run on the Orange and Alexandria Railroad. See map in Freeman, *Lee's Lieutenants*, 2:68.

34. General Richard Heron Anderson (October 7, 1821–June 26, 1879) was born at "Hill Crest," Sumter County, South Carolina. He was graduated from West Point in 1842 and served in the Mexican War. Anderson entered the Confederate army on March 26, 1861, with the rank of major, and by July had risen to brigadier general. Soon given division command in Longstreet's corps, he temporarily replaced that officer when Longstreet was wounded in the Battle of the Wilderness. Following the war, Anderson returned to his home in South Carolina. See Warner, *Generals in Gray*, pp. 8-9; and *CMH*, 1:691-93.

35. Gaines' Cross Roads, Virginia.

36. General George W. Taylor.

37. General Thomas Lafayette Rosser (October 15, 1836–March 29, 1910) was born in Campbell County, Virginia. Rosser was attending West Point when the war began, and he resigned two weeks prior to graduation to accept a lieutenancy in the Confederate service. Rosser became colonel of the Fifth Virginia Cavalry and on September 28, 1863, was promoted to brigadier general. He commanded Early's cavalry in 1864. Following the war, Rosser became chief of engineers of the Northern Pacific and Canadian Pacific Railroads. In 1898 he entered the United States Army as brigadier general of volunteers. See *CMH*, 3:658-60; *DAB*, s.v. Rosser, Thomas Lafayette; Warner, *Generals in Gray*, pp. 264-65.

38. General William Henry Fitzhugh ("Rooney") Lee (May 31, 1837–October 15, 1891), the son of R. E. Lee, was born at "Arlington," the family estate. Educated at Harvard, he was commissioned in the U.S. Army in 1857. In 1859 Lee resigned to take up agriculture, but he entered the Confederate army when the war began. He was colonel of the Ninth Virginia Cavalry, and in September, 1862, was promoted to brigadier general. Wounded at Brandy Station (June 9, 1863), Lee was captured while convalescing and was held prisoner until March, 1864. On April 23, 1864, he was promoted to major general. Following the end of the war, he became a farmer and for a time served in the House of Representatives. See *DAB*, s.v. Lee, William Henry; Warner, *Generals in Gray*, pp. 184-85; *CMH*, 3:625-27; *Biog. Dir. Amer. Cong.*, p. 1450.

39. Ely's Ford, Virginia.

40. General Roswell Sabine Ripley (March 14, 1823–March 29, 1887) was born at Worthington, Ohio. Graduated seventh in the class of 1843 at West Point, Ripley served with distinction in the Mexican War. His marriage and business alignments in Charleston, South Carolina, caused him to remain with that state when the war began. Ripley was in command of the South Carolina troops that occupied Fort Sumter in April, 1861. Following the war, Ripley engaged in business in Charleston. He was the nephew of James W. Ripley, chief of ordnance of the U.S. Army (1861-63). See Warner, *Generals in Gray*, p. 257; Freeman, *Lee's Lieutenants*, 1:273; *DAB*, s.v. Ripley, Roswell Sabine; Cullum, *Biog. Register*, 2:76-77. Ripley was the author of a history of the Mexican War which was entitled *The War with Mexico* (New York, 1849).

41. John Pelham (September 14, 1838–March 17, 1863) was born in Calhoun County, Alabama. Attending West Point when the war began, Pelham returned to Alabama and entered the army there. Ordered to Virginia, he soon commanded a battery of Stuart's Horse Artillery. He earned the name "gallant Pelham" for bravery at the Battle of Fredericksburg. He was mortally wounded in an engagement at Kelly's Ford, Virginia. There is a good sketch of Pelham in *CMH*, 7:48 (Alabama); and an early biography by Philip Mercer, *The Gallant Pelham* (Macon, 1929). More recent studies include William W. Hassler, *Colonel John Pelham: Lee's Boy Artillerist* (Richmond, 1960); and Charles G. Milham, *Gallant Pelham* (Washington, 1959).

42. Major William Patrick, Seventeenth Virginia Cavalry.

43. General Fitz-John Porter (August 31, 1822–May 21, 1901) was born at Portsmouth, New Hampshire. Graduated eighth in the class of 1845 at West Point, Porter served under Generals Scott and Taylor in Mexico. He was promoted to brigadier general on May 17, 1861, and served under McClellan and Pope. At the Battle of Second Manassas, Porter arrived late on the field and was ineffective. Pope had him court-martialed, and on January 21, 1863, he was cashiered from the service. After a long and persistent fight he was reinstated on August 5, 1880. For an account of Porter's career, see Otto Eisenschiml, *The Celebrated Case of Fitz-John Porter: An American Dreyfus Affair* (Indianapolis, 1950). The bibliography in *DAB*, s.v. Porter, Fitz-John, contains references to both sides of the case. See also Cullum, *Biog. Register*, 2:118-19.

CHAPTER FIVE

1. General Philip Kearney and General Isaac I. Stevens. See G. F. R. Henderson, *Stonewall Jackson and the American Civil War* (New York, 1937), pp. 480-81, and Douglas S. Freeman, *Lee's Lieutenants: A Study in Command*, 3 vols. (New York, 1944), 2:130-34, for a full discussion of this action.

2. General Daniel Harvey Hill (July 12, 1821–September 24, 1889) was born in York District, South Carolina. Though Hill was a graduate of West Point, he was primarily engaged in education prior to the war. Beginning the war as colonel of the First North Carolina Infantry, he rose by July, 1862, to be major general. Hill fought with distinction at the battles of the Seven Days, Second Manassas, and Sharpsburg. Following the war Hill published a magazine, *The Land We Love* (Charlotte, N.C., 1866-69), and wrote *North Carolina in the War between the States* (Raleigh, 1926). Still active in education, he was for a time president of the University of Arkansas (1877-84). Hill was a brother-in-law of T. J. Jackson. See *DAB*, s.v. Hill, Daniel Harvey; Ezra J. Warner, *Generals in Gray: Lives of the Confederate Commanders* (Baton Rouge, La., 1959), pp. 136-37; *CMH*, 1:681-83. See also Index to *Battles and Leaders* for articles by Hill.

3. This is probably the destination of Hill's command, since this is where Jackson crossed the Potomac River. Frank E. Vandiver, *Mighty Stonewall* (New York, 1957), pp. 375-76.

4. Jackson had accepted the horse gratefully, for "Little Sorrel" was temporarily missing. Kyd Douglas (*I Rode with Stonewall* [Chapel Hill, N.C., 1940], p. 148) erroneously says that Jackson never mounted the horse again. Lee suffered a similar accident in attempting to mount his famous horse, Traveler (Douglas Southall Freeman, *R. E. Lee: A Biography*, 4 vols. [New York, 1934], 2:340). Thus the South's heroes were invading Maryland riding in ambulances for at least a portion of the trip. For a general discussion of this incident, see Vandiver, *Mighty Stonewall*, p. 376.

5. Boonsborough, Maryland.

6. General John George Walker (July 22, 1822–July 20, 1893) was born in Cole County, Missouri. Walker was commissioned into the army in 1846 and remained in the service until July 31, 1861, when he resigned to join the Confederacy. Beginning service with the rank of major, Walker was by November, 1862, a major general. It was his command that took Loudoun Heights at Harpers Ferry. At the close of the war he commanded the District of Texas, New Mexico, and Arizona. See Warner, *Generals in Gray*, pp. 319-20.

7. General Lafayette McLaws (January 15, 1821–July 24, 1897) was born at Augusta, Georgia. Graduated from West Point in 1842, he served in the army without distinction until March 23, 1861. Entering the Confederate service as colonel of the Tenth Georgia Infantry, McLaws was by May, 1862, a major general. After the war he engaged in the insurance business in Georgia. See *CMH*, 6:431-34; and Warner, *Generals in Gray*, pp. 204-5.

8. Jackson's delay was due to a lack of communication with McLaws. A semaphore system proved inadequate to make contact with him, and couriers were finally used. For a discussion of this delay, see Vandiver, *Mighty Stonewall*, pp. 385-87.

9. Colonel Jesse Segoine commanded the 111th New York Volunteers. For his testimony on the surrender of Harpers Ferry, see *Official Records*, ser. 1, vol. 19, pt. 1, pp. 682-84.

10. Halltown, Virginia.

11. Colonel William Allan was chief ordnance officer of the Second Corps, Army of Northern Virginia. Hotchkiss was fond of Allan, and he allowed that officer to utilize his diary and topographical data in writing a study of the Valley Campaign. The resulting *Stonewall Jackson's Campaign in the Shenandoah Valley of Virginia* (London, 1912) remains a source of major importance.

12. Leetown, Virginia.

13. Opequon Creek is frequently misspelled by Hotchkiss.

14. Reverend James Graham.

15. Lieutenant H. J. Rogers was an engineering officer of Hill's staff. *Official Records*, ser. 1, vol. 12, pt. 2, pp. 650-51.

16. Probably Robert Sherrard.

17. Colonel William W. Glass commanded the Fifty-first Virginia Militia.

18. Hotchkiss had been in his youth a tutor to Mr. Forrer's children, and it was this gentleman who helped him establish the Mossy Creek Academy. See *Staunton* (Va.) *Daily News*, January 19, 1899.

19. Dunmore, Mt. Airy, was the home of General Gilbert S. Meem and his brother, Dr. A. Russell Meem. See John W. Wayland, *Stonewall Jackson's Way: Route, Method, Achievement* (Staunton, Va., 1940), p. 78.

20. "Carter Hall," erected in 1790-92 by Colonel Nathaniel Burwell, is located to the east of Millwood, Virginia. Wayland, *Stonewall Jackson's Way*, p. 199.

21. Manassas Gap Railroad.

22. Samuel R. Johnston was a captain, later major, of engineers assigned to the staff of General Lee. It was this officer who later became involved in a controversy with General Longstreet concerning the long delay on the second day at Gettysburg. For a discussion, see Freeman, *Lee*, 3:81-106. For Johnston's story, see Southern Historical Society, *Papers*, 5:183-84.

23. Robertson's River, Virginia.

24. "Saratoga" was the former home of General Daniel Morgan who fought in the American Revolution. Wayland, *Stonewall Jackson's Way*, p. 196.

25. Gaines's Cross Roads, Virginia.

26. General Wade Hampton III (March 28, 1818–April 11, 1902) was born in Charleston, South Carolina. Hampton was graduated from South Carolina College in 1836. He served in both houses of the state legislature, and at the beginning of the war was reputed to be the largest landholder in the South. He organized the Hampton Legion, a military group about the size of a regiment containing all three arms, and took it to Virginia in time to participate in the Battle of First Manassas. On May 23, 1862, he was promoted to brigadier general and placed in command of a brigade under Stuart. Severely wounded at Gettysburg, he later returned to service as major general. When Stuart was killed at Yellow Tavern, Hampton succeeded him in command of the cavalry corps, a position he held until the war's end. In 1876 he was elected governor of South Carolina and was instrumental in reclaiming that state from the Reconstruction regime. Hampton served in the United States Senate from 1879 until 1891. For short sketches on Hampton, see W. P. Snow, *Lee and His Generals* (New York, 1867), pp. 493-500; *CMH*, 1:697-99; Warner, *Generals in Gray*, pp. 122-23; and *DAB*, s.v. Hampton, Wade. For a longer treatment see Manly Wade Wellman, *Giant in Gray: A Biography of Wade Hampton of South Carolina* (New York, 1949). See Index to *Battles and Leaders* for articles by Hampton.

27. Headquarters were at "Saratoga," two and one half miles from Winchester on the Front Royal Road.

28. Possibly the Groveton, Virginia, road.

29. Richard Bickerton Pemell Lyons (April 26, 1817–December 5, 1887), second Baron and first Earl Lyons, was born at Lymington, Hampshire. A graduate of Oxford, he entered the diplomatic service in 1839. In December, 1858, Lyons was appointed minister to the United States. His diplomatic skill was instrumental in averting war in the Mason and Slidell affair, when an English ship was stopped and Confederate officials on board were forcibly detained. During his stay in the United States Lyons frequently visited English consuls in the South. See *DNB*, s.v. Lyons, Richard Bickerton Pemell.

30. Colonel, later General, Samuel S. Carroll commanded the Fourth Brigade of Shields's Division at the Battle of Port Republic. For Carroll's report, see *Official Records*, ser. 1, vol. 12, pt. 1, pp. 698-99.

31. G. F. R. Henderson (*Stonewall Jackson and the American Civil War*, p. 571) places Jackson's corps in Orange Court House one day previous to the date of this entry, or on November 27. Douglas Freeman (*Lee's Lieutenants*, 2:319) says

he is in error in this, but it should be noted that Freeman used the Hotchkiss Papers extensively to revaluate much of the work of Lee's army.

32. James Power Smith was Jackson's companion when they requested lodging at the home of Muscoe Russell Hinton Garnett. Garnett refused, not knowing the identity of his caller. When Smith revealed that it was Jackson who wished a place to sleep, the door was thrown open. For an account of Smith's conversation with Garnett, see J. P. Smith, *With Stonewall Jackson in the Army of Northern Virginia* (Richmond, 1920), Southern Hist. Soc., *Papers*, 43:25. Garnett had formerly been a member of the United States House of Representatives and had served in the first Confederate Congress. He was something of a critic of military prerogative, having sponsored an investigation of "how generals muzzled the press and fixed agricultural prices." See Wilfred Buck Yearns, *The Confederate Congress* (Athens, Ga., 1960), p. 153.

33. This is probably "Fairfield," the home of Thomas Coleman Chandler. It was to this place that Jackson would be brought on May 4, 1863, to recuperate from the wounds he received at the Battle of Chancellorsville. See Vandiver, *Mighty Stonewall*, pp. 487-88, and Freeman, *Lee's Lieutenants*, 2:636-43.

34. The road is probably an extension from one of the Potomac or Rappahannock ports. For a discussion of its value, see Freeman, *Lee's Lieutenants*, 3:346 and note.

35. Captain, later Colonel William W. Blackford. For an account of his war experiences with Stuart, see Blackford, *War Years with Jeb Stuart* (New York, 1945).

36. Probably Captain John Grant of the engineering corps, who made many maps for the army. See James L. Nichols, *Confederate Engineers* (Tuscaloosa, Ala., 1957).

37. There is a picture of the "old gray cap" in *Battles and Leaders*, 3:203. Mrs. R. E. Christian, of Deerfield, Virginia, has in her possession a statement signed by Hotchkiss rendering this conversation with Jackson about the hat a little differently. The only substantial difference is the manner in which Hotchkiss asks for the hat. In the signed statement he appears to have been more emphatic, and he says that the request met with immediate consent.

38. General William Barksdale (August 21, 1821–July 3, 1863), a graduate of the University of Nashville, was born in Smyrna, Rutherford County, Tennessee. From 1852 until the war began Barksdale was a member of Congress from Mississippi. Entering the Confederate service as a quartermaster, he was soon colonel of the Thirteenth Mississippi Infantry. Barksdale was promoted to brigadier general on August 12, 1862. He was seriously wounded at Gettysburg on July 2, 1863, and died the following day. See *Biog. Dir. Amer. Cong.*, p. 815; Warner, *Generals in Gray*, pp. 16-17; and *DAB*, s.v. Barksdale, William.

39. General John Bell Hood (June 29, 1831–August 30, 1879) was born in Owingsville, Kentucky. Hood's birth date is listed as June 1, 1831, in many sources, but his biographer, John P. Dyer, in *The Gallant Hood* (New York, 1950), p. 29, places it on June 29. Hood was graduated from West Point in 1853, and served in California and Texas. He entered the Confederate army in April, 1861. Hood advanced rapidly, and by October, 1862, he was promoted to major general with divisional command under Longstreet. He was severely wounded at Gettysburg and again at the Battle of Chickamauga. In February, 1864, he was appointed lieutenant general and in July succeeded Joseph E. Johnston in command of the Army of Tennessee. Defeated at Atlanta and Nashville, he was relieved of command in January, 1865. Following the war Hood lived in New Orleans. In addition to Dyer's biography, short sketches on Hood may be found in Warner, *Generals in Gray*, pp. 142-43; Snow, *Lee and His Generals*, pp. 405-19; *CMH*, 1:657-60; and Cullum, *Biog. Register*, 2:362. See Index to *Battles and Leaders* for articles by Hood and for references to campaigns. Hood's own story may be found in *Advance and Retreat*, ed. Richard N. Current (Bloomington, Ind., 1959).

40. Richmond, Fredericksburg and Potomac Railroad.

41. Rappahannock Academy was a small school in Caroline County. Joseph Martin, *A New and Comprehensive Gazeteer of Virginia* (Charlottesville, 1835), pp. 143-44, gives the location as sixty-four miles northwest of Richmond, or near Fredericksburg.

42. General William Buel Franklin (February 27, 1823–March 8, 1903) was born in York, Pennsylvania. Franklin was graduated first in the class of 1843 at West Point. He commanded a brigade in the Peninsula, and by July, 1862, was a major general. Following the Battle of Fredericksburg, Burnside held Franklin responsible for the Federal defeat. See J. L. Greene, *General William B. Franklin and the Operations of the Left Wing at the Battle of Fredericksburg* (Hartford, 1900); and *DAB*, s.v. Franklin, William Buel. See also Index to *Battles and Leaders* for articles by Franklin.

43. "Moss Neck" was the home of Richard Corbin, who served in the Ninth Virginia Cavalry as a private soldier. Jackson made Moss Neck his winter quarters, although he refused to stay in the house, choosing instead a tent in the yard. See Douglas, *I Rode with Stonewall*, p. 207, and Vandiver, *Mighty Stonewall*, pp. 443-54.

44. General William Edmunson ("Grumble") Jones (May 9, 1824–June 5, 1864) was born in Washington County, Virginia. He attended Emory and Henry College and was graduated from West Point in 1848. When the war began Jones organized a mounted group for Virginia, and after First Manassas he became colonel of the First and then the Ninth Virginia Cavalry. In late December, 1863, he led an unhappy cavalry raid in western Virginia. He was killed in the Battle of Piedmont. See Freeman, *Lee's Lieutenants*, 2:409-12; Warner, *Generals in Gray*, 166-67; and *CMH*, 3:616-18.

45. For a discussion of Pendleton and his anxiety over the promotion, see W. G. Bean, *Stonewall's Man: Sandie Pendleton* (Chapel Hill, 1959), pp. 78, 80. As Bean says (p. 89), the position of assistant adjutant general was tantamount to chief of staff.

46. In response to General Benjamin F. Butler's somewhat harsh occupation of New Orleans, Davis retaliated by proclaiming Butler and his officers to be felons "deserving of capital punishment." For the full proclamation, see Dunbar Rowland, *Jefferson Davis: Constitutionalist*, 10 vols. (Jackson, Miss., 1923), 5:408.

47. Probably James Beard.

48. Captain Franklin F. Sterrett.

49. For a discussion of aid and relief societies, see H. H. Cunningham, *Doctors in Gray* (Baton Rouge, 1958), pp. 141-45.

CHAPTER SIX

1. Possibly J. E. Johnson, at one time a member of Jackson's staff.

2. The Battle of Murfreesboro or Stones River was fought on the last day of 1862, and final actions were taken on the first day of 1863. The battle involved the Confederate Army of Tennessee, commanded by General Braxton Bragg, and the Union forces, commanded by newly appointed General William S. Rosecrans, successor to General Don Carlos Buell. After much urging from General Henry Halleck in Washington, Rosecrans finally moved on December 26, 1862, toward the Confederate encampment on Stones River, near Murfreesboro, Tennessee. Early on the morning of December 31 the Confederate left, under General William J. Hardee, attacked. Hardee was supported in the center by General Leonidas Polk, and General John C. Breckinridge was held in reserve on the right. The unusual tenacity of the Union forces under Generals Philip Sheridan, George H. Thomas, and Thomas L. Crittenden stopped the advance. Although he won the battle, Bragg retreated the next day and abandoned Murfreesboro to Rosecrans. For further reference to the Battle of Murfreesboro, see Joseph Mitchell, *Decisive Battles of the Civil War* (New York, 1955), pp. 111-16; Stanley F. Horn, *The Army of Tennessee: A Military History* (New York, 1941), pp. 190-210; Archer Jones, *Confederate Strategy from Shiloh to Vicksburg* (Baton Rouge, 1961); and Index to *Battles and Leaders* and *Official Records* for articles by participants and official reports.

3. General Henry Brevard Davidson (January 28, 1831–March 4, 1899) was born in Shelbyville, Tennessee. At fifteen he enlisted as a private in the First Tennessee Volunteers to serve in the Mexican War. For meritorious service at the Battle of Monterrey he received a field promotion, and after the war an appointment to West Point. Graduated with the class of 1853, Davidson served in the cavalry on the frontier. He resigned on July 20, 1861, to enter the Confederate service in the adjutant and inspector general's office. He served on the staff of Generals John Floyd, S. B. Buckner, and A. S. Johnston. Commissioned a brigadier general on August 18, 1862, Davidson served under General Nathan B. Forrest. He was with J. E. Johnston when he surrendered at Greensboro. Following the war Davidson was a deputy sheriff in New Orleans (1866-67), and in various state offices in California, including that of deputy secretary of state. See Cullum, *Biog. Register*, 2:355; Ezra J. Warner, *Generals in Gray: Lives of the Confederate Commanders* (Baton Rouge, 1959), pp. 67-68; and Eliot Ellsworth, Jr., *West Point in the Confederacy* (New York, 1941), pp. 323-24.

4. The brigade commanders here referred to are James Henry Lane, James Jay Archer, William Dorsey Pender, Charles William Field, Maxcy Gregg, and Edward Lloyd Thomas. For short biographical sketches of each, see Warner, *Generals in Gray*.

5. Hotchkiss refers to President Abraham Lincoln's celebrated Emancipation Proclamation, an executive order that declared free all slave property of those engaging in rebellion after January 1, 1863.

6. Major Norman R. FitzHugh, J. E. B. Stuart's chief of staff, was captured at Verdiersville and was at length exchanged. FitzHugh was a native of Stafford County, Virginia. He later served as divisional quartermaster. See Douglas S. Freeman, *Lee's Lieutenants: A Study in Command*, 3 vols. (New York, 1944), p. 441 and n.

7. Major Heros von Borcke is among the better-known Europeans who came to America following a war. Von Borcke had been an officer in the Third Dragoon Guards of the Royal Prussian army. He ran the blockade and made his way to Richmond in 1862, where J. E. B. Stuart gave him a place on his staff and recommended him for a commission. Despite an accent so Prussian he was sometimes difficult to understand, von Borcke served Stuart as adjutant and inspector general. He was severely wounded at Gettysburg. Following the war von Borcke again served in the Prussian army. He wrote of his Confederate experiences in a self-praising and often unreliable way. See Heros von Borcke, *Memoirs of the Confederate War for Independence*, 2 vols. (New York, 1938). For an informative note, see also Henry Kyd Douglas, *I Rode with Stonewall* (Chapel Hill, 1940), p. 371.

8. The story of the capture of Galveston Island by Federals and its subsequent recapture by General John B. Magruder, formerly of the Virginia theater, is admirably told in Earl Wesley Fornell's *The Galveston Era: The Texas Crescent on the Eve of Secession* (Austin, 1961), pp. 298-305. Using cotton-clad flat-bottomed vessels, Magruder's infantry was able to cross the bay and assault the island successfully; however, its location some distance from the mainland kept Galveston from being defensible and thus a really important installation for either side.

9. Colonel T. M. R. Talcott was an engineering officer assigned to the staff of General Robert E. Lee. Talcott later wrote of his war experiences with General Lee, printed as "General Lee's Strategy at the Battle of Chancellorsville," *Southern Historical Society, Papers*, 34:13.

10. Major George H. Bier was originally in the navy. Born in Maryland and appointed to the United States Navy from that state, Bier resigned his commission as lieutenant on April 23, 1861. He was commissioned a first lieutenant in the Confederate navy on November 13, 1861. Bier served at Sewell's Point, Virginia, in 1861, and later at the Jackson and Richmond Stations in 1862. During the winter of 1862-63 he was detailed to the staff of General T. J. Jackson as an artillery officer. Transferred back to the navy, Bier resigned his commission on June 22, 1863, and began running the blockade on a private vessel. He was captured aboard the *Greyhound* on May 10, 1864, off Wilmington, North Carolina. See *Register of Officers of the Confederate States Navy* (Washington, 1931), p. 14.

11. General Robert Emmett Rodes (March 29, 1829–September 19, 1864) was born at Lynchburg, Virginia. He was educated at the Virginia Military Institute, and after his graduation in 1848 he was continued at that institution as an instructor until 1851. From that date until the beginning of the war Rodes was a professional civil engineer. He entered the Confederate army as colonel of the Fifth Alabama Infantry, and his conduct in battle soon earned him a brigadier's rank. Wounded at Seven Pines, Rodes returned to fight well at Gaines' Mill, South Mountain, and Sharpsburg. For his service at Chancellorsville Rodes was promoted to major general. As a divisional commander he took a leading part in the actions at Gettysburg, the Wilderness, and Spotsylvania. Transferred to the Shenandoah Valley in June, 1864, he was mortally wounded at Winchester in September of that year. For short sketches of Rodes's life, see Warner, *Generals in Gray*, p. 263, and *DAB*, s.v. Rodes, Robert Emmett.

12. Captain Henry Richardson had formerly filled a similar post on the staff of General Richard S. Ewell.

13. Some New Yorkers felt themselves quite apart from the rest of the North, due to their close shipping and creditor relationship with the South. For an analysis of New York during the war, see Sidney D. Brumer, *Political History of New York State during the Period of the Civil War* (New York, 1911).

14. Following the Battle of Fredericksburg in December, 1862, Burnside persisted in his plan to cross the Rappahannock at Fredericksburg. Plagued by low morale and some seemingly disloyal subordinates, Burnside was at least blessed during the later part of December and early January with fair skies. When he finally ordered an offensive on January 20, the heavens opened up and dropped torrents of rain. The result was the demoralizing "Mud March," in which the army was literally mired to its axles. On January 25, Burnside was replaced in command by General Joseph Hooker. For a discussion of the command friction and the disastrous march, see Warren W. Hassler, *Commanders of the Army of the Potomac* (Baton Rouge, 1962), pp. 117-23; and *Battles and Leaders*, 3:118-19.

15. This intention was eventually gratified. Among Hotchkiss's published works are *Virginia: A Geographical and Political Summary* (Richmond, 1876), published in collaboration with William B. Rogers; *Historical Atlas of Augusta County* (Staunton, 1885), with Joseph A. Waddell; *Virginia*, vol. 3 of *CMH*; from 1880 until 1886 he edited *The Virginias* (Staunton), a technical magazine; and he contributed nearly one half of the Confederate maps to the *Official Records*. In addition, Hotchkiss both during and after the war was helpful to prospective writers about Jackson. His assistance to William Allan, both for his *The Army of Northern Virginia in 1862* (Boston, 1892) and for his *Stonewall Jackson's Campaign in the Shenandoah Valley of Virginia* (London, 1912), was significant, and help was extended upon request to J. P. Smith, R. L. Dabney, Hunter McGuire, and other associates who wrote about Jackson. His assistance to G. F. R. Henderson, whose *Stonewall Jackson and the American Civil War*, Amer. ed. (New York, 1937), stood for fifty years as the finest work on its subject, was acknowledged in this manner: "To the late Major Hotchkiss, his trusted staff officer, whatever of value these volumes may contain is largely due. Not only did he correct the topographical descriptions, but he investigated most carefully many disputed points; and in procuring the evidence of eyewitnesses, and thus enabling me to check and amplify the statements of previous writers, he was indefatigable" (p. xvii). This has been verified by Jay Luvass, *The Military Legacy of the Civil War: The European Inheritance* (Chicago, 1959), pp. 175-80, and Douglas S. Freeman, *The South to Posterity: An Introduction to the Writing of Confederate History* (New York, 1951), p. 161. An excellent example of the careful way Hotchkiss worked is to be found in the Thomas T. Munford Papers, Manuscript Division, Duke University Library. Hotchkiss repeatedly queried Munford in these letters regarding an alleged meeting between the two at the foot of Mount Sidney on the eve of June 19, 1862. The method by which the two resolved the problem of reconstructing the events of a brief encounter thirty years past in order that it might find its way into history is an interesting exercise in historiography.

16. General Joseph Hooker (November 13, 1814–October 31, 1879) was born in Hadley, Massachusetts. He was educated at the local Hopkins Academy and at the United States Military Academy. Hooker was twenty-ninth in the 1837 class of fifty. With the outbreak of the Civil War he offered his services to the Union, and on May 17, 1861, he became a brigadier general of volunteers. Hooker had divisional command under successive commanders of the Army of the Potomac, until he succeeded Ambrose Burnside under some question of disloyalty to his superior. Hooker commanded the army at the Battle of Chancellorsville and for approximately six weeks afterward. Supreme command seemed to change Hooker, and his caution, plus a new northern invasion by Lee, caused him to be replaced by General George Gordon Meade on June 23, 1863. For biographical references, see Cullum, *Biog. Register*, 1:536-38; Hassler, *Commanders of the Army of the Potomac*, 126-58; *DAB*, s.v. Hooker, Joseph; in addition there are numerous monographs relative to the actions in which Hooker took part. For a full biographical treatment, see Walter H. Hebert, *Fighting Joe Hooker* (Indianapolis, 1944).

17. The division commanded by General George Edward Pickett was a favorite of General James Longstreet, commander of the First Corps. Pickett was a dashing, cavalierlike commander, whose name is most frequently associated with the vain but glorious charge at Gettysburg. For a microscopic view of that action, see George H. Stewart, *Pickett's Charge* (Boston, 1959).

18. This probably refers to a social gathering of farmers at a member's residence. During this period many business establishments in agrarian communities were named "Farmer's" with an eye for business.

19. General Samuel Cooper (June 12, 1789–December 3, 1876) was born in Dutchess County, New York. He was graduated from West Point in 1815, and he remained in the army until he resigned to join the southern cause on March 7, 1861. His long service was rewarded in 1852 by his appointment as adjutant general. Marriage to the daughter of Virginia Senator James M. Mason and residence in that state impelled Cooper to devotion to the South. He was first appointed brigadier general, but within five months he was a full general. Cooper never exercised field command, but his administrative talents were utilized as adjutant and inspector general, and he was at all times ranking general in the Confederate army. Following the war Cooper retired to his farm near Alexandria, Virginia. For sketches of his life, see *DAB*, s.v. Cooper, Samuel; Warner, *Generals in Gray*, pp. 62-63; Cullum, *Biog. Register*, 1:158; Ellsworth, *West Point in the Confederacy*, p. 318.

20. Dr. Moses Drury Hoge (September 17, 1819–January 6, 1899) was born at Hampden-Sydney. Like his father, who had been a founder of the Union Theological Seminary, Hoge was all his life associated with administration and pastorship in the Presbyterian church. The voyage to Europe here referred to is an interesting one. Hoge left Charleston on December 29, 1862, for England on behalf of the Confederate Bible Society to purchase Bibles for the South. He enlisted the assistance of many prominent Britons and made a side trip to Paris to acquire theological materials. In the French capital Hoge met L. Q. C. Lamar, who tried unsuccessfully to persuade Hoge to join him in the mission to Saint Petersburg. Hoge used all the money the society had granted to him, plus that which he had raised in Britain. In sum, he acquired an inventory of about 250,000 items, including Bibles, Testaments, and tracts. He returned to Bermuda on September 23, 1863, and on October 10 steamed through the blockaders in broad daylight to Wilmington. Amid shot and shell, with everyone praying for divine assistance, the blockade runner reached its destination. Unfortunately, the bulk of the religious material did not make it. Hoge was one of the ministers who regularly served the Confederate senate as chaplain, and he officiated at the marriage of General T. J. Jackson's daughter. For a complete account of Hoge's activities and other Confederate religious matters, see Haskell Monroe, "Confederate Presbyterians" (Ph.D. diss., 1961, Rice University).

21. The Union had a kind of "limping draft" prior to this, under which the President, by the authority of the Militia Act, assigned quotas to the various states.

The inequity and inefficiency of such a system called for the first national, if not really efficient, conscription system. Enacted on March 3, 1863, it made all able-bodied male citizens between the ages of twenty and forty-five liable to military service. See Fred A. Shannon, *Organization and Administration of the Union Army, 1861-1865*, 2 vols. (Cleveland, Ohio, 1928), 2:31; J. G. Randall and David Donald, *The Civil War and Reconstruction*, 2d ed. (New York, 1969), pp. 313-18. Hotchkiss's reaction to conscription is typical of a volunteer, but is somewhat surprising since the Confederacy had used this method of filling their ranks first. See A. B. Moore, *Conscription and Conflict in the Confederacy* (New York, 1924), pp. 20-21.

22. In the second year of the war balloons were frequently used as observation posts for battles and for limited reconnaissance. The obvious difficulty of communication between balloon and ground made them less effective than they might have been, and they were of course hardly secret. Observations were customarily made at an altitude of one thousand feet; a higher altitude rendered an ascent valueless, and a much lower altitude would bring the balloon within range of enemy guns. Professor T. S. C. Lowe brought the balloon *Intrepid* to the front and, with Captain Richard T. Auchmuty, made numerous ascents. The Confederates also acquired a balloon later in the war. Denied the technological luxuries of the North, the South constructed its balloon of silk dresses donated by patriotic ladies, filled it with gas at Richmond, and towed it by railroad to the vicinity of its use. Its service was short; anchored to a coastal ship that grounded, it was captured by the Federals. See *Battles and Leaders*, 2:321, 513.

23. The Reverend Beverly Tucker Lacy was Jackson's unofficial chaplain general. He enjoyed a roving ecclesiastical commission, riding the circuit of command posts, preaching, directing other chaplains, and lending a religious influence to the army. Lacy and Hotchkiss became fast friends; it was to Lacy that Hotchkiss turned when his friend Boswell was slain. For further reference to Lacy, see Freeman, *Lee's Lieutenants*, 2:431-32, and Frank E. Vandiver, *Mighty Stonewall* (New York, 1957), p. 446.

24. Hotchkiss's inability to obtain a commission is difficult to understand. He had the unanimous and wholehearted endorsement of J. K. Boswell, his immediate superior, of Jackson, Ewell, Stuart, and Lee; letters from each member of this galaxy to Jeremy Gilmer, chief of the Engineer Bureau, are to be found in the Hotchkiss Papers. If influence could have secured the commission, surely here was the power. Gilmer's monotonous reply was that too many commissions had already been granted to residents of Virginia. Hotchkiss was never to receive officially what R. S. Ewell called "a simple act of justice." But he was customarily addressed as "Captain," and following the war as "Major."

25. Lee was not infrequently called to Richmond to keep President Jefferson Davis abreast of events in the field. This trip no doubt involved discussions relative to the spring campaign and the possibility of carrying the war to the North.

26. Winter quarters for the Second Corps, at Moss Neck, the home of Richard Corbin, was a happy place for Jackson. Corbin, although able to secure a commission, had preferred to serve as a private. His home was open to Jackson and his staff, but they maintained their headquarters in an office, or outbuilding, near the main house. This last long winter was full of enjoyment for Jackson, such as the merriment described by Freeman when Generals Lee and Stuart came to dinner and baited their very austere host by accusing him of dissipating in luxury (*Lee's Lieutenants*, 2:496-97); it was his last view of home life, where he observed the young Kate Corbin and Sandie Pendleton in romance, and where he befriended the young Janie Corbin and saw her as the little girl his own so recently born daughter might grow up to be. There is the final touching scene of Jackson removing the gold braid from his cap as a parting gift for Janie. For accounts of Jackson's winter sojourn at Moss Neck, see Vandiver, *Mighty Stonewall*; Lenoir Chambers, *Stonewall Jackson* (New York, 1959); Freeman, *Lee's Lieutenants*; W. G. Bean, *Stonewall's Man: Sandie Pendleton* (Chapel Hill, 1959).

27. No Lieutenant Long is listed on the roster of the Thirty-first Virginia, nor

is he listed as an officer in the list of regiments and battalions from Virginia. Perhaps Hotchkiss has accidentally given an incorrect unit name, or was misinformed.

28. Jackson had two sisters, Elizabeth, born in 1819, and Laura Ann, born on March 27, 1826, and the youngest of Jackson's family. The reference here is obviously to Laura Ann, because Elizabeth died in childhood. Laura Ann married Jonathan Arnold, and despite her husband's Whig politics and her own failure to profess Christianity, the Arnolds were very close to Jackson, even naming their eldest son for him. For his part Jackson never tired of trying to convert them respectively to Democracy and to the Lord. See Vandiver, *Mighty Stonewall*, p. 47.

29. Major Roberdeau Wheat commanded the battalion known as the "Louisiana Tigers." See Charles L. Dufour, *Gentle Tiger: The Gallant Life of Roberdeau Wheat* (Baton Rouge, 1957).

30. Colonel David B. Penn commanded the Seventh Louisiana.

31. Charles Welles Russell was born in Virginia in 1818. Educated at Jefferson College in Pennsylvania, he returned to Virginia to practice law. Russell served as a member of the Virginia legislature as a Democrat. He was an active secessionist, and he served in both the provisional and the permanent Congress of the Confederacy. Russell generally supported the administration. For reference to Russell or other matters regarding the Confederate legislative branch, see Wilfred Buck Yearns, *The Confederate Congress* (Athens, Ga., 1960), p. 243.

32. Colonel J. T. L. Preston had known Jackson for a long time. They had been together at the Virginia Military Institute, where Preston taught languages and English literature, and Jackson instructed the cadets in optics, analytical mechanics, acoustics, and astronomy. Preston was Jackson's brother-in-law by his first marriage; Jackson married Elinor and Preston married Margaret Junkin, daughters of the Reverend George Junkin, Presbyterian minister in Lexington. See Vandiver, *Mighty Stonewall*, p. 84.

33. John Esten Cooke (November 3, 1830–September 27, 1886), author and staff officer under General J. E. B. Stuart, was among Jackson's earliest biographers. A fine example of Virginia's leisure class, he served his state in time of war and then wrote several volumes about his experiences. His works are noted for a lively, picturesque style rather than for accuracy. In all he authored twenty-nine volumes and numerous articles. There is a good biographical sketch of Cooke by Philip Van Doren Stern in the Centennial Series reprint of Cooke's *Wearing of the Gray* (Bloomington, Ind., 1959). There is also a full biography by John Owen Beaty, *John Esten Cooke* (New York, 1922).

34. Lieutenant Colonel W. R. Peck of the Ninth Louisiana Infantry.

35. General Leroy Augustus Stafford (April 13, 1822–May 8, 1864) was born near Cheneyville, Rapides Parish, Louisiana. He was educated in Kentucky and Tennessee and then returned to Louisiana to become a planter. When the war began, Stafford organized a group known as the Stafford Guards, and he was elected its captain. The company was mustered into the Confederate army as Company "B" of the Ninth Louisiana Infantry, with Stafford as lieutenant colonel. He succeeded Richard Taylor as colonel in October, 1861, and led the regiment in Jackson's Valley Campaign, the Seven Days, Cedar Mountain, Second Manassas, Harpers Ferry, and Sharpsburg. In October, 1862, Stafford was transferred to the command of General Harry Hays, under whom he fought at Fredericksburg, Chancellorsville, and Gettysburg. Stafford was commissioned brigadier general on October 8, 1863, and assigned to command the Second Louisiana Brigade. On the first day of the Battle of the Wilderness he was mortally wounded. See Warner, *Generals in Gray*, pp. 287-88; see also Dr. G. M. G. Stafford, *General Leroy Augustus Stafford* (n.p., n.d.).

36. Captain R. H. T. Adams was signal officer with Hill's Division, and Captain Murray Taylor was an aide.

37. General Charles William Field (April 6, 1828–April 9, 1892) was born at "Airy Mount," Woodford County, Kentucky. He was graduated from West Point in the class of 1849 and served in the United States Army until he resigned in May,

1861. In the Confederate service Field was first colonel of the Sixth Virginia Cavalry, and on March 9, 1862, he was commissioned a brigadier general and transferred to the infantry. Field was severely wounded at Second Manassas, and during his lengthy convalescence he served in Richmond as superintendent of the Bureau of Conscription. He was promoted to major general in early 1864 and assigned to the First Corps. Following the war he served the Khedive of Egypt, was doorkeeper of the national House of Representatives, and was a civil engineer. For short sketches see Cullum, *Biog. Register*, 2:244; and Warner, *Generals in Gray*, pp. 87-88.

38. Jackson first learned Spanish while serving in Jalapa in the Mexican War. He took it up both as a diversion and for the practical purpose of meeting some nice ladies. During his first marriage Jackson was fond of referring to his wife in Spanish, calling her his *Esposa*. See Vandiver, *Mighty Stonewall*, pp. 30-31.

39. The battery was commanded by Captain A. C. Latham.

40. General Edmund Kirby Smith (May 16, 1824–March 28, 1893) was born at St. Augustine, Florida. He was educated at Benjamin Hallowell's Preparatory School in Alexandria, Virginia, and was graduated from West Point in 1845. Smith was commissioned into the infantry and soon won brevets of first lieutenant and captain for gallantry in the Mexican War. Between this action and the Civil War Smith served on the frontier and at the academy as a professor of mathematics. He resigned from the army on April 6, 1861, when Florida seceded. Smith was made a lieutenant colonel and stationed in the Shenandoah Valley under J. E. Johnston. He was commissioned a brigadier general on June 17, and on October 11 he was made a major general and given command of the District of East Tennessee. He became a lieutenant general on October 9, 1862, and from that date until the end of the war Smith commanded the Trans-Mississippi Department. Following the war he was president of the Pacific and Atlantic Telegraph Company, president of the Western Military Academy at Nashville, and chancellor of the University of Nashville; and at the time of his death he was a professor of mathematics at the University of the South, Sewanee, Tennessee. For short sketches see Warner, *Generals in Gray*, pp. 279-80; Cullum, *Biog. Register*, 2:127; and *DAB*, s.v. Smith, Edmund Kirby. An early biography is Arthur Howard Noll, *General Edmund Kirby Smith* (Sewanee, 1907). More recent is Joseph Howard Parks, *General Edmund Kirby Smith* (Baton Rouge, 1954).

41. Lieutenant Colonel James H. Skinner, Fifty-second Infantry Regiment.

42. Captain A. Elhart, a native of Rockbridge County, Virginia, began his Confederate service in the winter of 1862 as paymaster for General G. W. Smith's command. In the spring, when General T. J. Jackson was ordered to the Valley, he requested that Elhart be transferred to his command, a request that General J. E. Johnston denied because Smith would not consent to Elhart's release. Finally Jackson made a trip to Richmond in the company of Elhart and requested the secretary of war to transfer the paymaster to his staff. The obliging secretary expedited the matter easily, and Elhart served on Jackson's staff and that of the other commanders of the Second Corps until the end of the war. See T. J. Arnold, *Early Life and Letters of General Thomas J. Jackson* (New York, 1916), pp. 329-30, for a discussion of the general and the paymaster.

43. Major John Seddon commanded Campbell's brigade of Jackson's old division. *Battles and Leaders*, 2:511.

44. General Lawrence O'Bryan Branch (November 28, 1820–September 17, 1862) was born in Enfield, North Carolina. Branch was privately tutored by Salmon P. Chase, Lincoln's secretary of the treasury and chief justice, and was graduated from Princeton in 1838. Prior to the war he followed several professions, including law, newspaper editing, and politics. Branch joined his state when it seceded from the Union and was appointed quartermaster and paymaster general of North Carolina. Shortly he became colonel of the Thirty-third North Carolina Infantry, and on November 16, 1861, was promoted to brigadier general. Serving in A. P. Hill's "Light" Division, Branch's greatest service was at Harpers Ferry and Sharpsburg, where his brigade, along with those of Generals Archer and Gregg, arrived just in time to

block the final Union advance. In the evening of the battle, September 17, 1862, Branch was killed by a Federal sharpshooter. See Warner, *Generals in Gray*, p. 31; Douglas, *I Rode with Stonewall*, pp. 124-25; *Biog. Dir. Amer. Cong.*, p. 589.

45. This is in reference to General James Longstreet's activities in the southeast, around Suffolk, which included occupation of the area and, more importantly, foraging. See Donald B. Sanger and Thomas R. Hay, *James Longstreet: I Soldier; II Politician, Officeholder and Writer* (Baton Rouge, 1952), pp. 141-42.

CHAPTER SEVEN

1. Samuel J. Forrer was the son of Daniel Forrer, of Mossy Creek, Virginia. The elder Forrer had employed Hotchkiss in 1847 to tutor his children and had been instrumental in helping Hotchkiss found the Mossy Creek Academy in 1852. See John W. Wayland, *Stonewall Jackson's Way: Route, Method, Achievement* (Staunton, Va., 1940), p. 104.

2. This was to be the last meeting of Jackson with his family before he was wounded, and it was the first time that he saw his five-month-old daughter, Julia. The meeting was at Yerby House, the home of William Yerby, located two and a half miles up Massaponax Creek from Hamilton's Crossing. It was a warm family affair, with Jackson spending every possible moment that could be spared with his daughter; indeed, Anna Jackson seemed ignored as her husband enjoyed the privileges of fatherhood. It was arranged that Julia be baptized by Rev. Tucker Lacy and that her father be present. The entire army and the Yerby household were astonished to see the usually stiff Jackson unbend. A highlight of the visit was a call from General Robert E. Lee and his staff. When military matters forced Anna and Julia to leave, Jackson detailed Anna's brother Joseph Morrison, who was a member of his staff, to escort them to Guiney's Station and the railroad that would take them back to North Carolina. For tender and moving descriptions of Jackson's last happy days with his family, see Douglas S. Freeman, *Lee's Lieutenants: A Study in Command*, 3 vols. (New York, 1944), 2:519-23; Frank E. Vandiver, *Mighty Stonewall* (New York, 1957), pp. 451-54.

3. General Paul Jones Semmes (June 4, 1815–July 10, 1863) was born at Montford's Plantation, Wilkes County, Georgia. Educated at the University of Virginia, before the war Semmes was a banker and a planter at Columbus, Georgia. Semmes was captain of the Columbus Guards from 1846 until 1861, when he resigned to accept the elected captaincy of the Second Georgia Infantry. Transferred to Virginia and promoted to brigadier general on March 11, 1862, he served under General John B. Magruder and General James Longstreet. Semmes was at Sharpsburg and Marye's Heights, and he was mortally wounded on the second day at Gettysburg in Longstreet's attack on the Round Tops. He died eight days later. See Ezra J. Warner, *Generals in Gray: Lives of the Confederate Commanders* (Baton Rouge, 1959), pp. 272-73; Southern Historical Society, *Papers*, 33:54.

4. Hotchkiss makes a slight error in spelling. He obviously refers to General Lafayette McLaws.

5. There is some question about the identity of Battery Commander Graham. Jennings C. Wise, *Long Arm of Lee: The History of the Artillery of the Army of Northern Virginia* (New York, 1941), pp. 385, 985, 988, lists a Lieutenant Graham as commanding a section of artillery under Poague in the First Rockbridge Battery. Freeman, *Lee's Lieutenants*, 2:706n. refers to a Captain Joseph Graham as serving under Poague. It is of course likely that they both refer to the same person. However, Edward A. Moore, in his recollections, *The Story of a Cannoneer under Stonewall Jackson* (Lynchburg, Va., 1910), does not list a Graham in his roster of those who served with him in the First Rockbridge Battery.

6. General Stephen Dodson Ramseur (May 31, 1837–October 20, 1864) was born at Lincolnton, North Carolina. Educated at Davidson College and at West Point, he was graduated from the latter institution in 1860. He resigned from the U.S. Army on April 6, 1861, and entered the Confederate army as captain of the Ellis

Light Artillery. In a matter of days he was elected colonel of the Forty-ninth North Carolina. Promoted to brigadier general on November 1, 1862, he fought at Chancellorsville despite a severe wound suffered at Malvern Hill. Wounded again at Chancellorsville, he continued to serve under the successive commanders of the Second Corps until he was mortally wounded on October 19, 1864, only a short time after he had been appointed major general. At twenty-seven he was the youngest West Pointer to achieve that rank in the Confederate service. After he was wounded he fell into enemy hands and died the following day at Sheridan's headquarters. See Cullum, *Biog. Register*, 2:504; Eliot Ellsworth, Jr., *West Point in the Confederacy* (New York, 1941), pp. 413-14; *DAB*, s.v. Ramseur, Stephen Dodson; Warner, *Generals in Gray*, pp. 251-52.

7. General Ambrose Ransom "Rans" Wright (April 26, 1826–December 21, 1872) was born at Louisville, Jefferson County, Georgia. He became an attorney and was active in Georgia until the war began. Wright was commissioned colonel of the Third Georgia Infantry on May 18, 1861, and he served in North Carolina until he was promoted to brigadier general on June 3, 1862, when he was transferred to Virginia. His Georgia Brigade served with distinction from the Seven Days until the siege of Petersburg, and Wright was wounded at Sharpsburg leading the brigade in battle. On November 26, 1864, he was promoted to major general and ordered back to Georgia where he remained until the end of the war. See Warner, *Generals in Gray*, pp. 345-46.

8. General William Mahone (December 1, 1826–October 8, 1895) was born in Monroe, Southampton County, Virginia. Mahone was graduated from the Virginia Military Institute in 1847. He was for a time an instructor at the Rappahannock Military Academy while he studied engineering. Mahone was an engineer for several Virginia railroads, and in 1861 he was president of the Norfolk & Petersburg Railroad. Early in the war he was appointed colonel of the 6th Virginia Infantry. Although engaged in operations at Norfolk for a time, he served with the Army of Northern Virginia from the action at Seven Pines until the ultimate surrender. Mahone was promoted to brigadier general on November 16, 1861, and to major general on July 30, 1864. Following the war Mahone returned to railroading and to politics. He was elected to the U.S. Senate in 1880. For sketches of his life see Evans, *CMH*, 3:634-36, and Warner, *Generals in Gray*, pp. 208-9.

9. After a day of success at Chancellorsville, Jackson was in the dusk of twilight performing a personal reconnaissance of the Mountain Road, seeking a route that would allow him once more to flank Hooker and finish his conquest of the Federal forces. With a small detail from his staff, he was doing a task that any subordinate could have done. Suddenly there was a shot, and in the deepening darkness it was impossible to tell if friend or enemy had fired it. Unable to see, and apprehensive at their advanced position down the road from Chancellorsville, a North Carolina infantry regiment responded to a cried order to fire. Jackson, taking the first shot as a warning, wheeled his horse to return to the safety of his own lines and faced instead the opening volley of the North Carolina regiment. Jackson threw up his hands as if to stop the firing; Joe Morrison screamed: "Cease firing! You are firing into your own men." Unable to see who was thus pleading, the officer ordered his men to continue their fire. Jackson's outstretched hands had indeed stopped three of the bullets: one in the right hand and two in the left arm. "Little Sorrel" instinctively bolted away, and the rider lost control of his mount. A branch struck him viciously in the face, and he was almost thrown to the ground. Jackson came down in Wilbourn's arms, unable to help in the descent; his left arm was rendered useless by the severing of a main artery and the trauma of the blow. Jackson was barely conscious, but fighting to hold on. Hotchkiss, without knowing that his good friend J. K. Boswell had been instantly killed in the same volley, sped away to find Hunter McGuire to tend his commander's wounds. A. P. Hill arrived and cared for Jackson almost tenderly, compassionately, all of the past bitterness between them forgotten. Although Hill now succeeded to command, a wound would also soon temporarily remove him from ser-

vice. Thus in moments of confusion had the North Carolina regiment, in blameless error, accomplished what sharpshooters and countless Union dreamers had failed to do. For moving descriptions of these few minutes, see Freeman, *Lee's Lieutenants*, 2:566-81; Vandiver, *Mighty Stonewall*, pp. 478-81; and G. F. R. Henderson, *Stonewall Jackson and the American Civil War*, Amer. ed. (New York, 1937), pp. 678-80.

10. The other litter bearer was Captain R. E. Wilbourn, who had been at Jackson's side since the fateful volley. In addition to Smith and Wilbourn, two enlisted men were helping. See Vandiver, *Mighty Stonewall*, pp. 480-81.

11. The wounded litter bearer was hit in both arms by shell fragments. The litter was caught before the general fell completely to the ground, but the other enlisted man abandoned his burden when the danger became so acute. Further postponement of medical attention could not help but be harmful to the general; he had already lost much blood and was losing more. It was later the opinion of Hunter McGuire that this fall was the cause of the subsequent pneumonia complication that caused Jackson's death eight days later. The continuing cannonade made going on an invitation to another spill or perhaps even being wounded again. To prevent the latter event, Wilbourn, Smith, Joseph Morrison, and Captain Benjamin Leigh covered Jackson with their bodies until they could continue. Vandiver, *Mighty Stonewall*, p. 481.

12. Captain Joseph G. Morrison, a member of Jackson's staff, was dispatched on this duty because he was Mrs. Jackson's brother.

13. Morrison traveled in haste, but still it was four days before Anna Jackson could reach her husband. She had been in Richmond when the news came, and the enemy had temporarily occupied the avenues of travel to Guiney's and to the home of Thomas Chandler, where Jackson was to convalesce. The four days had been hard on Anna; the reports of Jackson's condition varied from near recovery to certain decline. Actually, until the day of her arrival Jackson seemed well on the road to recovery; his attitude was cheerful, and when Hotchkiss came to say goodbye Jackson expressed the opinion that he too would soon be rejoining the army. Then pneumonia appeared, and Anna arrived to find that her husband's condition confirmed her fears. He lived but three more days. For the finest description of Jackson's apparent recovery and subsequent decline, see Lenoir Chambers, *Stonewall Jackson* (New York, 1959), 2:424-69, "The Last March." For two firsthand accounts, see Mrs. Mary Anna Jackson, *Memoirs of Stonewall Jackson* (Louisville, Ky., 1913); and Hunter H. McGuire and George L. Christian, *The Confederate Cause and Conduct in the War between the States* (Richmond, 1907).

14. The Twelfth Mississippi Infantry, commanded by Colonel W. H. Taylor, was assigned to Nathanel H. Harris's Brigade, Third Corps.

15. Colonel William Proctor Smith, a native of Virginia, was graduated from West Point in 1857. Smith resigned from the army on April 27, 1861, and on the recommendation of General R. E. Lee was appointed captain of volunteers. He soon transferred to staff engineer work, serving under Lee as acting chief of engineers, and in 1864 as chief of engineers to General Jubal A. Early in his Valley Campaign. In 1865 Smith was back with Lee, serving with that officer until Petersburg. For sketches see Cullum, *Biog. Register*, 2:452; and Ellsworth, *West Point in the Confederacy*, pp. 435-36.

16. General John Sedgwick (September 13, 1813–May 9, 1864), born at Cornwall Hollow, Connecticut, was graduated from West Point in 1837. When the Civil War began Sedgwick was on the frontier. He was quickly transferred to the East to command first a brigade, then a division, and finally a corps in the Army of the Potomac. Sedgwick was killed by a Confederate sharpshooter while placing artillery at Spotsylvania. For biographical sketches see *DAB*, s.v. Sedgwick, John; Cullum, *Biog. Register*, 1:533-34; E. S. Welsh, *John Sedgwick, Major General* (New York, 1899).

17. General Raleigh Edward Colston (October 31, 1825–July 29, 1896) was born in Paris, France. In 1842 he was sent to the United States to attend the Virginia Military Institute, from which he was graduated in 1846. He remained at the institute

to teach French until 1861. Colston was first appointed colonel of the Sixteenth Virginia Infantry, and was promoted to brigadier general on December 24, 1861. In April, 1863, he was assigned a brigade in Jackson's corps. Following his unhappy command of Trimble's Division at Chancellorsville, Colston was transferred from Lee's army. Following the war he was variously employed as master of a military school in North Carolina and as a colonel in the Egyptian army. See Warner, *Generals in Gray*, pp. 58-59; William Crouper, *One Hundred Years at V.M.I.* (Richmond, 1939), 4:10.

18. General George Stoneman (August 8, 1822–September 5, 1894) was born in Busti, Chautauqua County, New York. He was graduated from West Point in 1846. Stoneman became a cavalry commander in the Army of the Potomac and in July, 1863, was called to Washington to command the Cavalry Bureau. See *DAB*, s.v. Stoneman, George.

19. This pleasant meteorological observation seems strangely out of place immediately following the words "Much to our grief General Jackson died today. . . ." Only the staunch faith that commander and engineer shared, plus the latter's definite sense of history, makes this seeming indifference understandable. Hotchkiss was not indifferent, but confident that Jackson had made his peace and was ready for death. Furthermore, he was still under the great shock he felt with the death of an even closer friend, James Keith Boswell, his messmate and immediate superior.

20. This is very probably the father of James Keith Boswell, come to hear from Hotchkiss of the death of his son and to claim his personal property that Hotchkiss had taken from the body prior to the burial.

21. A search fails to reveal that General George McClellan was actually a witness to the battle, but his interest must have been keen.

22. General Oliver Otis Howard (November 8, 1830–October 26, 1909) was born at Leeds, Maine. He was graduated in 1854 from West Point. In September, 1861, he was appointed brigadier general of volunteers, and he served for two years in the Army of the Potomac. In the fall of 1863 Howard was transferred to Tennessee. He is best remembered for his postwar administration of the Freedman's Bureau. See *DAB*, s.v. Howard, Oliver Otis; Howard, *The Autobiography of Oliver Otis Howard*, 2 vols. (New York, 1907); and *Who's Who in America, 1908-1909*.

23. An extension of time could easily have been obtained for such a human need, but Hooker was probably trying to protect himself from any further criticism. He was then catching it from all sides, including the President. Lincoln even paid the general a visit in the field in an attempt to ascertain the latter's fitness to continue in command. Hooker's failure at Chancellorsville would within a matter of weeks cost him his command. For a discussion of the controversy and doubt surrounding Hooker's performance, and a critical evaluation, see T. Harry Williams, *Lincoln and His Generals* (New York, 1952), pp. 240-59.

CHAPTER EIGHT

1. Later Colonel John J. Clark, who was for a time chief engineer of Longstreet's corps. See James L. Nichols, *Confederate Engineers* (Tuscaloosa, Ala., 1957), p. 100; and James Longstreet, *From Manassas to Appomattox* (Bloomington, Ind., 1960), p. 488.

2. George Edward Pickett (January 28, 1825–July 30, 1875), whose divisional command has been previously discussed, was born in Richmond, Virginia. He was graduated from West Point in 1846 at the bottom of his class. Prior to the war he served in the Mexican conflict and on the Texas frontier. With the coming of civil war he joined the Confederate service and was made a brigadier general on January 14, 1862. Pickett served in the Peninsular Campaign, at Gaines' Mill, and at Fredericksburg, but the high point of his career was the gallant charge of his division at Gettysburg on July 3, 1863. Pickett later commanded the department of Virginia and North Carolina and was one of the defenders at Petersburg. Following the war Pickett was in the insurance business in Norfolk, Virginia. See *CMH*, 3:650-54; Cullum,

Biog. Register, 2:179-80; Eliot Ellsworth, Jr., *West Point in the Confederacy* (New York, 1941), pp. 409-10; and Ezra J. Warner, *Generals in Gray: Lives of the Confederate Commanders* (Baton Rouge, 1959), pp. 239-40. George H. Stewart, *Pickett's Charge* (Boston, 1959), is an excellent study in microhistory.

3. Undoubtedly General Albert Gallatin Jenkins (November 10, 1830–May 21, 1864), who was born in Cabell County, now West Virginia. He was educated at Jefferson College in Pennsylvania (1848) and in 1850 was graduated from the Harvard Law School. He practiced law in western Virginia until elected to Congress in 1856, a post that he held until April, 1861, when he resigned to organize a cavalry unit for the southern cause. Jenkins served as colonel of the Eighth Virginia Cavalry until August 5, 1862, when he was promoted to brigadier general. He was wounded at Gettysburg; receiving another wound on May 9, 1864, in an action on Cloyd's Mountain in Pulaski County, Jenkins died twelve days later. For a brief sketch of his life, see Warner, *Generals in Gray*, pp. 154-55; *Biog. Dir. Amer. Cong.*, p. 1119.

4. The "Stonewall Brigade" is one of the better-known military units in American history. It was originally known as Virginia's First Brigade, but it was later officially changed to "Stonewall" in honor of its commander and its heroic action at the Battle of First Manassas. The brigade remained close to Jackson as he ascended the ladder to divisional and finally corps command, and he was always careful to select competent commanders for it. On the occasion of his promotion to major general, Jackson made his only known public address, a farewell, to this brigade. It is published in Henry Kyd Douglas, *I Rode with Stonewall* (Chapel Hill, 1940), p. 16. The muster of the brigade was mostly from the Valley of Virginia and numbered 2,600 in the beginning, although probably 5,000 served within its ranks during the course of the war. After 39 major engagements, only 210 remained to surrender at Appomattox with none above the rank of captain. This and other interesting information about Jackson's first command may be found in James I. Robertson, Jr., *The Stonewall Brigade* (Baton Rouge, 1963). The feeling of unit identification is best expressed in the lines of John Esten Cooke:

> And men will tell their children
> Tho' all other memories fade,
> How they fought with Stonewall Jackson
> In the old "Stonewall Brigade."

5. General John Brown Gordon (February 6, 1832–January 9, 1904) was born in Upson County, Georgia. He attended the University of Georgia but left without graduating to study law. Gordon turned to coal mining and was engaged in that activity when the war began. With no previous military experience or training, he was appointed captain of a company known as "Raccoon Roughs." He was assigned to the Army of Northern Virginia, and he served with that army until the surrender in 1865. Gordon was wounded severely several times. Promotions kept pace with his growing abilities; he was commissioned brigadier general on November 1, 1862, and major general on May 4, 1864. Following the war Gordon fought to redeem control of his state from outside political influence and thus began a successful political career. Twice elected to the U.S. Senate (1873-80; 1891-97) and once to the governorship (1886-90), he was a political power in Georgia for many years. Gordon was among the organizers of the United Confederate Veterans and was its first commander-in-chief. His own version of his war experiences is in *Reminiscences of the Civil War* (New York, 1903). A useful biography is Allen P. Tankersley, *John B. Gordon: A Study in Gallantry* (Atlanta, 1955). For shorter sketches see *Biog. Dir. Amer. Cong.*, p. 959; Warner, *Generals in Gray*, p. 111.

6. Chambersburg, Pennsylvania, had once before, in mid-October, 1862, been the object of one of Stuart's daring raids. Its purpose was to obtain horses and other supplies, but the raiders also destroyed approximately $250,000 in public and railroad property. See Henry B. McClellan, *I Rode with Jeb Stuart* (Bloomington, 1958),

pp. 136-66. This present raid was no doubt in preparation for the second great Confederate invasion that took Stuart away from Lee on the eve of Gettysburg. The commander was General A. G. Jenkins, who was merely to hold the line for Ewell to advance.

7. Gilbert Moxley Sorrel (February 23, 1838–August 10, 1901) was born at Savannah, Georgia. When the war began, Sorrel was a clerk for the Central Railroad of Georgia, and a member of the Georgia Hussars, a militia group. Following the capture of Fort Sumter he traveled to Richmond and became a captain and volunteer aide on the staff of General James Longstreet. Sorrel remained with Longstreet until the latter's wounding at the Wilderness, and eventually became his chief of staff with the rank of lieutenant colonel. On October 27, 1864, he was appointed brigadier general to command a Georgia brigade in the Third Corps. Following the war Sorrel was engaged in the steamship business in Savannah. For Sorrel's own story, see *Recollections of a Confederate Staff Officer* (New York, 1905). Bell Wiley has edited and republished this memoir (Nashville, 1958). See also Warner, *Generals in Gray*, pp. 286-87.

8. Boonsborough, Maryland, is near Sharpsburg.

9. "Contributions" is a quaint and slightly inaccurate way of hiding the real meaning—tribute. It will be remembered that a major reason for this invasion was to obtain supplies, and that a secondary reason was to carry the war to the North; the goal of Gettysburg was shoes. The foraging that Confederates committed was hardly as extensive as that practiced so expertly by Sherman's "bummers" in Georgia and South Carolina, but the motivation was the same. General Lee admonished his men to make war only on military men, however, for as he said in the General Order, "We cannot take vengence for the wrong our people have suffered, without lowering ourselves in the eyes of all whose abhorrence has been excited by the atrocities of our enemies, and offending against Him to whom vengence belongeth." Quoted in *CMH*, 3:401.

10. Probably Captain J. B. Richardson, artillery officer with Pickett's command.

11. It is surprising to note that Lee had pinpointed the location of probable enemy contact this far in advance of the actual engagement. The general impression is that the selection of Gettysburg as a battleground was largely in the hands of fate and that Ewell's advance more or less accidentally ran into the Federal forces. A study of the roads will reveal, however, that Gettysburg was something of a hub, and contact there was likely. Strangely each commander seemed to expect the other to head for the place, and each sought to block the other. Kyd Douglas identified Gettysburg as the army's destination as of June 27, but in *CMH*, 3:401, Hotchkiss says that Lee, because of the absence of his cavalry, did not know the exact location or intentions of his foe. As Lee and Meade approached the turning point of the war, neither seemed really certain of where the other was or what his intentions were.

12. Mummasburg, Pennsylvania, or just southeast of the town toward Gettysburg, was the scene of a preliminary engagement of troops. For descriptions of these early activities, see Jubal A. Early, *War Memoirs: Autobiographical Sketch and Narrative of the War between the States*, ed. Frank E. Vandiver (Bloomington, Ind., 1960), pp. 256-59.

13. General Junius Daniel (June 27, 1828–May 13, 1864) was born at Halifax, North Carolina. Graduated from West Point in 1851, he served briefly in the army and then resigned to return to agricultural pursuits in Louisiana. In 1861 Daniel was elected colonel of the Fourteenth North Carolina Infantry. He was promoted to brigadier general on September 1, 1862, and assigned to the division of Robert Rodes. Daniel performed distinguished service at the Battle of Gettysburg. He was killed at Spotsylvania Court House. See Cullum, *Biog. Register*, 2:300; and Warner, *Generals in Gray*, pp. 66-67.

14. The home of H. Spangler was located east of the Emmitsburg road, approximately 650 yards north of the Peach Orchard. Douglas S. Freeman, *Lee's Lieutenants: A Study in Command*, 3 vols. (New York, 1944), 3:154.

15. General Alfred Iverson, Jr. (February 14, 1829–March 31, 1911) was born in Clinton, Jones County, Georgia. Iverson served in the war with Mexico as a volunteer officer and was commissioned directly into the army on March 3, 1855. He resigned when his state seceded and was soon elected colonel of the Twentieth North Carolina Infantry. Iverson was commissioned brigadier general on November 1, 1862, and he led his brigade at Chancellorsville and Gettysburg. Following the war he was engaged in business in Georgia and in agriculture in Florida. See Warner, *Generals in Gray*, pp. 147-48.

16. The identity of this corps is found in Freeman, *Lee's Lieutenants*, 3:89.

17. General James Johnston Pettigrew (July 4, 1828–July 17, 1863) was born at "Bonarva" in Tyrell County, North Carolina. Educated at the University of North Carolina, he was awarded a position as assistant professor at the Naval Observatory in Washington in 1847. Pettigrew became a colonel of South Carolina militia in 1861 and subsequently served in Hampton's Legion. As colonel of the Twelfth South Carolina, he was soon ordered to Virginia and was commissioned a brigadier general on February 26, 1862. At Gettysburg Pettigrew commanded the division of Henry Heth with distinction. The failure here noted by Hotchkiss to sustain Pickett was not Pettigrew's fault; in the advance his horse was shot from under him and the canister and rifle fire was so heavy that it almost destroyed his command. Pettigrew commanded a section of the rear guard in the retreat from Gettysburg, and was wounded on July 14 by a Federal cavalryman at Falling Waters, Maryland. He died three days later. For a short sketch see Warner, *Generals in Gray*, pp. 237-38; for Pettigrew's part at Gettysburg, see Stewart, *Pickett's Charge*, pp. 198, 209.

18. General Henry Wager Halleck (January 6, 1815–January 9, 1872) had an illustrious military career. Graduated from West Point in 1839, he was third in a class of thirty-one. Halleck's military intellectualism earned him European tours as an observer at various conflicts there, and he was known for his *Elements of Military Art and Science* (New York, 1846). Halleck was in the beginning of the war a commander in the West, and his success there as an administrator soon caused his transfer to command the Army of the Potomac. In July, 1862, he was appointed general-in-chief. Halleck retained that post, although others commanded the field army, until Grant replaced him on March 12, 1864. He was retained as chief of staff, a liaison position between Lincoln, Secretary Stanton, and Grant. The most recent biographical and military study of Halleck is by Stephen E. Ambrose, *Halleck: Lincoln's Chief of Staff* (Baton Rouge, 1962); Halleck is also prominently treated in Kenneth P. Williams, *Lincoln Finds a General*, 5 vols. (New York, 1949-59), especially vols. 3 and 4; and T. Harry Williams, *Lincoln and His Generals* (New York, 1952), pp. 301-3, which contains an excellent analysis of Halleck's position and value as chief of staff.

19. Sampson B. Robinson, a native of England, served in the Seventh Louisiana until he was permanently detailed to Hotchkiss as a topographical assistant. Robinson and Hotchkiss were fast friends, and immediately following the war Robinson returned to Hotchkiss's home and was for a time employed by his host first at the Academy and then in the surveying business. He soon returned to Louisiana and was employed by Colonel David French Boyd at the University of Louisiana at Baton Rouge. A gloss on a picture in the Louisiana State University Archives, D. F. Boyd Papers, identifies Robinson as a clerk, "valuable worker, was good at almost anything." He died at Louisiana State University and is interred in Baton Rouge. Robinson's personal property became the object of a lively correspondence between Hotchkiss and Boyd and also between Nellie Hotchkiss and Boyd. Hotchkiss was greatly interested in the school and grateful that Boyd had taken care of his friend; Nellie, apparently enamored of Robinson, wrote for his property. Litigation on the part of Robinson's family apparently blocked her efforts to obtain it, or even a memento by which to remember him. Letters and pictures are located in the Fleming Collection, Louisiana State University Archives, in the Louisiana State University Collection of Pictures of Faculty, and in the Boyd Letterbooks: Hotchkiss to Boyd, October 16, 1871; Robinson

to Boyd, September 22, 1865; Nellie Hotchkiss to Boyd, April 17, 1876; Robinson to Boyd, December 10, 1866; and Robinson to Boyd, March 10, 1866, Louisiana State University Archives.

20. This reluctance to reengage the enemy is rendered more understandable by historical perspective. Meade's army had also been severely punished at Gettysburg; however, the lost opportunity to attack a weakened army that was trapped with a swollen river at its back undoubtedly prolonged the war. Lincoln was highly critical of Meade's immobility, characterizing it as being like an old woman shooing her geese across a creek. Indeed, Meade seemed to miss the entire military concept of the invasion and his victory when he wrote to Lincoln that the invader had been driven from northern soil. Lincoln's reaction showed clearly that he realized that the object of armies is to defeat armies. Moreover, it was not enough to chase out the invader, since the invader was also a revolutionary who needed to be positively defeated. Lincoln could only say: "Drive the invader from our soil! My God! Is that all?" Quoted in Williams, *Lincoln and His Generals*, p. 265, from David H. Bates, *Lincoln and the Telegraph Office* (New York, 1907), p. 402.

21. Probably Major McHenry Howard, who served on the staffs of Generals Winder, Trimble, Steuart, and Edward Johnson. Howard's *Recollections of a Maryland Soldier and Staff Officer* (Baltimore, 1914) is one of the more valuable personal narratives of military operations.

22. Thus in the small things that mean the most to the soldier in the ranks is the failure of the second northern invasion characterized. Partially undertaken in an effort to supply the army, it ended with a substantial portion of the command returning barefoot.

23. Williamson, like Robinson, was another of the revolving staff that assisted Hotchkiss in the preparation of topographical materials. His rank, however, was unusual; most of Hotchkiss's assistants were enlisted men.

24. This title was not new for Smith, but his duties had recently changed. Serving Lee's engineering and topographical needs was more than a one-man job. Therefore, on July 28 Smith was assigned to full-time staff work, and Major T. M. R. Talcott was promoted to command the engineer regiment. Nichols, *Confederate Engineers*, p. 94.

25. General George Gordon Meade (December 21, 1815–November 6, 1872), born in Cadiz, Spain, was graduated nineteenth in the class of 1835 at West Point. Meade was assigned a brigade of volunteers on August 31, 1861, and by November 29, 1862, he was a major general. He replaced Hooker in command of the Army of the Potomac on June 28, 1863, on the eve of the Battle of Gettysburg, and retained that command longer than any other man. Meade was made a major general in the Regular Army on August 18, 1864. Meade's own story is *The Life and Letters of George Gordon Meade*, 2 vols. (New York, 1913); an old biography is Richard M. Bache, *The Life of General George Gordon Meade* (Philadelphia, 1897); much more recent is Freeman Cleves, *Meade of Gettysburg* (Norman, Okla., 1960). Shorter sketches may be found in *DAB*, s.v. Meade, George G.; and Cullum, *Biog. Register*, 1:472-73.

26. Pisgah Church is located about four miles from the Rapidan on the road from Orange Court House to Sommerville Ford. See Early, *War Memoirs*, pp. 105, 285.

27. Major John M. Bell, an old friend of Hotchkiss's and a longtime Valley resident.

CHAPTER NINE

1. The romance between Sandie Pendleton and Catherine Carter ("Kate") Corbin was an outgrowth of the winter's residence of the Second Corps at the home of James Parke Corbin. They were married on December 29, 1863, and Sandie was dead within ten months. One month after his death Kate gave birth to their only child, a boy, who was christened in honor of his father. In an apparently healthy infancy little Sandie was stricken with diphtheria, and he died on September 1, 1865,

in the tenth month of his first year. In the words of W. G. Bean, Sandie's biographer, "The vicissitudes of this devoted couple reveal the heart-rending effect of the Civil War on the personal lives of those in the ardor of youth." Bean, *Stonewall's Man: Sandie Pendleton* (Chapel Hill, 1959), p. viii, and generally chaps. 6, 10, 11, and 13.

2. Hotchkiss's little department was growing. He began his assignment with Jackson in 1862 aided only by a driver, a wagon, and a team. Now at the command of a small topographical section creating and reproducing maps for several general officers, he is by this time established as the topographical clearinghouse of the field command.

3. Cooke's biography, "By a Virginian," published in Richmond in 1863, was the first of many. The Cooke biography was itself reprinted several times with the author's name attached. It was frankly eulogistic.

4. President Davis's proclamation, issued on July 25 for execution on August 21, enjoined the southern people to "receive in humble thankfulness the lesson which He has taught in our recent reverses, devoutly acknowledging that to Him, and not to our own feeble arms, are due the honor and glory of victory"; James D. Richardson, ed., *A Compilation of the Messages and Papers of the Confederacy*, 2 vols. (Nashville, 1906), 1:328.

5. General Stephen Dodson Ramseur, whose biography has been previously noted, was now twenty-seven and the youngest major general in the Confederate army. This is a significant example of how attrition had elevated the very young to high responsibility.

6. General Robert Frederick Hoke (May 27, 1837–July 3, 1912) was born at Lincolnton, North Carolina. A graduate of the Kentucky Military Institute, Hoke was engaged in business before the war. He entered the Confederate army as a second lieutenant of the First North Carolina Volunteers. Hoke advanced through the ranks until he was appointed brigadier general on January 17, 1863, and major general on April 21, 1864. He returned to North Carolina and was with J. E. Johnston at the final surrender. Ezra J. Warner, *Generals in Gray: Lives of the Confederate Commanders* (Baton Rouge, 1959), pp. 140-41.

7. Jackson had long felt assured of his eternal reward. He had been slow to associate himself with a particular denomination, but once he became a Presbyterian he accepted Calvinism completely and was confident from the day of his conversion that his destination was Heaven. See Frank E. Vandiver, *Mighty Stonewall* (New York, 1957), pp. 86-87. In the gloom of May 10, 1863, when told that he was soon to die, Jackson said that he preferred it, glad that the day was Sunday, the best of all days on which to die. Later when McGuire confirmed the inevitable, Jackson said, "Very good, very good, it is all right." See Hunter McGuire and George L. Christian, *The Confederate Cause and Conduct in the War between the States* (Richmond, 1907), p. 228; and especially Vandiver, *Mighty Stonewall*, p. 494.

8. General Edwin (Ned) Gray Lee, a distant kinsman of Robert E. Lee, was Sandie Pendleton's brother-in-law. He was a graduate of Hallowell Military Academy and of the College of William and Mary. Before the war he was a lawyer in Shepherdstown, Virginia. Ned Lee served in the Stonewall Brigade and in the Thirty-third Virginia Regiment. In 1862 he was on Jackson's staff for a short time. Because of ill health, he was forced to retire from the field in 1863, but he continued in semiactive status until he was promoted to general in charge of an army post at Staunton. In 1865 Lee was sent on a diplomatic mission to Canada. He died of tuberculosis in 1870. See Bean, *Sandie Pendleton*, p. 64 n; and Warner, *Generals in Gray*, pp. 177-78.

9. General Jubal A. Early was a difficult man to get along with. His *War Memoirs: Autobiographical Sketch and Narrative of the War between the States*, ed. Frank E. Vandiver (Bloomington, Ind., 1960), pp. 307 ff., relates an incident in which he is critical of Hays's Seventh Louisiana and their fortifications on the Rappahannock. He does, however, commend their valor.

10. Jackson's health, and his own ideas about it, have been given much atten-

tion by historians. His weak eyesight, for instance, and his absolute refusal to read by artificial light, his occasional elevation of an arm to stimulate circulation, and his frequent trips to resorts to "take the waters" all may seem eccentric. However, each of these examples reflects common sense and the contemporary ideas about the curative powers of mineral waters. While it is true that Jackson was never robust, his childhood, adolescence, and adulthood could generally be called normal from the standpoint of health. Mrs. Jackson's comment about his inability to endure hard work may well be true; but he was sufficiently healthy to endure the rigors of West Point, service in the heat of southern Texas, Mexico, and Florida, and two years of active field command in the Civil War.

11. General Benjamin F. Butler (November 15, 1818–January 11, 1893) was born at Deerfield, Massachusetts. He was educated at Waterbury (Colby) College in Maine, but he did not graduate. On the eve of the war he was elected brigadier general of militia, a position both earned and retained through political influence. Butler is undoubtedly best known for his command of the Department of Louisiana, especially the occupation of New Orleans. In 1863 he commanded the districts of eastern Virginia and North Carolina. Following the war Butler was elected to Congress where he was allied with the Radical Republicans. His own version of a colorful career is *Personal Reminiscences of Major-General Benjamin F. Butler: Butler's Book* (Boston, 1892); see also C. E. Macartney, *Grant and His Generals* (New York, 1953); *DAB*, s.v. Butler, Benjamin F.; *Biog. Dir. Amer. Cong.*, p. 638.

12. Governor William ("Extra Billy") Smith (September 6, 1797–May 18, 1887) was born at "Marengo" in King George County, Virginia. Educated in Virginia and in Connecticut, he became a lawyer and a mail contractor in Virginia. He offered daily service between Washington and points farther and farther south, extending finally to Milledgeville, Georgia. His peculiar name came from this rapid expansion and the "extra" payments that he received. In the antebellum period Smith served five years in the Virginia Senate, five terms in Congress, and one term as governor. He entered the war as colonel of the Forty-ninth Virginia Infantry, but was soon elected to Congress. He was appointed brigadier general on January 31, 1863, and major general on August 12, 1864. In the latter year he was again elected governor of Virginia. Following the war he was engaged in agriculture, and he served one final term in the state legislature. See Warner, *Generals in Gray*, pp. 284-85; *Biog. Dir. Amer. Cong.*, p. 1625.

13. This is a good example of how fast rumor, in this case true, can sweep an army. On August 31 Lee wrote to Longstreet and directed him to prepare for offensive operations. Longstreet replied advising against an offense at that time. He maintained that the army was not strong enough for such action, but he recommended that he be sent to Tennessee where there was a greater possibility of success. Word rapidly spread that he was going, and it also included the intelligence that he was supplanting Bragg in command of the Army of Tennessee. Actually, Longstreet had this in mind and was making a bid for independent command. President Davis did not wish Bragg to be thus handled, and of course he was not; but Longstreet went anyway, with a large part of the First Corps. For an account of the command maneuvers and Longstreet's sojourn in the west, see Douglas S. Freeman, *Lee's Lieutenants: A Study in Command*, 3 vols. (New York, 1944), 3:222-28.

14. Dr. Robert Lewis Dabney's biography, *Life and Campaigns of Lieutenant General Thomas J. Jackson*, was published in New York in 1866.

15. Apparently they were needed to aid in the defense of Charleston, which was under almost constant attack during the summer of 1863. For a detailed discussion of these activities see the various articles in *Battles and Leaders*, 4:1-75.

16. Major A. L. Pitzer was an aide on the staff of General Jubal A. Early. For a portrait, see Early, *War Memoirs*, p. 107.

17. Captain W. D. Brown commanded the Fourth Maryland, or "Chesapeake" Battery. See Jennings C. Wise, *The Long Arm of Lee: The History of the Artillery of the Army of Northern Virginia* (New York, 1941), p. 983.

18. Captain W. F. Dement commanded the First Maryland Battery.

19. Hotchkiss refers to "Springfield," built by Colonel Philip Slaughter in Culpeper County, Virginia.

20. It was charged that Lee was denied his "Eyes" in the midst of enemy territory by Stuart's absence on an independent cavalry raid and hence was unable to function with the celerity which was necessary for coping with such a situation. Freeman called the net gain of the raid, 125 wagons, the price of the campaign and perhaps of the war. The concluding sentence of chap. 4 of *Lee's Lieutenants* (3:51-72) is a searing indictment: "Other adventure was to be his, but nothing he had achieved and nothing he could hope to accomplish with his exhausted men could offset the harm which the events of the coming days were to show he already had done his chief and his cause."

21. The Battle of Chickamauga, September 19, 1863, was indeed a case of Bragg whipping Rosecrans. Bragg had been defending Chattanooga, Tennessee, when Longstreet was ordered west to assist him in an offensive move. Longstreet's reinforcements of 10,000 men brought Bragg's command to 62,000. Opposing him was the Army of the Cumberland, commanded by William S. Rosecrans, numbering 65,000. As Rosecrans approached, Bragg withdrew from the city about fifteen miles, and Rosecrans came after him. The battle raged throughout September 19. The Federal line was broken and driven into hasty retreat, including its commander, who fled to the safety of Chattanooga. General George H. Thomas protected the rear and in fact stopped the Confederate assault, earning the name "Rock of Chickamauga." For a detailed examination of the battle, see Joseph Mitchell, *Decisive Battles of the Civil War* (New York, 1955), pp. 169-73; and Indexes to Johnson and Buel, eds., *Battles and Leaders of the Civil War*, and the *Official Records*.

22. Mr. Jonathan Arnold, Jackson's brother-in-law, was apparently the antithesis of the general. He had little interest in religion and was not a military man, but apparently they got on well enough except at election time. Arnold was a Whig, Jackson a Democrat. Arnold's son was named for Jackson, and Jackson helped with his education financially and allowed him to live in his home in Lexington. Vandiver, *Mighty Stonewall*, pp. 47, 53, 94, and 121.

23. Gradually the full knowledge of Bragg's victory came across the mountains to cheer the veterans of Gettysburg. Bragg now had Rosecrans besieged in Chattanooga, and he held his forces fast for nearly two months. Finally Grant came to command the disheartened Union army and by the end of November, 1863, after the battles for Missionary Ridge and Lookout Mountain, the siege was lifted. Then the inevitable Confederate retreat began again. See Mitchell, *Decisive Battles of the Civil War*, pp. 174-81.

24. Louis Trezevent Wigfall (April 21, 1816–February 18, 1874) was born at Edgefield, South Carolina. He attended the University of Virginia and was graduated in 1837 from the South Carolina College. In 1848 Wigfall moved to Texas to practice law. He served in both houses of the state legislature and in the United States House of Representatives, and in 1859 he was elected to the Senate. An extreme secessionist attitude caused his expulsion from the latter chamber in July, 1861, but he was soon elected to the Confederate Congress. He was also commissioned a colonel in the First Texas Infantry, and on October 21, 1861, became a brigadier general. He resigned his military commission to serve in the Confederate Senate. See *DAB*, s.v. Wigfall, Louis T.; Warner, *Generals in Gray*, pp. 336-37; *Biog. Dir. Amer. Cong.*, p. 1813; for his legislative role in Richmond, see Index to W. B. Yearns, *The Confederate Congress* (Athens, Georgia, 1960).

25. Smith was successfully engaged in a campaign to be reelected governor of Virginia. He was inaugurated on the following January 1, 1864.

26. Lieutenant P. W. O. Köerner.

27. Entries for the period October 7 through 19, 1863, are inexplicably absent.

28. During the Bristow campaign of October, 1863, Imboden was instructed to move down the Valley and guard the mountain passes. On the 18th he captured and

held the garrison at Charlestown (West) Virginia, for which he was commended by General Robert E. Lee. See *CMH*, 3:423-30, 610.

29. On June 9, 1863, Brandy Station was the location of one of Stuart's most contested engagements. Here for the first time Union cavalry under the command of General Alfred Pleasonton held their own against the seemingly invincible Stuart.

30. General Harry Thompson Hays (April 14, 1820–August 21, 1876) was born in Wilson County, Tennessee, but lived his early years in Wilkinson County, Mississippi. He was educated at St. Mary's College in Baltimore, but he moved to New Orleans to practice law. Hays entered the Confederate service as colonel of the Seventh Louisiana Infantry and was commissioned a brigadier general on July 25, 1862. Hays was at First Manassas, in the Valley Campaign of 1862, at Sharpsburg, Fredericksburg, Chancellorsville, Gettysburg, and the Wilderness. After the war he practiced law in New Orleans and served briefly as sheriff of Orleans parish. See Warner, *Generals in Gray*, p. 130.

31. The now empty mansion of Jeremiah Morton, Virginia educator and politician, was located on the south bank of the Rapidan. Its owner had moved to safer territory. The mansion had been appropriated by General Ewell in the autumn of 1863 as quarters for Mrs. Ewell when she came to visit in the winter. See Freeman, *Lee's Lieutenants*, 3:331.

32. Major Campbell Brown, in addition to being Ewell's stepson by virtue of the General's marriage to the much younger Lizinka Campbell Brown, also served on his staff as Assistant Adjutant General. Freeman, *Lee's Lieutenants*, 3:331.

33. The plans for the Pendleton-Corbin wedding had to be postponed, now for the third time, from the November 25 date that the couple had finally settled on. Pendleton apparently was rushing to Moss Neck to smooth once again the ruffled feelings of his fiancée. The wedding was finally held on December 29, 1863. For the perils of wartime romance, see Bean, *Sandie Pendleton*, pp. 155-83.

34. This is further evidence that Hotchkiss planned to write following the war. Much of this copy work is in the Hotchkiss Papers, Manuscript Division, Library of Congress.

35. On November 25, 1863, the Federals succeeded in breaking the siege that Bragg had laid around Chattanooga. The decisive action for Missionary Ridge fought on that day saw the forces of General George H. Thomas once again distinguish themselves by sweeping the hills to the south of the city. Both Federals and Confederates were surprised at the ease with which it was done. See Mitchell, *Decisive Battles of the Civil War*, pp. 178-81.

36. Colonel John Thompson Brown (February 6, 1835–May 7, 1864) was born in Petersburg, Virginia. Thompson was a lawyer in civilian life, but he was now senior officer of artillery in the Second Corps. Freeman, *Lee's Lieutenants*, 3:367 and n.

37. Colonel Walter Herron Taylor (June 13, 1838–March 1, 1916) was born in Norfolk, Virginia. Taylor was educated at Norfolk Academy and at the Virginia Military Institute. He joined the staff of General Robert E. Lee in September, 1861, and served in that capacity throughout the war. Ultimately he became adjutant general of the Army of Northern Virginia. Taylor wrote of his experiences in *Four Years with General Lee*, originally published in 1877, and now reprinted with an introduction by James I. Robertson, Jr. (Bloomington, 1962).

CHAPTER TEN

1. General William Woods Averell (November 5, 1832–February 3, 1900) was born at Cameron, New York. He was graduated from West Point in 1855. He entered the war as colonel of a Pennsylvania regiment, but in September, 1862, he was chosen brigadier general for a cavalry unit. Averell's Raiders staged a series of sudden strikes in western Virginia in the summer and fall of 1863. The action of which Hotchkiss speaks was an attempt in December to cut the line of communication between Lee in Virginia and Bragg in Tennessee. Averell crossed the icy mountain

roads to destroy the Virginia and Tennessee Railroad at Salem. All the commands from Staunton to Newport were ordered out to capture the raider, but he managed to escape. In all, he covered 340 miles in thirteen days, destroyed invaluable railroad property, and captured 200 Confederates. See Cullum, *Biog. Register*, 2:411-12; *DAB*, s.v. Averell, William Woods; Jubal A. Early, *War Memoirs: Autobiographical Sketch and Narrative of the War between the States*, ed. Frank E. Vandiver (Bloomington, Ind., 1960), pp. 326-42.

2. General William Lowther ("Mudwall") Jackson (February 3, 1825–March 24, 1890) was born at Clarksburg, (West) Virginia. Jackson's legal career led him into public service as jurist, legislator, and lieutenant governor of Virginia. In 1861 he enlisted in the army as a private, but was soon elected colonel of the Thirty-first Virginia Infantry. He served for a period on the staff of his famous cousin, "Stonewall" Jackson, until he recruited the Nineteenth Virginia Cavalry and became its colonel. He was promoted to brigadier general on December 19, 1864. After the war Jackson lived briefly in Mexico, and then in Kentucky, where he practiced law and served as a judge. See Ezra J. Warner, *Generals in Gray: Lives of the Confederate Commanders* (Baton Rouge, 1959), pp. 154-55.

3. Though these maps were sent to Colonel William P. Smith at Lee's headquarters, copies were no doubt sent also to Jeremy Gilmer at the Engineer Bureau in Richmond. Hotchkiss also retained copies of his maps, most of which are still in the Hotchkiss Collection in the Library of Congress. Some were purchased for the army in 1866, and others were published in the *Atlas* to the *Official Records*. Of the 202 Confederate maps in the volume, approximately one-half were contributed by Hotchkiss. See Clara E. Le Gear, ed., *Hotchkiss Map Collection* (Washington, 1951), and Le Gear, "The Hotchkiss Map Collection," *Library of Congress Quarterly Journal of Current Acquisitions*, vol. 6.

4. Very probably Colonel D. B. Harris, engineering officer who was on the staff of General Beauregard.

5. Like Washington to the Confederates, Richmond seemed the goal of the war to the Federals. The lesson of modern war was well enough learned by then—that armies are the objectives of armies. But the natural value of capturing the enemy's capital made the effort worth it. Pictures taken by the early visitors from the North after the surrender resemble those taken in Berlin in 1945, so great was the destruction. For the story of Richmond and how it bore the dignity of a capital city in wartime, see Alfred Hoyt Boyd, *The Beleaguered City, Richmond, 1861-1865* (New York, 1946).

6. C. W. Oltmanns, who is variously referred to as "Olts." and "O.," was a draughtsman assigned to Hotchkiss. He worked for Hotchkiss until the end of the war.

7. General Martin Luther Smith (September 9, 1819–July 29, 1866) was born at Danby, Tompkins County, New York. Smith was graduated in 1842 from West Point and assigned to the topographical engineers. Except for a tour in Mexico during the war there, his service was spent almost entirely in the South. He therefore resigned from the army on April 1, 1861, to join the Confederate army. First a major of engineers, he also served as colonel of the Twenty-first Louisiana Infantry. Smith was appointed a brigadier general on April 11, 1862, and a major general on November 4, 1862. Ultimately he became chief engineer of both major Confederate armies. See Warner, *Generals in Gray*, pp. 282-83; Cullum, *Biog. Register*, 2:49; Index to James L. Nichols, *Confederate Engineers* (Tuscaloosa, 1957).

8. Early omits any discussion of the incident in his *War Memoirs*, but Freeman (*Lee's Lieutenants*, 3:333) discusses it at some length. The occasion for the arrest is not known, but the specification was for "conduct subversive of good order and military discipline." Freeman hints strongly that the real trouble lay in Early's ambition to succeed the ailing Ewell and in Mrs. Ewell's quite equal ambition for her husband and her desire to keep Early from getting his command. Lee dismissed the affair as being Early's fault, but he urged that harmony among officers was more important

than punishment. It apparently did not cause permanent hard feelings between the two officers, and Early eventually did get Ewell's command, when the latter retired from active command because of bad health.

CHAPTER ELEVEN

1. The Wilderness Campaign conducted in the summer of 1864 was one of the most costly of the war to both sides. It involved two armies for each side: Meade's Army of the Potomac and Butler's Army of the James for the Union, and for the Confederacy Lee's Army of Northern Virginia and a second force under Beauregard hastily formed to protect Richmond. Grant was the overall Union commander, and the campaign is customarily regarded as a struggle between the General-in-Chief and General Lee. It began on the eve of May 3 with the Battle of the Wilderness, and concluded on June 3 with the Battle of Cold Harbor. The heavy Union losses in the latter action caused a pause in the fighting. The toll was equally heavy on the Confederates, and in a way their loss was more severe, since their capacity to replace the casualties with able-bodied men was nearly gone. At the begining of the campaign Grant had approximately 110,000 men, while Lee had only 62,000. Losses to both sides were approximately 50 percent. One of the more serious blows to the Confederacy was the accidental wounding of General Longstreet by Southern soldiers, a wound that removed him from service for nearly six months. For studies of the campaign, see Joseph Mitchell, *Decisive Battles of the Civil War* (New York, 1955), pp. 189-92; Edward Steere, *The Wilderness Campaign* (Harrisburg, Pa., 1960).

2. According to Gordon it was only the darkness and not the resistance of Union soldiers that compelled the assault to stop. For Gordon's view of the campaign, see his *Reminiscences of the Civil War* (New York, 1903), pp. 235-61.

3. General Truman Seymour, a native of Vermont, was a graduate of West Point (1846). Seymour was exchanged on August 9, 1864, after being held prisoner at Charleston, South Carolina. Cullum, *Biog. Register*, 2:151-52.

4. General Alexander Shaler. Gordon credits both of these officers with gallantry for their attempt to rally their men. Panic had already seized the Federals, however, and most were captured. See Gordon, *Reminiscences of the Civil War*, pp. 248-50.

5. Captain Thomas T. Turner was an aide on the staff of General Richard S. Ewell. He was also engaged to marry Ewell's stepdaughter, Harriet Brown. For a humorous discussion of such nepotism, see Douglas Southall Freeman, *Lee's Lieutenants: A Study in Command*, 3 vols. (New York, 1944), 3:332.

6. Many of the European countries had press representatives with the armies observing and reporting the American fratricide. Hewson, evidently a gentleman who knew how to make friends, seems really to have impressed Hotchkiss with "delicacies" and conversation. His investment was no doubt repaid by the loquacious Hotchkiss with many items of news value.

7. General Cadmus Marcellus Wilcox (May 29, 1824–December 2, 1890) was born in Wayne County, North Carolina, but grew to manhood in Tipton County, Tennessee. He was educated at the University of Tennessee and at West Point, graduating from the latter institution in 1846. On June 8, 1861, he resigned from the Federal service and subsequently entered the Confederate army as colonel of the Ninth Alabama Infantry. He was promoted to brigadier general on October 21, 1861, and to major general on August 3, 1863. See Cullum, *Biog. Register*, 2:177-78; and Ezra J. Warner, *Generals in Gray: Lives of the Confederate Commanders* (Baton Rouge, 1959), pp. 337-38.

8. General Henry Heth (December 16, 1825–September 27, 1899) was born in Chesterfield County, Virginia. Graduated from West Point in 1847, he rose to the rank of captain before he resigned in 1861. Heth served in the Confederate army as colonel of the Forty-fifth Virginia Infantry until January 6, 1862, when he was promoted to brigadier general. He was commissioned a major general on February 17, 1864. He served in both major theaters of the war, under Kirby Smith in Kentucky and under A. P. Hill in Virginia. After the war he was in the insurance business in

Richmond. For short sketches of his life, see *CMH*, 3:601-3; Cullum, *Biog. Register*, 2:206; and Warner, *Generals in Gray*, p. 133.

9. General J. E. B. Stuart had been wounded on May 11 while directing the interception of General Sheridan's cavalrymen at Yellow Tavern. He was wounded in the abdomen, probably through the liver, by a trooper from the Fifth Michigan firing a pistol. Stuart refused a stimulant because he said he had promised his mother that he would never drink alcohol. All who were near tried to be reassuring, but Stuart knew from the first that his wound was mortal. For descriptions of Stuart's last days, of his constant urging of his fellows to fight on, and of the tributes paid to Stuart after his death, see Index to Henry B. McClellan, *I Rode with Jeb Stuart* (Bloomington, 1958), and William W. Blackford, *War Years with Jeb Stuart* (New York, 1945), for two accounts written by staff members. For a modern narrative see Freeman, *Lee's Lieutenants*, 3:424-31.

10. General Christopher Colon Augur (July 10, 1821–January 16, 1898) was a native of New York. He was graduated from West Point in 1843, and he served in the war with Mexico as an aide to Generals Hoping and Cushing. Augur was made a brigadier general of volunteers in 1861. On October 13, 1863, Augur was placed in command of the Department of Washington and of the Twenty-second Corps, not the Twenty-first as Hotchkiss reports. See Cullum, *Biog. Register*, 2:82-83.

11. General John Cabell Breckinridge (January 15, 1821–May 17, 1875) was born near Lexington, Kentucky. Graduated from Center College in 1839, Breckinridge studied law at Transylvania University and was admitted to practice in Lexington in 1845. Politics was a natural calling for Breckinridge; he served in the state legislature, 1849-51; in the House of Representatives, 1851-55; and in 1856 he was elected vice-president to James Buchanan. Although opposed to the act, if not the right, of secession, and opposed to war, he accepted a brigadier's commission in the Confederate army on November 2, 1861. He was promoted to major general on April 14, 1862. Breckinridge fought at Shiloh, Vicksburg, Murfreesboro, and Chickamauga. He commanded the Department of Southwest Virginia briefly during 1864, and in that year accompanied Early on his raid on Washington. On February 4, 1865, Breckinridge was appointed the final Confederate secretary of war. After the war he lived briefly in England but he returned to Kentucky in 1869. For short sketches, see Warner, *Generals in Gray*, pp. 34-35; *Biog. Dir. Amer. Cong.*, p. 592; *DAB*, s.v. Breckinridge, John C.; and Rembert W. Patrick, *Jefferson Davis and His Cabinet* (Baton Rouge, 1961), pp. 149-54. A full biography is Lucille Stillwell, *John Cabell Breckinridge: Born to Be a Statesman* (Caldwell, Idaho, 1936).

12. General Matthew Calbraith Butler (March 8, 1836–April 14, 1909) was born in Greenville, North Carolina. He was educated at South Carolina College. Butler was a member of the South Carolina legislature in 1861, but he resigned to become a captain in Hampton's Legion. He advanced through the ranks to become a brigadier general on September 1, 1863, and a major general on September 19, 1864. Butler commanded cavalry units under both Hampton and Stuart. Following the war he was elected to the United States Senate in 1876. He served as a major general in the war with Spain in 1898. See *DAB*, s.v. Butler, Matthew C., pp. 363-64; *Biog. Dir. Amer. Cong.*, pp. 639-40; and Warner, *Generals in Gray*, pp. 40-41.

13. Ramseur was appointed on the 27th to command the division of Jubal Early. Early then assumed command of the Second Corps, and Ewell was transferred to the more sedentary Department of Richmond. The change was the result of Ewell's incapacitation due to illness, age, and discomfort from his wounds. Though he was still an able general, his condition demanded that he be replaced. Early was promoted to lieutenant general on May 31 to provide appropriate rank for his new position. See Jubal A. Early, *War Memoirs: Autobiographical Sketch and Narrative of the War between the States*, ed. Frank E. Vandiver (Bloomington, Ind., 1960), p. 345; and Freeman, *Lee's Lieutenants*, 3:510-11.

14. General Johnson Hagood (February 21, 1829–January 4, 1898) was born at Barnwell, South Carolina. A graduate of the South Carolina Military Academy

(1847), Hagood studied law and was admitted to the bar in 1850. He was a brigadier general in the state militia, and in 1861 was elected colonel of the First South Carolina Volunteers when that unit took part in the attack on Fort Sumter. Hagood became a brigadier general on July 21, 1862, and was transferred to the Virginia theater, where he spent most of the war. At the end, however, he was back with Johnston in North Carolina. Hagood was active in South Carolina politics following the war, and he was elected governor of the state in 1880. A short sketch is in Warner, *Generals in Gray*, pp. 121-22; for Hagood's own story, see *Memoirs of the War of Secession* (Columbia, S.C., 1910).

15. General Joseph Robert Davis (January 12, 1825–September 15, 1896) was born in Woodville, Mississippi. Davis was educated at Miami University at Oxford, Ohio, and he practiced law in Madison County, Mississippi. He served briefly in the Mississippi Senate. He began his Confederate service as captain of a militia company but was soon the lieutenant colonel of the Tenth Mississippi Infantry. He was commissioned brigadier general on September 15, 1862. Davis's promotions were marked by charges of nepotism, since he was a nephew of President Jefferson Davis. Following the war he practiced law in Biloxi, Mississippi. For a sketch of his life see Warner, *Generals in Gray*, pp. 68-69.

16. General Joseph Finegan (November 17, 1814–October 29, 1885) was born in Clones, Ireland. In the mid-1830s he migrated to Jacksonville, Florida, and entered the lumber business. Finegan was commissioned a brigadier general on April 5, 1862, and assigned to command the District of Middle and East Florida. He was ordered to Virginia in May, 1864, and he continued to serve in that area until March, 1865. He was in Florida when the war ended. Finegan was active in business during the postwar years, particularly as a cotton broker, and he served one term in the Florida Senate (1865-66). See Warner, *Generals in Gray*, pp. 88-89.

17. Colonel T. M. R. Talcott, engineering officer assigned to the command of General Robert E. Lee.

18. This tribute to Jackson's preference for keeping his own counsel is ample evidence that the General's eccentricities were often beneficial, were well known, and were often respected. In the matter of military secrecy, Jackson took the biblical admonition literally and did not let his right hand, or flank, know what the left was up to. Hotchkiss frequently prepared maps days or even weeks in advance of a proposed move without knowing why, and certainly the remainder of the command knew no more.

19. The University of Virginia was and is located at Charlottesville. For an account of the events of this day and of the entire raid on Washington, see Frank Vandiver, *Jubal's Raid, General Early's Attack on Washington in 1864* (New York, 1960); and Early, *War Memoirs*, pp. 380-98.

20. General Arnold Elzey (December 18, 1816–February 21, 1871) was born at "Elmwood" in Somerset County, Maryland. He was graduated from West Point in 1837. Elzey served in the Seminole uprising and in Mexico, and at the time of the Civil War he was stationed in Georgia. He resigned to accept a captaincy in the Second Artillery, and on April 25, 1861, he became colonel of the First Maryland Infantry. He was promoted to brigadier general by President Davis on the field of First Manassas for his gallantry in the battle. Elzey continued to serve under Jackson until wounded in the Seven Day's fighting. Promoted to major general on December 4, 1862, Elzey commanded the Department of Richmond and helped to organize the defenses of that city. He was again wounded at Cold Harbor, and upon his recovery was sent to Hood and the Army of Tennessee as chief of artillery. Following the war Elzey farmed in Anne Arundel County, Maryland. See Cullum, *Biog. Register*, 1:539; Eliot Ellsworth, Jr., *West Point in the Confederacy* (New York, 1941), pp. 330-31; Warner, *Generals in Gray*, pp. 82-83.

21. General John McCausland (September 13, 1836–January 22, 1927) was born in Saint Louis, Missouri. He was educated at Point Pleasant, (West) Virginia, and at the Virginia Military Institute. McCausland was first in the class of 1857. After

further study at the University of Virginia, he returned to the Institute as an assistant professor of mathematics. McCausland served as colonel of the thirty-sixth Virginia, and was appointed brigadier general on May 18, 1864. Prior to this command he had served under John B. Floyd at Fort Donelson and in Virginia under Generals Loring, Echols, and Sam Jones. In 1864 he was with Early on the famous Washington raid and was the officer in charge of the burning of Chambersburg, Pennsylvania. Following the war McCausland lived in Europe, in Mexico, and finally in Mason County, West Virginia. See *DAB*, s.v. McCausland, John; and Warner, *Generals in Gray*, pp. 197-98.

22. Colonel John Singleton Mosby (December 6, 1833–May 30, 1916) was born in Edgemount, Powhatan County, Virginia. He attended the University of Virginia, but before being graduated he was forced to leave to serve a jail sentence for wounding a fellow student. In 1855 he was admitted to the bar, and he practiced law in Bristol, Virginia. Mosby entered the Confederate cavalry in 1861, and during the early years he served under Stuart. But his principal service began on January 2, 1863, when he was given independent command of a company of Rangers, or partisans. Mosby's Rangers were famed and feared for their daring raids and exploits both north and south of the Potomac. They were considered outlaws by the Union commanders. Following the war Mosby practiced law in Warrenton. He later joined the Republican party and served in various federal posts, including that of consul to Hong Kong, land agent, and assistant attorney for the Department of Justice. For Mosby's version of his wartime experiences see John S. Mosby, *Mosby's Reminiscences and Stuart's Cavalry Campaign*, ed. Virgil C. Jones (Boston, 1887; reprint Bloomington, 1959). The best biography is by Jones, *Ranger Mosby* (Chapel Hill, 1944). See also *DAB*, s.v. Mosby, John S.

23. The home of Francis P. Blair, postmaster general of the United States, was located near Silver Spring. Maps were not the only prizes provided by the luxurious home; the vintage wine in Blair's cellar was looted and enjoyed by the officers. Unfortunately the house burned on the night of the 13th, and although Early was blamed for it he stubbornly denied doing such a foolish thing. While it was richly deserved, he maintained, he would not have allowed such a spectacle to draw attention to his position. See Vandiver, *Jubal's Raid*, p. 152; and Early, *War Memoirs*, p. 395.

24. Early did indeed come to within sight of the Federal capitol, but the heat and the dusty roads had taken their toll. The raiders were unable to take their objective, but they did interject a large portion of fear into Washington. Kyd Douglas (*I Rode with Stonewall* [Chapel Hill, 1940], pp. 295-96) reported that Early said to him, "Major, we haven't taken Washington, but we've scared Abe Lincoln like hell!" Lincoln had been under fire when he went to observe the city's defenders holding Early's forces outside the limits of the town. But as Douglas also said, correcting the General, ". . . this afternoon when that Yankee line moved against us, I think some other people were scared as hell's brimstone." Early was forced to agree. For a discussion of this exchange, see Douglas, *I Rode with Stonewall*; Frank E. Vandiver, *Mighty Stonewall* (New York, 1957); and especially Freeman, *Lee's Lieutenants*, 3:567.

25. General Gabriel Colvin Wharton (July 23, 1824–May 12, 1906) was born in Culpeper County, Virginia. He was an honor graduate of the Virginia Military Institute (1847), and before the war he was an engineer in the West. Wharton was elected major of the Forty-fifth Virginia Infantry in July, 1861, and in August he became colonel of the Fifty-first Virginia Infantry. He was promoted to brigadier general on July 8, 1863, and temporarily placed in command of the Valley District. Wharton was with Early in the Valley and on the famous Washington raid. After the war he lived in Radford, Virginia, and engaged in mining and in state politics. See *CMH*, 3:684-85; and Warner, *Generals in Gray*, p. 331.

26. General John Crawford Vaughn (February 24, 1824–September 10, 1875) was born in Roane County, Tennessee. He served in the Mexican War as an infantry captain, but he was a merchant in Tennessee when the war began in 1861. He entered the Confederate army as colonel of the Third Tennessee Infantry, and on

September 22, 1862, he was made a brigadier general. During the Shenandoah Valley Campaign of 1864 Vaughn was given command of a cavalry brigade. On the Washington raid he was seriously wounded near Martinsburg. After the war he lived in Tennessee and in Georgia, and he served briefly in the Tennessee Senate. See Warner, *Generals in Gray*, pp. 316-17; and Freeman, *Lee's Lieutenants*, 3:526; Freeman lists Vaughn as a native of Grayson County, Virginia, although he was appointed as a general officer from Tennessee. However, Vaughn is not listed in *CMH*, 3, *Virginia*, as being from that state.

27. For an analysis of the meaning of these actions, see Freeman, *Lee's Lieutenants*, 3:571. He is particularly complimentary to Breckinridge, who "brilliantly led" Echols's Division.

CHAPTER TWELVE

1. This section of the journal has been published in the *Official Records*, ser. 1, vol. 43, pt. 1, pp. 567-88. An editor's note on p. 567 reveals that "strictly private matters" have been deleted; happily, the information that the editors considered expendable has been replaced in Hotchkiss's own hand in marginal glosses to the copy in his papers. These glosses are restored herein and are indicated by brackets. These pages discuss the Valley Campaign of 1864, involving the forces of Jubal Early and Philip Sheridan.

2. Colonel Henry A. Cole commanded the First Maryland Potomac Home Brigade, which was a unit of General Geremiah C. Sullivan's First Cavalry Division.

3. General Robert Ransom (February 12, 1828–January 15, 1892) was born in Warren County, North Carolina. He was graduated in 1850 from West Point, and his career was spent principally on the frontier until he resigned on May 4, 1861, to join the Confederate service. Ransom served as captain and then cólonel of the Ninth North Carolina Cavalry. He was commissioned brigadier general on March 1, 1862, and assigned to a command in Longstreet's corps. Ransom was promoted to major general on May 26, 1863, and transferred to eastern Tennessee for a brief period. He commanded Early's cavalry during the raid on Washington and during the fall of 1864 until forced by illness to retire. Following the war Ransom lived in New Bern, North Carolina. For references, see Ezra T. Warner, *Generals in Gray: Lives of the Confederate Commanders* (Baton Rouge, 1959), pp. 253-54; Cullum, *Biog. Register*, 2:263-64; and Eliot Ellsworth, Jr., *West Point in the Confederacy* (New York, 1941), p. 415.

4. General John Pegram (January 24, 1832–February 6, 1865) was born at Petersburg, Virginia. He was graduated from West Point in 1854 and served on the frontier until the war began. Pegram resigned on May 10, 1861, to become a lieutenant colonel in the Confederate service. Promoted to colonel, he served for a time as engineering officer on the staff of Generals Beauregard, Bragg, and later Kirby Smith. On November 7, 1862, he was promoted to brigadier general and assigned to the cavalry under the command of General Forrest. His sojourn in the west was short, and he was soon back commanding an infantry brigade under Early. He was mortally wounded in the fight at Hatcher's Run. Warner, *Generals in Gray*, pp. 232-33; *CMH*, 3:648-49; Cullum, *Biog. Register*, 2:374; and Ellsworth, *West Point in the Confederacy*, pp. 406-7.

5. Bryan's Battery, possibly commanded by Edward Brown, who at one time was a member of the Rockbridge Battery. It was principally organized from the area around Lewisburg, (West) Virginia. See Jennings C. Wise, *Long Arm of Lee: The History of the Artillery of the Army of Northern Virginia* (New York, 1941), p. 987.

6. Lowry's Battery, commanded by Captain William N. Lowry, was also known as part of the "Wise Legion."

7. This gallant officer was assigned to John B. Gordon's Division, and is credited by both John B. Gordon (*Reminiscences of the Civil War* [New York, 1903], p. 346) and Jubal A. Early (*War Memoirs: Autobiographical Sketch and Narrative of the War between the States*, ed. Frank E. Vandiver [Bloomington, Ind., 1960], p. 407) with taking and holding the mountain.

8. General Lundsford Lindsay Lomax (November 4, 1835–May 28, 1913) was born at Newport, Rhode Island. Although a native Virginian, his father was stationed in Rhode Island and attached to the Third Artillery. Lomax was educated in Richmond and Norfolk, and in 1856 he was graduated from West Point. He served in the cavalry on the frontier until April 25, 1861, when he resigned to accept a captain's commission in the service of Virginia. During the first half of the war Lomax was a staff officer with Generals Ben. McCulloch, J. E. Johnston, and Earl Von Dorn. He was transferred to Virginia as colonel of a cavalry regiment, and shortly after Gettysburg he was promoted to brigadier general. On August 10, 1864, Lomax was promoted to major general and assigned to command Early's cavalry. On March 29, 1865, he was assigned to command the Valley District. Following the war Lomax was variously engaged as a farmer, as president of Virginia Polytechnic Institute (1885-99), as an assistant in the compilation of the *Official Records* (1899-1905), and as commissioner of the Gettysburg National Military Park. For sketches of his life and service, see Cullum, *Biog. Register*, 2:430-31; Ellsworth, *West Point in the Confederacy*, pp. 380-81; *CMH*, 3:628-30; and Warner, *Generals in Gray*, pp. 190-91.

9. Augustus Forsberg's brigade of cavalry.

10. General Joseph Brevard Kershaw (January 5, 1822–April 13, 1894) was born at Camden, South Carolina. Kershaw was an attorney, but he had a brief military career as a lieutenant of the Palmetto Regiment in the Mexican War. He entered the Civil War as colonel of the Second South Carolina, but he was promoted to brigadier general on February 13, 1862. He was commissioned as a major general on May 18. Kershaw was assigned to the First Corps from First Manassas until Appomattox, except when temporarily detached to serve under Ewell in defense of Richmond. After the war he continued the practice of law. He served in the state senate, as a judge, and briefly as postmaster of Camden. See Warner, *Generals in Gray*, p. 171; and Douglas S. Freeman, *Lee's Lieutenants: A Study in Command*, 3 vols. (New York, 1944), 3:xlvi.

11. General William Terry (August 14, 1824–September 5, 1888) was born in Amherst County, Virginia. Terry was graduated from the University of Virginia in 1848. He was a teacher, a lawyer, and an editor of a local newspaper before the war. Terry entered the Confederate army as a lieutenant in the Fourth Virginia Infantry, and in September, 1863, he was appointed its colonel. He was commissioned a brigadier general on May 19, 1864, and he led his unit with distinction until severely wounded near the end of the war at Fort Stedman on March 25, 1865. Following the war he again practiced law and was active in politics. He served in the United States House of Representatives, 1871-73 and 1875-77. See *CMH*, 3:673-74; Warner, *Generals in Gray*, p. 302; and *Biog. Dir. Amer. Cong.*, p. 1700. It is easy to confuse Terry with William Richard Terry, also of Virginia, who also served in the eastern theater.

12. General Zebulon York (October 10, 1819–August 5, 1900) was born in Avon, Franklin County, Maine. Educated at Wesleyan Seminary at Kent's Hill, Maine, and at Transylvania University, Kentucky, he was graduated from the University of Louisiana (Tulane). York was an attorney and a planter at Vidalia, Louisiana, prior to the war, and was reputed to have owned six plantations and 1,700 slaves. He organized the Fourteenth Louisiana Infantry and served in its officer corps from captain through colonel until promoted to brigadier general on May 31, 1864. York was financially ruined by the war. He operated the York House in Natchez, Mississippi, until his death. See Warner, *Generals in Gray*, pp. 347-48.

13. General Clement Anselm Evans (February 25, 1833–July 2, 1911) was born in Stewart County, Georgia. Evans attended the public schools of Lumpkin, Georgia, and the Atlanta Law School. When the war began, Evans enlisted in the Thirty-first Georgia Infantry, and by April, 1863, he had advanced to become its colonel. He served under Generals T. J. Jackson, Jubal Early, and John B. Gordon, from the Peninsular Campaign until Appomattox. He was commissioned a brigadier general on May 19, 1864. After the war Evans was active in business and in the Methodist Episcopal church. Evans, like Hotchkiss, was vigorous in the battle of the books; his most notable

contribution was the twelve-volume *Confederate Military History: A Library of Confederate States History* (Atlanta, 1899), which he edited. For a sketch of his life, see Warner, *Generals in Gray*, p. 83.

14. General Williams Carter Wickham (September 21, 1820–July 23, 1888) was born at Richmond, Virginia. He was educated at the University of Virginia and admitted to the practice of law in 1842. Wickham was elected to the House of Delegates in 1849, and to the state senate ten years later. When the war began, he took his militia company, the Hanover Dragoons, into the Confederate army. In September, 1861, he became colonel of the Fourth Virginia Cavalry. He served under Stuart until that officer's death. Wickham was commissioned a brigadier general on September 1, 1863. He resigned his commission on November 9, 1864, to assume a seat in the Confederate Congress, and he continued to serve in that body until the end of the war. He was active in business and politics after the war, and he was associated with the Republican party. See *CMH*, 3:685-89; and Warner, *Generals in Gray*, pp. 335-36.

15. Captain John C. Carpenter commanded Carpenter's Alleghany Battery. See Wise, *Long Arm of Lee*, p. 889.

16. Continued reading of the entry for September 20 makes it obvious that Hotchkiss did not learn of the death of Rodes for another twenty-four hours. Apparently he inserted the intelligence at its proper chronological place in the journal for purposes of accuracy. The actions discussed here are portions of the Battle of the Wilderness on the Opequon.

17. General Cullen Andrews Battle (June 1, 1829–April 8, 1905) was born at Powelton, Hancock County, Georgia, but was moved at an early age to Eufaula, Alabama. Battle attended the University of Alabama and was admitted to the practice of law in 1852. Shortly following the secession of Alabama, he became lieutenant colonel of the Third Alabama, and after Seven Pines he became its colonel. Battle was promoted to brigadier general on August 20, 1863. He was with Early in the Valley Campaign of 1864. After the war he resumed the practice of law at Tuskegee. Despite his election to Congress in 1868, he was denied his seat in that body. See Warner, *Generals in Gray*, p. 20.

18. Pendleton was wounded at dusk on September 22, following a day of gallantry at the Battle of Fisher's Hill. He was wounded in the abdomen, the ball passing completely through. Pendleton believed himself to be mortally wounded and urged Kyd Douglas, who attempted to help him, to save himself. Douglas remained until Pendleton was secured in the home of a Dr. Murphy in Woodstock. Hunter McGuire, who had the sad duty of treating the vanishing staff of Jackson's old command, was summoned, but to no avail. The retreating Confederates were forced to leave Pendleton at Woodstock, and he was cared for by Federal surgeons. He failed to respond, however, and he died during the evening of September 23, five days before his twenty-fourth birthday. The best account of the affair is of course W. G. Bean, *Stonewall's Man: Sandie Pendleton* (Chapel Hill, 1959), pp. 210-23. For Douglas's part, see *I Rode with Stonewall* (Chapel Hill, 1940), pp. 312-13.

19. Captain William T. Hart, Corps of Engineers.

20. Lieutenant Charles R. Boyd, Corps of Engineers.

21. General George Armstrong Custer (December 5, 1839–June 25, 1876) was born at New Rumley, Harrison County, Ohio. Graduated from West Point with the class of 1861, Custer rose rapidly in rank to brigadier general of volunteers by June 13, 1863; and on October 2, 1864, he was given command of the Third Division of the Cavalry Corps. Following the war Custer was reduced to a captain in the regular army, an experience that embittered this overly ambitious man. On June 28, 1866, he was promoted to lieutenant colonel of the new Seventh Cavalry. In June, 1876, Custer and his entire command were killed by Sioux Indians at the Little Big Horn. See *DAB*, s.v. Custer, George Armstrong; Cullum, *Biog. Register*, 2:568-69; F. S. Dellenbaugh, *George Armstrong Custer* (New York, 1918); and G. A. Custer, *My Life on the Plains* (New York, 1874).

22. General James Conner (September 1, 1829–June 26, 1883) was born at

Charleston, South Carolina, and was a graduate of South Carolina College (1849). Before the war Conner was a leading South Carolina attorney. He entered the Confederate army as a captain in Hampton's Legion, but he was soon made colonel of the Twenty-second North Carolina. He was promoted to brigadier general on June 1. 1864. He commanded a brigade under Early in the Valley in 1864 until a wound at Cedar Creek on October 13 necessitated the amputation of his leg. Following the war Conner resumed the practice of law and was active in politics. He was elected attorney general of South Carolina in 1876. See Warner, *Generals in Gray*, pp. 59-60.

23. General Bryan Grimes (November 2, 1828–August 14, 1880) was born at "Grimesland," Pitt County, North Carolina. He was educated at the University of North Carolina (1848), and until the war he was active in farming, travel, and state politics. He entered the Confederate service as major of the Fourth North Carolina, and for most of the war he was assigned to the Army of Northern Virginia. On May 19, 1864, he was promoted to brigadier general, and on February 15, 1865, he was commissioned a major general. Grimes commanded one of the last attacks at Appomattox on the day of surrender. Following the war he returned to farming. He was killed by a hired assassin over a political grievance. A part of Grimes's correspondence is published in Grimes, *Extracts of Letters of Major General Bryan Grimes* (Raleigh, 1883). See also Warner, *Generals in Gray*, pp. 120-21.

24. Both Early and Gordon (*War Memoirs*, pp. 438-52; and *Reminiscences of the Civil War*, pp. 332-51) refer to this incident in their memoirs, as does every major secondary account. Early made his decision to attack Sheridan at Cedar Creek on the strength of this report by Gordon and Hotchkiss. They had located a road around Three Top that made the attack possible. The controversy that developed after the battle is largely responsible for the fame of the incident. Initially successful, the Confederates stopped their attack by Early's order on the very brink of a rout, or so it seemed to Gordon. Sheridan was absent from his command when the surprise attack came, and his troops were confused. A dramatic ride brought him to his army in time to organize a counterattack out of a rally that had already begun, and Early stopped the attack. Hotchkiss later reported that Early requested that he not inform Lee of this unfortunate hesitation. It is not revealed whether or not Hotchkiss kept this trust; in any case it was revealed with the publication of this portion of the diary in the *Official Records*. Early later claimed that the halt was necessary because of Gordon's delay in assuming his position on the field and because the troops were looting and straggling. Thus another controversy was born out of missed chances and lost opportunities.

25. Colonel Thomas Hill Carter, who commanded a battery, a battalion, and finally a division in the Second Corps, Army of Northern Virginia. See Wise, *Long Arm of Lee*, pp. 944, 963.

26. General William Henry Fitzhugh Payne (January 27, 1830–March 29, 1904) was born in Fauquier County, Virginia. A graduate of the Virginia Military Institute (1849), he also studied law at the University of Virginia. Payne began the war as a private, and he ended it as a brigadier general. He served from the first occupation of Harpers Ferry until Appomattox; he was wounded three times and captured three times. He was awarded his general's commission in recognition for exceptional cavalry service in the Army of Northern Virginia. Following the war he practiced law and was elected to the Virginia House of Delegates (1879). See *CMH*, 3:645-47; and Warner, *Generals in Gray*, pp. 230-31.

27. General Philip Henry Sheridan (March 6, 1831–August 5, 1888) was born at Albany, New York. He was graduated from West Point in 1853. He had risen to captain by 1861, but was soon the colonel of the Second Michigan Cavalry. By July, 1862, Sheridan was a brigadier general of volunteers, and by the end of the year he was a major general. He was singularly responsible for the reorganization of the Union cavalry that placed it on an equal, and ultimately superior, footing with its Confederate counterpart. In August, 1864, Sheridan was given command of the Army of Shenandoah, and he opposed Early in a devastating campaign against both military and agricultural resources. For short sketches, see Cullum, *Biog. Register*, 2:356-57;

and *DAB*, s.v. Sheridan, Philip H. Sheridan's *Personal Memoirs* (New York, 1888) give his own story. See also Joseph Hergesheimer, *Sheridan* (Boston, 1931).

28. General William Tatum Wofford (June 28, 1824–May 22, 1884) was born in Habersham County, Georgia. Prior to the war Wofford was a lawyer and was active in politics. He served in the state legislature from 1849 until 1853. Although he was opposed to secession, he entered the Confederate service as colonel of the Eighteenth Georgia Infantry. He took part in all the major campaigns of the Army of Northern Virginia. On January 17, 1863, Wofford was appointed brigadier general and designated to command T. R. R. Cobb's brigade. Until the end of the war he was assigned to the First Corps. Following the war Wofford was again active in Georgia politics and business. See Warner, *Generals in Gray*, pp. 343-44.

29. General Archibald Campbell Godwin was born in Nansemond County, Virginia, in 1831. He traveled widely before the war, but returned home to serve in the Confederate army. He was for a while stationed at Libby Prison and then sent to Salisburg, North Carolina, to organize a prison there. He recruited the Fifty-seventh North Carolina Infantry and was soon ordered back to Virginia. Godwin was promoted to brigadier general to rank from August 4, 1864, and he was fatally wounded on October 19, 1864. Warner, *Generals in Gray*, p. 108, erroneously gives the month of his death as September, but Hotchkiss's reference and citations in the *Official Records* prove that he died in October.

30. General Stephen Dodson Ramseur was wounded in the lungs; he was captured and taken to Sheridan's headquarters. Here were many former associates and friends from West Point, and they comforted and cared for Ramseur until he died.

31. Shorter was attached to the Regular Engineers.

32. Flood's pioneers were engaged in clearing a road and in other activities of march and camp maintenance.

33. The Honorable John Goode was born in Virginia in 1829. He was educated at Emory and Henry and at the Lexington Law School. Prior to the war Goode was an attorney and was active in Democratic politics. He was an ardent secessionist, and he was considered an administrative supporter in the First and Second Confederate Congresses. See Wilfred Buck Yearns, *The Confederate Congress* (Athens, Ga., 1960), p. 240.

34. General George Blake Cosby (January 19, 1830–June 29, 1909) was born at Louisville, Kentucky. Graduated from West Point in 1852, he served in the cavalry until May 10, 1861, when he resigned to enter the Confederate army. Cosby served generally in the west, first on the staff of General S. B. Buckner and later under General J. E. Johnston. He led a cavalry brigade for Earl Van Dorn, and during the final year of the war was stationed in western Virginia. Following the war Cosby moved to California. See Warner, *Generals in Gray*, p. 64; Cullum, *Biog. Register*, 2:314; and Ellsworth, *West Point in the Confederacy*, p. 319.

35. Later Colonel Green Peyton was a member of General John B. Gordon's staff.

36. The Sixth Corps, Army of the Shenandoah, was commanded by Major General Horatio G. Wright.

CHAPTER THIRTEEN

1. The first of the year was the customary time for arranging the annual hiring of servants. On this occasion, however, Hotchkiss went into debt to purchase William Gearing because he felt a moral obligation to the slave and to his owner. William, like many who went away to war, acquired vices. Drink had claimed him, and Hotchkiss felt that he must now shoulder the responsibility.

2. Colonel Albert W. Cook commanded the Eighth Virginia Cavalry.

3. *Joseph II and His Court* was a recently published historical novel by the distinguished German author Frau Klara (Muller) Mundt (1814-1873), who wrote under the pseudonym Louise Muhlbach. The book was originally published in Brandenburg, but the copy that Hotchkiss read was the translation of Adelaide de Von Chaudron and was published by S. H. Goetzel at Mobile in 1864.

4. General John Echols (March 20, 1823–May 24, 1896) was born at Lynchburg, Virginia. He was a graduate of Washington College, but he also studied law at Harvard. Echols practiced his profession from 1843 until the war, but he was also active in politics. He served as an attorney for the state, as a member of the general assembly, and as a delegate to the secession convention. He commanded the Twenty-seventh Virginia Infantry at the Battle of First Manassas and was soon promoted to colonel. After the Valley Campaign he was commissioned a brigadier general to rank from April 16, 1862. Following the war Echols was active in business in Virginia. See *CMH*, 3:591-93; and Ezra T. Warner, *Generals in Gray: Lives of the Confederate Commanders* (Baton Rouge, 1959), p. 80.

5. This court-martial grew out of a dispute between Munford and General Rosser. When the latter had prepared for a raid into western Virginia in 1865, he called on Munford for a cavalry detachment. With the conditions of both men and horses extremely poor, Munford requested a delay in order to allow supplies from Richmond to arrive. He was interested particularly in horseshoes to give his mounts better footing. The matter became personal, and Rosser placed Munford under arrest. At the court-martial Munford was acquitted and Rosser was "inferentially censured" for causing the action. Nevertheless, Munford was cast under a shadow and his promotion to brigadier general was in doubt. For a discussion of this incident, see Douglas S. Freeman, *Lee's Lieutenants: A Study in Command*, 3 vols. (New York, 1944), 3:667 and n. In rereading this passage in 1897, Hotchkiss's memory failed to respond with the particulars. In a letter to Munford on October 22, 1897, he queried: "Pray tell me what this trial was for. I have no remembrance of it, and what sort of evidence could I, or did I give?" A gloss at the foot of the letter, which is now in the Munford Collection at Duke University, reveals the essential facts of the trial. It is initialed, "CT."

6. On February 3, 1865, a conference was held aboard the Union transport *River Queen*, lying off Hampton Roads, in an attempt to bring the war to an end. The negotiators were important men: for the Union there were President Lincoln and Secretary of State Seward; for the Confederate government there were Vice-President Stephens, R. M. T. Hunter, and J. A. Campbell. Lincoln's terms were few, but they were important: reunion, emancipation, and the surrender of all forces hostile to the government. The matter of armistice was discussed but denied by Lincoln because it would not mean a real ending to the conflict. The conference ended without agreement, and both presidents reported to their respective Congresses that they were no nearer to resolving their problems than they had been four years earlier. The war lingered on for $3\frac{1}{2}$ more months. See J. G. Randall and David Donald, *The Civil War and Reconstruction*, 2d ed., rev. (New York, 1969), pp. 524-25; for a statement of the southern position and reasons for rejection of the terms, see Jefferson Davis, *Rise and Fall of the Confederate Government*, 2 vols. (New York, 1881), 2:608-25.

7. General John Pegram (January 24, 1832–February 6, 1865) was born at Petersburg, Virginia. He was graduated from West Point in 1854, and he served in the United States Army until May 10, 1861, when he resigned to become a Confederate lieutenant colonel under General R. S. Garnett. He was promoted to colonel and assigned to staff duty with Generals Beauregard and Bragg and finally to chief of staff under Kirby Smith. Appointed brigadier general on November 7, 1862, he continued in that rank until his death in 1865. He was mortally wounded at Hatcher's Run and died in the arms of his best friend, W. Gordon McCabe. See *CMH*, 3:648-49; Cullum, *Biog. Register*, 2:374; and Warner, *Generals in Gray*, pp. 231-32. For a touching story of Pegram's death and his friend's grief, see Freeman, *Lee's Lieutenants*, 3:673-74.

8. The burning of Columbia has spawned one of the bitterest historical controversies of the war. Sherman's reputation for destruction established by events in Georgia makes him the natural villain, but Wade Hampton also has his critics. The fire that destroyed a large part of the South Carolina capital apparently began in some

stored cotton. Confederates insisted that Sherman was responsible. Sherman was not so certain, and he offered two explanations. First, he charged that Hampton had set the fire; second, he claimed that he permitted the circulation of the first story in order to discredit Hampton. A stronger possibility is that the fire was accidentally set by Sherman's soldiers, without orders, as they pillaged the city. The propaganda value of the incident to both sides, during and since the war, served to make it a storm center. See James Ford Rhodes, "Who Burned Columbia?" *American Historical Review*, 7:485-93; and William Gilmore Simms, "The Sack and Destruction of Columbia," first published in the *Columbia Daily Phoenix*, then cited in the *Congressional Record*, May 15, 1930. See also Randall and Donald, *Civil War and Reconstruction*, pp. 433-34.

9. Charleston was abandoned by its Confederate defenders on February 17, 1865, approximately two months short of four years after the first shot of the war was fired there. This fact, plus South Carolina's position as the center of secession, made the conquest of this proud city important to the Union forces. For a complete discussion of the final defense of Charleston, see *Battles and Leaders*, 4:1-74.

10. Major General Benjamin F. Kelley, an officer in the Department of West Virginia.

11. Major General George Crook, an officer in the Department of West Virginia.

12. The capture of the two officers mentioned above was executed by the partisan cavalry company of Lieutenant Jesse McNeill that had formerly been commanded by Captain John H. McNeill, father to the current commander. With a raiding party of forty to fifty men, McNeill dashed into Cumberland, Maryland, in the dead of night and kidnapped the two generals plus a staff officer while several thousand troops in and around Cumberland slept. For a discussion of the incident, see Jubal A. Early, *War Memoirs: Autobiographical Sketch and Narrative of the War between the States*, ed. Frank E. Vandiver (Bloomington, Ind., 1960), p. 461.

13. This rosy picture of an enthusiastic crowd stirred by oratory to subscribe supplies and money contradicts the accepted picture of a defeated Southland. However, there was probably more emotion than fact in this presentation. Correspondence from Hotchkiss to his wife had for some time been revealing a despondency at the Confederate effort.

14. General Armistead Lindsay Long (September 3, 1825–April 29, 1891) was born in Campbell County, Virginia. Graduated from West Point in 1850, he served in the artillery until he resigned on May 20, 1861. Long entered the Confederate army as a major of artillery attached to the command of General Loring. He was soon transferred to Lee's staff to serve as a military secretary, but his artillery training soon caused his promotion to brigadier general (September 21, 1863) and his transfer to command the artillery of the Second Corps. Long's biography of his chief, *Memoirs of Robert E. Lee* (New York, 1866) is one of the best contemporary works. For references to Long, see *CMH*, 3:630-32; Cullum, *Biog. Register*, 2:263; Eliot Ellsworth, Jr., *West Point in the Confederacy* (New York, 1941), p. 381; and Warner, *Generals in Gray*, pp. 191-92.

15. General William Lowther Jackson had only recently been given brigade command, and he was thus a principal figure in one of the last engagements in the Shenandoah Valley. Many of the prisoners were civilians and convalescents from Staunton. Rosser pursued the caravan and, with the aid of Jackson's men, fell on their rear and drove them to Melrose. On the next day Smith's brigade arrived to help Rosser, and he again struck the Federals at Rude's Hill and nearly recaptured the Confederate prisoners. The next day McNeill's partisans circled to the front of the train, and at the bridge over the North Fork they brought converging fire upon the Federals, who, however, escaped by a farm road to the west. See *CMH*, 3:541.

16. Colonel William F. Arnett commanded the Twentieth Virginia Cavalry Regiment.

17. This "day of public fasting, humiliation and prayers" for "invoking the favor and guidance of Almighty God," proclaimed by President Jefferson Davis on January 25, 1865, was the last such commemoration. For the full text of the proclamation, see

James D. Richardson, *A Compilation of the Messages and Papers of the Confederacy, 1861-65*, 2 vols. (Nashville, 1906), 1:567-68.

18. General Jeremy Francis Gilmer (February 23, 1818–December 1, 1883) was born in Guilford County, North Carolina. He was graduated from West Point in 1839, and he served as an engineering officer until he resigned on June 29, 1861. His first post in the Confederate army was as chief engineer on the staff of General A. S. Johnston, and he was wounded at Shiloh. He was promoted directly from colonel to major general on August 25, 1863, to command the Engineer Bureau of the Confederate War Department. Following the war Gilmer was president of the Savannah Gas Light Company. Warner, *Generals in Gray*, p. 105; Cullum, *Biog. Register*, 1:574-75; and Ellsworth, *West Point in the Confederacy*, p. 344.

19. Major David J. Kyle of Culpeper, Virginia.

20. Richmond was occupied by the Twenty-fifth Corps, Army of the James, commanded by General Godfrey Weitzel, at the invitation of Mayor Joseph Mayo following the evacuation of the city by the Confederate government and its armed forces. Mayo requested the commanding general to preserve order and protect women and children and property. For a brief account of the day, see Alfred Hoyt Boyd, *The Beleaguered City: Richmond, 1861-1865* (New York, 1946), pp. 273-75; *Battles and Leaders*, 4:725-28; and Rembert Patrick, *The Fall of Richmond* (Baton Rouge, 1960).

21. General Robert Edward Lee, commanding the Army of Northern Virginia, met with General Ulysses S. Grant at Appomattox Court House, Virginia, on April 9, 1865, and arranged for the surrender. The actual marching of the troops to surrender took place three days later. While others continued to resist briefly, this single act all but ended the war. Within a day Lincoln walked in the streets of Davis's capital. There is no more moving description of the events of this fateful day than that by Freeman, *Lee's Lieutenants*, 3:726-52. Other accounts of the closing days of the war include Philip Van Doren Stern, *An End to Valor* (Boston, 1958); and Burke Davis, *To Appomattox* (New York, 1959).

22. When Lee surrendered, many units under his command did not immediately comply with his orders to disband. Some did so because they were out of communication; others were recalcitrant because they wished to retain their arms, join another unit, and continue fighting. Many tried to make it south to the Army of Tennessee, now once more under the command of Joseph E. Johnston; some even went to the Trans-Mississippi. For most, however, the war was over.

23. Major Conway R. Howard.

24. Major Thomas Rowland.

25. Colonel William Nelson, of Virginia, commanded an artillery battalion assigned to General Jubal A. Early.

26. General John C. Breckinridge had been secretary of war since February 4, 1865. He was the fifth to hold that office in four years.

27. Hotchkiss was unaware that Lincoln had been assassinated four days earlier, on April 14, while attending Ford's Theatre in Washington. The revolution in sentiment of which Hotchkiss speaks is understandable; the President's plans for Virginia did not call for punishment, but instead welcomed the state back into the Union as an equal.

Bibliography

MANUSCRIPTS

Chapel Hill, N.C. University of North Carolina Library. J. Howard Beckenbaugh collection of Henry Kyd Douglas papers.

Baton Rouge, La. Louisiana State University Library. David F. Boyd papers.

Baton Rouge, La. Louisiana State University Library. Walter L. Fleming collection.

Washington, D.C. Library of Congress. Jedediah Hotchkiss papers.

Chapel Hill, N.C. University of North Carolina Library. Thomas Jonathan Jackson papers.

Durham, N.C. Duke University Library. Thomas T. Munford papers.

Washington, D.C. Library of Congress. J. Addison Waddell papers and diary. Deposited with the Jedediah Hotchkiss papers.

PUBLISHED CORRESPONDENCE

CHAMBERLAYNE, G. C., ed. *Letters and Papers of an American Artillery Officer in the War for Southern Independence*. Richmond, Va., 1932.

GRIMES, BRYAN. *Extracts of Letters of Major General Bryan Grimes*. Raleigh, N.C., 1883.

DIARIES, MEMOIRS, REMINISCENCES, AND AUTOBIOGRAPHIES

ALEXANDER, E. P. *Military Memoirs of a Confederate.* Edited by T. Harry Williams. Bloomington, Ind., 1962.

BLACKFORD, WILLIAM W. *War Years with Jeb Stuart.* New York, 1945.

BUTLER, BENJAMIN F. *Personal Reminiscences of Major-General Benjamin F. Butler: Butler's Book.* Boston, 1892.

CASLER, JOHN O. *Four Years in the Stonewall Brigade.* Revised by Jedediah Hotchkiss. Marietta, Ga., 1951.

CHESTNUT, MARY BOYKIN. *A Diary from Dixie.* Edited by Ben Ames Williams. 2d ed. Boston, 1949.

COCKRELL, MONROE F., ed. *Gunner with Stonewall: Reminiscences of William Thomas Poague.* Jackson, Tenn., 1957.

COOKE, JOHN ESTEN. *Wearing of the Gray.* Edited by Philip Van Doren Stern. Bloomington, Ind., 1959.

CUSTER, GEORGE A. *My Life on the Plains.* New York, 1874.

DOUGLAS, HENRY KYD. *I Rode with Stonewall.* Introduction by Fletcher Greene. Chapel Hill, N.C., 1940.

EARLY, JUBAL A. *War Memoirs: Autobiographical Sketch and Narrative of the War between the States.* Edited by Frank E. Vandiver. Bloomington, Ind., 1960.

FRAZIER, HARRY. *Recollections.* Huntington, W. Va., 1938.

FREMONT, JOHN C. *Memoirs of My Life.* New York, 1887.

GORDON, JOHN B. *Reminiscences of the Civil War.* New York, 1903.

HOOD, JOHN B. *Advance and Retreat.* Edited by Richard N. Current. Bloomington, Ind., 1959.

HOWARD, MCHENRY. *Recollections of a Maryland Soldier and Staff Officer.* Baltimore, 1914.

HOWARD, OLIVER OTIS. *The Autobiography of Oliver Otis Howard.* New York, 1907.

JOHNSTON, JOSEPH E. *Narrative of Military Operations.* Edited by Frank E. Vandiver. Bloomington, Ind., 1959.

LONG, ARMISTEAD LINDSEY. *Memoirs of Robert E. Lee.* New York, 1866.

LONGSTREET, JAMES. *From Manassas to Appomattox: Memoirs of the Civil War in America.* 1896. Reprint. Bloomington, Ind., 1960.

MCCLELLAN, GEORGE B. *McClellan's Own Story.* New York, 1887.

MCCLELLAN, HENRY B. *The Life and Campaigns of Major General J. E. B. Stuart.* Boston, 1887.

MCGUIRE, HUNTER, and CHRISTIAN, GEORGE L. *The Confederate Cause and Conduct in the War between the States.* Richmond, Va., 1907.

MAURICE, SIR FREDERICK, ed. *An Aide-de-Camp of Lee, Being the Papers of Colonel Charles Marshall, Sometimes Aide de Camp, Military Secretary and Assistant Adjutant General on the Staff of Robert E. Lee.* Boston, 1927.

MEADE, GEORGE GORDON. *The Life and Letters of George Gordon Meade.* New York, 1913.

MOORE, EDWARD A. *The Story of a Cannoneer under Stonewall Jackson.* Lynchburg, Va., 1910.

MOSBY, JOHN S. *Mosby's Reminiscences and Stuart's Cavalry Campaign.* Edited by Virgil C. Jones. Bloomington, Ind., 1959.

QUARLES, CHARLES R., and BARTON, LEWIS N., eds. *What I Know about Winchester: Recollections of William Greenway Russell, 1800-1891.* Staunton, Va., 1953.

SHERIDAN, PHILIP HENRY. *Personal Memoirs.* New York, 1888.

SMITH, JAMES POWER. *With Stonewall Jackson in the Army of Northern Virginia.* Southern Historical Society, *Papers,* vol. 43. Richmond, Va., 1920.

SORREL, GILBERT MOXLEY. *Recollections of a Confederate Staff Officer.* New York, 1905.

SUMMERS, FESTUS P., ed. *A Borderland Confederate: The Diary of William L. Wilson.* Pittsburgh, 1962.

TAYLOR, RICHARD. *Destruction and Reconstruction.* New York, 1879.

TAYLOR, WALTER H. *Four Years with General Lee.* Edited by James L. Robertson, Jr. Bloomington, Ind., 1962.

TUNSTALL, VIRGINIA LYNE, ed. *Cornelia McDonald: A Diary, with Reminiscences of the War and Refugee Life.* Nashville, Tenn., 1934.

VANDIVER, FRANK E., ed. *The Civil War Diary of General Josiah Gorgas.* Tuscaloosa, Ala., 1947.

VON BORCKE, HEROS. *Memoirs of the Confederate War for Independence.* New York, 1938.

BIOGRAPHIES

ALFRIEND, FRANK H. *The Life of Jefferson Davis.* Philadelphia, 1868.

AMBROSE, STEPHEN E. *Halleck: Lincoln's Chief of Staff.* Baton Rouge, La., 1962.

ARNOLD, THOMAS JACKSON. *Early Life and Letters of General Thomas J. Jackson.* New York, 1916.

BACHE, RICHARD M. *The Life of General George Gordon Meade.* Philadelphia, 1897.

BASSO, HAMILTON. *Beauregard, the Great Creole.* New York, 1935.

BEAN, W. G. *Stonewall's Man: Sandie Pendleton.* Chapel Hill, N.C., 1959.

BEATY, JOHN OWEN. *John Esten Cooke.* New York, 1922.

BRIDGES, LEONARD HAL. *Lee's Maverick General: Daniel Harvey Hill.* New York, 1961.

BROOKS, ULYSSES ROBERT. *Butler and His Cavalry in the War of Secession, 1861-1865.* Columbia, S.C., 1909.

BUSHONG, MILLARD KESSLER. *Old Jube: A Biography of General Jubal A. Early.* Boyce, Va., 1955.

CHAMBERS, LENOIR. *Stonewall Jackson.* New York, 1959.

CLEVES, FREEMAN. *Meade of Gettysburg.* Norman, Okla., 1960.

CONRAD, BRYAN. *James Longstreet: Lee's War Horse.* Chapel Hill, N.C., 1936.

CONDON, W. H. *The Life of Major-General James Shields.* Chicago, 1900.

COOKE, JOHN ESTEN. *Stonewall Jackson: A Military Biography.* New York, 1866.

CUNNINGHAM, FRANK. *Knight of the Confederacy: General Turner Ashby.* San Antonio, 1960.

DABNEY, ROBERT LEWIS. *Life and Campaigns of Lieutenant General Thomas J. Jackson.* New York, 1866.

DAVIS, BURKE. *Jeb Stuart: The Last Cavalier.* New York, 1957.

DELLENBAUGH, F. S., *George Armstrong Custer.* New York, 1918.

DUFOUR, CHARLES L. *Gentle Tiger: The Gallant Life of Roberdeau Wheat.* Baton Rouge, La., 1957.

————. *Nine Men in Gray.* Baton Rouge, La., 1963.

DYER, JOHN P. *The Gallant Hood.* New York, 1950.

ECKENRODE, HAMILTON J. *George B. McClellan: The Man Who Saved the Union.* Chapel Hill, N.C., 1941.

————. *Jefferson Davis: President of the South.* New York, 1923.

————, and CONRAD, BRYAN. *James Longstreet: Lee's War Horse.* Chapel Hill., N.C., 1936.

EISENSCHIML, OTTO. *The Celebrated Case of Fitz-John Porter: An American Dreyfus Affair.* Indianapolis, Ind., 1950.

FISHWICK, MARSHALL WILLIAM. *Lee after the War.* New York, 1962.

FREEMAN, DOUGLAS SOUTHALL. *R. E. Lee: A Biography.* 4 vols. New York, 1934.

GOVAN, GILBERT E., and LIVINGOOD, JAMES W. *A Different Valor: The Story of General Joseph E. Johnston, C.S.A.* New York, 1956.

GREENE, J. L. *General William B. Franklin and the Operations of the Left Wing at the Battle of Fredericksburg.* Hartford, Conn., 1900.

HAMLIN, PERCY G. *Old Bald Head.* Strasburg, Va., 1940.

————. *The Making of a Soldier.* Richmond, Va., 1935.

HARRINGTON, FREDERICK H. *Fighting Politician: Major General N. P. Banks.* Philadelphia, 1948.

HASSLER, WARREN W. *A. P. Hill: Lee's Forgotten General.* Richmond, Va., 1957.

————. *Colonel John Pelham: Lee's Boy Artillerist.* Richmond, Va., 1960.

————. *Commanders of the Army of the Potomac*. Baton Rouge, La., 1962.

————. *General George B. McClellan, Shield of the Union*. Baton Rouge, La., 1957.

HEBERT, WALTER H. *Fighting Joe Hooker*. Indianapolis, Ind., 1944.

HENDERSON, G. F. R. *Stonewall Jackson and the American Civil War*. American ed. New York, 1937.

HERGESHEIMER, JOSEPH. *Sheridan*. Boston, 1931.

JOHNSON, ALLEN, and MALONE, DUMAS, eds. *Dictionary of American Biography*. 22 vols. New York, 1928-37.

JOHNSON, T. C. *Life and Letters of Robert Lewis Dabney*. Richmond, Va., 1903.

JOHNSTON, WILLIAM PRESTON. *The Life of General Albert Sidney Johnston*. New York, 1879.

JONES, VIRGIL C. *Ranger Mosby*. Chapel Hill, N.C., 1944.

LAMERS, WILLIAM MATHIAS. *The Edge of Glory: A Biography of General William S. Rosecrans, U.S.A.* New York, 1961.

McELROY, ROBERT M. *Jefferson Davis: The Unreal and the Real*. 2 vols. New York, 1937.

MEADE, ROBERT DOUTHAT. *Judah P. Benjamin: Confederate Statesman*. New York, 1943.

MERCER, PHILIP. *The Gallant Pelham*. Macon, Ga., 1929.

MILHAM, CHARLES G. *Gallant Pelham*. Washington, 1959.

National Cyclopedia of American Biography. 42 vols. New York, 1898-1959.

NEIMAN, SIMON I. *Judah Benjamin: Lawyer*. New York, 1963.

NEVINS, ALLEN. *Fremont: The West's Greatest Adventurer*. New York, 1928.

NOLL, ARTHUR HOWARD. *General Edmund Kirby Smith*. Sewanee, Tenn., 1907.

PARKS, JOSEPH HOWARD. *General Edmund Kirby Smith*. Baton Rouge, La., 1954.

PATRICK, REMBERT W. *Jefferson Davis and His Cabinet*. 2d ed. Baton Rouge, La., 1961.

RAND, CLAYTON. *Sons of the South*. New York, 1961.

RANDALL, J. G. *Lincoln the President*. 4 vols.; vols. 1-3 New York, 1945-52. Vol. 4 with CURRENT, RICHARD N. New York, 1955.

ROSS, ISHBELL, ed. *Rebel Rose: Life of Rose O'Neal Greenhow, Confederate Spy*. New York, 1954.

ROWLAND, DUNBAR. *Jefferson Davis: Constitutionalist*. 10 vols. Jackson, Miss., 1923.

SANGER, DONALD B., and HAY, THOMAS R. *James Longstreet: I. Soldier; II. Politician, Officeholder, and Writer*. Baton Rouge, La., 1952.

STILLWELL, LUCILLE. *John Cabell Breckinridge: Born to Be a Statesman.* Caldwell, Idaho, 1936.

STRODE, HUDSON. *Jefferson Davis.* 2 vols. New York, 1955-59.

TANKERSLEY, ALLEN P. *John B. Gordon: A Study in Gallantry.* Atlanta, Ga., 1955.

THOMASON, JOHN W. *Jeb Stuart.* Chicago, 1953.

TYLER, LYON GARDINER, ed. *Encyclopedia of Virginia Biography.* 5 vols. New York, 1915.

VANDIVER, FRANK E. *Mighty Stonewall.* New York, 1957.

WARNER, EZRA J. *Generals in Gray: Lives of the Confederate Commanders.* Baton Rouge, La., 1959.

WELSH, E. S. *John Sedgwick: Major General.* New York, 1899.

WILLIAMS, T. HARRY. *P.G.T. Beauregard: Napoleon in Gray.* Baton Rouge, La., 1955.

WELLMAN, MANLY WADE. *Giant in Gray: A Biography of Wade Hampton of South Carolina.* New York, 1949.

HISTORIES AND MONOGRAPHS

ALLAN, WILLIAM. *Stonewall Jackson's Campaign in the Shenandoah Valley of Virginia.* London, 1912.

————. *The Army of Northern Virginia in 1862.* Boston, 1892.

BATES, DAVID H. *Lincoln in the Telegraph Office: Recollections of the United States Military Telegraph Corps during the Civil War.* New York, 1907.

BAXTER, JAMES PHINNEY. *The Introduction of the Ironclad Warship.* Cambridge, 1933.

BOYD, ALFRED HOYT. *The Beleaguered City: Richmond, 1861-1865.* New York, 1946.

BRUMER, SIDNEY. *Political History of New York State during the Period of the Civil War.* New York, 1911.

BURGER, NASH KERR, and BUTTERWORTH, J. K. *South of Appomattox.* New York, 1959.

COMMAGER, HENRY STEELE, ed. *The Blue and the Grey.* 2 vols. New York, 1950.

CROUPER, WILLIAM. *One Hundred Years at V.M.I.* Richmond, Va., 1939.

CUNNINGHAM, H. H. *Doctors in Gray.* Baton Rouge, La., 1958.

DALY, R. W. *How the Merrimac Won: The Strategic Story of the C.S.S. Virginia.* New York, 1957.

DAVIS, BURKE. *To Appomattox.* New York, 1959.

DAVIS, JEFFERSON. *The Rise and Fall of the Confederate Government.* New York, 1881.

DAVIS, JULIA. *The Shenandoah.* New York, 1945.

DEADRICK, BARRON. *Strategy in the Civil War.* Harrisburg, Pa., 1946.

DUFOUR, CHARLES L. *The Night the War Was Lost.* New York, 1960.

ELLSWORTH, ELIOT, JR. *West Point in the Confederacy.* New York, 1941.

ESTES, CLAUD. *List of Field Officers, Regiments, and Battalions in the Confederate States Army, 1861-1865.* Macon, Ga., 1912.

EVANS, CLEMENT A., ed. *Confederate Military History.* 12 vols. Atlanta, Ga., 1899.

FISKE, JOHN. *The Mississippi Valley in the Civil War.* New York, 1900.

FLEMING, WALTER LYNWOOD, ed. *The South in the Building of the Nation.* 12 vols. Richmond, Va., 1909.

FORNELL, EARL WESLEY. *The Galveston Era: The Texas Crescent on the Eve of Secession.* Austin, Tex., 1961.

FREEMAN, DOUGLAS SOUTHALL. *Lee's Lieutenants: A Study in Command.* 3 vols. New York, 1944.

————. *The South to Posterity: An Introduction to the Writing of Confederate History.* New York, 1951.

HALLECK, HENRY WAGER. *Elements of Military Art and Science.* New York, 1846.

HAMLIN, AUGUSTAS CHOATE. *The Battle of Chancellorsville.* Bangor, Maine, 1896.

HILL, DANIEL HARVEY. *North Carolina in the War between the States.* Raleigh, N.C., 1926.

HORN, STANLEY F. *The Army of Tennessee: A Military History.* New York, 1941.

HOTCHKISS, JEDEDIAH. *Confederate Military History.* Vol. 3, *Virginia.* Atlanta, Ga., 1899.

————, and ROGERS, WILLIAM B. *Virginia: A Geographical and Political Summary.* Richmond, 1876.

————, and WADDELL, JOSEPH A. *Historical Atlas of Augusta County.* Staunton, Va., 1885.

JOHNSON, ALEXANDER KEITH. *The Physical Atlas.* Edenburgh, 1850.

JOHNSON, ROBERT UNDERWOOD, and BUEL, CLARENCE CLOUGH, eds. *Battles and Leaders of the Civil War.* 4 vols. 2d ed. New York, 1956.

JONES, ARCHER. *Confederate Strategy from Shiloh to Vicksburg.* Baton Rouge, La., 1961.

LUVASS, JAY. *The Civil War: A Soldier's View, a Collection of Civil War Writings by Col. G. F. R. Henderson.* Chicago, 1958.

————. *The Military Legacy of the Civil War: The European Inheritance.* Chicago, 1959.

McCARTNEY, CLARENCE EDWARD. *Grant and His Generals.* New York, 1953.

MARKS, J. J. *The Peninsula Campaign in Virginia.* Philadelphia, 1864.

MARTIN, JOSEPH. *A New and Comprehensive Gazetteer of Virginia.* Charlottesville, Va., 1835.

MARTION, BESSIE. *Desertion of Alabama Troops from the Confederate Army.* New York, 1932.

MITCHELL, JOSEPH. *Decisive Battles of the Civil War.* New York, 1955.

MOORE, A. B. *Conscription and Conflict in the Confederacy.* New York, 1924.

NEVINS, ALLEN. *The War for the Union.* Vol. 1, *The Improved War, 1861-1862.* New York, 1959. Vol. 2, *War Becomes Revolution.* New York, 1960.

NICHOLS, JAMES L. *Confederate Engineers.* Tuscaloosa, Ala., 1957.

OWSLEY, FRANK L. *King Cotton Diplomacy: Foreign Relations of the Confederate States of America.* 2d ed., rev. Chicago, 1959.

PATRICK, REMBERT. *The Fall of Richmond.* Baton Rouge, La., 1960.

RANDALL, J. G., and DONALD, DAVID. *The Civil War and Reconstruction.* 2d ed., rev. New York, 1969.

————. *Constitutional Problems under Lincoln.* New York, 1926.

RIPLEY, R. S. *The War with Mexico.* New York, 1849.

ROBERTSON, JAMES I., JR. *The Stonewall Brigade.* Baton Rouge, La., 1963.

SHANNON, FRED A. *Organization and Administration of the Union Army, 1861-1865.* 2 vols. Cleveland, Ohio, 1928.

SMITH, GUSTAVAS W. *The Battle of Seven Pines.* New York, 1891.

SNOW, WILLIAM P. *Lee and His Generals.* New York, 1867.

SPARKS, EDWIN ERLE. *National Development, 1877-1885.* New York, 1918.

STACKPOLE, EDWARD J. *Chancellorsville: Lee's Greatest Battle.* Harrisburg, Pa., 1958.

STEERE, EDWARD. *The Wilderness Campaign.* Harrisburg, Pa., 1960.

STERN, PHILIP VAN DOREN. *An End to Valor.* Boston, 1958.

————. *The Confederate Navy: A Pictorial History.* New York, 1962.

STEWART, GEORGE H. *Pickett's Charge.* Boston, 1959.

THOMPSON, SAMUEL B. *Confederate Purchasing Operations Abroad.* Chapel Hill, N.C., 1935.

TREXLER, H. A. *The Confederate Ironclad "Virginia" ("Merrimac").* Chicago, 1938.

VANDIVER, FRANK E. *Jubal's Raid: General Early's Famous Attack on Washington in 1864.* New York, 1960.

————. *Making of a President.* Richmond, Va., 1962.

————. *Rebel Brass: The Confederate Command System.* Baton Rouge, La., 1956.

WADDELL, JOSEPH ADDISON. *Annals of Augusta County, Virginia, from 1726 to 1871.* Staunton, Va., 1902.

WATKINS, N. J., ed. *The Pine and the Palm.* Baltimore, 1873.

WAYLAND, JOHN W. *A History of Rockingham County, Virginia.* Dayton, Va., 1912.

————. *Stonewall Jackson's Way: Route, Method, Achievement*. Staunton, Va., 1940.

————. *Twenty-Five Chapters on the Shenandoah Valley to Which Is Appended a Concise History of the Civil War in the Valley*. Strasburg, Va., 1957.

WESLEY, CHARLES H. *The Collapse of the Confederacy*. Washington, 1930.

West Virginia: A Guide to the Mountain State. New York, 1941.

WILEY, BELL I. *The Life of Johnny Reb: The Common Soldier of the Confederacy*. New York, 1943.

WILLIAMS, KENNETH P. *Lincoln Finds a General*. 5 vols. New York, 1949-59.

WILLIAMS, T. HARRY. *Lincoln and His Generals*. New York, 1952.

————. *McClellan, Sherman, and Grant*. New Brunswick, 1962.

WINTERS, JOHN D. *The Civil War in Louisiana*. Baton Rouge, La., 1963.

WISE, JENNINGS C. *The Long Arm of Lee: The History of the Artillery of the Army of Northern Virginia*. New York, 1941.

YEARNS, WILFRED BUCK. *The Confederate Congress*. Athens, Ga., 1960.

YOUNG, BENNETT H. *Confederate Wizards of the Saddle*. Boston, 1914.

NEWSPAPERS

Richmond Newsleader, Richmond, Virginia.

Staunton Daily News, Staunton, Virginia.

Welsh Daily News, Welsh, West Virginia.

PUBLIC DOCUMENTS

Biographical Directory of the American Congress, 1774-1949. Washington, D.C., 1950.

CULLUM, GEORGE W. *Biographical Register of the Officers and Graduates of the U.S. Military Academy, at West Point, New York, from Its Establishment, March 16, 1802, to the Army Reorganization of 1866-67*. 2 vols. New York, 1868.

LE GEAR, CLARA EGLI, ed. *The Hotchkiss Map Collection*. Washington, D.C., 1951.

Register of Officers of the Confederate States Navy (1861-1865). Washington, D.C., 1931.

RICHARDSON, JAMES D. *A Compilation of the Messages and Papers of the Confederacy, 1861-65*. 2 vols. Nashville, Tenn., 1906.

War of the Rebellion: A Compilation of the Official Records of the Union and Confederate Armies. 70 vols. in 127, and Index. 4 series. Washington, D.C., 1880-1901.

ARTICLES IN PERIODICALS

FREEMAN, DOUGLAS SOUTHALL. "An Address." *Civil War Review* 1 (1955):
7-15.

LE GEAR, CLARA EGLI. "The Hotchkiss Map Collection." *The Library of Congress Quarterly Journal of Current Acquisitions* 6 (1948): 16-20.

OSTERHOUT, CHARLES HOTCHKISS. "A Johnny Reb from Windsor, New York." *Courier Magazine*, January 1955, pp. 20-23.

Index